T0139824

Progress in IS

More information about this series at http://www.springer.com/series/10440

Kai Riemer · Stefan Schellhammer
Michaela Meinert
Editors

Collaboration in the Digital Age

How Technology Enables Individuals, Teams and Businesses

 Springer

Editors
Kai Riemer
Business Information Systems
University of Sydney
Sydney, NSW, Australia

Michaela Meinert
Department of Information Systems
University of Münster
Münster, Germany

Stefan Schellhammer
Department of Information Systems
University of Münster
Münster, Germany

ISSN 2196-8705   ISSN 2196-8713 (electronic)
Progress in IS
ISBN 978-3-030-06861-5   ISBN 978-3-319-94487-6 (eBook)
https://doi.org/10.1007/978-3-319-94487-6

Printed on acid-free paper

This Springer imprint is published by the registered company Springer International Publishing AG part of Springer Nature
The registered company address is: Gewerbestrasse 11, 6330 Cham, Switzerland

Preface

The proliferation of digital technologies has brought the world closer together but also created new barriers and divides. It is now possible to connect almost instantly and seamlessly with family, friends and co-workers across the globe. As a result, new forms of collaboration between individuals, teams and businesses have not only become possible, but a necessity to stay competitive in fast-changing markets.

At the same time, the emerging Digital Age brings with it new requirements and challenges for all involved:

- *Individuals* have to learn new skills for collaborating at a distance and find themselves in rapidly changing work environments;
- *Teams* need to develop new practices and engage in much, often hidden, 'collaboration work' to enable effective work across boundaries;
- *Executives and managers* face the challenge of having to lead teams and people that are dispersed across space and time zones;
- *Organisations* see new opportunities for transforming work using digital and social collaboration tools, but face new and unique challenges of introducing and adopting such 'social' technologies;
- *Businesses* are able to access resources in new collaborative inter-organisational networks, at the expense of new managerial complexity of engaging in multi-stakeholder arrangements;
- *New markets* proliferate with the advent of digital commerce, yet engaging with consumers in multiple channels requires new capabilities that challenge many traditional retailers.

This book brings together expert scholars to address these challenges. Across 14 chapters, our authors share their insights into new forms of work, team collaboration, enterprise social networking, management in a digital world, digital commerce, as well as various new inter-organisational forms of doing business such as in digital cooperatives, large project businesses and living labs.

We are confident that professionals and academics alike will regard this book a valuable resource for understanding the diverse power of collaboration in the Digital Age. The book is organised into three main parts that represent different levels at which such phenomena play out:

(1) The first part engages with *collaboration between people and in teams, on a work practice level*. It contains chapters that investigate co-working spaces, enterprise collaboration systems, virtual teams and management practices for the Digital Age.
(2) The second part widens the gaze and covers matters of *inter-organisational collaboration in business networks*, supply chains or entire industries. Chapters in this section introduce new forms of citizen cooperation in the health sector, the sharing economy, cooperation in large projects, supply chain innovation and 'living' infrastructures.
(3) The third part covers *digital commerce*, new forms of digital interactions between businesses and their customers, with a focus on online search and digital technology adoption among traditional 'high street' retailers.

Festschrift for Stefan Klein

This book is a Festschrift in honour of Stefan Klein, on the occasion of his 60th birthday.

Stefan Klein is Professor for Interorganizational Systems and a Director of the European Research Center for Informations Systems (ERCIS) at the Department of Information Systems, University of Münster. Stefan received his Ph.D. from the University of Cologne, Germany and his Habilitation from the University of St. Gallen in Switzerland. He also held positions with the German National Research Center for Computer Science (GMD); Harvard University; University of Koblenz-Landau, Germany; University of Linz, Austria; and University College Dublin, Ireland, where he was John Sharkey Chair in The Centre for Innovation, Technology & Organisation. Stefan has published widely in the discipline of Information Systems and held editorial positions with many of the top journals in the field.

Importantly, Stefan has been a positive role model for many colleagues, junior and senior alike, ourselves included. Many of those colleagues have keenly accepted our invitation,[1] and taken time out of their busy schedules to contribute their latest work and insights to this book. As a result, this book is as much a reflection of the quality of Stefan's network of collaborators, as it is of his own research interests and his approach to academic work and life more generally. If asked to describe Stefan with one word, many colleagues would provide as an answer 'collaboration' (or various derivatives thereof). This term describes at once Stefan's research interests, and his fundamentally open and cooperative attitude towards others.

The theme of the book 'Collaboration in the Digital Age' captures, in today's language, Stefan's long-standing research agenda which revolves around the impact of emerging new technologies, such as information infrastructures, inter-organisational systems, digital devices and communication technologies, on social phenomena of collaboration among businesses, teams, workers or even consumers. More specifically, the three parts of this book are a direct reflection of the three major research streams that characterise Stefan's academic career to date. He has made important contributions to each.

Stefan's core research area of *inter-organisational systems and network collaboration* is reflected in the second part of the book. His main contributions to this area include his Habilitationsschrift 'Interorganisationssysteme und Unternehmens-netzwerke' (Klein, 1996), as well as a number of high-profile journal papers on the configuration of inter-organisational relationships (Klein, 1996), the role of intermediaries in electronic markets (Giaglis, Klein, & O'Keefe, 2002), virtual organisations

---

[1] The editors would like to say a big 'thank you' to all who considered our invitation, including those who were unable to contribute, and apologise to anyone that we might have forgotten to invite.

(Riemer & Klein, 2008), as well as the evolution of inter-organisational information systems (Reimers, Johnston, & Klein, 2013), among many others.

The third part of the book reflects another of Stefan's research areas, that of *digital commerce*, or e-commerce. Since the emergence of the Internet, Stefan has shown a keen interest in understanding its impact on organisations and the ways we do business, which is reflected in a number of highly cited papers on electronic auctions (Klein, 1998; Klein & O'Keefe, 1999), local and global issues in electronic commerce (Klein & Steinfield, 1999), multi-channel retail (Müller-Lankenau, Wehmeyer, & Klein, 2006), electronic pricing strategies (Klein & Loebbecke, 2003), and his 1999 book on information technology and tourism (Werthner & Klein, 1999).

More recently, Stefan has taken to investigating how *team collaboration and work* itself are changing with the emergence of digital technologies and devices, which is reflected in the first part of the book. His work in this field focuses on the complexities of communication systems (Riemer, Froessler, & Klein, 2007) and their organisational adoption (Vehring, Riemer, & Klein, 2011), information overload and technology-induced occupational stress (Schellhammer & Klein, 2016; Schellhammer, Klein, & Ebner, 2017), or interruptions of work in collaborative environments (Lansmann & Klein, 2018).

Importantly, the contributions that his collaborators have selected for this volume, beyond reflecting Stefan's own research interests, are also a reflection more generally of Stefan's approach to academic research and to working with others. Reading the chapters is thus learning about Stefan Klein himself. For example, Stefan is a skilful collaborator, acutely aware of and experienced in the hidden work that goes into carefully crafting successful relationships, both at the collegial and at the project level. A number of chapters are dedicated to such practices, be it in teams (Chaps. 5 and 6), organisations (Chap. 4) or business networks (Chap. 11). In addition, his approach to working with junior colleagues has always been one of coaching and genuine mentorship; an approach illustrated in Chap. 7.

Stefan's scholarship is inquisitive, innovative and driven by curiosity and enquiry for its own sake, often breaking with tradition and unafraid of venturing outside the box, as it is best reflected in the kind of work reported in Chap. 12 on 'living infrastructure'. Methodologically, Stefan is pragmatic and undogmatic, employing methods that will yield answers. Not surprisingly, the chapters in this volume reflect a broad spread of research designs from conceptual, analytical or survey-based studies, to case studies, ethnography or dedicated philosophical work, all of which are part of Stefan's repertoire.

Moreover, Stefan's work is in many ways about bridging and uniting; associating disciplines, joining technical understanding with social and organisational implications, as well as connecting academia and industry. His work has always been grounded in rigorous, engaged scholarship with a strong practical angle, guided by the phenomenon at hand, never abstract or purely theoretical, but rich in thinking, reflection and theorising. Again, this is reflected in the research offered in this book, which balances theoretical insights with practical insights.

As a result, we are confident that you, Stefan, will find this book interesting and insightful, and so will our readers.

Happy Birthday, Stefan!

Sydney, Australia   Kai Riemer
Münster, Germany   Stefan Schellhammer
Münster, Germany   Michaela Meinert

References

Giaglis, G. M., Klein, S., & O'Keefe, R. M. (2002). The role of intermediaries in electronic marketplaces: developing a contingency model. *Information Systems Journal, 12*(3), 231–246.

Klein, S. (1996). *Interorganisationssysteme und Unternehmensnetzwerke Wechselwirkungen zwischen organisatorischer und informationstechnischer Entwicklung.* Wiesbaden: Deutscher Universitätsverlag.

Klein, S. (1996). The configuration of inter-organizational relations. *European Journal of Information Systems, 5*(2), 92–102.

Klein, S. (1998). The diffusion of auctions on the web. In C. T. Romm & F. Sudweeks (Eds.), *Doing business electronically* (pp. 47–63). London: Springer.

Klein, S., & Loebbecke, C. (2003). Emerging pricing strategies on the web: Lessons from the airline industry. *Electronic Markets, 13*(1), 46–58.

Klein, S., & O'Keefe, M. (1999). The Impact of the web on auctions: Some empirical evidence and theoretical considerations. *International Journal of Electronic Commerce, 3*(3), 7–20.

Klein, S., & Steinfield, C. (1999). Special section: Local vs. global issues in electronic commerce. *Electronic Markets, 9*(1–2), 45–50.

Müller-Lankenau, C., Wehmeyer, K., & Klein, S. (2006). Multi-channel strategies: Capturing and exploring diversity in the European retail grocery industry. *International Journal of Electronic Commerce, 10*(2), 85–122.

Reimers, K., Johnston, R. B., & Klein, S. (2013). An empirical evaluation of existing IS change theories for the case of IOIS evolution. *European Journal of Information Systems,* (advance online publication), 1–27.

Riemer, K., Froessler, F., & Klein, S. (2007). Real time communication—Modes of use in distributed teams. In *Proceedings of the 15th European Conference of Information Systems* (pp. 286–297). St. Gallen, CH. Retrieved June 07–09, 2007.

Riemer, K. & Klein, S. (2008). Is the V-form the next generation organisation? An analysis of challenges, pitfalls and remedies of ICT-enabled virtual organisations based on social capital theory. *Journal of Information Technology, 23*(3), 147–162.

Schellhammer, S., & Klein, S. (2016). Benefits and perils of virtual modes of organizing: a call for practical wisdom. In N. Dalal, A. Intezari, & M. H. Heitz (Eds.), *Practical wisdom in the age of technology: Insights, issues, and questions for a new millennium* (pp. 73–86). London: Routledge.

Schellhammer, S., Klein, S., & Ebner, E. (2017). Primary prevention for employees in the information age organization. *Health Policy and Technology, 6*(1), 72–82.

Vehring, N., Riemer, K., & Klein, S. (2011). "Don't pressure me!" Exploring the anatomy of voluntariness in the organizational adoption of network technologies. In *Proceedings of the 32nd International Conference on Information Systems*. Shanghai, China.

Werthner, H., & Klein, S. (1999). *Information technology and tourism: a challenging relationship*. Wien: Springer.

Contents

Chapter 1
Collaboration in the Digital Age: Diverse, Relevant and Challenging

Kai Riemer and Stefan Schellhammer

Introduction

Collaboration, the organisation of joint efforts among actors to achieve a shared goal, has always been an integral part of human life, given that we are social beings. Modern life however has increased both the necessity for and complexity of collaboration, bringing about complex production and political systems that require highly coordinated efforts for their functioning. The digital age, driven by the advent of network computing, the Internet, and mobile devices has added an entirely new layer of both opportunity and challenges. The ability to communicate, exchange information, and collaborate across space and time has given us new forms of working, new types of (virtual) organisation, and the reconfiguration of markets. This in turn has spurred innovation across different sectors of the economy, enabling never before possible collaboration across national and disciplinary boundaries. Yet, all of this comes at a cost. Collaboration online without face-to-face contact is not frictionless; it requires new skills and hidden 'collaboration work', above and beyond the 'actual work'. New, multi-stakeholder, network forms of organising come with new coordination costs, sources of conflict, and the need to renegotiate the fair distribution of value. In this book we take a look at a diverse range of issues of collaboration in the digital age, unpacking both opportunities and challenges. In this introductory chapter, we present results of a study into the global news discourse around 'collaboration', before we introduce each chapter of the book in more detail.

K. Riemer (✉)
The University of Sydney, Camperdown, Australia
e-mail: kai.riemer@sydney.edu.au

S. Schellhammer
WWU - University of Muenster, Münster, Germany
e-mail: stefan.schellhammer@ercis.de

© Springer International Publishing AG, part of Springer Nature 2019
K. Riemer et al. (eds.), *Collaboration in the Digital Age*, Progress in IS,
https://doi.org/10.1007/978-3-319-94487-6_1

1

The Global Conversation Around Collaboration in the Digital Age

The aim of this piece of research was to get a sense for how matters of "collaboration" are being discussed internationally and online. We report on a semantic text analysis that we have carried out using the text-analysis tool Quid (www.quid.com). Quid allows to run analyses of online news articles and blogs, unearthing thematic clusters of conversations that provide insight into what the main related topics, contexts, and areas of interest are in which the topic of interest, in this case "collaboration", is being discussed.

What Is Quid?

Quid refers to itself as "a platform that searches, analyzes and visualizes the world's collective intelligence to help answer strategic questions." The tool allows visualising and analysing the online conversations that mention and discuss 'collaboration' in various ways. Much like a web search engine Quid collects news articles and blog posts using a keyword or search phrase. It then analyses all text to identify key words, phrases, and names of people, companies, and institutions. In doing so, it compares words from each document to create links between them based on similarity in the language being used.

This process produces a network that shows how similar or different these documents are from each other. Each document is represented in the network as a node and connected to other nodes with which it shares similar language. The size of each node visualises the number of similar other nodes that a particular node is connected to. Importantly, nodes that are similar are grouped together in clusters represented by different colours. Less distance between clusters, e.g. clusters placed next to each other, indicates a high-number of inter-related topics. Nodes and clusters at the centre are core to the overall network, indicating central topics and bridging ideas, while peripheral nodes and clusters represent important niche topics. Dense clusters contain highly similar documents, while those that are spread out are more diverse in nature.

Methodological Considerations

For our analysis we simply used the keyword "collaboration" because we were interested broadly in how matters of collaboration manifest in the digital outlets affording today's global conversation. The results are quite revealing and interesting.

We experimented with a number of settings in the tool to see which ones would unearth what we were looking for. In the end, we included quite broadly news articles, blogs, trade and research publications, as well as press releases, but focused on English-speaking countries (United States, United Kingdom, Australia, Ireland, Canada), as these represent best both the group of authors contributing to this volume, as well as its intended readership.

The search with these settings led to an initial network of 5,398 documents for the period 8 May 2017 to 8 May 2018. After excluding from the network all documents that were not grouped into a cluster, as well as very small clusters (with less than 1% of the documents), the final network comprised 4,709 documents, divided into 18 clusters. We subsequently analysed and interpreted each cluster based on (1) the keywords that Quid identified as common for that cluster, and (2) the core articles in each cluster. This allowed us to name and describe each cluster. We argue that the 18 clusters provide a good overview of how "collaboration" features in the English-speaking online discourse, which of course is itself a product of the digital age. We describe the clusters in the following.

Findings: Overview of the Clusters

The visualisation of the resulting network is shown in Fig. 1.1; it shows all 18 clusters in different colours, as well as the percentages of the number of documents in each cluster. We note that there are two main groups of clusters: those that represent more generally conversations about collaboration as a, mostly digital, phenomenon (e.g. 'how to collaborate'), and those that report more specifically on concrete collaborative efforts, alliances and partnerships in various different industry sectors (e.g. fashion, health care, government, fintech, etc.).

Clusters Revolving Around Digital Collaboration and Collaborative Systems

We have grouped five clusters together, all of which are mostly concerned with collaboration as the main topic (see Table 1.1 for an overview). Hence, topics in these clusters revolve mainly around skills, practices, tools, systems and otherwise the 'how to', benefits, and mechanics of collaboration as a phenomenon in the digital age.

Firstly, we want to highlight a cluster we termed "The Future of Work and Digital Transformation", which is one of the most central clusters in the network, connecting with most other clusters. This cluster contains conversations about collaboration in the workplace, the use of technology to break down silos between organisational units, implications of collaboration for productivity, specific collaboration skills, as well as dedicated programs with collaboration at the centre, such as agile methodology.

Secondly, there is one cluster that presents as an outlier, since it revolves very specifically around "market research" on different matters of collaboration, chiefly

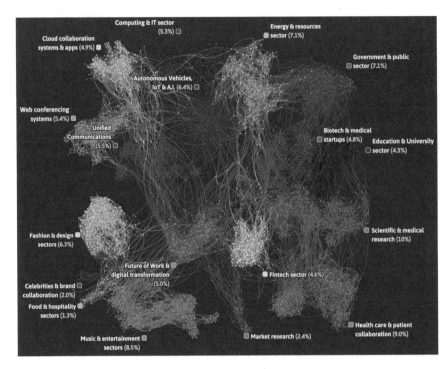

Fig. 1.1 The network of 18 clusters visualising the "collaboration" conversation

the market for collaborative systems. Not surprisingly, the most common keyword for documents in this cluster is the name of market research firm "Gartner".

Three more clusters represent different conversations around specific classes of collaboration tools, systems and platforms: "Cloud Collaboration systems and apps" comprises articles with a focus on software-as-a-service collaboration platforms of various kinds, many of which are also available as light-weight mobile apps, such as Slack, Microsoft Teams, Atlassian's Trello, Dropbox or various Google software. "Web conferencing systems" comprises news and documents about audio, video, and web conferencing systems with a strong focus on synchronous communication, such as Google Hangout, Zoom, and Microsoft Skype. Finally, "Unified Communications infrastructures" comprises articles and news about professional multi-channel communications infrastructures with a particular focus on telephony, as is apparent from the brand names discussed: Cisco, Broadsoft, or Avaya. Together, these three clusters represent the broad conversation around Enterprise Communication and Collaboration Systems.

Table 1.1 Clusters on collaborative systems, and collaboration as a topic

Cluster	# of docs	% of docs (%)	Important keywords	Typical article
Future of Work & Digital Transformation	237	5.0	Contributor, workplace, organisation, workers, silos, skills, productivity, agile	"Innovation: who owns it at your workplace?"
Market Research	115	2.4	Gartner, recommended reading, content collaboration, analysis, publications	"Box Named a Leader in the Gartner Content Collaborations Platforms Magic Quadrant"
Cloud Collaboration Systems & Apps	231	4.9	App, tool, chat, files slack, Microsoft, Dropbox, Trello, Google, Atlassian	"How Twist aims to compete against Slack with its own approach to collaboration"
Web Conferencing Systems	252	5.4	Audio conferencing, video collaboration, conference room, microphone, huddle, hd, Zoom, Skype	"Whose Zoomin who? Polycom is"
Unified Communications	260	5.5	Unified communications, communications and collaboration, contact center, Cisco, Broadsoft, Avaya	"BroadSoft Announces New BroadSoft UC-One SaaS Solution"

Clusters with a Focus on Concrete Collaboration in Different Sectors

The second group shares as a characteristic that articles in these clusters report predominantly on concrete collaborative arrangements among actors in different industries and sectors. Again, this group falls into two sub groups, which are also visually separated in the network. The first sub group, located to the right in Fig. 1.1, comprises collaboration in the sciences and technology sectors, including computing, AI, fintech, energy, biotech, and healthcare. The conversation in the second subgroup, located to the left in Fig. 1.1, revolves around consumer goods and retail, including fashion, food, music and entertainment. A different way of looking at the distinction is that the first sub group is about research and supply-side collaboration, whereas the second sub group is about marketing or demand-side collaboration.

We will not offer a detailed description of each of the clusters in Table 1.2, but want to give some general observations. First of all, collaborative research and the University sector feature quite strongly among those clusters, which is not surprising, given how much work in the academic world relies on collaboration these days, with many researchers working in cross-institutional, cross-disciplinary, and cross-industry projects. Secondly, health care features equally prominently, spanning the "Scientific & Medical Research", "Biotech & Medical startups" and "Health Care & Patient Collaboration" sectors. This demonstrates the complexity of this field, and the effort that currently goes into rebuilding health care globally, in the face of an aging population in most Western countries. Thirdly, a number of high tech sectors feature in this group of clusters, which does justice to the ways in which technology is developed in often complex multi-stakeholder networks. And finally, we want to highlight that the IT & Computing, as well as the artificial intelligence related clusters are located adjacent to the collaborative systems clusters, which is due to the fact that these clusters revolve around similar groups of companies (Table 1.2).

The last sub group comprises four clusters, all of which have a strong focus on partnerships between actors in customer-focused, demand-side collaboration; accordingly, we refer to them as marketing alliances (Table 1.3). For example, in the "Food & Hospitality Sectors" we find announcements about partnerships between hotels or restaurants and emerging new craft breweries. In the "Fashion & Design Sectors" we learn about various designers and fashion labels entering into collaborative partnerships. Partnerships in "Music & Entertainment" are often about musicians collaborating on a recording project, or movie franchises partnering on a blockbuster movie. Finally, we find a dedicated cluster about collaboration between celebrities and consumer brands; a typical partnership constitutes the collaboration between a make-up brand and an online influencer, such as Kim Kardashian.

In sum, our analysis of the global conversation revolving around "collaboration" has unearthed a diverse set of clusters that represent quite well, not only the three main facets of collaboration in the digital age: (1) the mechanics, tool-support and outcomes of collaboration as a practice, (2) collaboration in various multi-stakeholder arrangements across industries, as well as (3) the demand-side collaboration in industries focused on end consumers, but also the sectors that are currently most prominently characterised by ongoing collaboration efforts. In the following, we will use this platform to introduce the contributions in this volume.

Overview of the Book

We begin by noting that the three main groups of clusters we identified from our semantic cluster analysis correspond loosely with the three parts of this volume:

1. The first part focuses on collaboration at the work and team level, with a particular focus on the use of collaboration tools. For example, Chaps. 2, 5, 6, and 7 talk directly to matters that fall within the "future of work and digital transformation" cluster, such as coworking as novel work practice, as well as the skills needed for collaborating in emerging virtual teams or the digital age more broadly. Chapters 3 and 4 have at their core the adoption and use of enterprise social network platforms, which fall into the "cloud collaboration systems & apps" cluster.

Table 1.2 Clusters comprising concrete collaboration in research, science, and technology

Cluster	# of docs	% of docs (%)	Important keywords	Typical article
Scientific & Medical Research	472	10.0	Shares, drug, alliance therapeutics, discovery, cancer, pharmaceuticals	"Novartis Partners With Harvard To Develop Biomaterial Systems"
Education & University Sector	201	4.3	Students, school, education, learning, college, classroom, event, educators	"Flipped classroom instruction for inclusive learning"
Government & Public Sector	336	7.1	Minister, Brexit, EU, UK, government, European, international, nations	"India teams up with World Bank to boost healthcare sector"
Energy & Resources Sector	333	7.1	Supply chain, supply, oil, gas, plant, production, energy, logistics, construction	"Rio Tinto signs collaboration agreement with Minmetals"
Biotech & Medical Startups	225	4.8	Forward looking statement, production candidates, tsx, cannabis, antibody, venture	"Seattle Genetics and Pieris Pharmaceuticals Announce Multi-Program Immuno-Oncology Collaboration"
Health Care & Patient Collaboration	425	9.0	Care, health, patient, study, practice, physicians, findings, analysis, evidence, methods, clinical, hospital	"Vidyo Integrates with Allscripts FollowMyHealth Patient Engagement Platform to Provide High Quality Telehealth Visits"
Fintech Sector	218	4.6	Fintech, banks, blockchain, banking, financial services, payments, transactions	"German Asset Management: A model for collaboration"
Autonomous Vehicles, IoT & A.I.	300	6.4	Vehicles, autonomous, IoT, AI, car, driving, electric, semiconductor, machine learning	"Interview: Head Of Volvo R&D On Uber Collaboration And Automaker's Autonomous Vehicle Plans"
Computing and IT Sector	251	5.3	Cyber security, Sharepoint, lifecycle, threats, Microsoft azure, server, storage, marketers	"New Box Admin Experience Extends Visibility and Advanced Insights Into Content, Collaboration and Security"

Table 1.3 Clusters comprising concrete collaboration in retail, marketing and advertising

Cluster	# of docs	% of docs (%)	Important keywords	Typical article
Music & Entertainment Sector	399	8.5	Music, song, album, fans, track, singer, billboard, twitter	"What's Your Favorite Demi Lovato Collaboration? Vote!"
Fashion & Design Sectors	296	6.3	Collection, fashion, designer, pieces, brand, shoes, stores, inspired, style	"River Island launch Holly Fulton designer collaboration range—and these are our top picks"
Celebrities & Brand Collaboration	95	2.0	Beauty, Kim Kardashian, Kylie Jenner, Instagram, makeup, wearing, cosmetics, fashion	"Quay eyewear taps Kylie Jenner for new sunglass collaboration"
Food & Hospitality Sectors	63	1.3	Craft beer, special edition, hotel, luxury, guests, food, drink, restaurants, flavors	"Hard Rock International Announces Collaboration with GiG to Build Online Casino"

2. The second part comprises chapters that discuss various forms inter-firm collaboration in networks and alliances in different sectors. Chapter 8 for example discusses new cooperative arrangements for patients to share their health data, and thus speaks directly to the "Health Care & Patient Collaboration" cluster. Chapter 10 focuses on large project businesses, a common form of organising in the construction, energy and resources sectors, while Chap. 11 discusses a particular form of cross sector collaboration in an academic, public sector-industry arrangement for innovating in complex cross-country trade settings.
3. The third part focuses on digital commerce, the use of digital technology reshaping retail and forms of collaboration with end consumers. Chapter 14 for example falls squarely within those clusters that focus on demand-side collaboration, as it discusses new forms of digital retail practices, which can increasingly be found in the fashion or entertainment industries.

   In the following three subsections we will further unpack the three parts of the volume and provide brief introductions to each chapter.

Part 1: Digital Work and Team Collaboration

Collaboration refers to a set of social practices; it is a phenomenon that always starts with people and increasingly involves the use of various dedicated communication and collaboration technologies. New forms of collaboration in turn have the potential to significantly change the ways in which we work and live, in teams, organisations, and society more broadly. Naturally, in this first part of the book, we have grouped together studies that investigate collaboration at the 'micro level', with a focus on how people work together, how teams organise, how organisations take on board new collaborative technologies, and how new forms of work in organisations proliferate.

In Chap. 2, Nathalie Mitev and colleagues report on their latest research into new work practices in the collaborative economy that mushroomed on the back of new digital collaboration technologies, as well as the kind of agile work practices popularised by the high tech sector itself. The study sheds light on the relationship between co-working spaces and the configuration of city workforces in terms of waged and independent workers, such as entrepreneurs. The authors find that alternative work spaces and new forms of work spur a change in employment patterns, whereby young people in particular adopt more flexibility in moving between traditional and new forms of work.

The next two chapters are dedicated to Enterprise Collaboration Systems (ECS) within organisations, in particular the increasingly popular phenomenon of Enterprise Social Networking (ESN). In Chap. 3, Petra Schubert provides a detailed state-of-the-art overview of the Enterprise Collaboration Systems space. Firstly, she outlines the transition of collaborative technologies from more traditional groupware software to social networking platforms and discusses which characteristics and features make such systems "social". Secondly, the author outlines the unique challenges of implementing ECS. She argues that ECS require very different techniques compared to traditional enterprise systems. This is due to their malleable nature and their need to be shaped through use. Finally, the author consolidates case study research undertaken in 20 organisations to derive a framework of archetypes of ECS uses. The framework provides a timely overview of the practical usefulness of such systems.

Chapter 4 builds on the previous one and hones in on the topic of Enterprise Social Network adoption in organisations. Specifically, Kai Riemer and Ella Hafermalz investigate the challenging role of the so-called community manager, a person tasked with the roll-out and adoption of ESN in their organisation, who finds themselves "stuck in the middle" between management expectations, who demand successful adoption, and those of workers who have to make sense of this new technology. A case study of an inter-organisational ESN where community managers are able to strategize with each other in a safe space provides unique insight into this role in the process of ESN adoption.

The next two chapters both deal with the challenges and practices of virtual, geographically dispersed teams. The first of those, Chap. 5 by Russell Haines, Nadine Vehring and Malte Kramer, takes on the problem of awareness in virtual teams. Unlike co-located ones, virtual teams have to invest effort and develop practices to create and maintain awareness of each other's whereabouts and activities. The authors find that maintaining awareness goes beyond improving coordination and has a significant additional effect on a team's social motivation through increased feelings of connectedness.

Chapter 6, by Mary Beth Watson-Manheim, is dedicated to the unseen and unaccounted for effort required to perform work in virtual collaboration. It builds on the insight that successful collaboration takes dedicated, skilful, and time-consuming work. This is true for co-located settings, but even more so for virtual teams where people do not share the same physical environment. Members of virtual teams have to expend much additional effort to stay connected to each other and coordinate joint tasks. They need to engage in, what the author terms 'articulation work', work that allows actual work to occur successfully.

The final chapter of the first part (Chap. 7), written by Camilla Noonan, Séamas Kelly and Geoff Pelham, tackles an important aspect of successful collaborative work—a coaching style of management that contrasts with a more conventional directive style of management found in more hierarchical settings. Based on a case study of a UK social housing organisation, the authors unpack in detail the practices involved in bringing about a genuine coaching style of management, and how these practices helped re-shape broader cultural practices within the organisation. The insights provided by this work are useful for any organisation that wants to transition to a more open and collaborative work culture.

Part 2: Digital Networks and Inter-organisational Collaboration

Collaboration extends beyond the inter-personal level to collaboration between businesses, organisations, and other legal entities. Technology enables the emergence of new forms of transactions and activities between organisations that require new forms of cooperation and the reconfiguration of inter-organisational network constellations. In the second part of the book, authors take a closer look at various novel forms of inter-organisational collaboration, in citizen cooperatives, sharing economy networks, large project organisations, and supply chain 'living labs'. They investigate how incentives between players in such networks are distributed to achieve sustainable and equitable outcomes, as well as how we can arrive at new network forms of organisation, new ways of collaborating and of distributing value within inter-organisational networks in the first place.

Chapter 8 by Joan Rodon Mòdol, delves deep into emerging issues of collecting and re-using of personal data in the health care sector. The author identifies the need to rethink the way in which we commonly organise access to and use highly sensitive data. He shows that existing models of personal data reuse fail to balance the interests of public and private health providers with that of individuals, because those models do not guarantee that subjects have a say over how their personal data is re-used. As a potential solution the author proposes a new collaborative network form, which he terms 'data cooperatives'. Data cooperatives offer a new logic of cooperation, in that subjects voluntarily pool their personal data and, importantly, participate in the governance of its re-use. While grounded in the health care sector this model in principle offers insights into the collaborative use of 'big data' in society more broadly.

The topic of Chap. 9, by Theresia Theurl and Eric Meyer, is the sharing, or gig economy. Using transaction cost economics, the authors begin by demonstrating the reasons for why the sharing economy emerges, why people increasingly both 'share' or 'rent' certain assets such as cars or living space, instead of owning them outright. Yet the core of their argument revolves around questioning critically how interests in this new form of collaborative consumption are currently balanced, given that the most prominent examples, such as Uber or AirBnb, represent increasingly powerful platforms that use sophisticated algorithms to organise activity between platform participants. While lowering transaction costs, the authors argue that such platforms come with new dependencies, because they tend to become monopolies over time that exploit their dominant position at the expense of platform users. Again, the authors find a potential solution in cooperatives as an organisational form, whereby the platform is owned by its users, thus significantly rebalancing the users' position in the network.

In Chap. 10, Klaus Backhaus and Ulf König investigate particularly interesting, and rather mature forms of inter-organisational collaboration: large project businesses, often employed in the construction, energy and resources sectors, and for large-scale civil engineering projects. The authors find that this sector is undergoing a revolution on the back of increased collaboration and digitization. They uncover how three trends drive changes: negotiation of contracts using software agents, changes in the ways in which governance is organised, and the adoption of digital collaboration tools that alter the way in which business partners collaborate on a day-to-day basis.

Chapter 11, written by authors from the European research project consortium ITAIDE, reports on experiences with the first supply chain "living lab", established to "analyse and improve complex cross-border trade and logistics challenges using innovative information technology". The living lab idea follows the insight that real-life experimentation is needed for developing and testing innovative technology to change large-scale institutional networks, such as in cross-border trade. The article reports on the main learning from the Beer Living Lab, which reveals the importance of continuous negotiation and sense-making, and knowledge broking and establishing close working relationships for making living labs successful.

The final chapter in this part extends and deepens the thinking of the previous one. In Chap. 12, Kai Reimers and Robert B. Johnston present the notion of "living infrastructure" as a way to challenge the established understanding of infrastructure as a material system that merely coordinates the activities of diverse practices. When understood genuinely as 'living', infrastructure constitutes an 'opening' of socio-material practices, where complex social interactions, such as those in health care, are able to productively and continuously change and thrive over time. The authors present nothing less than a fundamental rethinking of how we can understand generative, or creative, change in complex, inter-organisational social settings.

Part 3: Digital Commerce and Consumer Experience

The final part of our book covers 'digital commerce', the ways in which digital technologies re-configure transactions and relationships between businesses and consumers, in particular in retail. This section contains two chapters, each dealing with one of the most relevant digital commerce aspects: (1) online search, which has fundamentally changed the way in which consumers make decisions about what and where to purchase, and (2) the combination of traditional and digital ways of interacting with consumers in hybrid retail models.

In Chap. 13, Christopher P. Holland revisits the broad body of theories from different disciplines that explain consumer search behaviour. The author argues that in order to do justice to the often ad hoc and haphazard ways in which consumers search, a bricolage model that combines different search theories will best be able to make sense of and explain actual search behaviour in digital commerce.

In the final chapter of the book (Chap. 14), Jörg Becker and colleagues, take on the challenges that traditional "high street" retailers face in adopting and integrating digital technologies in order to compete with dedicated digital commerce retailers. The authors present ways for such bricks and mortar retailers to adopt digital commerce through making use of alliances and digital platform ecosystems, in which "retailers join forces to provide digital touchpoints and boundary-spanning service to the customer". The paper brings to life the topic through a hypothetical comparison in the near future of two cities in which retailers have each adopted different strategies towards digital commerce.

Part I
Digital Work and Team Collaboration

Chapter 2
Co-working Spaces, Collaborative Practices and Entrepreneurship

Nathalie Mitev, Francois-Xavier de Vaujany, Pierre Laniray, Amélie Bohas and Julie Fabbri

Introduction

The current transformation of work and society is taking multiple forms: globalisation (Giddens, 2000), the growth of entrepreneurship, independent work, telework and mobility (Raffaele & Connell, 2016), digital nomads (Gussekloo & Jacobs, 2016), self-production, value co-creation and social innovation (Bizzarri, 2014). Entrepreneurs and independent workers are assembled and disassembled, depending on market demand and on-going projects. Beyond the logic of a peripheral job market and firms outsourcing their activities, digital, legal and organisational structures are also aggregating and disaggregating. Digital transformation, new workspaces and project management are facilitating this evolution and collaborative co-working has the potential of creating a new kind of economy that supports community and innovation (Davies & Tollervey, 2013). Tounes and Fayolle (2006) argue that entrepreneurs are mobilised culturally and socially during periods of economic turmoil and social

N. Mitev (✉)
King's College London, London, UK
e-mail: nmitev@btinternet.com

F.-X. de Vaujany
Paris-Dauphine University, Paris, France
e-mail: devaujany@dauphine.fr

P. Laniray
Poitiers University, Poitiers, France
e-mail: planiray@poitiers.iae-france.fr

A. Bohas
Aix Marseille University, Marseille, France
e-mail: amelie.bohas@univ-amu.fr

J. Fabbri
Ecole de Management de Lyon, Écully, France
e-mail: fabbri@em-lyon.com

© Springer International Publishing AG, part of Springer Nature 2019   15
K. Riemer et al. (eds.), *Collaboration in the Digital Age*, Progress in IS,
https://doi.org/10.1007/978-3-319-94487-6_2

change. Merkel (2015) states that co-working spaces can be regarded "as a new form of urban social infrastructure enabling contacts and collaborations between people, ideas and connecting places". In order to understand this evolution, we explore the emergence and practices of collaborative spaces, communities and movements.

We define collaborative communities as collectives of individual entrepreneurs, project workers and managers who build lasting collaborations in order to share practices. They consist of co-workers, makers, 'fabbers' and hackers who rely on digital infrastructures, collaborative spaces and places, and temporal structures. Their work is less easily defined than traditional work or occupational communities whose boundaries and identities they often question. We describe research carried out in several European cities to understand better these collaborative communities and movements in the context of digital work transformation. We suggest that policy decision-makers move from policies for to policies through collaborative communities and collaborative spaces.

A specific concern is the border between waged employment and entrepreneurship, and we found that new work practices make this border more and more porous, as illustrated by the emergence of professional trajectories based on alternate entrepreneurship. We also found that waged workers in traditional organisations not only suffer from stress but from boredom (Sundsted, Jones, & Bacigalupo, 2009). For the last 15 years or so, work practices have been transformed through the collaborative economy and new forms of collaboration. We explore the implications for workers and individuals, work collectives, social movements, and urban and societal dynamics. For individual workers, collaborative work spaces can lead to new competences, prospects, and sometimes new lives. For communities, collectives are important in work transformations. In the collaborative economy, entrepreneurship, independent work and mobility fragment working lives: belonging to a community becomes vital in providing practical, professional, identity and most importantly emotional support. A community can help address a crisis of meaning, fight boredom and loneliness for entrepreneurs. Finally social movements such as hackers/makers display governance and regulation models which can be of value to traditional organisations and public policy-makers.

Since the 1990s, digital actors-entrepreneurs have contributed business models disruptive of national and local interests. They endeavour to be actors in the city and many start-ups address citizens and communities through their extended value co-creation processes. They are often located in third spaces, such as WeWork,[1] which are reinventing ways to gather and aggregate workplaces, co-working and co-living practices in many cities,[2] disrupting the system of production of legitimate actors and discourses in the city. Beyond the sustainable, equitable and ethical aspects of digitally-based business models, collaborative spaces could have a role to play as they are at the heart of the city and its communities. Pressure now centres on individual activities and projects, where incentives to innovate have become stronger, through

---

[1] https://www.wework.com/.

[2] See for instance the support of the former Mayor of London for the Fish Island Village project: http://www.huffingtonpost.com/adi-gaskell/londons-leading-role-as-a_b_9367478.html.

continuously evolving digital assemblages. However, this can only be maintained through communities which are difficult to envisage in a context where consumption and production take place primarily in homes and on the move.

This chapter offers a synthesis of empirical research carried out in 2014–16 by the Research Group on Collaborative Spaces (RGCS[3]). It is an international informal network of researchers interested in new work practices in the context of the collaborative economy with the aim of exploring collaborative spaces and communities. We engaged with entrepreneurs-makers and co-working space members through a series of visits, seminars and working groups on new work practices and work spaces in several major cities. Our overall purpose is to gain an understanding of practices and discourses about entrepreneurship, new innovative places, third-places and collaborative movements in cities and their public territorial policies linked to innovative places and collaborative spaces.

Our empirical material consists of field notes and documents from seminars, workshops and visits and an online questionnaire (378 respondents), involving approximately 1000 people in 8 cities (Paris, London, Montreal, Lyon, Grenoble, Barcelona, Amsterdam and Berlin). Seminars and meetings were carried out, and participants also communicate through a collaborative platform, a blog and Twitter. Some seminars were run inside collaborative spaces; participants included practitioners such as managers of and workers in third-places, members of collaborative communities and representatives of public city organizations.

This chapter is based on these events and encounters and some of the online questionnaire results. We first briefly review the rise of co-working spaces, their features and relationship to independent workers and entrepreneurs; we then present our findings according to the individual, community and societal levels of work practices associated to the collaborative economy and their spatial and temporal aspects. To conclude we highlight the need for better coordination between public actors, and between public actors and collaborative communities. Collaborative communities require a stronger coupling of public policies and should be seen at the heart of economic, educational, industrial and cultural policies targeting the city, aiming at collaborating and sharing.

[3] See RGCS website at https://collaborativespacesstudy.wordpress.com/a-propos/ email at collaborativespaces@gmail.com and Twitter @collspaces. This research is the result of a collaborative initiative and did not benefit from any public or private funding. We thank Sebastien Lorenzini, Gregor Bouville, Stefan Haefliger and Helene Bussy-Socrate for their help in designing the questionnaire. We also wish to thank all the RGCS local coordinators for their help in organising seminars, workshops and visits, in particular Stefan Haefliger, Julie Fabbri, Viviane Sergi, Annie Camus, Anna Glaser, Pierre Laniray, Anouk Mukherjee, Fabrice Periac, Sabine Carton, David Vallat, Boukje Cnossen and Paula Ungureanu.

The Rise of Co-working Spaces

Beyond Co-working Spaces: Diverse Third Places

The number of co-working spaces in the world multiplied 32 times between 2007 and 2013.[4] According to Ross and Ressia (2015) they are a highly relevant area of research in relation to the future of work in an era of deregulated labour markets, telework and rapid technological change. The term 'co-working' appeared from the first time in the literature in a 1999 article by Bernie DeKoven (2002), a video games designer, as the phenomenon of "working together as equals" in a workspace and Spinuzzi (2012) defines it as "working alone together".

Raffaele and Connell (2016) state that telecommuting has increased exponentially in recent years: The US has one of the highest rates of telecommuting adoption in the world, with approximately 16 million US employees working from home at least 1 day per month—about 10% of all employees. In Australia, it has been estimated that in 2013, 5.6 million adult Australians aged 18 years and over were 'digital workers', representing 51% of the total employed workforce. They argue that co-working practices have the potential to overcome some of the issues that telecommuting poses both from individual and organisational perspectives.

Co-working spaces are also regarded as 'serendipity accelerators', designed to "host creative people and entrepreneurs who endeavour to break isolation and find a convivial environment that favours meetings and collaboration" (Moriset, 2014). According to William van den Broeck, cofounder of the Mutinerie[5] co-working space in Paris, co-working spaces are "a sustainable and clearly identified solution for entrepreneurs and freelancers looking to build a network and collaborate with like-minded people". For example, Hurry (2012) found in his qualitative study that owners and users of the Canadian Halifax hub[6] felt that it decreased isolation, offered networking opportunities, supported bootstrapping functions, and assisted with ideation and productivity. He concludes that co-working "could function as a platform for social engineering and activism through leveraging its networking capabilities to fully engage with the community, positively affecting the economic viability of the local area".

A main characteristic of co-working places is a physical workspace, but their members often refer to a place, a time, a community. As well as a workspace, co-workers are looking for a 'third place', described by Oldenburg (1989, p. 16) as a place hosting "the regular, voluntary, informal, and happily anticipated gatherings of individuals beyond the realms of home and [corporations]." Indeed, these places represent more than cheap working spaces and co-working is often associated with a strong attachment to a space and emotional support (Gerdenitsch, Scheel, Andorfer, & Korunka, 2016). Spreitzer, Bacevice, and Garrett (2015) found that people who

---

[4]https://www.bureauxapartager.com/blog/le-24-mai-rangez-vos-bureaux/.

[5]http://mutinerie.org/.

[6]http://thehubhalifax.ca/.

use co-working spaces see their work as meaningful, they have more job control and they feel part of a community.

Reflecting this need, their members have over time increased in diversity. Users of co-working spaces include a wide range of actors. Large companies enable their teleworkers or teams of teleworkers to use them; SMEs may use them in a closed (e.g. using a whole floor) or open space fashion (sharing the space with other SMEs, for example a small communication agency at Coworking Republic[7]); co-workers and individuals in small groups (around 10 people), who can be said to be 'micro' organisations; or a range of independent workers, freelancers, micro-entrepreneurs, contract staff, students, the unemployed, seniors, mobile workers and teleworkers, trainees, 'indie' workers, small businesses, non-profit workers (DeGuzman & Tang, 2011) and many others. Holienka and Racek (2015) found that members of co-working spaces are mostly young professionals, predominantly men, who act as small businesses with the dominance of IT, creative and knowledge-intensive areas; that the perceived benefits are often the reason for selecting specific co-working spaces; and that the general satisfaction rate among co-working members is very high. However, they also signal that "co-working members may lack in ability to benefit from knowledge exchange and access to job/business opportunities".

The Paradox of Community-Building

Co-working spaces also represent a paradox. Indeed, co-working is associated with flexibility and mobility due to ongoing organisational and work transformations and the disappearance of a traditional workplace (Pennel, 2013; Dale & Burrell, 2007) and the rise of flexible independent activities. Nevertheless, extending "the times and spaces of work into ever more aspects of everyday life (…) simultaneously attempts to obscure this colonisation" (Massey, 1995). Gandini (2015) also offers a critical review of the spread of co-working into a "buzzword with increasingly high expectations concerning the improvement of the socio-economic conditions of workers in the knowledge economy" and warns that it is important to interpret the co-working phenomenon in the landscape of the knowledge labour market, as it is connoted with the expectation of being the new and only model of work.

But simultaneously, there is an expressed need by co-workers to go beyond an 'office to rent', and belong to a social group or community; how can a community develop a more permanent identity in a context of constant fluidity? Leaderless communities have been discussed by Brafman and Beckstrom (2006) as:

- Self-organising, describing the capability of individuals to choose various ways of functioning and their level of autonomy and responsibility;
- Care of each other;
- Sense of ownership;
- Integration of new members.

---

[7]http://coworkingrepublic.com/.

Creating a social link is the challenge, but also maintaining and nurturing both strong and weak links leading to a sense of belonging to a community. Co-working spaces are an interesting recent new development in which to explore the potential for such community-building and collaboration.

Furthermore, in Westernised societies of the global North, many once-foundational jobs have been resigned to the past, are in short supply or have been dispatched offshore. According to Butcher (2016) "a new spirit of entrepreneurial-ism has emerged to fill the void". He argues that co-working can sustain citizens' entrepreneurial identity and help construct a "symbolic expression of unconven-tional and anti-organisational work" (i.e. in opposition to neoliberal and bureaucratic organisations). Co-working spaces are therefore particularly relevant to d'Andria and Gabarret (2017)'s argument that the entrepreneur can no longer be seen as solitary but as embedded in society, and their stress on the importance of networks of social relations to develop entrepreneurship.

Additionally, there is a growing recognition of agglomerations as key to supporting economic growth and the importance of cities in growth processes. Reuschke, Mason, Syrett, and Van Ham (2015) have studied business and household decisions in relation to business strategies, notably how household characteristics and strategy influence the development of new business and business growth in cities. However, they state that, at both theoretical and policy levels "there has been a disjuncture between perspectives on how people work, start-up businesses and innovate".

Co-working and Entrepreneurship

Indeed, there is limited, if growing, literature on the role of co-working spaces for entrepreneurs. van Weele, Van Rijnsoever, and Steinz (2014) claim that "although the number of incubators, accelerators, co-working spaces and science parks is rapidly increasing around the world, little academic attention has been paid to the start-up communities that these initiatives create." They respond to recently made calls for in-depth research in a study of start-up communities in three cities in Australia, a country that has seen a rapid growth in entrepreneurial activity. They found that "incubators and co-working spaces have an influence by introducing community managers and selection processes and creating optimal circumstances for start-up communities to prosper".

Next we outline recent work which is striving to explore links between third places and entrepreneurship in various parts of the world, from quantitative to qualitative perspectives, and related to a range of issues such as: measuring entrepreneurial orientation and economic outcomes, studying urban ecosystems and entrepreneurial spatial distribution, the development of entrepreneurial social skills and learning pro-cesses, hackerspaces governance mechanisms, makerspaces and innovative thinking and knowledge sharing.

Co-working and Entrepreneurial Orientation

Gertner and Mack (2017) explore the differences in the 'entrepreneurial orientation' of different types of business support to entrepreneurs such as incubators, accelerators and co-working spaces and their results show variations related to their organisational context and suggest indicators for measuring different dimensions of entrepreneurial orientation. In a study of entrepreneurial hacker and co-working spaces Assenza (2015) examines how space, defined not only as physical space, but also as social context, and as a conceptual space within which production occurs, can contribute to new venture creation and offers a model for empirical measurement of interaction between spatial configuration and ultimate economic outcomes.

Co-working Entrepreneurs in Urban and Rural Spaces

In a qualitative study and survey of urban high tech entrepreneurs in Munich, Marx (2016) related co-working spaces functionally and spatially in the city, and the importance of co-working as a new paradigm of work for the entrepreneurs. He shows that numerous actors, big companies, universities and co-working operators, contribute in different ways to the positive development of the start-up scene in this dynamic ecosystem and that the spatial distribution of entrepreneurial activities is particularly taken into account.

Fuzi (2015) carried out an empirical exploration in Wales in the UK of whether co-working spaces can promote entrepreneurship in regions with sparse entrepreneurial environments by "creating the hard infrastructure particularly designed in such a way that the soft infrastructure necessary for entrepreneurship can also emerge". She found that these spaces provide support (moral, emotional, professional, financial) and facilities (infrastructure) to enable entrepreneurs to start and grow their businesses.

Co-working and Network Skills

Drawing on ethnographic data gathered in a large case study of co-working spaces in Australia, Waters-Lynch and Potts (2017) demonstrate that the "main margin of value a co-working space provides is not price competition with serviced offices, or a more pleasant environment than working at home, but a focal point for finding people, ideas and other resources when you lack the information necessary for coordination." Burret and Pierre (2014) examined how the co-working space La Muse in Geneva[8] helped develop entrepreneurs' social skills. They found that this type of organisation enabled the emergence of a peer network effect; this stimulates "the development of their abilities and their level of engagement in their project, as well as the opportunity to affect its development through interaction without significant start-up capital". In

---

[8]http://www.la-muse.ch/coworking/geneve/.

her qualitative doctoral study of three co-working spaces in Paris, Fabbri (2015) found that, as well as improving knowledge transfer, belonging to a co-working space increased entrepreneurs' credibility and provided them with access to partners through a 'labelling' and 'window' effect.

Co-working and Learning Processes

Bouncken and Reuschl (2016) show that entrepreneurial performance improves by the learning processes among co-working users that take upon the individual efficacy, trust and community among co-working users. They also warn that opportunism, often as knowledge leakage, will directly and indirectly spoil learning processes and entrepreneurial performance as it reduces their antecedents trust and community building. Allen (2017) studied hackerspaces and hackers as 'proto-entrepreneurs' and uncovered private governance mechanisms such as graduated social ostracism, collective action processes and nested hierarchies of rules. He concludes that "hackerspace anarchy may be a comparatively efficient institutional solution to the earliest stages of the entrepreneurial innovation problem compared to firms, markets and states."

In an exploration of makerspaces in different countries and how they contribute to business generation and sustainment, Van Holm (2015) also found that the maker movement presents multiple avenues to increase access to tools, with potential for impacts on the quantity and nature of entrepreneurship. It attracts more individuals into product design, and thus may launch more "accidental entrepreneurs". It also creates "dense but diverse networks, creating new ideas and innovative thinking (…) lowers the costs for prototyping, making early sales and acquiring outside funding more realistic".

Co-working and Knowledge Sharing

Soerjoatmodjo, Bagasworo, Joshua, Kalesaran, and van den Broek (2015) explore how knowledge sharing occurs in co-working spaces through semi-structured interviews with entrepreneurs from small and medium enterprises who are users of two co-working spaces in Jakarta. Occurring informally and voluntarily, and motivated by personal and business development, knowledge sharing amongst entrepreneurs in these co-working spaces involves donating and collecting tacit knowledge, shared around points of interaction such as pantry/kitchenette and coffee-makers and during lunch and/or afternoon coffee breaks, and endorsed through community culture formally declared in membership agreement and promoted by co-working space hosts. Knowledge not shared in these co-working spaces is trade secret-related. Subjects also admit that they refrain from sharing knowledge to direct competitors and knowledge sharing is also discouraged when the majority of available tables are dominated by particular companies.

Different Co-working Spaces Business Models: From Convenience Sharing to Collaborative Community-Building

Co-working spaces can be categorised into various forms. Some of the first actors were associations which initiated and participated in their development, opening them to the general public and becoming legitimate representatives of this movement through labels and certifications; for example the association Actipôle 21[9]; or participative 'collectives'[10] such as the cooperative Tiers Lieux,[11] which set up collective spaces for mainly independent workers in a spirit of co-opetition and community-building, with the aim of opening civic spaces for debate. Maker spaces (Dougherty, 2012; Hatch, 2013) and fab labs (Diez, 2012) are typical of this movement with the aim of empowering the "collective mind" and "redefining the future of production for mankind and its relation with the environment" and reshaping and reconfiguring "new models of production and creation" (Diez, 2012).

Traditional organisations have paid attention to the co-working phenomenon, as indicated by Pompa (2017) who shows how using digital platforms and co-working spaces may facilitate a company's human resource management and assist the work of HR managers, especially with the conception and implementation of recruitment and motivational processes.

Institutional actors such as local authorities, regional councils or universities have financed spaces, partially or entirely. For example, the Mairie de Paris[12] has created 19 spaces for student-entrepreneurs; the University of Paris-Saclay[13] has set up 7 innovation fab labs. Lumley (2014, see also Winkler, Saltzman, & Yang, 2016, about the rise of the 'entrepreneurial university') reports on a co-working project in a campus library to create a space to encourage student, faculty, and entrepreneur collaboration and interaction while demonstrating the economic value of the library. Frick (2015) describes key government initiatives in Norway to establish public incubators and co-working spaces to provide the necessary infrastructure for entrepreneurs to succeed with their innovations.

More broadly, Bouncken, Clauss, and Reuschl (2016) state that limited understanding exists on how coworking-space providers can design their business models for the differing user demands and their business models. They suggest "four layers of value creation and several value capture approaches to configure their business models along a continuum from rather basic efficiency-centered to novelty-centred full-service business models". Castilho and Quandt (2017) explore the development of collaborative capability in co-working spaces, as perceived by the main stakeholders in fourteen co-working spaces, located in six Asian countries, involving 31 stakeholders. Their results indicate that "convenience sharing" co-working spaces

---

[9]http://actipole21.org/en/.

[10]http://www.le-50.fr/tag/coworking-reseau-collaboratif-collectif-participatif/.

[11]https://coop.tierslieux.net/.

[12]https://api-site-cdn.paris.fr/images/94119.

[13]https://www.universite-paris-saclay.fr/fr/les-fablabs.

are mostly related to knowledge sharing and supporting collective action towards an effective execution, whereas 'community building' co-working spaces are more related to enhancing a creative field and supporting individual actions for collective results, showing a clear influence of a collaboration capability in 'community building' spaces.

However, the market for co-working spaces has now exploded and private, global enterprises, banks, real estate or investors are capitalising on the trend. Frick (2015) states that rapid changes took place in Norway when private companies started their own hubs. This is leading to competitive pressures and, according to some, "industrialising the market and losing the original values of the co-working movement" (Co-working Manager Interview, June 2016 in Dandoy, 2016).

Methodology

The RGCS network started in June 2014 and after two years of activities included groups in 8 cities, with around 1000 people participating in events organised by core members. The profiles of participants are varied: academics in management, economics, sociology, political sciences, design, ergonomics, architecture, urban studies; managers and owners of third spaces; consultants in organisational design and strategy; open innovation managers and project managers; representatives of public institutions such as boroughs, town halls, municipalities, regional councils, universities, urban conurbations; students, representatives of civic society and associative movements.

52 events were organised, such as seminars, workshops and meetings in cities in 6 countries (Paris, Lyon and Grenoble in France, London in the UK, Montreal in Canada, Barcelona in Spain, Amsterdam in Holland, and Berlin in Germany) with a range of participants, usually combining practitioners and academics. Before or after these events and on other occasions, visits of 82 co-working spaces, maker spaces, fab labs and hacker spaces took place in 8 countries (Paris, Lille and Lyon in France, London in the UK, Montreal in Canada, Berlin in Germany, Barcelona in Spain, Lisbon in Portugal, Singapore and Sydney in Australia). A demonstration in Berlin was organised in July 2016.[14] These events provided us with the opportunity to meet and talk to a large number of entrepreneurs and co-workers. 46 semi-structured interviews with managers of and workers in collaborative spaces were carried out in 10 countries (Germany, England, Australia, Canada, Spain, US, France, Italy, Portugal, Singapore), 1450 photos and 30 short films of collaborative spaces and their surroundings were taken, and 900 pages of field notes were produced by a number of RGCS members. The material gathered allowed us to compare a range of spatial designs, business models, work practices, city dynamics and public policies.

---

[14]See #visualizinghacking.

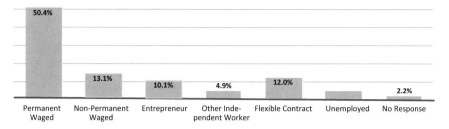

Fig. 2.1 Professional status

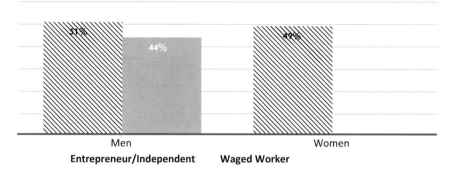

Fig. 2.2 Gender and professional status

Based on these activities, discussions, encounters and exchanges, RGCS published various online documents to report to its participants and beyond.[15]

This chapter is based on the analysis of these activities and of an online survey carried out in May 2016. The questionnaire can be found on the RGCS website[16] and focuses on new work practices and collaborative spaces. The target was recent graduates as we thought this category may include a higher proportion of young entrepreneurs and/or workers with experience of collaborative spaces. This targeting was opportunistic, no scientific sampling was intended. We gained access to alumni email databases from our RGCS academic contacts in three major cities, London, Paris and Montreal. We received approximately 1500 responses, but only processed 378 responses in an initial analysis, by selecting a sample based on age (21–30 years old) and academic qualifications—people who had studied in at least two countries, which we thought could be more likely to have adopted new work practices. This sample includes tele-workers, co-workers and most are in permanent employment. Permanent and non-permanent workers represent 63% of this sample, whereas entrepreneurs and independent workers 15% (see Fig. 2.1). Men and women are almost equally represented in each category (see Fig. 2.2).

---

[15]https://halshs.archives-ouvertes.fr/halshs-01426513/document.

[16]https://collaborativespacesstudy.files.wordpress.com/2016/10/synthese_des_recherches_rgcs_2 015_2016_vff.pdf see pp. 25–34.

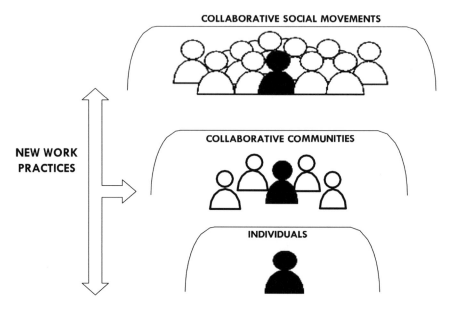

Fig. 2.3 Three levels of analysis of new work practices in the collaborative economy

The focus of the questionnaire was work transformation and collaborative spaces and it included filter questions to identify individuals with experience of collaborative spaces in order to probe them further. Our aim was to gain an understanding at the following three different levels (see Fig. 2.3). At the individual level, we wanted to elicit people's viewpoints about their current work practices in relation to their professional status, positions and activities. The community level (e.g. co-workers, managers or owners of co-working spaces) was important to consider the collective aspects of work practices. At the societal level, we aimed to gain insights into any social movement thinking underlying the emergence of these working practices, for instance from hackers/makers/fabbers, and their implications for communities and public policies. For each level, we paid attention to the spatial and temporal dimensions of work practices: space-time, i.e. how personal and collective time is managed; space-place, i.e. how third spaces organise space; and space-territory, i.e. whether and how third spaces are embedded in a city and their networks.

Findings

Field Notes, June 2014, London Technology Week[17]

We are attending this exhibition, it is early in the morning. I am taking photos and filming short video clips of visitors arriving through the main entrance. There are hundreds, thousands of people. An entire city is pouring into these old industrial wharves; I am listening to a group of 3 people nearby, talking about their start-up. I realise that most of these thousands of individuals are entrepreneurs. Only a few are waged workers, in the digital or IT industry, public relations, marketing or communication. This is a trigger for me, probably experienced by RGCS participants and other academics. Beyond statistics and a frame of mind, this is becoming tangible: work is being transformed, entrepreneurship is spreading and becoming commonplace, together with a culture of 'doing'. A few days later I attend an event in Shoreditch, which I do not recognize from 15 years ago. All around me there are new co-working spaces, entrepreneurs, hipsters; the atmosphere is playful and jolly. Exchanging glances with some people I can sense that there probably is another side to this coin, a less glamourous reality, but the seeds are planted. Many questions spring to my mind: is our university teaching still adapted to this evolution? Does our understanding of entrepreneurship correspond to this reality? Can we still delegate this transversal and manifold competence to a single 'entrepreneurship' colleague or course? Is our teaching reference point, the enterprise rather than assembled entrepreneurs, still relevant? What about our research in management? Have enterprises, big and small, understood the challenges of this transformation? Have citizens, beyond media reports and fears, realised what is happening? Despite these questionings, it is worth remembering that the large majority of workers are still in waged employment. For instance, out of 25.8 million workers in France, 22.8 million are waged (INSEE, 2014). Common products are still made in large numbers by traditional firms, far away from fab labs and maker spaces. Will future changes come from enterprises themselves, or from urban collaborative communities? (*RGCS Academic*).

---

[17]https://londontechweek.com/.

Individual Work Practices: Waged Versus Independent Employment?

New Professional Trajectories

Commonly found views in the media and management worlds (e.g. human resource management, see Pompa, 2017) tend to oppose the waged worker-follower-performer to the entrepreneur-innovator-creator. Accordingly, there are only two incompatible life choices, 'being' a waged worker or 'becoming' an entrepreneur. The latter are adventurous, operate in loose communities and multiple projects, take risks and have precarious lives. On the other hand, the former benefit from job security, attachment to an organisation, social status, and the comfort of a stable role and hierarchical structures. Entrepreneurs, and independent non-waged workers at large, are seen as an unavoidable solution to the economic crisis—also argued by some as due to a lack of entrepreneurial spirit and freedom. Current issues such as universal income, the 'uberisation' of economies and digital transformation (with some well paid big data workers but many less secure 'pickers' and software analysts down the chain) have instigated a rather dichotomous debate about waged and independent workers. The question of 'forced' entrepreneurship and independent work was frequently discussed in our workshops and seminars in many places. According to the Global Entrepreneurship Monitor (2017) reports, around 40% of entrepreneurs who have created a company had no real choice: their job searches were unsuccessful, they were fired, 'span off', or more or less forced to become intrapreneurs. We are not contesting these figures but our findings paint a more nuanced picture.

People in our seminars and workshops, especially in London and Paris, discussed time and professional trajectories (past and planned) extensively; many young people do not oppose waged work to entrepreneurship. Questionnaire responses displayed equal concerns from both waged and independent workers about time management. In both cases, new work practices are provoking the same difficulties in separating professional and personal lives and blurring the boundary between waged and independent work. Laurent (2016) reports research findings showing that an entrepreneur works more than an average waged worker but less than an executive; entrepreneurs enjoy less holiday time, which together with higher pressures, has long-term repercussions on their health. In some cases, it is worth noting that time pressures are experienced more negatively by waged workers, and that independent workers do not feel overwhelmed by time constraints (Fig. 2.4). Responses to questions about feeling involved at work, thinking about professional problems when waking up, considering organisational problems as one's own, or sacrificing too much for one's work, show, surprisingly, little difference between waged and independent workers.

'Slashers' or workers cumulating several jobs, often a waged activity and an entrepreneurial activity through an organisation or an association, represent for instance 2 million people in France of which 70% do so willingly (INSEE, 2014). It shows the emergence of alternate professional trajectories which can take the following shape. A new graduate creates a start-up. S/he develops competencies essential to

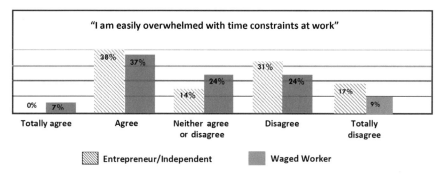

Fig. 2.4 Perceptions of time constraints in entrepreneurs and waged workers

most management professions: managing projects and managing through projects; the capacity to formulate and communicate the goals to a diverse range of communities; and resistance to stress and loneliness… In our conversations with young graduates attending our events, we found them very aware of the demand for such transversal competencies. An engineering graduate told us "*I want to become an entrepreneur to become a waged salaried employee*" which seems paradoxical but in fact is not contradictory. Another spent one year working on a start-up after graduating, and then got recruited by a large consulting group as open innovation manager. Once recruited, it is then possible to apply and refine these competencies and extend one's network, in order to then become again an entrepreneur 2 or 3 years later—based on what could be an overall strategy or simply an opportunity, a spin off, intrapreneurship or a change in personal circumstances. Individuals in the third loop of Fig. 2.5 are slightly older (25–30 years), have had first a short entrepreneurial experience and then 3–4 years of waged employment. Some express strong ambitions: "*I think this will help me climb up… move to an executive position, in project management or digital transformation*". This is different from chosen or enforced entrepreneurship.

Some insights were provided in our interviews and encounters: "Fight against boredom… I saw my father get bored to death in his professional career, which has been a straight road"; "Progress fast, move, be disruptive in my employment like in my start-up"; "The labour market will appreciate entrepreneurial behavioural more and more". And Fig. 2.6 shows that in terms of well-being, entrepreneurs or independent workers seem happier at work, even very happy, than waged workers in our respondents.

From the perspective of third spaces, we found that some already integrate the career loops we suggest in Fig. 2.6. A manager of a co-working space, also housing an incubator, told us his business was "*becoming a human resources management consulting firm*". Beyond their projects and start-ups themselves, the entrepreneurs they host are recruitment targets, because of their individual competences and employability. This manager was planning to organise events such as recruitment fairs, although this may be still an unusual case.

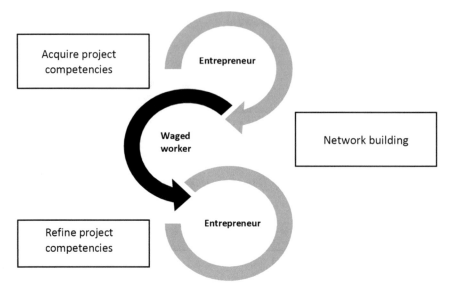

Fig. 2.5 Alternate entrepreneurship

"How do you feel at work?"

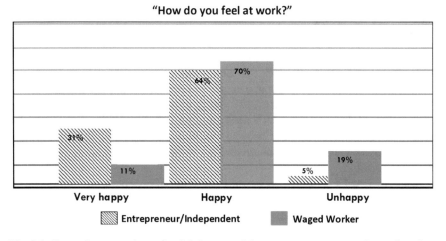

Fig. 2.6 Comparing perceptions of well being at work between entrepreneurs and waged workers

In the French case, public policies have contributed to this development, for instance through the new status of 'student-entrepreneur',[18] probably with the sole aim of facilitating the first career loop rather than the two following ones we suggest. New French university alliances, particularly in business and management education, have supported such initiatives in order to gain legitimacy and differentiate

---

[18]http://www.enseignementsup-recherche.gouv.fr/cid79926/statut-national-etudiant-entrepreneur.html.

themselves from traditional universities. Like universities in many other countries, they are investing in labs, incubators, accelerators and co-working spaces and are recruiting students with profiles and ambitions amenable to these new professional trajectories.

An Emotional Dimension to New Work Practices

Our interviews and visits to third spaces revealed an emotional dimension to their time-space arrangements, which is rarely found in traditional work environments. These new workers express a need for an almost familial cell structure which some called "*a community*", "*a gang of friends*", "*an extension of students' associations and parties*" or even "*a tribe*". Many of our questionnaire respondents come from outside the cities where they carried out their secondary education. Their families, childhood friends and acquaintances are often far away. Going to universities in the big cities, they feel "*catapulted*" far from home and hang on to their newly found "*gang of friends*" for talking, exchanging and managing emotions such as stress, loneliness, and the hardships of an entrepreneurial project: "*Talking on Skype is OK, but having a beer with other entrepreneurs from the workspace is better... And many have found partners here [laughter]*" (see also[19]).

Third spaces can be seen as emotional communities as much as communities of practice. When asked to define a community, managers of third spaces use the following terms: "*people you can trust*", "*a group of people helping each other*", "*shared and convergent values*", "*friendly atmosphere and mutual help*", so beyond a good work climate. For managers of third spaces, what is at the core of a community is reciprocal exchanges (47%) rather than spatial (20%) or technological (13%) aspects, or events (13%). This is confirmed by a GCUC (2016) global survey of co-working spaces which found that co-workers' feeling of being part of a community has increased from 58% in 2011–12, to 61% in 2013–14 and 70% in 2015–16.

During some of our visits, we also learnt that waged workers enjoy participating to the life of 'corporate' third spaces (or 'corpo-working'), for instance hackathons and training events where they mix with invited external entrepreneurs and innovators, which they find "*entertaining*" and "*disruptive*". These spaces are also used to manage geographic mobility for national and international workers and teleworkers. Beyond managing a space and enterprise social networks, their managers see themselves as 'community managers' and emphasise "*horizontality and transversality*", "*mutual exchanges*", "*rejection of hierarchies*", "*facilitating rather than organising*", and "*community management*". This represents a shift from hierarchy and coordination to relational logics.

Several interviewees talked about the 'post-wage' status of community managers. Similarly to a project manager, a community manager assembles internal and external waged workers and independent workers; this requires flexible interacting with actors in third spaces, elsewhere and on electronic social network platforms, and also with

---

[19]https://www.bureauxapartager.com/blog/les-chiffres-du-coworking-en-2014/.

consumers who are becoming ever present. The community manager's roadmap and necessary competences are therefore challenging: *"community management… its meaning keeps changing as I manage it"*.

New Work Practices and Communities

The notion of communities is far from new for business academics and practitioners alike, and there are many terms to describe them such as occupational or professional communities, communities of trade, or communities of practice, amongst many. Much is hoped for from informal collective communities forming at the intersection of formal organisations in terms of innovative potential, knowledge management, and a more humane and local human resource management. In our constantly assembled and disassembled digital 'entrepreuneurialised' economies, communities have come to represent the community-based innovative stitching of micro-coordination which seems to happen in third spaces. A co-worker tells us how happy he is in this space. He plans his comings and goings according to not only his projects but his appointments and his mood: *"when I feel a little low, I come more often, the energy here is great."* In an artists' maker space in Barcelona,[20] the manager tells us she does not organise events but parties. The space we visit looks like a musical or theatre stage setting.

Throughout the day, personal working times mingle with collective events such as breakfasts, coffee breaks, pitches, training sessions, hackathons, sharing reflexions, coaching, games and challenges between teams, etc. Event calendars are displayed on websites, walls and newsletters. There is evidence of intergenerational approaches mixing different age groups or with specific events for children (*"coding and cakes"*) or seniors (*"digital lunches for oldies"*).

Community managers play an essential role. A fab lab manager tells us of how his successor was taken by surprise when people came to him for chats, confided in him, shared their problems and *"unwind"*, as they had done with her before. Tech Hub in Berlin[21] has a 'Chief Happiness Officer'. Two thirds of third space managers in our questionnaire stated that their communication material promises to make members feel part of a community. The role of community managers can be underestimated: 88% of our questionnaire respondents state that they facilitate the emergence of collaborations, 50% that they establish relations with the neighbourhood and local communities and 67% say they *"look after everything"*. 82% think that relational skills are absolutely essential, compared to 59% for technical and 47% for financial and administrative competences.

Visiting third spaces is also carefully organised and is seen as entering a community: it starts with the kitchen, the coffee machine, meeting people, telling anecdotes about the furniture and the rooms and the social events. Commonly used sentences during visits are *"you will join our community"*, *"community members often meet…"*,

---

[20]https://hangar.org/en/hangar/que-i-com/.

[21]http://berlin.lafrenchtech.com/.

"*the events we organise are at the heart of our community*". Of course, the quality of the equipment, machines, IT facilities, physical layout, open and working spaces and the infrastructure matter, with a wide range of design, working and cultural styles across different spaces. Overall the dominant emphasis is on "*spaces for competence-building, creativity and innovation*".

The spaces are also envisaged as "*windows*" into larger communities or territories. For instance, the Internet of Things Start-up Ecosystem[22] accelerator space is situated in the IoT Valley in Toulouse and was created by an association aiming to "*develop IoT excellence and productivity across regional entrepreneurs, industrialists and academics*". They act as intermediary or boundary objects between start-ups, business angels, large enterprises, support structures and political institutions, concentrating know-how and creativity.

A "*tourism industry of collaborative spaces*" (interview with a hacker) is also emerging in many places, for instance in Berlin. To promote their region, public bodies, regional and local authorities, universities and consulting firms are joining forces to organise tours of several spaces together, or "*learning expeditions*". These are offered as "*experiences, a time to reflect and make contacts*" and are charged for through a fee or a donation. There appears to be a growing demand for these, which is clearly capitalised on by third spaces managers, but at the risk of disturbing the peace and quiet for workers (our hacker above was ironical in his description of a 'tourism industry'!) and increasing community managers' workloads.

The issue of open innovation is a part of this phenomenon. It is an important challenge, as indicated in our survey with 73% of managers of third spaces deeming it crucial. From our visits and interviews, we suggest that there are currently three scenarios to support open innovation: relocation, 'excubation', and transition.

- Relocation involves seconding waged workers to a corporate or independent third space for several days, weeks or even months. Some of the expected benefits are new collaborations, learning new techniques and business intelligence.
- Excubation is about relocating parts of a project or an organisation, with its members and some resources, to a third space. Expected benefits are similar to the ones for relocations.
- Transition concerns waged or independent workers who travel long-distances for projects, and allocated a subscription to a third-space situated in a geographically convenient place, or are located for episodic stays in their clients' internal third spaces. For instance, the Mixer innovation hub[23] in Paris offers seven 'flex offices' to their collaborators visiting their headquarters.

As well as practical solutions, these spaces and mechanisms provide emotional support above all, which was expressed to us strongly in hackerspaces and makerspaces such as Noisebridge,[24] a non-profit educational technical-creative hack-

---

[22]http://www.iot-valley.fr/.

[23]http://www.urlab.eu/news/.

[24]https://www.noisebridge.net/.

erspace based in San Francisco, C-Base,[25] an early digital activists hackerspace in Berlin, the Open Innovation Space in Berlin[26] and Hangar, an artists' makerspace in Barcelona, already mentioned above. Hackerspaces and makerspaces are more inspired by social movement ethics, but are often reduced by managers to hackathons, mainly run by corporate third spaces, or to a vague principle of hacking: *"we now need to hack management..."* Hackerspaces in particular, but also some makerspaces, run on new forms of governance, based on 'hacker ethics' centred on the community. This means agreeing on and regulating the value of a hack (a bit like academic peer-reviewing) as a collective. This implies long and time-consuming discussions aiming at a consensus (voting is seen negatively), listening, talking, observing and equalising speech times. This often takes place in the biggest open space.

Hackers regulate themselves by and through their professional community which shares and renders matters explicit during multiple collective exchanges. Group endogenous control is part and parcel of exogenous control by a bigger community outside the specific space, and a larger social movement. The hacker communities we observed were very heterogeneous: independent workers, freelancers, students, waged workers, academics; more entrepreneurs and co-workers during the day, and more hackers and makers in the evenings. Clearly, these practices may also have limitations when groups break away from exogenous control and run the risk of becoming inward-looking and sectarian, or if social movements rigidify.

Collaborative Movements and New Work Practices

Our third level of analysis is societal. Makerspaces, hackerspaces and fab labs were easily associated to a well-known social movement in the discussions we witnessed. Co-working is different. This phenomenon was more commonly referred to as an *"industry"*, a *"societal trend"*, or *"innovation-related"*. Some co-working movements, for instance the French collective of third places,[27] the Associacio de Coworking de Catalunya[28] or Coworking Europe,[29] strive to structure and incarnate a social movement. However, many of the people we interviewed and talked to during our events were not convinced. Collaborative movements can be split into two categories which seem in opposition to each other: the activists and participants in the hacker/maker social movement; and the managers looking for *"disruptive experiences"* and in search of innovation. Makers, hackers and fabbers nurture the common good and promote open knowledge to move away from enterprise closed systems, and for them capitalist business enterprises and relentless innovation are ambiguous. Doing and learning together are more important.

---

[25] https://wiki.hackerspaces.org/c-base.

[26] https://www.openinnovationspace.com/en/.

[27] https://www.helloasso.com/associations/collectif-des-tiers-lieux.

[28] http://www.cowocat.cat/.

[29] https://coworkingeurope.net/tag/2017/.

Field Notes and Discussion in a Paris Makerspace, June 2016
I spend over an hour with a group of enthusiastic makers who talk about their drone. They have spent hundreds of hours building it together. They tell me about their ideas, tricks, reuses and adaptations… They have clearly sacrificed many evenings for this project. The little plane is impressive and beautiful. It shows scars of much tinkering. Before leaving them to go to another project I ask them whether it could fly. "No, it is far too heavy!" (*RGCS Academic*).

We saw many unfinished prototypes in the makerspaces and hackerspaces we visited—although there may be more entrepreneurial hackers pushing for completion of projects. Endless and aimless learning can sometimes lead to real and useful innovations. During one of our seminars, a fab lab manager mentioned the case of someone who had come to his corporate space to produce a photo frame using a 3D printer; he came out with a renewed vision of technical processes which led to managing his projects using 3D multiple prototypes as intermediary objects for his team members. Some makers and hackers have also finalised processes for bypassing built-in technical obsolescence in lightbulbs, computers and home appliances, which corresponds well to their ethical aims. Sometimes the aim is even more ambitious, like the French ICI Montreuil[30] manager who sees his maker space as an "*engine for reindustrialisation*".

The purist hackers are often very critical about corporate third spaces. A manager of a university fab lab told us: "if these were real fab labs, I could easily go there without making an appointment and they would share their knowledge and procedures with everyone… even their competitors! Everything I do in my fab lab is open, even to our university and academic rivals! Here is the proof! [pointing to a researcher sitting there]".

On the other hand, business enterprises draw heavily from collaborative movements, and innovative entrepreneurship and intrapreneurship are major strategies—to the point of sometimes not really having a clear strategic vision; this has been described to us by some managers in our events as "*a strategic smokescreen*". Makers, hackers and co-workers are seen as obvious (easy?) solutions to focus on professional communities, "*hack management*", induce tinkering and serendipity, and 'free' the enterprise from its walls and hierarchies. Corporate hacking is articulated by some we encountered as a means to "*move the lines*", "*provide a sense of opportunity and organisational improvisation*", "*a positive diversion from established practices*". Corporate hackers aim to improve and transform enterprises rather than challenge their raison d'être.[31]

Nevertheless importing hacking and co-working practices to corporate environments can be innovative (e.g. for research and development, see Fuzi, Clifton, &

---

[30]http://www.icimontreuil.com/stages/manager-un-fablab-makerspace.
[31]https://hacktivateurs.co/2016/04/05/corporate-hacking-quest-ce-que-cest/.

Loudon, 2014). In a context of increasing workers' mobility, third spaces can help build a network of stopovers for urban and rural workers and managers. Joint corporate third spaces, with partners and even competitors, independent third spaces to relocate workers or excubate projects, can stimulate business intelligence and innovative potential. They can help become aware of emerging projects and gain from coaching with seniors (who may also benefit from 'reverse mentoring'). It is possible to set up open innovation approaches including external entrepreneurs, student-entrepreneurs, resident hackers, workers from distant places, etc.

Conclusion

Collaborative movements are often expected to provide a disruptive impetus for traditional business organisations, where there is talk of 'hacking' management, enterprises, their language, procedures and tools. The emergence of the 'bore out' syndrome or exhaustion through boredom in traditional organisations seems to originate from pressures to conform which curtail personal development and creativity (Gino, 2016). Some companies are trying to stimulate innovative behaviour and creativity, for instance Google[32] policy of 20% time, leaving a day a week free for employees to work on their own projects.

Learning to become innovative happens not only by learning about it but through practicing it. Our research survey on third space co-workers and managers in cities in several countries found that, although the divide between waged and independent workers remains large, we are witnessing the emergence of professional trajectories in young people alternating waged and independent work across lifetimes; and there is also existing evidence of slashers cumulating waged and entrepreneurial activities across short-term time and space spans.

Collaborative third spaces such as co-working spaces, makerspaces, hackerspaces, fab labs, incubators or digital labs can mix waged and independent workers through new governance models such as excubation, transition, relocation, open innovation, and community management. This is closely related to hacker social movements, which are attracting interest from traditional organisations. These two worlds collide, cross over and feed each other. Some argue that the hacker community spirit and ethics of collaborative social movements may get lost when captured and colonised by business organisations (Richard, 2014). Opting for open source, running hackathons, setting up corpo-working spaces, or instigating corporate maker cultures are signs of a management which seeks meaning and 'free itself' which may well be utopian and often relies on techno-utopian entrepreneur heroes (Anderson, 2012). In this respect, the activist counter culture in collaborative movements (Lallement, 2015; Bottolier-Despois, 2012, see also the growth of cooperative and participative associations[33]) may well inspire a rethinking of work practices and a return to communities and

---

[32]http://uk.businessinsider.com/google-20-percent-time-policy-2015-4.

[33]http://www.les-scop.coop/sites/fr/ and https://www.uk.coop/.

collaborative practices. Our research aimed to transcend existing dichotomies and better understand emerging work practices, manifest in third spaces.

Further work could focus on the relationships between third spaces and local, city, regional and public planning authorities. The latter tend to have outdated pre-suppositions about new and future work practices, as found in our discussions with the Reinvent Paris[34] project and TechCity in London. Capdevila (2015, 2017) argues that co-working spaces contribute "to the interaction between co-located actors through the articulation of places, spaces, projects and events" and he suggests that public policies could support "the emergence and development of innovation by foster-ing innovative processes outside firms" and the "innovative and creative capacity of cities". Topics such as co-living (e.g. WeWork[35]), the growth of co-working spaces erected by private building contractors, the strong links with some large food-catering companies (e.g. Starbuck), transport issues (e.g. French railways and its co-working spaces[36]) show that a range of business actors are more and more present in the 'market' of collaborative spaces. Indeed, Gandini (2015) alerts us to an emerging 'co-working bubble' given that co-working is being increasingly used for branding, marketing and business purposes. Faced with these business actors, public institu-tions are currently rather disjointed and EU structural funds, regional, district and metropolitan authorities still think in terms of major material investments and long-term irreversible choices which may hamper the collaborative economy.

The choice of location is and may become more structuring of urbanism, city spaces and mobility. Some effects can be gentrification and unwelcome changes to real estate costs and housing rentals. Mariotti, Pacchi, and Di Vita (2017) recently stated that "location patterns and the effects co-working spaces generate on the urban context are issues that have been neglected by the existing literature". To fill this gap about the location patterns of these new working spaces and their urban effects at different scales, both in terms of urban spaces and practices, they focus on Milan, the core of the Italian knowledge-based, creative, digital, and sharing economy, and the city hosting the largest number of co-working spaces in Italy. Their field research illustrates how the participation of workers in co-working spaces in local commu-nity initiatives can contribute to urban revitalisation trends and micro-scale physical transformations. Waters-Lynch et al. (2016) also suggest future research directions on co-working spaces by "linking relevant extant theory with key questions across the fields of economic geography, urban planning economics and organisational studies".

Overall we concur with Houtbeckers (2017)'s view that there is a "need for alter-natives to the heroic representations of entrepreneurship (…) which affect how the phenomenon is represented in academic and public discussions". Her ethnographic study reflects on the "shifting positions manifested in the entanglement of stories of the researcher and the people met during the fieldwork". The stories she unveiled show how "for some the co-working space was a place for hope while for others it caused distress and even burnout". She found that despite its failure in the form of a

---

[34]http://www.reinventer.paris/fr/sites/.

[35]https://www.wework.com/.

[36]http://www.sncf-developpement.fr/actualites/des-espaces-de-co-working-en-gare-8799.

bankruptcy, the co-working cooperative succeeded in enabling social innovation in the form of hope and personal development—also for the researcher herself.

Finally, based on this initial research, we suggest some practical recommendations for various co-working stakeholder groups in Table 2.1 in order to make the most of the innovative and collaborative community-building potential of third places.

Table 2.1 Practical suggestions

Public bodies and institutional actors (Policy decision-makers, local authorities, regional councils, universities, etc.)	• Move from policies *for* to policies *through* collaborative communities • Coordinate with a range of actors (e.g. companies, SMEs, universities, co-working operators) to link innovation and territorial policies to entrepreneurial practices • Develop and support collaborative infrastructures necessary for entrepreneurship to emerge • Join forces (public bodies, regional and local authorities, universities, firms, co-working operators) to promote cities and regions, for instance by organising tours of third spaces • Go beyond using co-working spaces for branding and marketing purposes
Corporate actors	• Use co-working spaces to facilitate human resource management for the conception and implementation of recruitment and motivational processes • Enable teleworkers or teams of teleworkers to use external co-working spaces and/or corporate third spaces ('corpo-working', for instance hackathons and training events with invited external entrepreneurs, hackers and innovators) • Consider different scenarios to support open innovation (relocation, excubation and transition) • Be open to governance and regulation models used by hackers/makers for the early stages of entrepreneurial innovation
Work collectives (Hackerspaces, makerspaces, fablabs, etc.)	• Build dense but diverse networks to support innovative thinking • Act as intermediary between start-ups, business angels, large enterprises, support structures and political institutions • Shape and configure new models of production and creation • Support prototyping, early sales and outside funding • Regulate the collective through professional communities and multiple exchanges • Beware from breaking away from exogenous control and becoming inward-looking and rigidifying

(continued)

Table 2.1   (continued)

Co-working spaces owners/Managers	• Consider the range of business models (from basic efficiency-centred to novelty-centred full service)
	• Focus on collective meaning, which can be orientated towards practice, professional identity, and emotional support to address loneliness and sense-making
	• Think through 'leaderless' organising principles
	  – Self-organising (the capability of individuals to choose various ways of functioning and their level of autonomy and responsibility)
	  – Care of each other
	  – Sense of ownership
	  – Integration of new members
	• Develop HR management skills to understand individual competences and employability (e.g. organise events such as recruitment fairs, assemble internal and external waged workers and independent workers)
	• Interact flexibly with actors in third spaces, elsewhere and on electronic social network platforms
	• Support a community culture through convivial spatial design such as pantry/kitchenette, coffee-machines and collective spaces
	• Organise collective events such as breakfasts, coffee breaks, pitches, training sessions, hackathons, sharing sessions, coaching, games and challenges between teams, etc. Display event calendars on websites, walls and newsletters. Think of intergenerational approaches mixing different age groups or with specific events for children or seniors, in collaboration with local actors
	• Develop relational skills (as well as technical and financial and administrative competences)
	• Beware of industrialising the market and losing the original values of the co-working movement

Co-working spaces members	• Think about the difficulties in separating professional and personal lives and blurring the boundary between waged and independent work • Engage with the co-working space community-building culture to avoid distress and even burnout and bring hope, trust and personal development • Be open to networking opportunities and collaborative prospects
SMEs	• Use co-working spaces in a closed (e.g. using a whole floor) or open space fashion (sharing the space with others)

(continued)

Table 2.1 (continued)

Entrepreneurs	• Envisage alternating between waged employment and own entrepreneurial ventures • Consider transversal competencies and integrating career loops • Develop networks of social relations to increase credibility and innovative potential • Knowledge sharing amongst entrepreneurs in co-working spaces involves donating as well as collecting tacit knowledge • Beware of opportunism which may spoil learning processes and entrepreneurial performance as it reduces antecedent trust and community building

References

Anderson, C. (2012). *Makers: The new industrial revolution*. New York: Crown Publishers.

Assenza, P. (2015). If you build it will they come? The influence of spatial configuration on social and cognitive functioning and knowledge spillover in entrepreneurial co-working and hacker spaces. *Journal of Management Policy and Practice, 16*(3), 35–48.

Bizzarri, C. (2014). The emerging phenomenon of coworking. A redefinition of job market in networking society. In K. Müller, S. Roth, & M. Zak (Eds.), *Social Dimension of Innovation* (pp. 195–206). Prag; Linde. Available at SSRN: https://ssrn.com/abstract=2533911.

Bottolier-Despois, F. (2012). *FabLabs, makerspaces: entre nouvelles formes d'innovation et militantisme libertaire*. Observatoire du Management Alternatif, Cahier de Recherche, HEC Paris. http://appli6.hec.fr/amo/Public/Files/Docs/276_fr.pdf.

Bouncken, R. B., & Reuschl, A. J. (2016). Coworking-spaces: How a phenomenon of the sharing economy builds a novel trend for the workplace and for entrepreneurship. *Review of Managerial Science*, 1–18.

Bouncken, R. B., Clauss, T., & Reuschl, A. J. (2016). Coworking-spaces in Asia: A business model design perspective. In *Conference: Strategic Management Society Special Conference, Contextualizing Strategic Management in Asia: Institutions, Innovation and Internationalization*, Chinese University of Hong Kong, 10–12 December.

Brafman, O., & Beckstrom, R. A. (2006). *The starfish and the spider: The unstoppable power of leaderless organizations*. New York: Penguin.

Burret, A., & Pierre, X. (2014). The added value of co-working spaces in the area of business development support: Encouraging peer networks. *Revue de l'Entrepreneuriat, 13*(1), 51–73.

Butcher, T. (2016). Co-working communities. In R. Horne, J. Fien, & B. B. Beza (Eds.), *Sustainability citizenship in cities: Theory and practice* (pp. 93–103). Earthscan Routledge: London, New York.

Capdevila, I. (2015). Co-working spaces and the localised dynamics of innovation in Barcelona. *International Journal of Innovation Management, 19*(03), 28 pp.

Capdevila, I. (2017, June 7). Knowing communities and the innovative capacity of cities. *City, Culture and Society*.

Castilho, M. F., & Quandt, C. O. (2017). 'Convenience Sharing' or 'Community Building': Collaborative capability in coworking spaces. In *28th ISPIM Innovation Symposium*. Composing the Innovation Symphony, 18–21 June, Vienna.

Dale, K., & Burrell, G. (2007). *The spaces of organisation and the organisation of space: Power, identity and materiality at work*. Basingstoke: Palgrave Macmillan.

d'Andria, A., & Gabarret, I. (2017). The entrepreneurial connection. In A. d'Andria & I. Gabarret (Eds.), *Building 21st century entrepreneurship* (pp. 73–92). London: Wiley.

Dandoy, A. (2016). *Les défis de l'émergence et de la pérennité des communautés dans un contexte transitionnel, Le cas des espaces de coworking*, Rapport d'Avancement 1ere année, Atelier Doctoral, Département DRM M&O, Université Paris-Dauphine.

Davies, A., & Tollervey, K. (2013). *The style of coworking: Contemporary shared workspaces.* Munich: Prestel Verlag.

DeGuzman, G. V., & Tang, A. I. (2011). *Working in the unoffice: A guide to coworking for indie workers, small businesses, and nonprofits.* San Francisco: Night Owls Press LLC.

DeKoven, B. (2002). *The well-played game: A playful path to wholeness.* Bloomington: iUniverse.

Diez, T. (2012). Personal fabrication: Fab labs as platforms for citizen-based innovation, from microcontrollers to cities. *Nexus Network Journal, 14*(3), 457–468.

Dougherty, D. (2012). The maker movement. *Innovations, 7*(3), 11–14.

Fabbri, J. (2015). *Les espaces de coworking pour entrepreneurs. Nouveaux espaces de travail et dynamiques interorganisationnelles collaboratives.* Doctoral Dissertation, Centre de Recherche en Gestion, Ecole Polytechnique, Palaiseau.

Frick, J. A. (2015). A comparative study of entrepreneurial clusters and co-working spaces in Norway: The sudden boom of private initiatives from 2010–2015. In *Operations Management for Sustainable Competitiveness, 22nd Conference of European Operation Management Association (Euroma 2015),* June 26–July 1, Neuchatel, Switzerland.

Fuzi, A. (2015). Co-working spaces for promoting entrepreneurship in sparse regions: The case of South Wales. *Regional Studies, Regional Science, 2*(1), 462–469.

Fuzi, A., Clifton, N., & Loudon, G. (2014). New in-house organizational spaces that support creativity and innovation: the co-working space. In *R&D Management Conference* 2014, 3–6 June, Stuttgart.

Gandini, A. (2015). The rise of coworking spaces: A literature review. *Ephemera: Theory & Politics in Organizations, 15*(1), 193–205. http://www.ephemerajournal.org/contribution/rise-coworkin g-spaces-literature-review.

GCUC. (2016). Global coworking survey. In *Global Coworking Unconference Conference,* Los Angeles, May 6. http://canada.gcuc.co/wp-content/uploads/2016/presentations/DESKMAG%2 0GCUC%20GLOBAL%20COWORKING%20SURVEY%20PRESENTATION%202016%20 SLIDES.pdf.

Gerdenitsch, C., Scheel, T. E., Andorfer, J., & Korunka, C. (2016). Coworking spaces: A source of social support for independent professionals. *Frontiers in Psychology, 7,* 581.

Gertner, D., & Mack, E. (2017). The Entrepreneurial Orientation (EO) of incubators, accelerators, and co-working spaces. *International Journal of Regional Development, 4*(2), 1–24.

Giddens, A. (2000). *Runaway world: How globalization is reshaping our life.* New York: Routledge.

Gino, F. (2016). Let Your Workers Rebel (Special Issue on The Big Idea). *Harvard Business Review,* 3–25. http://www.hbs.edu/faculty/Publication%20Files/Let%20your%20workers%20rebel_b87 d0da9-de68-45be-a026-22dee862e6e4.pdf.

Global Entrepreneurship Monitor. (2017). *Global Report 2016/17.* London: Global Entrepreneurship Research Association, London Business School. http://gemconsortium.org/report.

Gussekloo, A., & Jacobs, E. (2016). *Digital nomads: How to live, work and play around the world.* New York: Esther Jacobs & André Gussekloo. http://www.digitalnomadbook.com/.

Hatch, M. (2013). *The maker movement manifesto: Rules for innovation in the new world of crafters, hackers, and tinkerers.* New York: McGraw Hill Professional.

Holienka, M., & Racek, F. (2015). Coworking spaces in Slovakia. *Management Review, 9*(2), 29–43.

Houtbeckers, E. (2017). Researcher subjectivity in social entrepreneurship ethnographies: The entanglement of stories in a co-working cooperative for social innovation. *Social Enterprise Journal, 13*(02), 128–143.

Hurry, C. J. (2012). *The Hub Halifax: A qualitative study on coworking.* MBA Research Project, St. Mary's University, Halifax, Nova Scotia.

INSEE (2014). *Une photographie du marché du travail en 2014*, Paris: Institut National de la Statistique et des Etudes Economiques. https://www.insee.fr/fr/statistiques/1560271.

Lallement, M. (2015). *L'âge du faire: Hacking, travail, anarchie.* Paris: Seuil.

Laurent, S. (2016). La vie d'un entrepreneur est-elle plus dure que celle d'un salarié? *Le Monde*, 20 January 2016. http://www.lemonde.fr/les-decodeurs/article/2016/01/20/la-vie-d-un-entrepreneu r-est-elle-plus-dure-que-celle-d-un-salarie_4850512_4355770.html.

Lumley, R. M. (2014). A coworking project in the campus library: Supporting and modeling entrepreneurial activity in the academic library. *New Review of Academic Librarianship, 20*(1), 49–65.

Mariotti, I., Pacchi, C., & Di Vita, S. (2017). Coworking spaces in Milan: Location patterns and urban effects. *Journal of Urban Technology*, 1–20.

Marx, A. (2016). *The ecosystem of urban high-tech entrepreneurs in Munich. Coworking spaces and their spatial configuration.* Master Thesis, Urbanistik Fakultät für Architektur, Technische Universität, München.

Massey, D. B. (1995). *Spatial divisions of labor: Social structures and the geography of production.* New York: Routledge.

Merkel, J. (2015). Coworking in the city. *Ephemera: Theory & Politics in Organizations, 15*(1), 121–139.

Moriset, B. (2014). Building new places of the creative economy. The rise of coworking spaces. In *2nd Geography of Innovation International Conference 2014*, Utrecht University, Utrecht, 23–25 January 2014, 24.

Oldenburg, R. (1989). *The great good place: Cafés, coffee shops, community centers, beauty parlors, general stores, bars, hangouts, and how they get you through the day.* Vadnais Heights, Minnesota: Paragon House Publishers.

Pennel, D. (2013). *Travailler pour soi: quel avenir pour le travail à l'heure de la révolution individualiste?.* Paris: Seuil.

Pompa, L. (2017). From the unusual to the useful: Digital platforms and co-working spaces as instruments for human resource management in emerging economic and organizational environments. *International Journal of Business and Management, 12*(8), 143–159.

Raffaele, C., & Connell, J. (2016). Telecommuting and co-working communities: What are the implications for individual and organizational flexibility? In J. Connell & J. Burgess (Eds.), *Flexible work organizations: The challenges of capacity building in Asia* (pp. 21–35). London: Springer.

Reuschke, D., Mason, C., Syrett, S., & Van Ham, M. (2015). Connecting entrepreneurship with homes and neighbourhoods. In C. Mason, D. Reuschke, S. Syrett, & M. van Ham (Eds.), *Entrepreneurship in cities: Neighbourhoods, households and homes* (pp. 1–18). Cheltenham: Edward Elgar Publishing.

Richard, S. (2014). *L'entrepreneur hacker.* L'ethos de travail des entrepreneurs web: Mémoire de Maitrise, Department of Communication, University of Montreal.

Ross, P., & Ressia, S. (2015). Neither office nor home: Coworking as an emerging workplace choice. *Employment Relations Record, 15*(1), 42.

Soerjoatmodjo, G. W. L., Bagasworo, D. W., Joshua, G., Kalesaran, T., & van den Broek, K. F. (2015). Sharing workspace, sharing knowledge: Knowledge sharing amongst entrepreneurs in Jakarta co-working spaces. In *International Conference on Intellectual Capital and Knowledge Management and Organisational Learning*, Bangkok, Thailand, 05–06 November, Kidmore End, Reading, Academic Conferences International Limited (pp. 259–267).

Spinuzzi, C. (2012). Working alone together: Coworking as emergent collaborative activity. *Journal of Business and Technical Communication, 26*(4), 399–441.

Spreitzer, G., Bacevice, P., & Garrett, L. (2015). Why people thrive in coworking spaces. *Harvard Business Review, 93*(7), 28–30.

Sundsted, T., Jones, D., & Bacigalupo, T. (2009). *I'm Outta Here: How co-working is making the office obsolete.* Lulu.com.

Tounes, A., & Fayolle, A. (2006). L'odyssée d'un concept et les multiples figures de l'entrepreneur. *La Revue des Sciences de Gestion, 4*, 17–30.

Van Holm, E. J. (2015). Makerspaces and contributions to entrepreneurship. *Procedia-Social and Behavioral Sciences, 195*, 24–31.

van Weele, M. A., Van Rijnsoever, F. J., & Steinz, H. (2014). Start-ups down under: How start-up communities facilitate Australian entrepreneurship. In *DRUID (Dynamics of Organizations, Industries, Systems and Regions) Society Conference,* Copenhagen Business School, Copenhagen, June 16–18 (27 pp.). https://www.researchgate.net/profile/Marijn_Van_Weele/publicati on/271846389_Start-ups_down_under_How_start-up_communities_facilitate_Australian_entre preneurship/links/54d4a0060cf2464758060991.pdf.

Waters-Lynch, J., & Potts, J. (2017). The social economy of coworking spaces: A focal point model of coordination. *Review of Social Economy*, 1–17.

Waters-Lynch, J. M., Potts, J., Butcher, T., Dodson, J., & Hurley, J. (2016). *Coworking: A transdisciplinary overview* (58 pp.). Available at SSRN: https://ssrn.com/abstract=2712217 or http://dx. doi.org/10.2139/ssrn.2712217.

Winkler, C., Saltzman, E., & Yang, S. (2016). Investigating student coworking as a catalyst for entrepreneurial success. In *United States Association for Small Business and Entrepreneurship. Conference Proceedings* (pp. FB1–FB29). Boca Raton: United States Association for Small Business and Entrepreneurship.

Chapter 3
Joint Work and Information Sharing in the Modern Digital Workplace: How the Introduction of "Social" Features Shaped Enterprise Collaboration Systems

Petra Schubert

Background to the Research: Center for Enterprise Information Research (CEIR)

In the first part of this chapter, I will discuss the background to the studies, the structure and nature of Enterprise Collaboration Systems (ECS) and discuss the origin of the word "social" and what it means for ECS. In the second part, I will present findings from a longitudinal research programme on the adoption of ECS, discuss differences in the implementation process and introduce typical forms of use (I will call them "archetypes of use"), which I identified in these studies.

Figure 3.1 shows an overview of the contents of this chapter.

The research presented in this chapter was conducted by the **Center for Enterprise Information Research (CEIR)**, a joint project I co-founded with my colleague Professor Susan P. Williams at the Computer Science Department of the University of Koblenz-Landau. The goal of CEIR is to conduct high quality research in the area of IT-enabled business change and the Digital Workplace (www.ceir.de). The research team working in CEIR is committed to evidence-based research and to translating that evidence into theoretical and actionable outcomes. Figure 3.2 shows an overview of the CEIR research programme on the adoption of ECS.

Since the year 2010, the research group has been collecting field data with the help of a University-Industry Collaboration named **IndustryConnect**. IndustryConnect is a collaboration project between CEIR and a group of practitioners from companies and public agencies, who all use the same, integrated Enterprise Collaboration System (ECS). At the point of writing this chapter, 29 organisations are members of IndustryConnect. The Online Community has 72 members (practitioners, professors, Ph.D. students). The participating practitioners are committed to sharing their

P. Schubert (✉)
University of Koblenz-Landau, Koblenz, Germany
e-mail: schubert@uni-koblenz.de

© Springer International Publishing AG, part of Springer Nature 2019   45
K. Riemer et al. (eds.), *Collaboration in the Digital Age*, Progress in IS,
https://doi.org/10.1007/978-3-319-94487-6_3

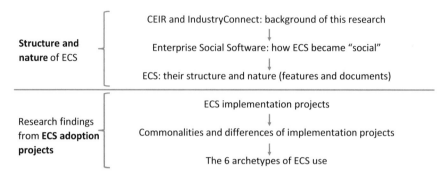

Fig. 3.1 Overview of this chapter

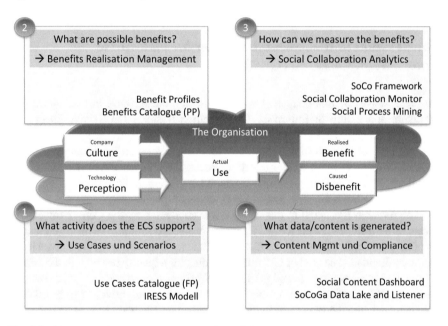

Fig. 3.2 CEIR research programme on enterprise collaboration systems

knowledge and experience about the adoption of their ECS with their peers and with the researchers by means of active participation in workshops, questionnaires and interviews. The data is captured using the eXperience Method for writing research cases on IT implementations (Schubert & Wölfle, 2007). At its heart, the eXperience Method is a *method for data collection*, which means that supplemental methods are required for the *analysis of the data* and thus the generation of research findings from the cases. Over the years, the research team has used eXperience cases e.g. in combination with *grounded theory* (coding approaches) or *cross-case analysis* and has created *in-depth narrative research cases* from them. Whilst eXperience cases capture in-depth information about the reasons and experiences from a tech-

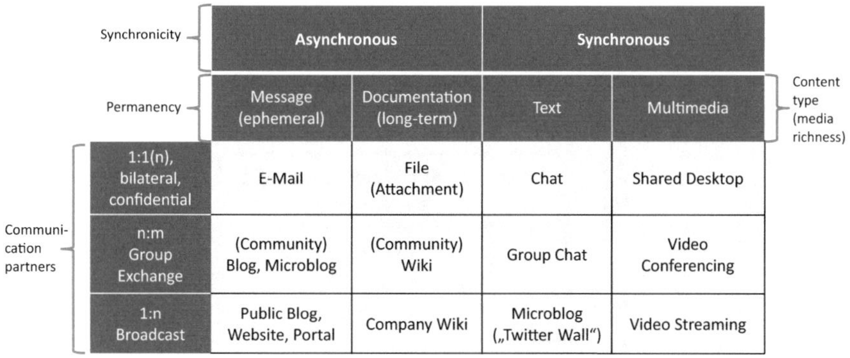

Synchronicity	Asynchronous		Synchronous		Content type (media richness)
Permanency	Message (ephemeral)	Documentation (long-term)	Text	Multimedia	
1:1(n), bilateral, confidential	E-Mail	File (Attachment)	Chat	Shared Desktop	
n:m Group Exchange	(Community) Blog, Microblog	(Community) Wiki	Group Chat	Video Conferencing	
1:n Broadcast	Public Blog, Website, Portal	Company Wiki	Microblog („Twitter Wall")	Video Streaming	

(Communication partners)

Fig. 3.3 Software components for communication depending on collaboration context

nology introduction project (reasons, participants, processes and systems) they can normally only provide a reflective account at *a point in time*. To address this, the researchers involved in IndustryConnect use eXperience cases along with a *complementary method*—the "milestories" method (Williams & Schubert, 2017).

The longitudinal nature of the IndustryConnect initiative allowed us to study the adoption of a new form of Enterprise Collaboration Systems in depth and over time. The following sections discuss the nature and structure of ECS, their functionality and content and present findings from our research.

Enterprise Collaboration Systems

Enterprise Collaboration Systems (ECS) are socio-technical systems that support employees in their daily work and facilitate functionality for workgroup collaboration. In large companies, the ECS is a commercial integrated software system that bundles many of the required collaborative features into a single system.

ECS provide a range of different features for the Digital Workplace including the support of everyday work activities (commonly known as Groupware) such as group calendars, task management, sharing of documents (files) and functions supporting the joint work on documents. In addition, ECS also support employees in synchronous and asynchronous communication, such as chat, video conferencing or e-mail (Fig. 3.3). Whilst information portals usually contain rather static content (e.g. quarterly reports, background reports on the company), ECS provide an authoring tool for employees allowing them to share content with colleagues and inform them about open issues, work results, activities, ideas or plans.

The increasing use of Social Media and their "social software features" in private life has changed the way people communicate and exchange information and has stimulated expectations on the side of employees regarding the use of similar software features in their workplace (Williams & Schubert, 2015). Large software ven-

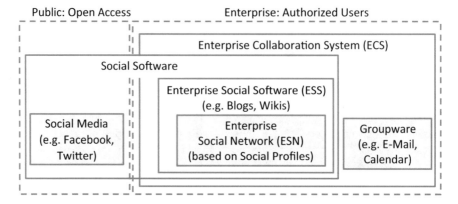

Fig. 3.4 Terminology of enterprise collaboration systems (Schwade & Schubert, 2017)

dors such as IBM, Microsoft and Atlassian have responded to the perceived demand for *socially-enabled* software with *Enterprise Social Software (ESS)* (e.g. IBM Connections, MS Yammer & SharePoint and Atlassian Confluence & Jira), a special form of collaboration software that provides *social software features*. Enterprise Social Software (ESS) has become an integral part of companies' Enterprise Collaboration Systems (ECS). Typical social features include subscribing (following) information or people, commenting or tagging contributions, or short expressions such as recommendations or likes. These systems are often equipped with extensive "*awareness features*", which help to recognize new and possibly relevant content. Figure 3.4 shows the terminology in the area of Enterprise Collaboration Systems.

The Evolution of the Word "Social" in Social Software

As laid out above, the word "social" in this context has its origin in Social Media where it is an indication of the features that allow people to engage, interact and share information in a virtual environment. Whilst the use of the word "social" is, without doubt, adequate in Social Media (which are by definition environments for social activity), it has led to some irritation among employees in companies where such "Social Software" was introduced. The workplace is usually not seen as a "social environment" but one that is focused on productivity and "getting the job done". However, not least stimulated by IBM's marketing campaign on "Social Business" in the years following the release of their software product IBM Connections, "Social" became the code word for the introduction of this new type of collaboration software. According to IBM, Social Business is about building and supporting the "human connections" of employees and partners (IBM Corporation, 2011) notwithstanding that the term "Social Business" had already been in use to describe a management style that strives to solve social problems (Yunus, 2008).

Social Features in Enterprise Social Software

The features that make a software "social" are usually centred on the "*Social Profile*" of a user. Social profiles are "*enhanced*" *user profiles* that include information that was traditionally only available in the HR record of an employee, such as skills and education, organisational role and affiliation, etc. Depending on the richness of information contained in the social profile, they can be used for expert search. They are also the basis for the so-called "*Enterprise Social Networks*" *(ESN)*. The social feature "follow" enables users to establish relationships between their own social profile and those of other employees regardless of physical location or organisational affiliation. ESN are an important facilitator for knowledge management in a company because they make skills and competencies transparent (thus addressing the issue of "if my company only knew what it knows"). Whilst ESN are emerging structures and thus represent static content, there is another group of social features that enables a more dynamic interchange of information and increases the awareness of what is going on in the workplace. Software features such as recommend (like), @mention, tag, comment are used to add meta information to content items. These features are quick and easy to use (lightweight) and are powerful *awareness markers*. The subtle ingenuity is on the receiving end because other users can follow certain content (e.g. a Blog or a whole community) or social profiles (thus specific authors) and receive notifications of new, individually-tailored content in their "*activity stream*" (or in an e-mail newsletter). The activity stream is an awareness feature in social software that allows the user to see alerts to posts, changes, recommendations and other additions or changes to content on the platform. When set up properly, these notifications make the workplace much more information rich and can at best lead to an increased degree of serendipity, that is, the encountering of unexpected useful information. The feature that has the greatest potential for *user-tailored information integration* is the activity stream. At the time of writing this chapter, most activity streams are only collecting and displaying activities in their native software system. However, there is also the useful potential to add alerts from other Enterprise Information Systems (e.g. ERP Systems). The collaboration software is a natural candidate for information integration and new integration approaches, and our research group at CEIR is currently investigating and testing integration approaches such as Enterprise Knowledge Graphs (Stokman & de Vries, 1988) or the Social Network of Business Objects (Gewehr, Gebel-Sauer, & Schubert, 2017).

So in a nutshell, "*social*" is a term that was adopted from Social Media and describes the view of connected users in modern Enterprise Collaboration Systems. The so-called "*social features*" support workplace collaboration, i.e. the information exchange and coordination among employees and increase the user awareness of what is important and relevant. Table 3.1 shows the most important social content types with likely features and purpose.

Table 3.1 Social content types, their features and purpose

Content type	Social features	Purpose
Social profiles	Tag, follow, pinboard	Enterprise social network
Microblog	Recommend (like), comment	Ephemeral messages (often informal)
Blog	Recommend (like), comment, @ mention, tag, file attachment	Publishing and informing
Wiki	Recommend (like), comment, @ mention, tag, file attachment, versioning	Collecting and preserving information

Social Documents

Social documents are the containers for the content that is generated in Enterprise Social Software. Most ESS offer different possibilities for creating documents or simple messages. Finding the right type of message for a given purpose can be challenging for an inexperienced user. Figure 3.5 shows a possible decision tree for message types depending on the nature (informal, formal, hyperlink), the need for a response (broadcast or bidirectional), and the need to be editable by others (multi-authoring).

Most social business documents are **compound documents** that contain an aggregation of different content elements (Hausmann & Williams, 2015). A Wiki page consists of a core item and can be supplemented by attached components such as comments or attachments. It can also have "*social markers*" such as tags, recommen-

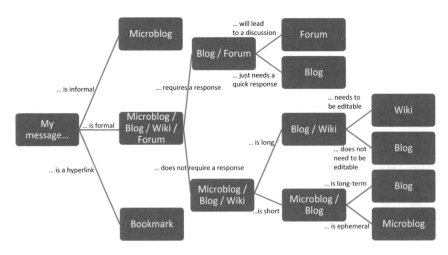

Fig. 3.5 Decision tree for message types in an Enterprise Social Software

dations or @mentions. Wiki pages are organised in a hierarchical structure, in which one Wiki page can have multiple sub Wiki pages. Such aggregations of dependent Wiki pages form a "*collection*".

Does "Social" Lead to Increased Collaboration?

An interesting question for the long-term management of *social business documents (SBD)* in ESS is the degree of collaboration that can be observed in the system. It is possible to show the degree of collaboration (employees interacting/engaging with each other) by looking at the components of compound SBDs and analysing the number of users that have interacted with this content.

Figure 3.6 is a screenshot of a dashboard that was developed by the CEIR research team to show the degree of collaboration of communities by looking at the structure and the authors of SBDs (Mosen, 2017). The displayed index of "2.4" indicates that an average of more than two users have worked on the entirety of social business documents in a given community. The right side of the graphic shows the size of SBDs. The larger the circle, the more compound elements are contained in the document. The higher the circle is located on the y-axis, the more users have participated in extending and editing this document. The graphic shows that in some cases more than 11 users contributed to a single SBD.

The nature of social software does not fit every kind of company culture. Due to its innate focus on "sharing" and "engaging", the software requires employees to actively engage with each other and share information openly. In the second half of this chapter, I present the findings from implementation projects (with a focus on the software adoption). The data was provided by the 29 user companies of the initiative IndustryConnect and was documented and analysed in longitudinal in-depth case studies.

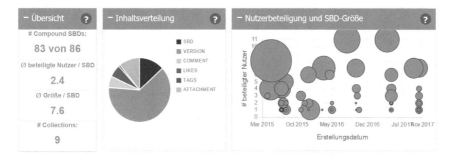

Fig. 3.6 Content Dashboard showing compounds and "collaborativity" of social business documents (Mosen, 2017)

Commonalities of ESS Implementation Projects

ESS implementation projects differ from *ERP implementation projects* mostly in terms of their much longer adoption phase. Whilst ERP software supports well-defined business processes, ESS provides interpretive flexibility (Doherty, Coombs, & Loan-Clarke, 2006) for the user, which means that the actual use of the software is dependent on the purpose and the proficiency of the user.

Structured guidelines (or "models") for the implementation of *ERP Systems* have existed for more than two decades. The most well-known methodology is the Architecture of Integrated Information Systems (ARIS) developed by the team of Professor Scheer at the University of the Saarland (Scheer, 1999). Within our CEIR research programme, we aimed to provide similar guidance for the *implementation of ECS*. The result was the IRESS model (Identification of Requirements for Enterprise Social Software), which helps to identify collaboration needs, to define Use Cases and Collaboration Scenarios and to conduct a structured software comparison based on software features (Glitsch & Schubert, 2017) (Fig. 3.7).

ARIS and IRESS are similar on a meta level because the implementation of both software types, ERP Systems and Enterprise Collaboration Systems, follows the same general steps of an IT project (c.f. Fig. 3.8). The implementation begins with the initial analysis of requirements, followed by the evaluation of commercial software

Organisation	**Use Cases**	Knowledge sharing Internal employee communication Project organization Document management Workshop organization	Team organization Event organization Idea and innovation management Internal communications Management accounting	Human resource management Sales opportunity and quotation Software development ...	
	Collaboration Scenarios	Administering documents Alerting to news Conducting a meeting Conducting a poll Conducting a survey Organizing a meeting	Creating meeting minutes and tasks Discussing topics Documenting information Enriching information Finding an expert Joint authoring	Posting news Rating information Retrieving information Sharing files Sharing information ...	
	Actions	**Person, Social Business Document, ...**	Search Edit Rate Label	Clarify Share Notify ...	
Software Support	**Collaborative Features (C⁴)**	**Communication** Asynchronous text message Asynchronous voice message Blogs Broadcast Chat Comments, annotations Discussion forums Message boards Microblogging Unified Communication Video conferencing	**Cooperation/Collaboration** Markup of changes Ratings, rankings Screen sharing/shared desktop Shared authoring Shared workspaces User profiles Workspace awareness	**Content Combination** Collecting feedback Content collection Content management Content subscription Data aggregation Data integration Document management Linking Pointers or references to content Search Tagging, Folksonomies Visualization of tags	**Coordination** Document and version control Graphical flow Group calendar, deadline planning Polls and voting Presence awareness Reminders, triggers, alerts Resource planning Roles Shared tasks User directories Workflow support
	Software Components	Workspace Blog Wiki	Forum Tasks Files	Calendar Microblog	

Fig. 3.7 IRESS framework—identification of requirements for enterprise social software (Glitsch & Schubert, 2017)

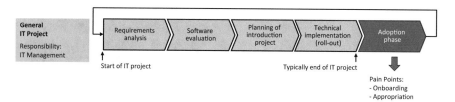

Fig. 3.8 The general IT project is similar for ERP systems and enterprise collaboration systems

packages, the signing of a (licence) contract, planning of the actual implementation project and the final technical implementation (roll-out).

Whilst ERP systems typically involve intensive training before the actual go-live, ECS are frequently made available ("installed") and then gradually rolled-out ("adopted"). ERP systems need to be fully functional from day one after their go-live because they support mission-critical business processes and even short downtimes can harm a business. Collaboration systems, on the other hand, aim at improving work efficiency (i.e. a non-mission critical support function) and their adoption may (and does) need longer time.

The analysis of the implementation projects of our IndustryConnect members shows that the ECS is sometimes almost "dormant" in the company, offered to employees for "voluntary use" and their introduction might require (but does not always get) "accompanying measures" to motivate the users to actually use the software. In some cases, we could observe a trial phase during which they are made available only to selected user groups in the company. In general, ECS tend to have a very long "adoption phase", some of our case companies reported to be still in the adoption phase five years after go-live (Williams & Schubert, 2015). After go-live, the responsibility of an ECS project is normally handed over from the IT Department to a specialised team, the "Enterprise Collaboration Team".

Figure 3.9 shows the typical steps of the *adoption phase* in an ECS implementation project. After go-live, companies gradually provide employees with their user accounts, inviting them to join the platform (onboarding). The onboarding process is sometimes supported by a basic user training, often with the help of exemplary use cases for best practice. This phase is normally followed by a gradual appropriation during which users are exploring the features of the software and finding their way as how to best use the software to fulfil their everyday tasks.

Most ECS implementation projects are characterised by a decline in use during the adoption phase sometimes almost leading to the discontinuation of the platform operation. At this point, some user companies reported a "restart" of their collaboration project, following a more structured and guided approach the second time. The adoption phase ends when the tool becomes an integral part of the digital workplace and users have appropriated it for their own purposes. A similar chronological sequence was identified in a study by Riemer, Overfeld, Scifleet, and Richter, (2012) and was visualised in the SNEP model.

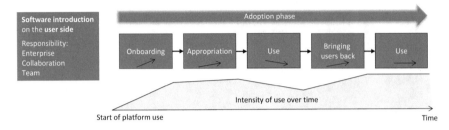

Fig. 3.9 Typical steps of the adoption phase in an ECS implementation project

Table 3.2 Companies starting with different features have different concerns

Companies starting with…	Typical concerns	Functional areas
Social profile (to build up an ESN)	Finding out what my company knows, "working out loud"	Human resources
Wikis	Collective writing availability of information, preserving information collectively	Information and quality management
Blogs	Workforce better informed about what's going on	Management, internal communications, service
Activities	Task management, coordinating project activity and ideation	Organisation, project management
Microblogs	Quick exchange of questions and ideas	Internal communications

Differences in ESS Implementation Projects

The analysis of our longitudinal cases involving 29 early adopters of large-scale, integrated ECS with the aim of creating a "Social Business" shows that there are differences in the approaches that the companies take which, as a consequence, lead to differing outcomes. An important influencing factor is the *initial reason* or motivation (aims/goals/expectations) for the introduction of a socially-enabled ECS. It could be observed that the "seed functionality", i.e. the first functionality that stimulated the use of the platform, impacts on the adoption and the way employees perceive the platform. Table 3.2 shows some "typical" paths into ESS adoption that could be observed in our real-world projects.

Archetypes of ECS Use

The initiative IndustryConnect (Williams & Schubert, 2017) provided an ideal data source for the analysis of "archetypes" of ECS use. Eight years after the introduction

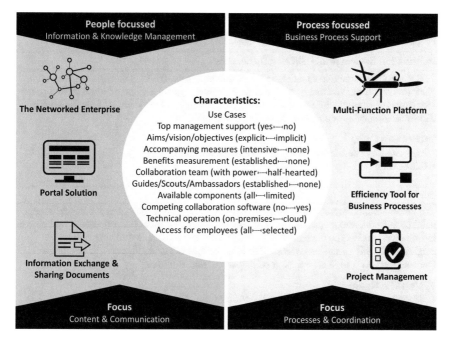

Fig. 3.10 Archetypes of ECS Use

of the commercial Enterprise Collaboration System IBM Connections, the CEIR team performed a cross-comparison among the *actual forms of use* of this particular ECS in the early adopter companies. The cross-comparison showed that even though the 20 companies had been using exactly the same integrated ECS, there are remarkable differences in the actual use of the system. The differences can be traced back to the specific context of the business (industry sector), historical path (e.g. motivation/pain points for starting the project, previously used collaboration software) and, interestingly, the nature of the implementation project (resources dedicated to the introduction). The analysis suggested six distinctive "archetypes of use", which are presented in the following.

The six archetypes were identified by examining the actual ECS use or in other words the "Use Cases" (Schubert & Glitsch, 2016) that are supported with the help of the ECS in the organisation. The centre of Fig. 3.10 shows the characteristics of the implementation projects that were analysed in the study. The findings show that the *actual use* of the integrated ECS and thus the emerging archetype(s) can be largely explained by three phenomena: (1) The *industry sector* (= the products and business activity of the organisation), the (2) *IT situation* at the point when the decision was made to implement the ECS (e.g. existing collaboration software) and the (3) existing *company culture* (e.g. a general openness or scepticism towards sharing ideas and knowledge).

Table 3.3 People focussed archetypes of ECS Use (left side)

People focussed: "Information and Knowledge Management"

Information Exchange and Sharing Documents

This archetype describes a situation, in which employees use the ECS mostly as an exchange platform for information that is needed to do their jobs. Typical use cases for this archetype are inter-employee communication (e.g. in discussion forums) and the sharing of files—activities that some companies describe as "Knowledge Management"

Typical Use Cases
• Inter-employee communication (e.g. in discussion forums)
• File sharing

Portal Solution

The Portal Solution represents a situation, in which the ECS is mostly used as a central access point for information on specific topics of interest for employees. It is the "gateway" to internal information provided by the internal communications department as well as by fellow employees. In this group, we typically find ECS platforms that were introduced to replace outdated Intranet solutions by a more participatory "Social Intranet"

Typical Use Cases:
• Corporate communications (making information centrally available)
• Internal communications
• Internal information organisation and exchange in a department

The Networked Enterprise

The Networked Enterprise is the archetype closest to the original vision of IBM at the time of launch of their product "IBM Connections". It describes a situation in which employees in a (frequently) globally distributed (large) organisation have access to information-rich social profiles, actively follow each other and the software is bridging groups, departments and even countries thus making work in this organisation a truly global experience with exchange of information and ideas

Typical Use Cases:
• Expert Search
• Knowledge Management
• Ideation
• Plus: Potentially all Use Cases for Portals and Information Exchange

As can be seen in Fig. 3.10 the six archetypes were assigned to two groups. The three archetypes on the left are *people focussed* supporting mostly "Information and Knowledge Management" and have an emphasis on "Content and Communication". The second group on the right side is *process focussed* leaning more towards "Business Process Support" and has its emphasis on "Processes and Coordination". The six archetypes are described in Tables 3.3 and 3.4.

It is important to note that the archetypes are not mutually exclusive and that their characteristics overlap in practice; one organisation is likely to assign their ECS to more than one archetype. However, the archetypes are a useful lens for the discussion of aims and objectives in an ECS introduction project. The archetypes have

Table 3.4 Process focussed archetypes of ECS Use (right side)

Process focussed: "Business Process Support"

Project Management

This archetype describes a situation, in which the main use of the ECS is for project management. This archetype has a focus on classical group work such as project planning, ideation, meetings and minutes and tasks assignment. The platform is, to a large extent, used for the coordination of information, people and tasks

Typical Use Cases
- Project support
- Joint work on documents
- Audit planning
- Quality management
- Employee suggestion systems

Efficiency Tool for Business Processes

This archetype describes a situation, in which the organisation is using the ECS for selected and sometimes very business-specific business processes

Typical Use Cases
- HR Management
- Event Management
- Store management
- Workshop organisation
- Exchange of information and files with external partners

Multi-Function Platform

The Multi-Function Platform integrates data and functionality from different business software systems and gives a uniform access to different functional areas of the company. Like the Portal Solution, it serves as a central entry point but in this case, it goes beyond mere access to information also providing certain functionality for workflows or business processes (e.g. working time recording or approval of orders in the procurement system). The activity stream (as an awareness feature) is an important element of the Multi-Function Platform because it shows events from the integrated software systems (e.g. a request to approve an order)
Typical use cases for this archetype are the general exchange of information and ideas, access to information that is spread over multiple information systems and most importantly, the integration of other applications (e.g. the HR module and the sales database of the ERP System)

Typical Use Cases
- Special: Integration of other applications (e.g. the HR module and the sales database of the ERP System)
- Access to information that is spread over multiple information systems
- General exchange of information and ideas
- Potentially all other Use Cases in the other two archetypes on this side

been through a process of review and evaluation with our participating organisations. Each of the organisations was clearly able to identify the current state of their ECS project and assign their organisations to one (or more) of these archetypes.

Conclusions

A limitation of the current body of ECS research is that it contains few in-depth, longitudinal empirical studies enabling us to understand and theorize about the degrees of similarities (and differences) in use across contexts and how they are being achieved (Monteiro & Rolland, 2012).

Our research has shown that even with the same kind of Enterprise Collaboration System, organisations develop different ways of using this software and there is a broad range of different Use Cases depending on industry, culture and existing IT infrastructure.

In addition, for most organisations, the Digital Workplace comprises a range of different collaboration software with redundant functionality. Their use is mostly voluntary and organisations rarely make one or the other software mandatory. The problems that arise from this "freedom of choice" are manifold and the proficiency in the use of social software in companies will still be improving remarkably in the years to come.

References

Doherty, N. F., Coombs, C. R., & Loan-Clarke, J. (2006). A re-conceptualization of the interpretive flexibility of information technologies: Redressing the balance between the social and the technical. *European Journal of Information Systems, 15*(6), 569–582.

Gewehr, B., Gebel-Sauer, B., & Schubert, P. (2017). Social Network of Business Objects (SoNBO): An innovative concept for information integration in enterprise systems. In M. M. Cruz-Cunha, J. E. Q. Varajão, R. Rijo, R. Martinho, J. Peppard, J. R. S. Cristóbal, & J. Monguet (Eds.), *Procedia computer science* (Vol. 121, pp. 904–912). Barcelona: Elsevier B.V.

Glitsch, J. H., & Schubert, P. (2017). IRESS: Identification of requirements for enterprise social software. In Procedia Computer (Ed.), *Science* (pp. 866–873). Barcelona: Elsevier B.V.

Hausmann, V., & Williams, S. P. (2015). Social business documents. *Procedia Computer Science, 64*, 360–368. Retrieved from http://www.sciencedirect.com/science/article/pii/S1877050915026 356.

IBM Corporation. (2011). Using IBM social business to take your business relationships to the next level: A game changer for small, medium, and large businesses. *IBM Redbooks*. Retrieved from http://www.redbooks.ibm.com/redpapers/pdfs/redp4746.pdf.

Monteiro, E., & Rolland, K. H. (2012). Trans-situated use of integrated information systems. *European Journal of Information Systems, 21*(6), 608–620.

Mosen, J. (2017). *Social business document monitoring*. Master Thesis. University of Koblenz-Landau.

Riemer, K., Overfeld, P., Scifleet, P., & Richter, A. (2012). *Oh, SNEP! The dynamics of social network emergence—The case of Capgemini Yammer* (Working papers—Business Information Systems (BIS) No. WP2012-01). Sydney. Retrieved from http://hdl.handle.net/2123/8049.

Scheer, A.-W. (1999). *ARIS—Business process modeling* (2nd ed.). Berlin et al.: Springer.

Schubert, P., & Glitsch, J. H. (2016). Use Cases and Collaboration Scenarios: How employees use socially-enabled Enterprise Collaboration Systems (ECS). *International Journal of Information Systems and Project Management, 4*(2), 41–62.

Schubert, P., & Wölfle, R. (2007). The eXperience methodology for writing IS case studies. In *Americas Conference on Information Systems (AMCIS)* (pp. 1–15). Retrieved from http://aisel.a isnet.org/cgi/viewcontent.cgi?article=1855&context=amcis2007.

Schwade, F., & Schubert, P. (2017). Social collaboration analytics for enterprise collaboration systems: Providing business intelligence on collaboration activities. In *50th Hawaii International Conference on System Sciences (HICSS)* (pp. 401–410). Hilton Waikoloa Village, Hawaii, USA.

Stokman, F. N., & de Vries, P. H. (1988). Structuring knowledge in a graph. In G. C. van der Veer & G. Mulder (Eds.), *Human-computer interaction* (pp. 186–206). Berlin, Heidelberg: Springer.

Williams, S. P., & Schubert, P. (2015). *Social business readiness survey 2014*. Working Report of the Research Group Business Software. Koblenz: University of Koblenz-Landau.

Williams, S. P., & Schubert, P. (2017). Connecting industry: Building and sustaining a practice-based research community. In *Proceedings of the 50th Hawaii International Conference on System Sciences (HICSS)* (pp. 5400–5409). Hilton Waikoloa Village, Hawaii, USA.

Yunus, M. (2008). *Creating a world without poverty: Social business and the future of capitalism.* New York: Perseus Books.

Chapter 4
The Go-Betweens: Backstage Collaboration Among Community Managers in an Inter-organisational Enterprise Social Network

Kai Riemer and Ella Hafermalz

Introduction

Enterprise Social Networks (ESNs) are increasingly considered a legitimate workplace tool. A level of ambiguity however remains as to whether time spent on an ESN is 'productive' or 'social' time. Will employees be judged harshly if they are seen to frequently post and reply on the company ESN? Are they 'slacking off' or are they being good organisational citizens, answering questions and contributing to innovative solutions? This ambiguity is central to the 'problem' of ESN implementation, not because it needs 'resolving' but because it requires a strategy that allows for both 'realities' of ESN use to exist at once, as they speak to different stakeholder groups within the organisation. Here we take note of the difficult task that falls on the role of the 'community manager'. A community manager is a member of the organisation whose job is to cultivate ESN adoption and use. They are usually not executives, nor are they amongst the worker cohort that they are trying to tempt onto the ESN. The community manager is 'stuck in the middle'.

They are tasked with brokering not only interest in the ESN but also the messaging around its value to the organisation. This message may need to be bifurcated, so that executives and managers are presented with stories of time saved and solutions found, while workers are shown how the ESN allows them to have their voice heard amongst peers and management. The community manager thus occupies a kind of role that is familiar to middle managers: they are a "go-between" (Goffman, 1959), a "master and victim of double talk" (Roethlisberger, 1945), who is burdened with

K. Riemer (✉)
The University of Sydney, Camperdown, Australia
e-mail: kai.riemer@sydney.edu.au

E. Hafermalz
Vrije Universiteit Amsterdam, Amsterdam, The Netherlands
e-mail: ella.hafermalz@sydney.edu.au

© Springer International Publishing AG, part of Springer Nature 2019
K. Riemer et al. (eds.), *Collaboration in the Digital Age*, Progress in IS,
https://doi.org/10.1007/978-3-319-94487-6_4

trying to influence two groups who have influence over them, while having only limited grounds for status and legitimacy themselves.

The anxiety that a "go-between" faces in trying to please two cohorts with sometimes opposing interests has been previously examined. In the following case we show how this phenomenon relates to ESN implementation. Using case material, we show how community managers are able to cope with the challenges of their go-between role by remotely coming together in an inter-organisational ESN of their own. We draw on the work of Erving Goffman to theorise how such a 'backstage' space operates and what it offers the community managers in their efforts to roll out ESNs in their organisations.

Background: ESN Adoption and Sense-Making

Enterprise Social Networks (ESN) are a set of technologies that include the foundational features associated with social network sites but which, sanctioned by management, are implemented within and have the ability to restrict membership to certain members of an organization (Ellison, Gibbs, & Weber, 2015).

ESNs are said to hold great promise for organisations. According to a report by McKinsey (2012), effective use of such technologies can result in a 20–25% improvement in the productivity of knowledge workers. Another study by Forrester Research in a large organisation found a return on investment of 365% on an investment in an ESN platform over three years (Dodd, 2011). Not surprisingly, enterprise social networks have gained increased interest from organisations, with more and more businesses adopting such platforms (Bughin, 2015).

At the same time, decision makers have voiced concerns that by employing social media within the organization, businesses are at risk of importing some of the typical behaviours associated with the use of social media on the public Internet (e.g. Howlett, 2009), such as hedonistic, egocentric, and leisure-focused behaviours observed on Facebook or Twitter (Naaman, Boase, & Lai, 2010). It is not surprising then that management in charge of the roll-out of ESNs are often highly focused on demonstrating economic returns from employing ESNs and similar technologies. The confusion and debate over ESNs and their role in organisations can be taken as evidence that although they are quite well understood from a technical perspective (i.e. as a fairly familiar instantiation of Web 2.0), what exactly ESNs 'are' and the role that they play in work practices is anything but settled. While the ambiguity inherent to ESNs is in its own right a worthy topic of investigation, we here focus on how community managers, who are tasked with gathering support for ESN adoption, come to collectively learn how to draw on this ambiguity in a strategic way in order to convince both management and worker cohorts, in different ways, that the company ESN is worthy of their time and attention.

Enterprise Social Networks

ESNs are platforms, typically accessed through a web browser or mobile app, that allow people to (1) communicate messages with their coworkers or broadcast messages to everyone within the organisation; (2) explicitly indicate or implicitly reveal particular coworkers as communication partners; (3) post, edit, and sort text and files linked to themselves or others; and (4) view the messages, connections, text, and files communicated, posted, edited and sorted by anyone else in their organisation at any time of their choosing (Leonardi, Huysman, & Steinfield, 2013).

As such, ESNs can be viewed as a subset of the Enterprise 2.0 phenomenon (McAfee, 2009), which refers to the application of social software more generally (von Krogh, 2012), such as social networking sites, blogs, wikis, or group communication services (Razmerita, Kirchner, & Nabeth, 2014), in an organisational context. Today's ESN applications, such as Yammer, Workplace, Slack, Chatter, Jive or IBM Connections resemble public social network sites in that they are aggregations of different tools including instant messaging, wikis, and microblogging.

ESNs have been linked directly to individual employee performance in recent research. Riemer, Finke, and Hovorka (2015) found that individuals draw social capital and associated benefits from their use of ESNs in day-to-day work. Further research found that ESNs can help overcome the challenges associated with knowledge sharing, such as locating of expertise, motivation to share knowledge and developing and maintaining social ties with knowledge bearers (Fulk & Yuan, 2013).

Hence, the business case for introduction of an ESN generally involves benefits that derive from better connectedness between employees. Indeed, past research has shown a variety of organisational ESN uses, such as for communication and collaboration (Riemer, Richter, & Böhringer, 2010), knowledge management (Levy, 2009) or crowdsourcing (Schlagwein & Bjorn-Andersen, 2014). ESN benefits are linked to increased efficiency as employees communicate and solve problems more quickly. A more ambitious hope is that improved communication will lead to the generation of more innovative ideas, because issues are made visible and accessible to a diversity of people and functions within the business; some early research has shown applications of ESN in contexts such as open innovation (Dahlander & Gann, 2010) or open strategy (Tavakoli, Schlagwein, & Schoder, 2015).

Essentially, ESNs serve as infrastructure that enable digitally supported work in many different ways. But while its open infrastructure character is at the heart of an ESN's capacity to support many different uses and contexts, this characteristic is not without problems when it comes to the adoption of ESNs.

ESN Adoption Challenges

Since any organizational benefits of ESNs will materialize only through sustained use of the platform (DeLone & McLean, 1992), and given its network nature, it is important that ESNs are adopted by a significant number of users within an organization. Adoption of ESNs however has proven elusive in many organizations. An important reason for this is that ESNs are "malleable" technologies (Richter & Riemer, 2013) that afford many different uses and can be appropriated for a variety of purposes, but for this very reason require an active process of interpretation, sense-making and appropriation to find a place within a particular organisation (Riemer & Johnston, 2012).

Malleability also implies that any efforts to 'prescribe' ESN use in a top-down way are bound to be problematic as it is difficult to determine ex-ante and at a distance how an ESN might best be used in a given context (Richter & Riemer, 2013). Rather, what an ESN will become in use within a particular organisation, or organisational unit, can ultimately only be uncovered through experimenting and local sense-making in concrete business practices, bringing about what Orlikowski, 2000) refers to as "technologies-in-practice". Consequently, unlike more traditional technologies that are employed to support the core business processes of the organisation, and thus are always associated with a concrete task and purpose, ESNs are best understood as infrastructure that is not intended to support specific predetermined tasks (Riemer, Steinfield, & Vogel, 2009). In other words, as malleable technologies ESNs are intended as platforms upon which users explore and negotiate *new* ways of working (Richter & Riemer, 2013). Consequently the proliferation of ESNs in the enterprise typically follows, at least in parts, a bottom-up approach of implementation, a more inclusive and egalitarian process (Schneckenberg, 2009), referred to as appropriation (Carroll, Howard, Peck, & Murphy, 2002) during which potential uses are discovered in a process of practical sense-making (Riemer & Johnston, 2014).

However, while top-down approaches to implementing ESNs appear antithetical to the open nature of the technology, our understanding of how bottom-up processes of sense-making and appropriation unfold in organisations is still in its infancy. Significantly, it is even less clear how such a process can be actively managed or guided to achieve positive and lasting outcomes for the organisation. Investigating how the roll-out of an ESN can be managed or guided is all the more important given typical managerial scepticism around 'social' technologies, concerns that social technologies lead to unproductive "wasting of time" or that economic benefits and return on investment are fundamentally unclear initially. One response to this challenge, which has not yet received significant research attention, is the hiring of so-called community managers, employed by organisations to look after their internal ESN implementation/adoption processes.

ESN Community Managers

Community managers are a relatively new role created to aid the implementation of ESNs, a person tasked with promoting and supervising the adoption and use of an ESN. The role is essentially caught between the notions of implementation and adoption—the community manager is employed by management to 'implement' a technology by stimulating the grass-roots 'adoption' of workers in the organisation. Because an ESN is supposed to involve members of the organisation at all levels and across divisions in daily conversational interactions, for the ESN to be successful, the community manager will need to wrangle support from individuals and cohorts who have not directly endorsed the introduction of the ESN. The biggest challenge facing the community manager is thus to, on the one hand inspire participation amongst workers, and on the other hand maintain support and even participation from managers/executives.

The malleable nature of ESN and the open nature of the adoption process is a double-edged sword for community managers, as this openness can be drawn upon in promoting the technology in different ways to different audiences, but this can also cause problems, for example when management promotes an ESN based on certain instrumental expectations of its benefits for collaboration and productivity, community managers are faced with the task of reconciling an open-ended process of sense-making and appropriation, so that the ESN can unfold its potential for local work practices in the best possible way, with management expectations of clear economic benefits in terms of return-on-investment of the 'ESN project'.

We further note that these complexities and struggles are usually burdens that are carried alone. It would be unusual for a company to hire more than one community manager. The position itself is somewhat precarious, as it depends on the 'success' of ESN implementation and adoption and therefore the support of both management and worker cohorts. Although ESNs are productively thought of as open-ended and in need of gradual, localised nurturing, community managers face an existential need to speed up the adoption process and communicate this in terms of 'value' to different stakeholders. Against this backdrop, in this paper we investigate the following research question: How do community managers deal with their conflicted position in the process of ESN implementation and adoption?

Case Study: A Community of ESN Community Managers

For this study we had access to data from Beta,[1] an international ESN provider. Beta provides a typical ESN platform, which is hosted as a software service in the cloud. Corporate clients will create their own private network on the platform, so that employees from each organisation become members of the network belonging to that organisation. Additionally, clients are able to also create dedicated inter-organisational networks, to which anyone can be invited. Each network on the Beta platform comes with a 'General stream' as the default for sending messages, but users can also create groups which are either public (accessible to anyone who wants to join) or private (protected and only open upon invitation). The particular data set we had access to for this study came from an inter-organisational network that was

---

[1]The name of the company, its products, and any other aspects have been changed to ensure anonymity.

managed by Beta itself in the form of an electronic hierarchy (Klein, 1996), in that this ESN was administered and controlled by Beta, with membership made up of those employees from each of its corporate clients serving in community manager (or similar) roles and a number of Beta employees. True to its make-up this network was called the Beta Community Network (BCN).

Data Collection: The Beta Community Network (BCN)

For Beta, the BCN was a strategic device for providing help and advice to its corporate clients. One of Beta's stated aims was to use the BCN to drive user adoption and engagement within its client networks. The BCN served at once as a suggestion box and discussion space for new product features and as a community for client community managers, tasked with the roll-out, and more generally the success, of the Beta ESNs within their organisations.

Accordingly, Beta made available via the BCN a range of different employees, most notably product managers and so-called Beta community network advisors (CNAs). Yet, rather than merely establishing bilateral relationships between client community managers and 'their' CNAs, Beta—out of a deep belief in transparency and the usefulness of its ESN for facilitating discussion—opted to create a space in which CNAs and client community managers were able to freely communicate and share their experiences with each other. It is this communal aspect of the BCN that is of most interest to our study.

We obtained from Beta a structured file of all public messages exchanged on the BCN between January 2011 and April 2013. This data set contained a total of just over 90K messages, around 15K of which were automatically generated bot messages. For each message the data set contained the actual message content, a time stamp, the ID of the sender of the message, the ID of the message it was in reply to, and a thread number that allowed sorting messages into communication threads to follow unfolding conversations. It also indicated if a message was posted in a group and the group name. To protect the privacy of its clients, the data set did not contain any identifying details about its users or their organisations, beyond numerical IDs.

The data is suitable for our study for a number of reasons. Firstly, it provides unique access to the first hand conversations among ESN community managers which allows studying the sense-making process of this group of people as they are involved in the roll-out and appropriation in their organisations. Secondly, the data stems from a period (2011–2013) when ESN was making inroads into organisational workplaces as an innovation that had yet to be fully understood. This time period is thus ideal to study how community managers jointly coped with the resulting ambiguity and uncertainty that each faced in their organisations. And thirdly, the data set includes the voice of Beta itself, in the form of the CNAs and other Beta employees.

Data Analysis and Initial Findings

As our interest in this paper lies with studying how community managers go about dealing with the conflicting requirements of stakeholders involved in the roll-out and adoption/implementation of ESN in their organisations, we focused on the ways in which they shared experiences regarding those matters within the BCN, rather than other conversations, such as those about technical ESN matters. Given the subject matter we proceeded with a qualitative, iterative analysis approach. Due to the size of the dataset this involved in a first step the identification of those conversations relevant to the topic. We began with one author reading the entirety of the main feed of the BCN, making notes of what stood out as surprising and interesting (Alvesson & Sandberg, 2013). The resulting set of conversations was then discussed with her co-author in an attempt to make sense of what was found and to identify a suitable lens through which to understand what was going on in the data (Timmermans & Tavory, 2012; Weick, 2012).

   In our initial reading of the material we found a number of different conversations in which community managers reported on tensions that stem from what we came to understand as a 'caught in the middle' position in their organisations, in that they had to rehearse different ways of communicating the value of ESN to different cohorts. This was most notable in a number of discussions that revolved around the following matters:

- *How do managers and the broader workforce view the ESN?* Some community managers reported that it was surprisingly difficult to convince managers of the benefits of employees using the ESN, as any such benefits were predominantly parsed through a productivity lens, at the expense of a broader understanding that included 'socialising' among employees, which was conversely often used as a drawcard to motivate employees to join the ESN.
- *How are benefits of the ESN demonstrated to the two stakeholder groups?* On the one hand, community managers saw a strong need to be able to defend the ESN's worth in terms of economic value vis-à-vis corporate managers. For example, a published report commissioned by Beta that reported on a particularly high ROI when employing Beta's ESN was said to be useful in doing so. This helped them construct the ESN as a *productivity tool* that was 'good for business' because it could be linked to efficiency and ultimately profitability. At the same time, BCN members also discussed the ESN as a *discussion space* with the capacity to break down silos and encourage workers to voice their opinions and get to know one another across business functions, regardless of status. Given that those two framings are at odds with each other, it led to visible confusion, anxiety and discussion among the community managers.
- *How is participation in the ESN viewed?* The differences in understanding of the ESN were further reflected in discussions about how 'engagement' on the ESN was perceived differently in different organisations. In one organisation, a high engagement score (meaning many workers were performing at least some actions on the ESN) could be taken to mean that workers were being *unproductive,*

as they were wasting time on a "social" platform. In another organisation high engagement scores could be seen as a success indicator in that the ESN was supporting productivity.

- *Should management participate in the ESN?* There was also disagreement among community managers about whether it was desirable to have executives join their local networks. Some thought that the presence of executives was a necessary way of lending credibility to the use of the ESN as a work tool, while other community managers thought that an executive presence would hamper workers in speaking their mind or deter them from contributing altogether for fear of being seen as lazy or unproductive.

Given the ways in which the ESN was portrayed very differently not just across organisations, but more importantly within the same organisation, by different stakeholder groups, meant that community managers had to at least juggle, if not reconcile those conflicting viewpoints. These initial insights reinforced that the community manager role is indeed characterised by a need to sustain more than one message at a time while coping with the pressures that such a selective and strategic presentation of information requires. This led us to search for an appropriate theoretical lens that would aid us in interpreting and theorizing the role of the ESN community managers, as the nexus of ESN appropriation practices. We were particularly interested in the kind of work that was being performed by the community managers on the BCN, and making sense of what was happening when community managers shared their frustrations, tips, strategies, and suggestions with one another and with Beta representatives.

In Search of a Theoretical Lens

The situation of the community managers being 'stuck in the middle' reminded us of the story of the "foreman" as reported in some of the early management literature (Roethlisberger, 1945). This literature typified the foreman's dilemma as stemming from being both the "master and victim of double talk". The foreman had to deal with being 'stuck in the middle'; between management and the factory floor, an awkward position that Roethlisberger associated with a near constant state of anxiety. Today, this position is commonly associated with the 'middle manager', who similarly needs to keep two cohorts happy at once, even when the aims of these two groups (management and workers) are in conflict with one another.

The notion of the foreman thus provided a starting point for illuminating the community managers' problems, and the way in which the community managers frequently appealed to their CNAs, and to one another, for help in 'managing the message' in a dual direction. We sought to further understand this middle manager perspective and found that sociologist Erving Goffman (1959) drew on Roethlisberger's ideas and developed a detailed theoretical discussion of the foreman role, which he characterised as an example of a 'go-between'. Thus informed by the work of Roethlisberger and Goffman, we developed a perspective with which we were able to ask new questions in a second, more targeted, analysis of the data. In this analysis we became sensitised to the uniqueness of the BCN setting: as a *place* or 'region' (Goffman, 1959) where community managers could come together, to share the burden of their position and to develop strategies with which to more effectively "talk out of both sides of his mouth at the same time—to become a master of double talk" (Roethlisberger, 1945, pp. 7–8).

We found that our data offered the opportunity to employ theoretical categories from Goffman to shed light on the community manager role. Further, this perspective enabled us to see the BCN as a particular kind of space which allows community managers to privately come together and make sense of ESNs and develop strategies that support the complex 'performances' involved in gaining and sustaining support for ESN implementation and adoption. In the following section we introduce several conceptual tools from Goffman (1959) that we subsequently put to work in interpreting our case data to gain insights about the community manager role and how the BCN supported their ability to cope with both the ambiguity of ESN and their two-sided role in promoting its use. In the subsequent section we work with this theory to make sense of our data, bringing in further concepts from Goffman (1959) where needed to analyse our case material.

Goffman's Theatre Metaphor for Theorising Social Life

Goffman's *The Presentation of Self in Everyday Life* outlines a way of understanding everyday life through the metaphor of theatrical performance. His concepts of 'front stage' and 'backstage' regions have found some purchase in Information Systems literature concerned with unofficial 'backchannel' communications (Orlikowski, 1996). Goffman's wider corpus and reference to the materiality of social life has also been championed as useful to scholars interested in technology by Pinch and Swedberg (2008). Overall however Goffman's influence in Information Systems and Organisational research remains marginal and we acknowledge that readers may not be familiar with the nuances of his approach. We therefore introduce key concepts and give brief context to his thinking here. Our introduction to Goffman is attuned to those aspects that we find relevant to the study of ESN, and we recognise that this precis is selective and is of course interpreted in a particular way. We direct interested readers to the original text as a primary source with, we argue, the potential to inspire further thinking and research on the topic of ESN use and implementation in particular and IS more broadly.

Table 4.1 Performances require information control

Term	Definition
Secrets	The concealment of destructive information is necessary for teams to maintain a particular impression of reality; teams keep one another's secrets and conceal destructive information from their audiences through impression management techniques
Destructive information	Provided by facts that, if attention is drawn to them, would discredit, disrupt or make useless the reality that the performance fosters in relation to a particular audience
Information control	A key problem for performing teams is to prevent the audience from acquiring destructive information; "a team must be able to keep its secrets and have its secrets kept"

Performances and Secrets

Goffman (1959) uses the metaphor of theatre to study and understand the dynamics of everyday life. He claims that we are always engaged in a performance of one kind or another, in relation to a particular audience. A performance is the endeavour of enacting a particular reality in relation to others (Goffman, 1959; Hafermalz, Riemer, & Boell, 2016). This is usually a collective effort—for example a team of consultants help one another in enacting professionalism and authority in relation to their client. These impressions that are fostered in the process of performance are however always partial and fragile, meaning that a team needs to work together to emphasise information that supports the reality they are trying to sustain, while de-emphasizing and concealing information that is incongruent with it. As a consequence performances to a large extent rely on the keeping of *secrets*—the suppression of certain facts from the audience to whom one is performing (Table 4.1).

A key aspect of being part of a performing team in the Goffmanian sense is that teammates help keep each other's secrets, explicitly or even at times without being consciously aware that such secrets are in play. *Secrets*, characterised by the containment of destructive information, can only be kept when there are adequate means of separating teams from one another, in that there needs to be a degree of separation between the performing team and the audience, so that the performing team has ways in which they can present certain realities while concealing others (for example costumes hanging in a theatre dressing room or piles of laundry in an expensive hotel). Secrets cannot be kept when there are no boundaries between performing teams and audiences. It is thus in relation to secrets that the notions of the 'front stage' and 'backstage' become important.

The notion of performances and secrets is relevant to our case because it provides us with a way of understanding the interaction between community managers on the BCN. Access to the BCN is restricted, and it is this privacy that supports the sharing of 'destructive information' that is useful to fellow community managers but could be harmful if it were to be accessed by workers or managers in their respective organisations. We also note that privacy achieved through restricted access to ESNs is important, and that it is possible to see the 'same' ESN platform as being very different in practice, depending on what cohorts have access to it and what kind of information is shared there.

Regions for Information Control

Goffman's notion of 'front stage' and 'backstage' are often introduced in a purely spatial sense, to delineate between one geographic area and another. What is often missed is that it is a need for information control that drives the construction of the boundaries that generate the front/backstage distinction. More than a fixed cordoned off place, backstage regions are a *means* of enabling the concealment of certain facts, or secrets, in the process of staging performances. Storerooms, changing rooms, and bathrooms are typical architectural examples of dedicated backstage spaces where individuals or groups of people exercise 'information control' by concealing 'tools of their trade', whether it be stacks of an item of clothing that on the store floor is presented as 'one of a kind', or an office lunchroom where workers take a break, relax, and speak candidly about the daily goings-on of the organisation.

Temporal and spatial separation between groups allows for the alternate conceal-ment and strategic presentation of information in a team's pursuit of sustaining "the definition of the situation that its performance fosters" (Goffman, 1959, p. 141). *Backstage regions* are thus primarily of importance because they offer a mechanism that affords concealing a team's secrets from the audience they perform to. Any reader who has had the experience of being shown 'backstage' after a performance will know that what is revealed there interrupts (sometimes to disappointing effect) the illusion that was fostered during the staged performance.

The analogy of a backstage can and has been translated to technologically-enabled environments. We have long used spatial metaphors to discuss online communication venues, e.g. a 'chat room' and scholars have explicitly used Goffman's work to describe situations where an online communication environment is used as a kind of 'backstage' that allows users to communicate in an informal capacity about what is happening on the 'front stage' (Hafermalz & Riemer, 2016; Orlikowski, 1996).

Under this analytical lens, both secrets and the spaces that enable their confidential transmission and concealment are essential elements of performance, both in the theatre and in everyday life. While prior IS research has focused on the spatial aspect of this point by discussing particular types of space or 'regions' for communication (see Table 4.2), so far the link to the importance of *secrets* in the wider process of staging a performance that involves technologically enabled communication has not been fully explored. As we will show however, appreciating the importance of secrets is key to understanding another element of Goffman's framework, "roles". Goffman's analysis of roles is closely linked to the concepts of regions and information control, and his notion of "discrepant roles" in particular proves useful to our analysis of community managers.

Table 4.2 Regions and their translation to the case

Term	Definition	Goffman example	Case example
Region	'any place that is bounded to some degree by barriers to perception' more or less bound, e.g. a room with glass panels (aurally bound) versus brick walls (visually and aurally bound)	Doctor's consulting room	Beta ESN: 'general stream', or group
Front region (front stage)	The place, relative to a given performance, where the performance is given, where aspects of activity congruent with the impression of reality that the performing team is trying to maintain are expressively accentuated and discrepant information is suppressed	Floor of a shop	The client ESNs; a boardroom during a meeting with executives; at-desk training sessions with employees
Back region (backstage)	A place, relative to a given performance, where the impression fostered by the performance is knowingly contradicted as a matter of course. Commonly located near but away from where the performance is located, cut off by a partition and guarded passageway	A hotel kitchen	The BCN network; private ESN groups

Discrepant Roles

Goffman (1959) posits that in relation to a particular performance, everyone takes on a particular *role*. The main roles, found in most performances, are that of: performer, audience, and outsider (see Table 4.3). Usually the staging of a performance requires that people fall clearly into one of these roles (keeping in mind that both roles and regions are never essential to a person or place, they derive their meaning from their position within the performance): (1) A *performer* is a member of the performing team and possesses the most information about the performance; (2) *audience* members have access to the information that is presented to them, but may also be able to glean insight to destructive information through careful observation (for example by noticing a misplaced prop). (3) There are also always *outsiders* who are excluded from both the front stage and backstage and generally have no knowledge of the performance.

The need for regions to be accessible by different kinds of people at certain times is common to everyday life because "destructive information" (Table 4.1) needs to be kept concealed from the audience to whom a team performs if a particular enactment of reality is to be maintained. So both in a theatre performance and in 'real life', backstage spaces are generally protected and only accessible to the performing team (e.g. a 'staff only' sign on a hotel door). However some roles are more complicated than those shown in Table 4.3. In some cases, an audience member may be 'in' on

Table 4.3 Main roles in relation to a performance

Role	Information possessed	Accessible regions	Case example
Performer	Impression they foster and destructive information about the show	Front stage and backstage	Community managers traverse both their organisation's ESN and the BCN
Audience	What they have been allowed to perceive and what they can glean from close observation	Front stage	Managers and workers who use the company ESNs do not have access to the BCN
Outsider	Neither the secrets of the performance nor the appearance of the reality fostered	Excluded from both regions	ESN non-adopters

the performance, for example a 'shill' in a circus surreptitiously plays along with the circus performers in order to facilitate the exploitation of the 'marks'. The shill has knowledge of the performers' secrets even though she acts as if she is a member of the audience.

Goffman is interested in such exceptions and refers to all such roles, which do not fit neatly into the categories shown in Table 4.3, as "discrepant roles". *Discrepant roles* are roles where peculiar *vantage points* lead to incongruences in the categories shown in Table 4.3. Such roles are possible when someone has access to more regions, and therefore information, than is usually available to either a single performing team or single audience, e.g. the shill. Another example of a discrepant role that we will focus on in this chapter is called a mediator, or "go-between". A *go-between* is characterised by access to some of the backstage regions and secrets of *two* teams. This is different from the shill, who only has access to the secrets of one performing team. Instead, the go-between is an example of a discrepant role because they perform to two audiences and are knowledgeable of aspects of both of these teams' secrets. Go-betweens are in essence 'double-shills' (Goffman, 1959, p. 93).

One famous organisational example of a go-between, which we mentioned earlier, is the factory foreman. The foreman was a fairly new, prominent, and curious position in Goffman's time. Building on a well-known article by Roethlisberger (1945), Goffman writes:

> One illustration of the go-between's role appears in recent studies of the function of the foreman. Not only must he accept the duties of the director, guiding the show on the factory floor on behalf of the managerial audience, but he must also translate what he knows and what the audience sees into a verbal line which his conscience and the audience will be willing to accept (Goffman, 1959, p. 159).

Here we get a sense of how the foreman must be a part of two performances that occur in different places and in relation to two different audiences—one in the manager's office to management and one on the factory floor to workers. The foreman as go-between is aware of secrets which one team does not wish to share with the other, and must be very careful in what facts he presents and conceals to either team. The foreman as go-between is thus an historical example of a discrepant role and illustrates the complexities that come from needing to act out one's role in relation to different teams and performances where the concealment, sharing, and maintenance of secrets through the use of spatial divisions is vital to fostering a successful impression of reality and keeping the show going.

We have already characterised the community managers as playing the role of such 'go-betweens'. They occupy a discrepant role that has them caught between management and worker cohorts. They have special access to the 'secrets' of each of these cohorts, and need to be careful about how they exercise information control both in relation to their own and their two audiences' performances. As we will explore in the following, the BCN offers a unique opportunity for these go-betweens to gather in a space that affords them the privacy needed to carefully share such destructive information in a candid and constructive way. We will show that this sharing not only of information but of *secrets* plays a vital part in the construction of a collegial relationship that supports them in the local performances of their roles.

Analysis: Interplay of BCN, Community Managers and CNAs

Encouraged by our initial insights we set out to better understand the nature of the BCN from a theoretical perspective, by employing Goffman's regions and roles concepts. Making use of Goffman's concept of the go-between made it possible for us to appreciate the uniqueness of the BCN as a space for this cohort to congregate, interact, and collaborate. It was also initially unclear to us what role the CNAs played in this arrangement, as a group of people dedicated to assisting the community managers (as go-betweens) to better manage the duality of their message. We find that Goffman (1959) provides a way of analysing our data that accounts for the complexities of these roles by offering concepts that are sensitive to spatiality. In the following we show how the BCN is constructed as a "backstage" space for community managers who are geographically dispersed and we consider how use of this space facilitates them in making sense of ESN and how to facilitate its adoption in their respective companies.

The BCN as a Backstage for Sharing "Secrets"

We introduced concepts from Goffman's work on performances in some detail because we found that this perspective assists our analysis of the BCN case. We first draw on Goffman's notions to argue that in our case, the BCN acts as a backstage space for community managers, who we come to understand as go-betweens.

We found that there is a tendency for the content of the community managers' conversations to directly pertain to these groups and their respective 'secrets'. For example, in the interaction in Fig. 4.1 between community managers, the challenge of getting leaders and executives to participate in ESNs is discussed. These community managers come from different (perhaps even competing) companies, and yet here they are exchanging suggestions and insights about how to present information (about ESN use) to one of their audience cohorts (executives/management). The advice centres on how to craft and sustain a particular reality in relation to this audience. In the exchange below, certain 'destructive information' pertaining to management audiences is shared—for example, the notion that executives are susceptible to flattery is discussed as a tactic for assisting other community managers in sustaining the impression that Beta is a worthwhile tool for executives; while another community manager reveals that their manager is insecure about being seen to condone unprofessional behaviour at work and that this needs to be overcome if Beta is to be seen as worth adopting.

The above exchange demonstrates how the BCN provides a 'backstage' space that permits the candid sharing of secrets pertaining to community managers' management audience, for example in relation to the strategies that community managers use to 'manage upwards' in influencing their executives. Because the BCN is accessible only to those who have been invited to it, there is little chance that the audience members to whom the community managers usually perform will 'walk in' and see that they are being talked about. It is therefore a private space where performers can run through their performance and rehearse how to best enact a particular reality when they will be 'on stage'.

We have already explained that such backstage spaces are integral to all performances as all performing teams need to keep secrets from their audiences in order to sustain the "illusion" that their performance fosters. However appreciating the uniqueness of the BCN case requires a consideration of what it means for community managers as *go-betweens* to have a space to gather, engage in sense-making, and share secrets about their dual audiences.

The ESN Community Managers as "Go-Betweens"

The role of the go-between is one marked by anxiety (Roethlisberger 1945), to do with needing to manage two impressions at once and needing to gain the "spontaneous cooperation" of the workforce, while meeting managerial imperatives at the same time. The excerpt below in Fig. 4.2 illustrates a discussion where the need for this kind of worker co-operation in the face of managerial imperatives leads to an exchange of advice. The community managers share their strategies and suggestions for engaging employees in the use of their company ESNs.

We interpret this exchange as the community managers collectively making sense of ESN and rehearsing different impressions of what the ESN is and what it can offer workers, seemingly in preparation for a future front stage performance (i.e. on the

User ID	Message	Time stamp
4315712	Starting a new thread about convincing execs to participate in an open and realtime format. I'd imagine that can cause some discomfort. How do you convince people otherwise?	2012-10-02,15:40:27
10489280	I think that helping your leader understand the value, first, is key. Stress to them that they can really connect with employees in a new and effective way. Then, draw a comparison that you think will appeal to them. I've used "online press conference" before; I've also said that it's like them being in New York's Central Park, being that cool guy who's playing five games of chess at once. I also assure them that I'll be there with them to support and help. They're not doing this alone; I engage subject matter experts ready to watch and be called or jump in.	2012-10-02,15:43:20
7242819	We had to work hard with this one particularly with our parent company, [client name removed], actually. They were worried because Beta had such a 'facebook' feel to it, but we emphasised that our code of conduct still applies to this the same way it applies to emails, etc... As far as getting a tricky question, we did some practice runs where I asked the exec some of the worst ones I could think of (or that I got from some of our brokers in the past) and showed him that no matter what people ask, as long as it's not offensive (in which case we'd delete the comment and they'd have a serious word from their manager) then we were very capable of answering any question. For example we've had complaints about the sales budgets being set too high and it gave a great opportunity to demonstrate how the targets are set and what factors are taken into account.	2012-10-02,15:44:30

Fig. 4.1 The BCN as a backstage space that permits the sharing of secrets

ESN itself or in training meetings or company presentations). What is noteworthy about it is that the community managers are not actually technically on the same performing team—they do not work in the same company, and so are never 'on stage' together when performing their role in relation to either management or other workers. Whether we take 'on stage' to refer to company ESNs or physical organisational spaces, the community managers are only ever in the same space when they interact on the BCN—they do not share the same front stage, because their daily performances (managing their respective company's social networks) are geographically, temporally, and organisationally separated. How then are we to understand the community managers' relationship to one another? This question leads us to consider an additional term from Goffman's vocabulary: that of the "colleague".

User ID	Message	Time stamp
1487147343	That would be great to see [User:1366087]. We're struggling with the same behavioral shift here at [client name removed]. We're about to launch Beta ESN to the enterprise and I'm struggling with how to communicate it's benefits to a population of 160K plus who have very particular ways of doing what they do...	2012-10-18,09:49:12
1366087	In October one of my HR colleagues set a Beta ESN Challenge to all HR colleagues - to go into Beta ESN and like a message, follow someone, post something or make a comment. We had a huge spike in activity which seems to be sticking!	2012-10-18,09:49:32
9558806	I'm working with a company who has consultants that have to jump from project to project at a moments notice. I've been talking to them about the benefits of moving their project comms to Beta ESN because it makes their project activity available more quickly to people as they move from team to team. Having project conversations happen in email distribution lists silos it off and slows down the onboarding process for new team members. So, if you have employees that have to move between projects fluidly, Beta ESN can really help get them up to speed on projects MUCH more quickly than before.	2012-10-18,09:49:45
1366087	Maria, we established a group of Social Media Champions late last year who help to promote the use of the network, demonstrate responsible behavior, connect people, answer questions, train, etc. You should consider this for your rollout. It's been huge for us!	2012-10-18,09:50:47
1366087	And, Karyn, we are constantly reminding people it's not about the tool it's about the behavior. Because if you don't change your behavior, the tool (Beta ESN) won't work for you. We hear "it's just another thing to check" but it's not if you change how you work. It's part of your workflow and can save you time. Good luck!	2012-10-18,09:52:07

Fig. 4.2 Discussing audience secrets

The BCN as a Place for Fostering "Collegiality"

Goffman (1959, p. 159, our emphasis) describes the colleague relationship as follows. We quote him at length because our findings suggest that this relationship of collegiality is significant for understanding and appreciating the work of the ESN community managers more fully:

Colleagues may be defined as persons who present the same routine to the same kind of audience but who do not participate together, as team-mates do, at the same time and place before the same particular audience. Colleagues, as it is said, share a community of fate. In having to put on the same kind of performance, they come to know each other's difficulties and points of view; whatever their tongues, they come to speak the same social language. And while colleagues who compete for audiences may keep some strategic secrets from one another, they cannot very well hide from one another certain things that they hide from the audience. The front that is maintained before others need not be maintained among themselves; relaxation becomes possible.

Here we find in Goffman's work an insightful and useful way of thinking about the nature of collaboration that emerges on the BCN between community managers.

We argue that, in being able to communicate with other community managers from all over the world and from different organisations using the BCN, the community managers are able to "come to speak the same social language" (Goffman, 1959, p. 159) *about* ESN community management. As this is quite a new job title/position, the opportunity to make sense of their own role and identities, and to discuss the nature of their performances, audiences, and the challenges they face, allows them to devise implementation strategies and to give voice to their anxieties, while being able to relax in the knowledge that others share similar experiences. As Goffman points out, while they may not tell each other everything, it is futile to try to fully keep up appearances as certain trade secrets would be familiar to all. We found evidence of the 'venting' aspect of the collegial dynamic in the way in which community managers would complain in an almost exasperated tone about the challenges of their role and equipment—reluctant executives, paranoid employees, poorly executed updates.

At first, this exchange seems to indicate a negative tone in the BCN interactions, but employing Goffman's description of collegiality we find in these calls for help and advice evidence of collegial relationships emerging. The episode in Fig. 4.3 illustrates how community managers share their frustrations and experiences, engage in sense-making to devise strategies and pass on 'narratives' that each can use in local performances to be successful in their roles. It is significant that these community managers refer to one another as "we", and share details of their experiences in a way that reveals a degree of vulnerability, which comes from struggling with their go-between positions.

Here again Goffman (1959, p. 160), now quoting Hughes (1945, pp. 168–169), offers a way of understanding the nature of these confessional interactions that take place between colleagues, where privately sharing experiences and 'tricks of the trade' helps to build a bond that in turn facilitates ongoing work:

Part of the working code of a position is discretion; it allows the colleagues to exchange confidences concerning their relation to other people. Among these confidences one finds expressions of cynicism concerning their mission, their competence, and the foibles of their superiors, themselves, their clients, their subordinates, and the public at large. Such expressions take the burden from one's shoulders and serve as a defence as well. The unspoken mutual confidence necessary to them rests on two assumptions concerning one's fellows. The first is that the colleague will not misunderstand; the second is that he will not repeat to uninitiated ears.

User ID	Message	Time Stamp
8779454	Just finished an interesting phonecall from one of our ESN members. A new member, keen to see what this "social media/ESN stuff" was all about. He called me as he couldn't understand why his ESN feed was full of "people I don't follow". I explained that those he followed had contributed to other user's posts, and Beta was bringing these posts to his attention. He didn't like this approach, and said that with all the noise, he would probably not be much of a [social media user] after all. He has quite a small and selective group that he follows, and I think his expectations were that he would only see "main posts" from these people, and not the threads that they had contributed to too. And as such, I think we may have lost him! So what can we do? Is there an option that allows him to only see the threads that the people he follows have started? I appreciate that the way the Beta ESN operates now means you get to see those conversations you might have missed, but it does confuse the follower network principles for some.	2012-01-05,03:42:36
6862681	Does he have his my feed settings set to "top message threads" or "followed message threads"	2012-01-05,06:51:53
6717568	He could try following Groups, but no people, or he could hide conversations that are not of interest. You could explain to him that, just like in the office, he will sometimes "overhear" a conversation or be cc-ed on an email that is not relevant to him or to his work. But sometimes overhearing a conversation is beneficial - he'll learn info that he otherwise wouldn't have learned.	2012-01-05,09:34:49
8779454	Thanks [User:6717568], that's the angle I went with - overhearing and picking up on things that are useful. But he's quite firmly in the 'only want to see what I want to see' camp, which is at odds to the fluid nature of Beta ESN conversations! [User:6862681] - he had 'followed message threads' ticked, but again it appears the Beta ESN pulls in *anything* any of his network posts, even if it's only a comment in a wider thread. To be honest I think it's more a shift in his thinking and behaviours that is needed, and I wonder how best to make this shift?	2012-01-06,02:36:56
8751865	I have been facing exactly the same issue with members of my Team and am still confounded on how to resolve this. Part of me feels that there will be a level of early adopters that "get it" straight away and then there will be a gradual shift towards mass adoption as it becomes more apparent that this technology is not going away. I'm sure there must have been a level of reluctance to embrace email when it first became available and now I believe there isn't a single employee within our organisation that doesn't use it. Maybe we have to take the approach that we can't convert everyone overnight and that some people will make the decision in their own time?	2012-01-06,03:09:58

Fig. 4.3 Forging collegial relationships

Here Hughes highlights the importance of secrets (and the 'spaces' that allow them to be kept) for the development of collegial relationships. When read through this theoretical lens we see that the BCN offers community managers an opportunity to bond, to share and make sense of their mutual struggles. As a consequence of sharing destructive information, they become responsible to one another and this plays a role in helping them to build a community of colleagues, that we suspect in turn helps them to improve their performance. Although at times negative in tone, we find that the BCN conversations between community managers may in fact be a sign of the process by which collegiality is established.

We have so far shown how our analysis, using Goffman, allows us to productively interpret the community managers as 'go-betweens', a type of discrepant role that is marked by the burden of performing to two audiences at once, without much existential space for a sense of being one's own kind of team. By offering a private space where secrets can be shared between go-betweens, the BCN affords the development of collegial relationships and thus of a community of geographically and organisationally disparate community managers. In order to give a fuller picture of the role of the BCN, we now consider the remaining participants on the platform—the CNAs, who are employees of Beta tasked with advising the community managers via the BCN platform, along with additional on-phone and in-person support. To do so we draw on Goffman's notion of a 'service specialist'.

The CNAs as "Service Specialists"

Service specialists, according to Goffman (1959), help their clients (members of the performing team) to present their performances. Service specialists are not a part of the performing team and do not go on stage. Instead they assist with the construction, repair, and maintenance of the show their clients maintain before other people. In the theatre, service specialists include set designers and costume makers, whose job is to support the performance and not to be seen by the audience. 'Real world' examples are architects, stylists, and consultants who specialize in supporting performing teams in presenting a particular impression to their audiences, again by assisting in the concealment of certain 'facts' and the strategic presentation of others.

We theorise that the CNAs who interact on the BCN are directly involved in helping the community managers in their performances, particularly in maintaining the dual impression of the Beta ESN as both a productivity tool in relation to management, and as a social tool in relation to employees. The CNAs and other Beta employees who participate in the BCN are responsible for assisting the community managers in managing the complexity of their performances. Although there is a separate help desk available for technical problems, the CNAs listen to the community managers' stories and help to identify their needs. In response to requests for support, the CNAs create training videos and presentation slide decks that community managers then use to help 'stage' their performances, as discussed in the interaction between community managers and CNAs in Fig. 4.4.

User ID	Message	Time stamp
2672589	Question re. training videos, narrated PowerPoints w/ screen shots, user documentation, etc. -- any updates as to ETA? [User:3525521] [User:1365639] I think I remember reading that videos and some other material would be ready by early Feb. Any updates?	2011-02-04,09:09:36
2604000	Hi Tina, I've requested our marketing team provide updates for all mentioned above. We are all chomping at the bit :)	2011-02-04,09:25:24
3525521	We are on schedule for delivery of these materials. We will be approving internally end of next week and will have materials ready for distribution the following week. Things are looking good I believe everyone will be happy.	2011-02-04,11:28:55
2672589	Great, Stephen! Can you give us a sense of what will be made available in a couple weeks in terms of format and topics? (e.g. video modules on X, Y, Z; narrated PPT with screen grabs covering A, B, C; Word doc with FAQs -- etc.) I know there was a long wish list; just curious about what we can look forward to seeing in this wave. Thanks much.	2011-02-04,13:20:48
3525521	Of course I should have mentioned it in the first place: Instructional Videos and One Sheeters for... The Network Feed, Profiles, Follow Buttton, Groups and Topics. Also we will be providing assets and a suggested layout for an intranet landing page. We are also working on an animated Beta ESN overview video that is several weeks away. We are in production on everything above but will need final internal approval before we can release them. Following the delivery of these materials we will be working with your CNAs to select the next round of materials. Hope this helps.	2011-02-04,13:39:44

Fig. 4.4 Discussing 'staging' with 'service specialists'

To better appreciate the role that the CNAs play in our case we learn from Goffman (1959, p. 152) that service specialists are in a unique position because "they are like members of the team in that they learn the secrets of the show and obtain a backstage view of it". This is indeed the case in our data—the CNAs are party to all discussions taking place on the BCN and are 'let in' on trade secrets and privileged information. However, because these service specialists do not themselves need to partake directly in the ESN implementation performances, "the specialist does not share the risk, the guilt, and the satisfaction of presenting before an audience the show to which he has contributed" (Goffman, 1959, pp. 152–153). So, while the service specialist learns secrets about members of the performing team, "the others do not learn corresponding secrets about him" (Goffman, 1959, p. 153). This imbalance leads to a phenomenon where clients try to convert their service specialists into what Goffman refers to as confidants.

Walking a Fine Line—Turning CNAs into "Confidants"

With the *confidant* role Goffman describes someone who shares their secrets with others, without a transactional basis for the relationship (Goffman, 1959). Goffman observes that often clients will try to turn their service specialists *into* confidants. This comes to bear due to the information asymmetry or power imbalance that emerges in the service specialist/client relationship, whereby the 'weaker' party over time tries to break down the power distance by establishing interactions that are more informal or intimate in nature than the relationship between the parties would otherwise warrant (Goffman, 1959). Hairdressers provide a good non-theatrical illustration here: a client who has been disclosing destructive information to her hairdresser (as service specialist) for years may eventually try to coax the hairdresser into a friendship relationship, where services are no longer paid for and the hairdresser divulges their secrets to their (former) client in equal measure.

We see some evidence of such attempts to convert CNAs as service specialists into 'confidants' in our data as well—on the platform, community managers emphasise experiences of meeting their CNAs at conferences and events and often encourage interactions that are personal in tone, for example making jokes and recollecting memorable events. Towards the latter sections of our data, the interactions between CNAs and community managers become more and more friendly and familiar in tone. The following excerpt gives evidence of one such exchange where community managers and CNAs exchange praise and flattery, breaking down barriers by voicing their intentions to meet in person outside of the BCN (Fig. 4.5).

This exchanges provides evidence of how community managers and CNAs over time have come to appreciate their mutual presence and collaboration, which results in active attempts to break down the transactional distance between the two groups, so that members of the two groups come to interact in ways more befitting of colleagues than of clients and service specialists. We note that the initiative for such attempts to reduce distance and engage in more informal exchanges usually come from within the community manager group.

According to Goffman this renegotiation of boundaries may occur in part because there is an asymmetry of information that develops over time, as service specialists gain access to secrets about their clients' performances and audiences, all the while not being required to offer much in the way of confidential information in return. We can thus read the shift towards a more familiar tone as a possible attempt to restore a sense of informational balance between the two cohorts, as well as potentially an effort on behalf of the community managers to obtain 'extra' assistance, special treatment, or insider information in relation to Beta and its future plans. We speculate that as a result of these tendencies, the dynamics of such relationships (i.e. between service specialists and their clients) will change over time, and that it is therefore unlikely that the dynamics that we identified in the BCN can be manufactured, or at least not sustained indefinitely. We thus find that even in the primarily digital setting of the BCN there is a 'fine line' between service specialist and client that is open to negotiation, and which is sometimes crossed.

User ID	Message	Time stamp
1488746532 {CM}	[Tag:1994679] time! To parlay off of a Wednesday activity from a few weeks ago... Who is the one person you have NOT met from the BCN but would most like to meet? Make sure you tag them in this post!	2013-04-10,06:19:27
1488746532 {CM}	To kick things off... I would like to meet [User:5565721{CNA}] Anyone who puts a period at the end of their name means business! Not to mention, I bet you'd have a lot of stories to tell from "behind the scenes".	2013-04-10,07:16:50
5565721 {CNA}	It's true. Its amazing how much you can get done when your name is a one-word sentence. Obvs, id like to meet [User:1488746532 {CM}] as well, but id like to have more than a friendly nod across a sea of people with [User:5464938 {CM}].	2013-04-10,08:09:11
1495290168 {CM}	This activity has risk of being flagged by HR... haha! Of course I'd like to meet [User:1488746532 {CM}] - but I'll call out [User:4315712 {CNA}] and [User:1488164017 {CM}] as being high on my list. Also [User:3413805 {CM}].	2013-04-10,08:41:03
1366110 {CM}	I have been so lucky in being able to meet so many great people from the BCN but I must say that there are two that come to mind. [User:9034364 {CM}] has help so many on the BCN and has published brilliant analytical data regarding ESN's, including the BCN. The other is [User:6126537 {CM}] because in the many years we have been members and as many times as we have collaborated together and given the fact that we live in the same state/city I have need actually met her in person.	2013-04-10,09:16:26

Fig. 4.5 Reducing distance between community network advisors {CNA} and community managers {CM}

Summary: The Value of a Community of Go-Betweens

Through a Goffmanian lens, we have come to see the BCN as a 'backstage' space that is uniquely able to facilitate relationships of collegiality amongst the geographically and organisationally disparate community managers. As such, it is important that such a space is not accessible by either the management or worker 'audience' cohorts to whom the community managers 'perform'. The restricted permissions of the BCN thus played an important role in rendering the platform a place where secrets could be shared and kept. It was through this sharing of secrets (for example about how community managers 'pitch' ESN as a different kind of technology depending on who they are speaking with) that the grounds for collegiality was established. In turn, this collegiality made it possible for community managers to share tips, vent, and rehearse and improve their subsequent 'performances' pertaining to the implementation of ESN in their respective organisations.

We note that the BCN worked as a backstage space *because* there was grounds for collegiality amongst its participants: the community managers shared a 'community of fate' because they all have a stake in implementing ESN, and can share their experiences of staging the kinds of performances that this activity involves. Because they serve similar kinds of audiences and share the experience of being 'stuck in the middle', sufficient common ground exists for collegiality to be established, and the BCN provides the space for this kind of relationship to develop over time.

We further found that the presence of the CNAs, as 'service specialists' was important in two ways. Firstly, the service specialists treat the community managers as clients, which gives these otherwise put-upon individuals a sense of status and identity. The presence of the service specialists creates an opportunity for the go-betweens to be a collective: the CNAs want to impress *them*, and for once they can complain and make demands and assert a degree of power. Secondly on a pragmatic level, the CNAs as service specialists are tasked with assisting the community managers in staging their complex performances. Upon request, training materials, videos, slide decks, and even an occasional system alteration to the Beta ESN platform itself are created to improve the credibility of the 'impressions of reality' in relation to ESN use, that the community managers are working to maintain in their organisations.

Finally, we found that the tendency, which Goffman identifies, for clients to try to convert service specialists into *confidants* also appears to occur in our online case context. Over time, and driven by the group of community managers, the conversations between them and the CNAs became more and more personal and convivial.

Conclusion and Implications

In this paper we have investigated the role of the 'community manager' that emerged recently in response to the challenges of implementation and adoption of Enterprise Social Networks (ESN). ESNs are malleable technologies and thus come with the need to be interpreted and appropriated by workers into their local business practices. This requirement brings about a tension between the expectations of managers and executives as the sponsors of ESN roll-out and those of the workers who have to engage in an active process of experimentation and sense-making to find appropriate use for the ESN in their practices. This puts the community manager in the position of a "go-between", who has to mediate and manage the tensions between the expectations of these two groups. Consequently, we set out to investigate the following research question: How do community managers deal with their conflicted position in the process of ESN implementation and adoption?

We had access to a unique data set for studying how community managers communicate and collaborate to help each other make sense of and cope with their roles, in the form of communication data from the Beta Community Network (BCN), a dedicated, inter-organisational ESN made up of community managers of Beta's corporate ESN clients and Beta employees. An initial analysis of our case data made us reach for the work of Goffman (1959), as a way to understand the particular role and place of the community managers in the process of ESN implementation, as well as the role of the BCN in facilitating coordination among them. The answer to our research question lies in the insight that community managers cope with the demands of their position by seeking to build a community of their own, which serves as a place for joint strategizing and identity-building with their 'colleagues'.

Implications for Practice

Our findings have surfaced useful implications for various stakeholders involved in the development, implementation and use of ESN specifically, and malleable technologies more broadly (see Table 4.4 for a summary). For organisations implementing malleable, infrastructure-like technologies (such as ESN) we note that such technologies require organisations to coordinate a multi-stakeholder process of sense-making and appropriation to find appropriate uses for the technology. Often a dedicated role is created and put in charge of this process—so-called community managers in the case of ESNs, who not only observe, encourage and curate communication on the ESN itself, but otherwise work with stakeholders to find appropriate uses for the ESN and encourage adoption.

  Our study was motivated by the observation that the in-betweenness of such roles can be challenging and uncomfortable. We reasoned that people in such go-between roles will benefit from connecting and collaborating with people in comparable roles in other organisations, with positive effects on their respective implementation and adoption projects. If suitable spaces for building a community of go-betweens do not exist, people in such roles might want to consider creating dedicated inter-organisational online spaces that are restricted to people in comparable positions in other organisations, in order to provide a safe space for collegial exchange between them. Such spaces can be private groups in public social media, or dedicated inter-organisational ESNs.

  For providers of malleable technologies our case shows that organising such an online community of go-betweens can be a valuable business strategy, in particular when the provider makes available personnel who encourage, facilitate and support the sense-making activities of the community managers. More broadly we argue that providers of malleable technologies will benefit from explicitly recognising the open platform or infrastructure character of their technologies, subsequently treating it as a service rather than a product, which deserves explicit support to increase the success rate of implementation and adoption in client organisations. Finally, we note that the tendency of client go-betweens to try and reduce the distance between them and the service managers presents a potential risk that the transactional nature between the provider and the client company representatives is compromised.

Table 4.4 Practical implications for stakeholders involved in malleable technology implementation

Stakeholder group	Advice
Client organisations	Malleable technologies, as open and flexible platforms, require user experimentation and sense-making to find appropriate uses
	Looking after such a process of experimentation and sense-making requires the creation of a dedicated go-between role
Go-betweens	People tasked with the success of malleable technology implementation find themselves in a challenging position between diverging management and worker expectations
	Given their precarious position people in this role will benefit from exchanges with people in comparable positions in other organisations
	The building of a private community of go-betweens affords strategizing and identity building for the benefit of both the go-betweens and their implementation projects
Technology providers	Providers of malleable technologies might consider building and moderating a community of go-betweens for the added benefit of learning and client relationship building
	Creating of a dedicated service or relationship manager role will benefit the sense-making of the group of client go-betweens and thus might drive success of the technology in client organisations
	A risk is presented by the tendency of client go-betweens to make service managers their confidants, thus compromising the otherwise transactional nature of the relationship

Implications for Future Research

Our work has direct implications for the future study of ESN. We have drawn on a unique data set that allows us to see ESN operating as a private inter-organisational space, rather than only as a public, company-wide activity stream that facilitates impression management more explicitly. We have shown that an ESN can act as an important, and to an extent protected/private, space where an otherwise disparate 'community of fate' can come together to work on understanding the complexities of their role in a way that informs refinement of their performance in another context. Future research could investigate these ideas by interviewing and observing network members in their everyday work to better understand how the sense-making that takes place online informs broader practice and vice versa. In particular we suggest that seeing such an inter-organisational network as 'a backstage space for go-between collegiality and community' can inform further research concerned with ESN use and implementation. As we have shown, there is still an unresolved tension in organisations that are trying to understand the use value of ESNs—are they a productivity tool, or a social infrastructure?

More broadly, our work suggests that Goffman's analytical framework, as we have introduced it here, can generate further insights in future research on ESN because his theatre metaphor lens is sensitive to the relationship between space, boundaries, information, and roles. These elements are all relevant in an ESN because there are always dynamics of information concealment and display. While Goffman is often considered in relation to impression management (Gardner & Martinko, 1988; Wiesenfeld, Raghuram, & Garud, 2001), we argue that his work is concerned with the social and material production of reality more fundamentally. ESN data gives us a unique opportunity to see the process of such productions play out in a relatively 'naturalistic' way over significant periods of time.

References

Alvesson, M., & Sandberg, J. (2013). *Constructing research questions: Doing interesting research.* London: SAGE.

Bughin, J. (2015). Taking the measure of the networked enterprise. *McKinsey Quarterly, 51*(10), 1–4.

Carroll, J., Howard, S., Peck, J., & Murphy, J. (2002). A field study of perceptions and use of mobile telephones by 16 to 22 year olds. *Journal of Information Technology Theory and Application, 4*(2), 49–61.

Dahlander, L., & Gann, D. M. (2010). How open is innovation? *Research Policy, 39*(6), 699–709.

DeLone, W. H., & McLean, E. R. (1992). Information systems success: The quest for the dependent variable. *Information Systems Research, 3*(1), 60–95.

Dodd, L. (2011). Study reveals huge ROI when using yammer. *Strategic Communication Management, 15*(6), 7.

Ellison, N. B., Gibbs, J. L., & Weber, M. S. (2015). The use of enterprise social network sites for knowledge sharing in distributed organizations: The role of organizational affordances. *American Behavioral Scientist, 59*(1), 103–123.

Fulk, J., & Yuan, Y. C. (2013). Location, motivation, and social capitalization via enterprise social networking. *Journal of Computer-Mediated Communication, 19*(1), 20–37.

Gardner, W. L., & Martinko, M. J. (1988). Impression management in organizations. *Journal of Management, 14*(2), 321–338.

Goffman, E. (1959). *The presentation of self in everyday life.* New York: Anchor Books for Doubleday.

Hafermalz, E., & Riemer, K. (2016). The work of belonging through technology in remote work: A case study in tele-nursing. In *24th European Conference on Information Systems (ECIS)*, Istanbul, Turkey.

Hafermalz, E., Riemer, K., & Boell, S. K. (2016). Enactment or performance? A sociomaterial reading of Goffman. In L. Introna, D. Kavanagh, S. Kelly, W. Orlikowski, & S. Scott (Eds.), *Beyond interpretivism? New encounters with technology and organisation.* Springer.

Howlett, J. (2009). Enterprise 2.0: what a crock. ZD Net: http://blogs.zdnet.com/Howlett/?p=1228.

Hughes, E. C. (1945). Dilemmas and contradictions of status. *American Journal of Sociology, 50*(5), 353–359.

Klein, S. (1996). Interorganisationssysteme und Unternehmensnetzwerke: Wechselwirkungen zwischen organisatorischer und informationstechnischer Entwicklung. Wiesbaden: Springer Verlag.

Leonardi, P. M., Huysman, M., & Steinfield, C. (2013). Enterprise social media: Definition, history, and prospects for the study of social technologies in organizations. *Journal of Computer-Mediated Communication, 19*(1), 1–19.

Levy, M. (2009). WEB 2.0 implications on knowledge management. *Journal of Knowledge Management, 13*(1), 120–134.

McAfee, A. (2009). *Enterprise 2.0: New collaborative tools for your organization's toughest challenges.* Boston: McGraw-Hill Professional.

McKinsey. (2012). The social economy: Unlocking value and productivity through social technologies. Retrieved 12, February 2014, from http://www.mckinsey.com/insights/high_tech_telecom s_internet/the_social_economy.

Naaman, M., Boase, J., & Lai, C.-H. (2010). Is it really about me?: Message content in social awareness streams. In *Proceedings of the 2010 ACM Conference on Computer Supported Cooperative Work*.

Orlikowski, W. J. (1996). Improvising organizational transformation over time: A situated change perspective. *Information Systems Research, 7*(1), 63–92.

Orlikowski, W. J. (2000). Using technology and constituting structures: A practice lens for studying technology in organizations. *Organization Science, 11*(4), 404–428.

Pinch, T., & Swedberg, R. (2008). Living in a material world. In *Economic sociology meets science and technology studies*. Cambridge: MIT Press.

Razmerita, L., Kirchner, K., & Nabeth, T. (2014). Social media in organizations: Leveraging personal and collective knowledge processes. *Journal of Organizational Computing and Electronic Commerce, 24*(1), 74–93.

Richter, A., & Riemer, K. (2013). Malleable end-user software. *Business & Information Systems Engineering, 5*(3), 195–197.

Riemer, K., & Johnston, J. B. (2014). Rethinking the place of the artefact in IS using Heidegger's analysis of equipment. *European Journal of Information Systems, 23*(3), 273–288.

Riemer, K., & Johnston, J. B. (2012). Place-making: A phenomenological theory of technology appropriation. In *International Conference on Information Systems*, Orlando, United States.

Riemer, K., Finke, J., & Hovorka, D. (2015). Bridging or bonding: Do individuals gain social capital from participation in enterprise social networks? In *International Conference on Information Systems*, Fort Worth, United States.

Riemer, K., Richter, A., & Böhringer, M. (2010). Enterprise microblogging. *Business & Information Systems Engineering, 2*(6), 391–394.

Riemer, K., Steinfield, C., & Vogel, D. (2009). eCollaboration: On the nature and emergence of communication and collaboration technologies. *Electronic Markets, 19*(4), 181–188.

Roethlisberger, F. J. (1945). The foreman: Master and victim of double talk. *Harvard Business Review, 23*(3), 283–298.

Schlagwein, D., & Bjorn-Andersen, N. (2014). Organizational learning with crowdsourcing: The revelatory case of LEGO. *Journal of the Association for Information Systems, 15*(11).

Schneckenberg, D. (2009). Web 2.0 and the empowerment of the knowledge worker. *Journal of Knowledge Management, 13*(6), 509–520.

Tavakoli, A., Schlagwein, D., & Schoder, D. (2015). Open strategy: Consolidated definition and processual conceptualization. In *International Conference on Information Systems (ICIS)*, Fort Worth, USA.

Timmermans, S., & Tavory, I. (2012). Theory construction in qualitative research: From grounded theory to abductive analysis. *Sociological Theory, 30*(3), 167–186.

von Krogh, G. (2012). How does social software change knowledge management? Toward a strategic research agenda. *Journal of Strategy Information Systems, 21,* 154–164.

Weick, K. E. (2012). Organized sensemaking: A commentary on processes of interpretive work. *Human Relations, 65*(1), 141–153.

Wiesenfeld, B. M., Raghuram, S., & Garud, R. (2001). Organizational identification among virtual workers: The role of need for affiliation and perceived work-based social support. *Journal of Management, 27*(2), 213–229.

Chapter 5
Social Motivation Consequences of Activity Awareness Practices in Virtual Teams: A Case Study and Experimental Confirmation

Russell Haines, Nadine Vehring and Malte Kramer

Introduction

Thanks to advanced information and communication technology (ICT), groups of geographically and/or temporally disbursed individuals can be brought together virtually to work on collaborative tasks. Such teams come with the promise that members with the best talent available can be brought in and taken away as needed, without incurring the expense and trouble of relocating members. However, the reality of virtual teams often does not meet this promise of seamless collaboration—virtual team members are frequently observed to be distrustful and unmotivated (e.g., Jarvenpaa & Leidner, 1999; Sarker & Sahay, 2003; Watson-Manheim & Bélanger, 2007; Piccoli & Ives, 2003). These *social motivation losses* (e.g., social loafing) in virtual teams can have dramatic effects, such as the incident when two U.S. Army black hawk helicopters were misidentified as enemy helicopters and destroyed (Snook, 2000, p. 135).

Social psychology research suggests that if one's effort can be identified and evaluated, motivation losses are reduced (Parks & Sanna, 1999, p. 86). When one is face-to-face with others, the notion of "mere presence" carries with it the connotation that others can observe and evaluate one's activities, which thereby increases motivation and performance (Zajonc 1965). However, awareness of the activities of others is not as easily achieved in virtual teams. When the members of a virtual team

R. Haines (✉)
Old Dominion University, Norfolk, VA, USA
e-mail: rhaines@odu.edu

N. Vehring · M. Kramer
WWU - University of Muenster, Münster, Germany
e-mail: Nadine_vehring@web.de

M. Kramer
e-mail: malte.kramer@uni-muenster.de

© Springer International Publishing AG, part of Springer Nature 2019
K. Riemer et al. (eds.), *Collaboration in the Digital Age*, Progress in IS,
https://doi.org/10.1007/978-3-319-94487-6_5

are geographically dispersed,, the lack of physical presence denies them access to important identification and comparison information (Greenberg, Ashton-James, & Ashkanasy, 2007), which increases the likelihood of motivation losses. Indeed, one might think of a virtual team setting where members use mediated communication (e.g., email, instant messaging) as similar to a face-to-face setting in which another is observable bodily, but whose back is turned such that his/her activities cannot be directly observed. In such a setting, one might observe the presence of the other and the outcomes of the other's work but not the extent to which the other is making an effort. This notion is prominent in virtual teams research, which suggests that dispersal affects the development of trust to the extent that many teams are unable to effectively perform their assigned task (Jarvenpaa & Leidner, 1999; Sarker & Sahay, 2003).

An inability to compare oneself with others via computer mediated communication (CMC) is thought to lead virtual team members to choose "less than ideal" sources of social comparison information, causing problems when perceiving fairness and experiencing negative affect about other team members (Greenberg et al., 2007). Based on the preceding, it is no surprise that social motivation losses have been shown to occur in a wide variety of experimental CMC studies, including electronic brainstorming (Shepherd, Briggs, Reinig, Yen, & Nunamaker, 1996, Pinsonneault, Barki, Gallupe, & Hoppen, 1999) and group decision making (Chidambaram & Tung, 2005).

The purpose of this paper is to examine how awareness of the activities of others via CMC affects the motivation of geographically distributed virtual team members. We present a case study of a financial services firm in which members of geographically dispersed teams developed and refined practices for maintaining awareness of the availability of other team members. These practices in turn affected their attitudes toward their team and their work. Using the results of the case study, we developed hypotheses about the effect of activity awareness on social motivation. These were tested a laboratory experiment, the results of which are presented in the second part of this paper. The paper begins with a theoretical foundation, which discusses the role of awareness practices in coordinating behavior in teams and includes a brief review of the theories and empirical CMC studies of social motivation losses. We conclude the paper with a general discussion of the results of both studies, along with implications for researchers and software designers.

Theoretical Foundation

When individuals are assigned to a team and given a task that must be accomplished by their collective efforts, the total amount of effort exerted is often less than what the individual members would be capable of if they were working alone. The difference between a team's performance and the sum of their individual capabilities is called *process losses* (Steiner, 1972). Process losses can further be divided into *coordination losses*, which are the result of team members' efforts not being used fully or not contributed at the best time, and *motivation losses*, which are the result of individual team members not exerting their full effort on behalf of the team.

Coordination Losses

Team coordination can be defined as "managing dependencies between activities" (Malone & Crowston, 1994, p. 90)—a team might have a shared resource and have to schedule its use, or there might be a task-subtask relationship in which certain subtasks have to be performed before others. Coordination encompasses the management of task/subtask dependencies in a team context where various team members need to perform different activities in order to achieve an overall team task or goal. For a given subtask, a team and its members need to know: what to do, who should do it, and when it should be done. If a team and its members do not understand how their work will be coordinated, it results in tasks not being completed, duplicated efforts, and/or team members interfering with each other.

Awareness

In order to coordinate his/her efforts with others, a team member needs to obtain information about the other members of the team, what they are working on, and how those activities will be coordinated (Gross, Stary, & Totter, 2005). This "understanding of the activities of others, which provides a context for your own activity" (Dourish & Bellotti, 1992, p. 107) has been broadly termed *awareness*. Maintaining awareness has been identified as a critical factor in ensuring that team members are able to coordinate their efforts in a variety of face-to-face contexts, including air traffic control (Harper, Hughes, & Shapiro, 1989) and subway control rooms (Heath & Luff, 1992). Awareness here is somewhat broader than "situational awareness," which is typically limited to task-oriented information that helps to coordinate activities in the present. We choose a more broad conception of awareness because information about others' past activities and background is used to infer the reasons behind their present behavior (Cooper & Haines, 2008) and therefore affects social motivation.

In face-to-face settings, awareness is maintained by observing others directly, meaning that one can gather awareness information without it being explicitly communicated by others. For example, when working on an assembly line, one may be able to directly observe that the person from whom one receives raw materials is engaged in a heated conversation with a supervisor. Thus, one is aware that the arrival of raw materials will be delayed at least until the conversation is finished. Awareness information places one's own activities in the context of other activities (e.g., you will not be able to begin your assembly work until after the conversation is over), and also provides context about the others with whom one works (e.g., the other is being disciplined for being late to work for the last five days).

When interacting via CMC, awareness information must either be provided explicitly by other team members or communicated by the mediating technology. Extending our example, if one is not able to directly observe the person from whom one receives raw materials, one can only speculate about the reasons why raw materials have been delayed (cf., Cooper & Haines, 2008). One will not be able to form a realistic expectation about when raw materials will arrive, nor will one have an explanation for why the other is unable to complete his/her work in a timely manner unless and until the other communicates what is happening or has happened.

Mitigation of Coordination Losses via CMC

To deal with this lack of easily obtainable awareness information, members of distributed virtual teams can employ awareness practices using communication technology. For example, features of an instant messaging (IM) application can be employed to create and maintain awareness of team members' presence or activities (Riemer, Klein, & Frößler, 2007). Based on this information, a distributed team may be able to better coordinate their individual activities in order to ensure the achievement of an overall team goal (Gutwin & Greenberg, 2002, Gross et al., 2005). For example, providing activity awareness information via CMC has been shown to help reduce the harm caused by interruptions by enabling team members to more carefully time when they interrupt another team member (Dabbish & Kraut, 2008).

Motivation Losses

In contrast with coordination losses, which occur when one is not sure *when* to apply one's efforts on behalf of the team, motivation losses occur when one questions *whether* to apply one's best efforts. For example, members of a tug-of-war team win based on the efforts of the entire team, but a given member might not necessarily pull as hard as he/she could. The primary individual drivers of motivation losses are dispensability and low involvement (Parks & Sanna, 1999). A perception of dispensability occurs when a team member feels that his/her efforts are not necessary for achieving the team's goal, such as a tug-of-war team member that feels that there are enough strong members to defeat the other team. Low involvement is evidenced when a team member contributes little to the team's effort because he/she has little interest in accomplishing the task and/or does not feel motivated to achieve the team reward, such as a tug-of-war team member who does not care whether their team wins the contest or not. When either of these occurs, a team member may not exert their full effort.

In a team context, motivation losses typically only occur when team members feel their individual efforts cannot be observed and evaluated separately from the effort of the team as a whole. Thus, the principal way to reduce motivation losses is to make individual efforts more visible. For example, if the members of a tug-of-war team can see how hard an individual member is pulling, the other members of the team would know and could sanction when one was shirking, and one could also see when the team would benefit from a little more effort (Kerr & Hertel, 2011). The implications of awareness information on motivation have received relatively little attention in the information systems literature (e.g., Shepherd et al., 1996).

Motivation Losses via CMC

In geographically distributed contexts where team members interact via computer-mediated communication (CMC), the influence of others is believed to be reduced because of the lack of physical presence of others (Greenberg et al., 2007; Short, Williams, & Christie, 1976), and reduced even more when team members communicate anonymously (McLeod, Baron, Marti, & Yoon, 1997; Haines, Hough, Cao, & Haines, 2014). Furthermore, motivation losses have been shown to occur during CMC brainstorming sessions (Shepherd et al., 1996; Kahai, Sosik, & Avolio, 2003), and have been observed in distributed teams when team members must post status reports (Watson-Manheim & Bélanger, 2007; Piccoli & Ives, 2003).

This suggests a rather bleak view of distributed work—researchers should expect to see situations where the members of a large proportion of distributed teams are reluctant to put forth their best effort toward their team's goal, are likely to focus on the failings of other team members and not to trust each other, and ultimately be ineffective at accomplishing their assigned task (e.g., Jarvenpaa, Knoll, & Leidner, 1998; Sarker & Sahay, 2003; Piccoli & Ives, 2003). One study goes as far as to suggest that mandatory reporting of activities via weekly status reports, rather than motivating members to work harder, actually *reduces* social motivation in distributed teams because it only serves to make the failings of team members evident (Piccoli & Ives, 2003). However, in spite of these results, the same researchers also note that virtual teams have become an integral part of real world organizations.

Thus, the question of whether and how communicating via CMC affects social motivation in distributed teams remains unanswered. Our case study, which is presented next, revealed that adopting and appropriating a communication system could have positive motivational effects on members of geographically distributed virtual teams. Our case study results suggest a more nuanced model of how using CMC affects motivation in teams, which was tested in a laboratory experiment. Following our analysis of the experimental results, we present overall conclusions and implications for researchers and practitioners.

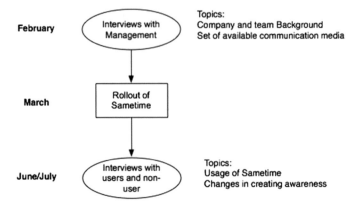

Fig. 5.1 Overview of data collection

Case Study

The case study involved the members of back office teams in a medium-sized financial services company in Germany, which hereafter is identified by the pseudonym
MUFIN. We conducted interviews at different organizational levels of the company
(e.g., managers and employees) during the period immediately surrounding the roll
out of Lotus Sametime (see Fig. 5.1). Our goal for the case study was to investigate the adoption and development of usage practices for Sametime at the individual
and team level. The interview topics centered how Sametime was used at MUFIN,
and whether Sametime changed the ways that employees routinely communicated,
coordinated, and collaborated.

Data Collection and Analysis

One month before the Sametime rollout, we conducted interviews with managers of
the IT department to get a good overview of the company and team background as
well as the existing set of available communication technology. Several months after
the rollout of Sametime, we conducted semi-structured interviews with 13 members
belonging to ten different teams in the finance division. The demographics of the
participants are summarized in Table 5.1. We tape-recorded the interviews with the
team members and the head of department and transcribed them.

A grounded theory approach was used, meaning that the interviewers did not
formulate hypotheses in advance to guide their questioning. Instead, a preliminary
analysis of the earlier interviews focused the questions in the later interviews. The
overall objective of understanding the adoption and development of CMC usage
practices was the central phenomenon of interest in the interviews. Our finding that
these practices had an impact on motivation in the teams was revealed in a post hoc

Table 5.1 Demographics of study respondents

Total in operating department		182
Total selected for interviews		13
Gender	Females	6
	Males	7
Job type	Team leader	1
	Deputy team leader	4
	Case worker	8
Sametime user type	User	12
	Non-user	1

analysis of the case study data, but was consistently noted by the study participants. Because the potential for communication practices to improve motivation has not been observed in the distributed teams literature, we thought it deserved a separate examination and experimental testing.

One key question of the interviews was: Why and how are different technologies used to create awareness of other team members' presence and availability? The interviews were transcribed and first analyzed by looking for points in time where the interviewees described changes in team awareness practices. Next, we identified the factors that led to the changes in the practices. Finally, we re-read the interviews to identify outcomes of the new practices. The outcomes of the practices are the focus of the analysis. In the text below, the quotes presented are highlights from the interviews and are translated from the original German.

Case Setting

The headquarters of MUFIN houses the IT department and several operating departments. The operating departments are subdivided into several divisions, each of which consists of approximately 15 teams with about 8–12 team members. These teams provide day-to-day support for the decentralized sales organization, whose members are spread over the entire country. Besides processing standard files for the sales agents, the daily work of the employees in these teams also involves communicating with sales agents, customers and colleagues inside or outside their teams. Normally, a single team member is responsible for processing his/her own set of standard files in a timely fashion, meaning efforts within a team only need to be coordinated to the extent that someone must be present when a sales agent or customer calls.

The physical structure of the workplace for the teams consisted of small offices, each with two work stations, which meant that team members were not physically co-present, even when all members were working in the headquarters building. Furthermore, most of the investigated teams included team members that practiced alternating telework, meaning that team members alternated between one workday at home (home office) and a workday in the headquarters office. Two team members with complementary rhythms normally shared a desk and thus only met face-to-face at team meetings.

Over the time period covered by the case study, employees could draw on a variety of communication technology: telephone, email, and instant messaging (IM). Telephone was the dominant communication medium for team members, especially when communicating with people outside their team. Every team member had his/her own telephone number that could be used at the headquarters office or forwarded to their home office. In addition, every team had a team telephone number. If someone called the team number, the call rang the phone of all team members who had connected to the team number at that moment. Team members normally had to answer both types of calls—their own phone number and any team calls. Furthermore, if a team member would not be able to answer his/her own telephone (e.g. they were going to be in a meeting), he/she could forward their telephone number to the team number.

Basis for Awareness Practices: Team Goal

Because the employees in the headquarters function as the back office for the sales organization, it is important that incoming calls from the sales organization are answered immediately to ensure prompt, personal service. All interviewees stated that it was important to know the availability of their colleagues in order to provide the right information when a sales agent called. As the manager of the IT department put it:

> Sales agents often are at the customer's house and can't strike the deal, because they don't know a particular legal detail or contract feature. If they leave the customer and need to make a new appointment … deals are lost because of that.

Thus, being informed about the absence of other colleagues was essential when deciding whether one could leave the office, as it was crucial that there always be at least one team member to answer the telephone. In the late nineties, MUFIN's management decided to improve telephone response rates at the team level by including it as one of the performance measures in the calculation of the annual team bonus. The head of the department explains:

> In the late 1990s we did some intensive optimizing of the telephone response rate. It is like a kind of registration authority. When you leave, when you arrive, when you shift your phone, all these things had been a little loose. We had always monitored these things, but in 1999 we added them to the variable salary. […] We monitored it for every team, the telephone response rate, and then we compared all teams.

At this point, achieving a 100% telephone response rate became one of the teams' top goals to assure the highest bonus. Now, teams had to coordinate telephone availability. In order to do this, team members depended on receiving awareness information about the comings and goings of their other colleagues to decide on their own availability.

Awareness Practices Using Instant Messaging

Coordinating 100% availability at the team level was difficult during the time period immediately following the new requirement, as the head of the department remembered:

> … they really obsessed about this and started to scream at each other: 'Why haven't you shifted your telephone? Man! You have to shift it to the team number when you leave your office.

At this point, it became obvious to the team members that the physically distributed nature of their workplace made it difficult for them to be aware of their colleagues' presence or absence from their workstation. Because being aware of others was essential when deciding on one's own presence or absence, teams started to use their instant messaging system to inform each other about an absence by sending a message to all group members. The head of the department continued:

> This is why there is an incredible huge sensitization about telephone: 'I will be gone for a few minutes or I won't be available'. And we don't have open-plan offices. Thus people might have said: 'I don't know about the others. It seems that I am the last one doing business and answering the telephone.' … and to avoid this: 'Before others might think that I am intentionally not answering the phone, I prefer to give notice of my departure'. This is why this practice evolved.

With instant messaging, employees sent short messages to individuals by addressing the ID number of this person. This ID number contained the number of the person's team (e.g. 45), meaning it was possible to send a message to an entire team by addressing it to the team ID followed by a wildcard (e.g. 45*). Thus, team members developed a practice of using instant messaging to send messages to their team whenever they needed to leave their workplace, informing their team members about their absence and its duration. MUFIN later implemented email, which was used in a similar way to maintain awareness, with the disadvantage that emails did not always arrive at a person's in box instantly, sometimes taking as long as 2 h.

Awareness Practices Based on Sametime

Although the employees had been familiar with practices for communicating awareness information via instant messaging that could simply evolve to fit the Sametime chat feature, Sametime's presence feature was new to them and led to the creation of new practices.

Awareness Practices using Chat Feature: As the employees had perceived some downsides of using email for signaling their comings and goings, most of them welcomed Sametime as an alternative that was similar to instant messaging. Thus, there were some teams where members simply changed from using email to using Sametime for signaling availability via text messages.

Awareness Practices using Presence Feature: Sametime's presence feature, although ostensibly quite simple, enabled new methods of signaling. Prior to the introduction of Sametime, availability could only be signaled by composing and sending an instant message. Afterward, it became possible to signal availability using the presence feature: for example, by actively changing one's presence status from "available" to "away" or "in a meeting" when one left the workplace. Furthermore, members of some teams added additional text to their status information. One employee reported:

> Right now, the additional label for my status information says: 'I am available @MUFIN.' I was the one that wrote this … and if I was working from home, it would say: 'I am available @home'.

Besides the active forms of signaling (changing the status and/or entering an additional text label), automatic forms of signaling were also reported, like when the computer was inactive for a certain time or when someone has logged off by pulling out his/her identification card from his/her computer. One employee explained, "[…] when I pull out my card, the status automatically changes to 'not available' and that's it."

Monitoring changed the most dramatically as a result of Sametime's presence feature. Prior to the introduction of Sametime, awareness about someone's availability had always depended on the active signaling of that person via text messages. After the introduction of the presence information feature of Sametime, employees could monitor the availability of their colleagues at any time under the assumption that they were available to answer the phone when their status showed available on Sametime, whether they were at home or in the office. The presence feature was perceived by some employees as a possible instrument for surveillance:

> I don't like the idea of big brother watching me. I don't know. I mean if they can see when I am online, it makes you wonder what else they can see.

However, many of the interviewees emphasized the advantages of using Sametime to better create an awareness of other's availability. This allowed them to better coordinate team availability and to manage their telephone response rate. Some of them stated:

> I always have a look at my buddy list to see who is online when I arrive in the morning. Starting at 8 a.m., we have to answer the telephone. If I arrive at 8.15 a.m. and no one is online, I know that I am the only one and that I have to connect to our team number.

> We use the presence information of our team members to coordinate availability. It is not okay to leave the work place for lunch or a cigarette break if half of the team is already absent.

Motivational Effects of Sametime Practices: Because the Sametime status changed automatically when a team member's identification card was inserted or removed, it began to be viewed as a proxy for availability. However, beyond simply coordinating availability, this feature affected the teams in ways that led to a new level of visibility and connectedness. As one employee put it:

> You always notice. When I have pulled my card out of my computer, people rarely call. In other words, if it says "I am not available" or "I am in a meeting" … no one calls. When I

put in my card and people can see that I am suddenly there, my telephone suddenly rings and then 'I have seen that you have just logged into Sametime' …

The ability to monitor comings and goings via the presence feature also motivated members to make themselves more available. One employee reported:

…I don't know, after 5 p.m. when it is normal that one called it a day and then someone sees…'Hey! You are still working. That's why I have thought that I could call you to clarify some things'. Thus, one knows who is there and one can get through to someone quickly …

… it is really interesting in the evening at about half past 5, who is still there. I think I have never seen all 27 people - belonging to my buddy list - being online at the same time. Right now, 18 out of 27 are online and at about half past five it will be about four, then three, then two. One day I just said; 'Today, I work till such time as I am the last one being online.' I really did this and then… I found it really funny and I really managed it.

The employees increasingly assumed that just being connected and available on the Sametime system indicated that the other team members were working. The team members reported that this assumption was made because team members were under individual pressure to process case files over the course of the day, and assumed that others were under similar pressure.

Case Study Discussion

Drawing a line through the changes in practices occurring from the time before the first messaging system was adopted to the current state shows how team awareness practices evolved as team members adapted to altering circumstances, additions to the available technology, or changes in team structure. Initially, team members developed a practice for communicating their availability so that their teams could deal with management's monitoring of the team telephone response rate and the inclusion of the response rate into the calculation of the annual bonus. Before this time, no practices were in place because coordination was not explicitly considered. With the change in the incentive structure, employees experienced the need to coordinate their availabilities and, by extension, their activities. Thus, they started to use the instant messaging system for sending short chat messages to their team members in a "push"-oriented fashion to inform them about their availability. Sametime initially enabled team members to reproduce their practice of using instant messages to signal their team members. Over time, however, the presence features in Sametime enabled them for the first time to *monitor* the presence status of other team members using a "pull"-orientation.

Coordination Gains

The driving force behind these changes was a desire to reach 100% availability. The earliest driver of change was the implementation of the team bonus for telephone availability, which gave the team members a financial reason to be coordinated. To a great extent, the later changes in communication practices were made in order to maintain or improve their efficiency at maintaining 100% availability. For example, less effort had to be exerted using Sametime than instant messages because team members could rely on others knowing they were away after simply removing their badge from the card reader.

Motivation Gains

At the time that management first incorporated the teams' availability into the calculation of their annual bonus, the team members realized that their distributed context meant that they needed to coordinate availability using mediated communication practices. In the beginning there were no awareness practices about availability; however, there was a demand to answer the team line, so some team members became rather upset with how other team members behaved about being available. With virtually no visibility about whether other team members' had switched their own numbers to the team line, members indicated they had the feeling of being the only one answering the team line, and reported that some team members had been yelling at each other. At this point, the lack of awareness information was demotivating for the teams.

Motivation gains came with the introduction of practices that enabled more visibility into the comings and goings of team members, first with instant messaging and ultimately with the presence feature of Sametime. This contrasts with prior research, in which members of distributed teams were observed to manipulate awareness information to the extent that it had demotivating effects (Watson-Manheim & Bélanger, 2007; Piccoli & Ives, 2003). The practices at MUFIN led to reported decreases in frustration within the teams, and the synchronous nature of the Sametime presence feature seems to have had the added effect of increasing feelings of what we term *connectedness*, and thereby the biggest positive impact on motivation within the teams.

Case Study Limitations

There are limitations to the case study that present opportunities for future research. The bulk of the interviews were conducted after the Sametime roll out, meaning that new practices had been developed and evaluated by the participants. In addition, we relied primarily on interview data, which might be affected by recall bias. Finally, team members in MUFIN had the motivation to maintain awareness about the availability of others because availability formed the team goal. However, in a context where the team goal was the completion of a collaborative document or project, availability awareness practices might be considered an unwelcome distraction and not fit with the task. We emphasize that this could be as much or more a task-practice fit than task-technology fit because team members might be able to choose whether or not to be prompted by such messages and/or use that information for purposes not intended by the designers of the technology. For example, being aware of the comings and goings of other team members might be viewed as a proxy for how much effort was being made and increase social motivation—members of a software development team might view the checking in and checking out of code from a repository as a means for gauging the effort of other team members and adjust their social motivation accordingly. Thus, we recommend further research into how awareness practices affect motivation in other contexts.

Case Study Conclusions

The emerging practices for coordinating availability could be described as merely an evolution in team communication practices. However, these changes influenced the performance of the teams, the efficiency of the teams' coordination, the motivations of the team members, the team members' attitude toward their team, and their relationship with each other. For example, using Sametime, team members only send instant messages when urgent, there is a "pull" observation of colleagues' status, and the presence status has been enriched with taken for granted information about availability and activity that gives team members a sense of how much effort that others are exerting (cf., Carroll, Rosson, Convertino, & Ganoe, 2006). Instead of feeling solely responsible for their team's success and phone availability, team members felt more connected as they could now see at a glance who was online and able to cover the phone. Based on the positive experience of being connected to a team and not alone, a motivational side effect emerged: employees made themselves more available and started to work more.

As noted earlier, social motivation *losses* seem to be the rule for virtual teams (Watson-Manheim & Bélanger, 2007), so finding that awareness practices increased social motivation at MUFIN was an unexpected result. Social motivation gains are ignored in the predominant workspace awareness frameworks (Teruel, 2014; Gutwin & Greenberg, 2002; Gross, 2013; Gross et al., 2005), beyond saying that "it might not only enhance the mutual understanding of group members, but also direct individuals or the group to follow certain goals or procedures" (Gross et al., 2005, p. 341). The prior studies that found only social motivation losses in CMC contexts also offer nothing to explain why users would alter their IM screen names (Smale & Greenberg, 2005) or maintain a long term Skype connection (Riemer et al., 2007). The results of the case study therefore mark an important first step toward examining the potential for awareness practices to lead to social motivation gains in distributed contexts. We suggest that motivational factors should be considered when studying the use of mediated communication for awareness creation.

We further suggest that there are certain organizational contexts where social motivation losses are reduced by increasing activity awareness. The organizational context of our case study seems to differ from contexts where losses were observed in the following key ways: (1) team members had clearly defined roles and objectives,

(2) team members understood how their portion of the team task would lead to team level rewards, (3) all team members were skilled at performing their portion of the team task, and (4) teams were allowed to create their own communication and coordination practices. In such a context, we suggest that individuals gauge the extent to which the efforts of team members are comparable based on the amount and kind of effort they observe them to make instead of on other factors like physical appearance. Members of distributed virtual teams interacting via CMC would therefore be able to experience social motivation gains when using a technology tool that simply shows if someone is online or not. Our experimental study, presented next, simulates such an organizational context and tests whether social motivation gains occur when activity awareness technology and practices are employed. By examining this experimentally, we hope to provide additional evidence and insights into how social motivation gains can be encouraged by managers of distributed teams and designers of awareness technology.

Experimental Study

The notion that activity awareness practices can lead to social motivation gains has intuitive appeal. However, we have already noted prior research that observed negative effects of activity awareness practices on social motivation (Watson-Manheim & Bélanger, 2007; Piccoli & Ives, 2003). In order to confirm that our observed increase in motivation was not idiosyncratic to a particular set of individuals at MUFIN using only Sametime, we developed and conducted an experimental study. In the experimental study, we examined the extent to which a user interface element that presents activities of other team members increased feelings that one is aware of the activities of others, how this in turn affects feelings of being connected to one's team, and the extent to which this in turn increases team performance. In the following subsections, we discuss how specific findings of the case study informed hypotheses that were then tested via the experiment.

Awareness Technology as a Facilitator of Awareness Practices

When working in a co-located (face-to-face) environment, where open offices or cubicles make spaces relatively open and accessible, one may be able to directly experience co-workers' presence and observe their activities. In a distributed work context like the case study, one may be unable to observe one's colleagues in their physical work environment and only indirectly be able to observe colleagues' presence and activities. Thus, information about the activities of others must be obtained by other means than direct observation.

In the case study, virtual team members compensated for others being unable to directly observe them by providing awareness information by CMC channels, such as status indicators or messages via IM, or through other, more general channels, such as including information about one's activities in an email. System designers can add user interface elements that automatically show information about the activities of others (Gutwin & Greenberg, 2002), which would make such practices easier to implement (Haines & Riemer, 2011). However, we emphasize that user practices are necessary in order for the technology's intended purpose to be realized (Orlikowski 2000), meaning that a direct link between a technology and other group factors like connectedness and performance is mediated by perceived awareness of the activities of others. Thus, we suggest:

> H1: A user interface element that automatically provides information about the activities of other team members will be more likely to lead to practices that heighten perceived awareness of the activities of others.

Awareness as a Facilitator of Feelings of Connectedness

In a face-to-face context, team members may take for granted that they can observe the activities of others and be relatively unreflective about the importance of such information in facilitating attachment. However, in a distributed work context, one can only indirectly observe colleagues' presence and activities, and when practices that provide this information are not employed, the information may not be available at all and decrease understanding of the behavior of others (Cooper & Haines, 2008). Because of this, one is likely to feel less connected to one's colleagues (Greenberg et al., 2007).

Increasing the amount of information that is passed when interacting via mediated communication can compensate for a lack of awareness, enabling one to experience colleagues' presence and activities virtually (Walther, 1992; Haines & Riemer, 2011). Rationally knowing that one belongs to the same team, being aware of colleagues' presence and activities, and knowing that others are working on the same or similar tasks and potentially able to communicate all work together to reinforce a feeling of being "in touch" or being connected with the team. Thus, we hypothesize:

> H2: Higher perceived awareness of the activities of other team members will lead to higher feelings of connectedness.

Connectedness as a Faclitator of Motivation

Simply being more aware of the activities of other team members should increase one's own effort because of increased social comparison. However, we noted earlier a case where mandatory reporting of activities via weekly status reports, rather than motivating members to work harder, actually reduced social motivation in distributed teams because it made the failings of other team members more evident (Piccoli &

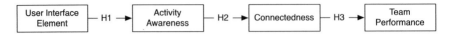

Fig. 5.2 Experimental study research model

Ives, 2003). In a case study of another organization with a lower trust environment (Watson-Manheim & Bélanger, 2007), employees reported that that "using email is not sufficient for relationship development," and instead must be combined with other, more personal media (p. 12), and reported instances of employees "copying email to colleagues and management to show 'how busy I am'" (p. 14).

In our case study, team members indicated that motivation increased when team members received activity information from others, reporting increased feelings of being connected with their team. Based on the case study results, we expect that social motivation will be increased the more one feels connected to the other members of one's team via the mediating technology. This occurs because the virtual presence of the others is heightened (Sarker & Sahay, 2003), meaning that the other team members more strongly become referent others (Greenberg et al., 2007). Thus, we hypothesize that simply having the additional information about the activities of others is not enough—feelings of connectedness mediate the link between awareness of the activities of others and increased social motivation:

> H3: Higher feelings of connectedness are associated with higher team performance.

The research model for the experimental study is summarized in Fig. 5.2.

Experimental Design

Similar to our case study context, management research suggests that social motivation losses are the exception rather than the rule under certain organizational conditions: (1) when teams have a specific goal rather than just "do your best," (2) team members are aware of the presence of other members (3) team members are free to communicate, and (4) team members know each other and might work together in the future (Erez & Somech, 1996). Under such conditions, regularly monitoring others inspires higher levels of performance from team members (i.e., "the Kohler Effect" Kerr & Hertel, 2011). We emphasize that condition #2 emerges as a result of awareness practices in a distributed environment, and awareness of others' activities cannot be taken for granted via CMC like it can in a face-to-face context. Our experimental setting was therefore designed such that teams needed to develop activity awareness practices and connectedness in order to experience social motivation gains.

In contrast with a context where motivation losses are expected in team members, these organizational conditions imply the converse of the normal hypothesis about why motivation losses occur. In many ad hoc experimental contexts, motivation losses are mitigated by enabling others to observe one's individual effort (Parks,

1999), meaning that individuals are expected to increase their efforts in the team situation because they worry about sanctions when their efforts are judged by others to be too low (a.k.a., evaluation apprehension). In situations such as those, a researcher should expect individuals to only perform to a *minimum* standard (i.e., social loafing). In an environment where all four of the above conditions are present, our analysis of the case study suggests an alternative explanation for a reduction in motivation losses: individuals increase their efforts because they see how much others are contributing; in essence, they evaluate their *own* efforts in comparison with the work of others when judging how much to contribute (cf., Erez & Somech, 1996). In a context where team members can trust each other, or at minimum wish to maintain their reputations, awareness should lead to performances that are measured against a *maximum* standard.

Participants in the experimental study were recruited from information systems courses offered by the business school at a public U.S. university. All communication within the teams took place via mediated communication.

Experimental Task

The experimental task simulated the process of making a medical diagnosis. This context proved to be meaningful to the participants, in contrast with contexts they might feel were artificial (e.g., the prisoner's dilemma), or that they did not understand (e.g., processing cases for a financial services company). In health care contexts, patient diagnosis and treatment is a process that involves communication among many health care providers, including paramedics, triage nurses, general practitioners, surgeons, and specialists (Anantharaman & Han, 2001; Bal, Mastboom, Spiers, & Rutten, 2007; Ng, Wang, & Ng, 2007). In general, the process of diagnosis and treatment begins with a first responder, usually a triage nurse or a paramedic, who collects and passes information to other, more specialized health care providers. The more specialized health care providers use this information as a basis for their own examinations and/or request that other health care providers do further examinations (e.g., a laboratory test of fluids, a radiological exam).

The medical conditions and symptoms for this experiment were simplified so that a team of college students could complete the medical diagnoses of a hypothetical patient with the assistance of a job-specific expert system. Three different jobs were filled by team members in this study: (1) nurse, (2) doctor, and (3) specialist. The nurse completed his/her job by "interviewing" a patient and received a patient's primary symptom and vital signs as output. The doctor completed his/her job by entering a patient's primary symptom and vital signs as received from the nurse, then "examining" the patient to receive more specific symptoms. The specialist entered the patient's primary symptom, vital signs, and specific symptoms, and received a "final diagnosis" as output, which was the final step in the process. Each interview, examination, or diagnosis appeared after a 15 s wait. This delay was chosen because

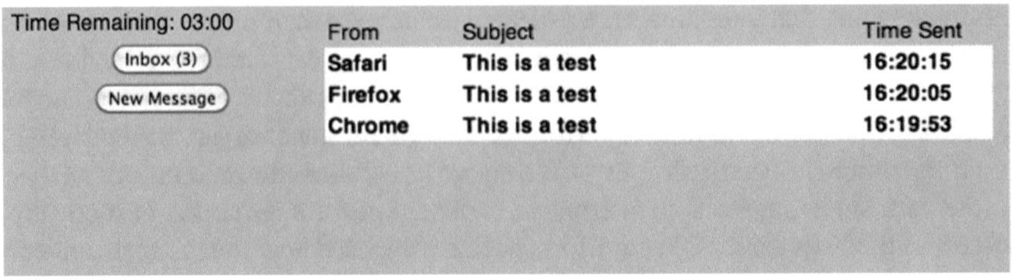

Time Remaining: 03:00	From	Subject	Time Sent
Inbox (3)	**Safari**	**This is a test**	**16:20:15**
New Message	**Firefox**	**This is a test**	**16:20:05**
	Chrome	**This is a test**	**16:19:53**

Fig. 5.3 Email screen for non-treatment team

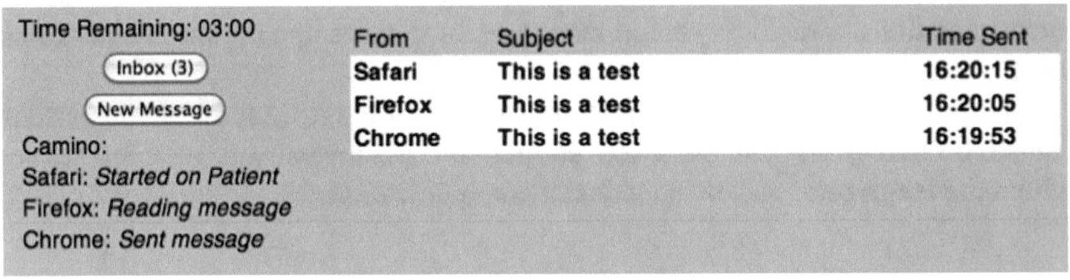

Time Remaining: 03:00	From	Subject	Time Sent
Inbox (3)	**Safari**	**This is a test**	**16:20:15**
New Message	**Firefox**	**This is a test**	**16:20:05**
	Chrome	**This is a test**	**16:19:53**
Camino:			
Safari: *Started on Patient*			
Firefox: *Reading message*			
Chrome: *Sent message*			

Fig. 5.4 Email screen for treatment team

it allowed team members a few seconds of idle time beyond the time that was required to exchange messages with other team members in pilot studies.

During the diagnosing period, participants used an email system to communicate that was integrated into the experimental application. The email screen was modeled after recent web-based email systems. It displayed an inbox that listed all of the messages that the participant had received during that period, the text of which was displayed below the list when that row was clicked (Figs. 5.3 and 5.4). The participants addressed messages using a drop down list that contained the names of their team members. The expert system that was used to interview, examine, or diagnose a patient was located below the status display on the left side of the screen.

The participants were rewarded at the conclusion of an experimental session based on the number of patients that were correctly diagnosed by the teams in which they worked. The participants whose teams diagnosed the most patients overall won a nominal cash prize.

Experimental Procedures

The experiment was completed during normal classroom hours as a class exercise illustrating online collaboration. First, the participants indicated their informed consent and filled out a demographic questionnaire. Next, the computer totaled the number of participants in the session and randomly assigned the participants to a job. When the class size was not an even multiple of three, the remaining participants were given the role of lab technician, meaning some teams had four members. The specialist on four member teams had to enter the results of a lab test before a patient diagnosis could be completed. The data for this study includes only teams that had three members.

The participants were given verbal instructions about the different jobs on the team, the task the teams needed to complete, and how to use the messaging system. Finally, each participant read instructions specific to their particular job: how to use the expert system, from whom they needed to receive information, and to whom they needed to send information. After all of the participants had read these instructions and any questions were answered, they were told that they would be meeting in a chat room for 5 min, and instructed to use the time to decide on a process for completing a patient diagnosis. All of the participants in the session were then randomly assigned to teams and met in the chat room. When the 5 min had elapsed, the participants completed a post chat questionnaire and then began the diagnosing period.

During the diagnosing period, the team members communicated via email. Typically, information flowed from the nurse to the doctor, then from the doctor to the specialist for final diagnosis. After 4 min, the diagnosing period ended, and the participants completed another questionnaire, which included the items used in this study.

Over the course of the session, each participant was part of three different teams. After the end of the first diagnosing period and post-diagnosis questionnaire, the participants were randomly assigned to a second team. The new teams returned to the chat room to decide on their process for diagnosing patients, then diagnosed patients again. After the second diagnosing period the participants completed the questionnaire again and were assigned to a third team. During the second and third chat periods, teams were given 3 min to chat because they were more familiar with their jobs and the diagnosing process. The shorter time period did not seem to affect the teams in any way, and a longer time period likely would have meant 2 min of idle time and/or off topic chatting.

Throughout the exercise, chat and email messages were identified by first names, which were entered by the participants at the time they indicated informed consent. This enabled team members to potentially recognize people they had worked with before. On the second and third teams, each participant performed the same job, but potentially worked with new people. This meant that a person could be on a team that was the same size but with one or more different team members, or be on a team with a different number of members. In that way, the second and third rounds simulated an environment where an individual is expert at their own task, but is working with new members and/or with new steps in the process. The data used in this study were collected after the participants worked with their third team.

Experiment Study Variables

The email interfaces were identical with the exception of an on-screen indicator that showed the activities of team members for teams with the experimental treatment (Fig. 5.4). Members of control group teams did not see the indicator (Fig. 5.3), making this a between-groups design. The status on this indicator automatically changed each time a team member clicked on an item on their screen (e.g., clicked the Interview Patient button, clicked on a message in their inbox, clicked on the New Message button, etc.).

Unless otherwise noted, the scales used were developed specifically for this study. The scales for each construct were reduced and/or modified from a larger set of items based on data collected from two pilot test sessions. All of the items are seven point Likert-type scales anchored Not At All—To A Great Extent. *Activity awareness* is defined as one's feeling that one knows when the other people on the team are working. Five items were used to measure activity awareness, which are based on the scale developed by George (1992):

(1) I could tell when the other people on this team were occupied with work.
(2) I knew when the other people on this team were busy.
(3) I knew whether or not I should wait before sending a request or information to another person on this team.
(4) I was aware of when the other people on this team were doing something.
(5) I recognized when the other people on this team were working versus not working.

Connectedness is defined as one's feeling that others in the team are virtually present. Four items were used to measure connectedness:

(1) I felt like the messaging system connected me to the other people on this team.
(2) I felt like the people on this team were connected through the message system.
(3) The message system linked me with the other members of this team.
(4) It seemed like we were linked together as a team.

Performance is the number of patients correctly diagnosed by the team during the third round. As noted earlier, participants were rewarded based on the total number of patients that all of their teams diagnosed.

Experiment Results

The data used for this study comes from questionnaire responses gathered after participants completed the experimental task with their third team. The data were analyzed using Partial Least Squares (PLS Graph build 1130). Significance of paths was determined using the bootstrap resampling technique (500 subsamples). The tests shown use data at the group level (n = 76), but we note here that the statistical significance of the tests is the same using individual level data (n = 228). Of the

Table 5.2 Means (standard deviations) of study variables by treatment

	n	Activity awareness	Connectedness	Performance
No indicator	41	4.70 (1.29)	5.03 (1.17)	1.88 (1.63)
Indicator	35	5.21 (0.98)	5.31 (1.05)	1.69 (1.83)

Table 5.3 Composite reliability and correlations of latent variables (square root of AVE on diagonals)

	Composite reliability	Activity awareness	Connectedness	Performance
Activity awareness	0.966	0.921		
Connectedness	0.968	0.873	0.939	
Performance	N/A	0.391	0.482	N/A

participants that were included in the analysis, most were business majors. Just over half were male (55%). The average age was 22 years old, and the average participant was between his/her second and third year of college. The means and standard deviations of the study variables by treatment are shown in Table 5.2. The values shown are the average of the responses to the items that comprise each seven point scale. Higher values represent a higher feeling of the underlying construct. For example, a higher value for Activity Awareness indicates that participants felt like they were more aware of the activities of others. Cell sizes for the treatments are not equal because of the design of the overall study.

All of the scales exhibited adequate reliability, with composite scale reliabilities equaling or exceeding 0.966. Convergent validity for the scales was supported because the correlations of the latent variables were lower than the square root of the average variance extracted for a given variable (shown in Table 5.3). The constructs of activity awareness and connectedness are strongly linked in the participants' minds, as proposed by hypothesis 2. However, discriminant validity was supported because individual scale items loaded higher on their own latent variable than their correlation with other latent variables (shown in Table 5.4) (Chin 1998). Furthermore, a model with a link from the user interface element to connectedness was not significant, indicating that feelings of connectedness arise more from communication practices than from user interface elements.

An alternative ordering of the research model with reversed causation of activity awareness and connectedness in predicting performance was also not supported. The correlation between activity awareness and performance is lower than the connectedness and performance (0.391 vs. 0.482). In addition, when performance is predicted only by activity awareness, its path coefficient is lower than when performance is predicted by connectedness (0.42 vs. 0.50), and the amount of variation in performance explained is lower (r-squared 0.174 vs. 0.247).

The results show that members of teams with the on-screen indicator had a significantly higher level of perceived activity awareness (Hypothesis 1: b = 0.215, t = 2.10,

Table 5.4 Loadings and cross loadings of items on latent variables

	Activity awareness	Connectedness
Act1	**0.918**	0.789
Act2	**0.927**	0.782
Act3	**0.890**	0.794
Act4	**0.951**	0.841
Act5	**0.920**	0.811
Conn1	0.799	**0.944**
Conn2	0.845	**0.960**
Conn3	0.794	**0.927**
Conn4	0.837	**0.925**

Fig. 5.5 PLS results

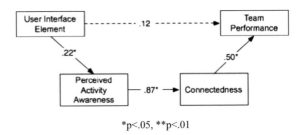

*p<.05, **p<.01

p=0.0359), confirming that the user interface element heightened activity awareness for participants. In turn, higher levels of perceived activity awareness were associated with a higher level of connectedness (Hypothesis 2: b=0.873, t=28.59, p<0.0001). Finally, higher values of connectedness were associated with higher levels of group performance (Hypothesis 3: b=0.498, t=6.8446, p<0.0001). Figure 5.4 graphically summarizes the results (Fig. 5.5).

Experiment Discussion

The experimental results confirm our hypotheses: a user interface element that provides activity awareness information about other team members led to increased feelings of awareness of the activities of others. This in turn led to higher feelings of connectedness; and higher connectedness was associated with higher team performance. This occurred in a team context where distributed members were expert at their own task and were working with a new team of people that were similarly experts. Thus, we suggest that the effects on coordination and motivation that were reported in the case study were indeed caused by increased feelings of connectedness that arose because of the practices developed to increase activity awareness.

Experiment Limitations

The experimental task was relatively clearly defined and took place over a short period of time. In more general organizational conditions, team tasks may be accomplished over the course of several hours or days and development of connectedness might take several months. In addition, our user interface element was relatively unsophisticated in its reporting of activities; however, the user interface element in the case study showed that conveying something as simple as "I am connected to the organization's Sametime system" was enough to convince other team members that one is working and thereby increase feelings of connectedness. Similar information about the activities of employees have formed the basis for staffing decisions (Carlson 2013).

General Discussion and Conclusions

As we noted in the Theoretical Foundation section, effective teams need information about the activities of team members in order to reduce coordination losses. In the case study, team members shared information about when they would be in meetings, taking breaks, etc. and needed others to cover the team phone. In their context, practices for communicating availability of team members had the additional effect of increasing social motivation as evidenced by the declining levels of frustration with other team members when awareness practices were introduced. With the introduction of Sametime, team members developed additional awareness practices that relied on automatic status changes resulting from removing the identification card from one's computer. Although these practices weren't directly aimed at increasing motivation, they had an impact on team performance because team members used this information to gauge the extent to which they and others were working (cf., Carlson 2013). The experimental results confirmed a causal relationship between activity awareness, connectedness, and performance.

Taken together, the results of the case study and experiment suggest that relatively simple technologies can be used to develop practices for increasing awareness of the presence and activities of others. Such practices might be developed with a goal of improving the coordination of team availability and thus team effectiveness (i.e., reduction of coordination losses). However, such practices might additionally lead to feelings of being connected to other members of the team in certain organizational contexts. We further suggest that team members that are more aware of the activities of others are better able to compare themselves with others. This can motivate them to work harder and longer for their teams because they feel other team members are doing the same (i.e., social motivation gains). The practical implications of these results are summarized in Table 5.5, and explained in detail in the following sections.

Table 5.5 Practical implications

	Managerial implications	Tool designer implications
1. A shared team goal is a critical antecedent to creation of awareness practices	A shared team goal motivates the development of awareness practices	A shared team goal motivates incorporation of available tools into awareness practices
2. Awareness practices that emerged from team interactions increased connectedness	Management-dictated awareness practices might not increase connectedness and lead to distrust	Sophisticated awareness technology may not have beneficial side effects
3. Awareness practices become more sophisticated over time	As team members internalize activity awareness practices, point of comparison shifts from others to self	Given sufficient time and message exchanges, simple-seeming awareness tools may be enough
4. Awareness practices leverage high trust environment	In a high trust environment, positive outcomes occur with activity awareness practices. In a low trust environment, activity awareness practices seem to make things worse	Context is important: users combine technology signals with taken-for-granted awareness information to determine meaning of signals
5. Awareness technology signals should be focused on the team	When users trust that their signals are private to their team, team-level social motivation increases. When signals are reported to and used by management, system gaming and demotivating effects are likely to occur	If the array of signals is too broad, it may overcome the information processing abilities of the users. Users should be able to limit the scope and narrow the frequency and amount of signals they receive

Managerial Implications

A shared/team goal is likely a critical antecedent to whether a team member will wish to be aware of the activities of others. In the case study, practices for monitoring availability did not emerge until after a goal was given. Once the goal was introduced, team members showed frustration with the lack of availability information, which motivated the development of awareness practices using the available technology. Team members likewise had a shared goal in the experimental study. In this case, the information shown in the on-screen indicator would not necessarily improve coordination, but an effect of activity awareness on connectedness and performance was shown.

We note that the practices for providing awareness of availability observed in the case study emerged from team interactions. Management clearly had the option to simply develop a system for ensuring that enough team members would be available to answer the phone. For example, management could have developed a schedule that ensured hour-by-hour coverage and dictated when each employee could take breaks for lunch, etc. We speculate that a management-dictated system would not have increased connectedness, and would not have had the motivating effects that the team developed availability awareness practices had. Thus, if management dictates practices rather than simply goals, employees will simply follow the practice and fewer beneficial side effects may occur.

A "between the lines" interpretation of the attitudes of the team members also emerged in the case study: as time passed and awareness practices became more sophisticated, team members seemed to use positive rather than negative language about efforts. Moreover, the point of evaluation seemed to shift from judging the efforts of others, to judging the efforts of oneself—descriptions of the later awareness practices were accompanied by statements about feeling more motivated to work harder, while the earlier practices were associated with statements about ensuring that others were working hard enough. Thus, we suggest that activity awareness might be necessary in order for social motivation gains to occur under organizational conditions where team members are expert at their tasks and may be working with their current team members again in the future (cf., Kerr & Hertel, 2011).

Finally, we note that, although our case involved members of ten different teams within MUFIN, teams in other organizations with different cultures might react differently. We noted earlier that Watson-Manheim & Bélanger (2007) suggested in their case study that "using email is not sufficient for relationship development," and instead must be combined with other, more personal media (p. 12), and reported instances of employees "copying email to colleagues and management to show 'how busy I am'" (p. 14) in a relatively low trust environment. We contrast this with our user above that eagerly worked after the end of business hours in order to give the signal to his/her group members that they were the last one online. Thus, we suggest that activity awareness should be treated as private, team-level information, and caution that when managers use activity awareness as a means for social comparison in low trust environments, members are likely to attempt to "game the system" instead of actually increasing their performance.

Tool Designer Implications

When designing interfaces for supporting communication and collaboration in a team context, designers should be aware of the importance of information about the activities of the different users. The presence indicator and status messages in Sametime as well as the on-screen indicator used in the experiment were relatively simple tools for providing awareness of the activities of others. However, in both environments, team members developed practices for increasing awareness to meet their shared goal, and reported higher connectedness with other team members. This higher connectedness seems to be durable over longer time periods—participants in our experiment still reported higher levels of activity awareness with the tool after working with their third group. This suggests that some, ostensibly simple, tools might not be taken for granted over time and still be used to provide awareness to team members (cf., Oemig & Gross, 2007), and reaffirms that subtle differences indeed count in the design of collaboration systems (cf., Huber 1990). Furthermore, sophisticated workspace awareness systems may provide unnecessary or unwanted information and might simply be ignored.

The status indicator provided with many messaging systems automatically provides information about whether the application on the users computer is connected with the messaging service, and many also indicate whether the user has recently moved the mouse or pressed a key on the keyboard. Simply saying that a person is online, however, does not necessarily provide a feeling of connectedness to others; rather, users need more information about the context in which the person resides (cf., Majchrzak, Malhotra, & John, 2005). One might wish to know where the other is—at a restaurant, in the office, and at home, meaning that whether they are available and/or when they will be available has some relevance when determining how much effort the other is making. In some contexts, then, a status indicator may be enough to indicate that a user is engaged in team-related work and thereby heighten willingness to work in others. However, this would require one to combine the status indication with other taken-for-granted information, such as assuming that another would only use that particular mediating application when performing team-related tasks.

We do not necessarily suggest that designers of mediating technologies need to add detailed information about team members' activities—a la the Facebook "news feed." Indeed, such information might unnecessarily overload the information processing abilities of the team members (cf., Dabbish & Kraut, 2008). Rather, technology designers should recognize that users wish to obtain activity information about others, and provide the flexible means for users to add context and implement practices that communicate such information. Practices that involve changing IM screen names (Smale & Greenberg, 2005) or status messages (Riemer et al., 2007) to indicate activity provide evidence that flexibility is desired.

Furthermore, it may be undesirable in some cases to provide others with what might be considered private information by an individual. The experiment's results show a positive relationship between our user interface element and team productivity and member satisfaction. In the case study, Sametime was only used in the work context. A user interface element that reported private information might be considered intrusive. We also speculate that such a user interface might be associated with indifference or perhaps user dissatisfaction in a context in which individual performance is rewarded.

Finally, we note that the team members in our experiment could only see the activity information about their own team members, and the team members in the case study could limit their viewing to only their team members. Thus, in both cases, team members knew at least part of the context in which the other users resided—they were members of their team. In this way, the information presented by an activity information tool could be combined with information about the known border of the group (cf., Gross et al., 2005) and information that the user might be able to recall from memory (e.g., that a particular person was the Nurse, or that a particular person was a smoker). Thus, we speculate that systems should allow for work unit differences—members of a particular team might feel more connectedness when they can see information about their *own* team members' activity, but activity information about *outsiders* (i.e., persons outside the team) would probably be deemed irrelevant and might only distract one from being able to understand whether and how hard their team members are working. For members of an organization that are outside of a particular individual's work area, it may only be necessary to provide what is typically considered presence information, and perhaps desirable to restrict the number of others about which one would observe more detailed information.

Implications for Future Research

Researchers in the area of computer mediated communication (CMC) have embraced the notion of process losses, and much attention has been given to the need for awareness to reduce coordination losses (Gutwin & Greenberg, 1996; Carroll et al., 2006). However, there has been little attention paid to the role of awareness in mitigating social motivation losses. Based on what we observed in the case study and experiment, we propose that social motivation gains can occur when IT artifacts are introduced, and might occur spontaneously when awareness practices are adopted that enable users to reliably track comings and goings (e.g., the Sametime presence feature, the experiment's on-screen indicator). Normally, the presence feature of IM applications is considered by technologists to indicate simply whether or not the person is able to communicate. Our case study shows that such a tool can mean much more than that to team members. In the case study, we found that team members observed when others' status changed and used this information not only to determine when others were available for work, but also as a means for determining how much they were working. In addition, we found some evidence that team members are motivated to be sure that their efforts measure up when compared with others. Thus, we suggest that the adoption of social software such as life streaming, microblogging, wikis and online communities will likely have implications for social motivation among the participants.

Prior researchers have noted the importance of presence awareness via CMC as a means to monitor others (Cameron & Webster, 2005). Here, we show that being aware of what other people are doing has implications for feelings about one's team and team performance, meaning the lack of bodily presence in a mediated context has additional implications beyond simply "Is anyone there?" For teams working in distributed contexts, members are unable to directly observe others, and must rely on what is they receive via CMC in order to compare efforts (Greenberg et al., 2007). In addition to our results, knowing who is there and being able to differentiate among them has been shown to improve decision-making and increases a team's ability to reach consensus (Cooper & Haines, 2008).

Thus, what normally is termed *presence* awareness in mediated communication (cf., Shaw, Scheufele, & Catalano, 2007; Kekwaletswe & Ngambi, 2006; Bønes, Hasvold, Henriksen, & Strandenæs, 2007) has an additional subcomponent of *activity* awareness (cf., Carroll et al., 2006). Researchers have observed that users wish to communicate information about their presence—when they will be able/unable to communicate (Shaw et al., 2007; Smale & Greenberg, 2005). However, when users indicate their presence, they are, in many cases, implicitly including information about their activities. Depending on the context, the Skype status message "in a meeting" could also be an indication of another's effort exerted, while observing that another's icon changed in the company's Sametime application, meaning he/she has just connected to the system, could indicate that the other has begun his/her workday. The observed benefit of online status in instant messaging (IM) as indicating whether one is "idle or away" (Shaw et al., 2007) implicitly acknowledges the potential usefulness of knowing whether another is engaged with work. Similarly, some of the screen name changes observed in IM contexts show activity information rather than just one's presence (e.g., "House hunting!", "reading at my desk/disregard (Away) status", "60% done my portfolio" Smale & Greenberg, 2005). Our results suggest that such user practices would improve feelings of connectedness and in turn increase effort.

Finally, we suggest activity information is often *imputed* from what is ostensibly presence information. Our examples above about meeting attendance or beginning of a workday involved a user interpreting the status update and/or status change as indicating another's activity. This happened because the user combined that new information with taken for granted assumptions about the other's context to impute awareness about their activities (cf., Garfinkel 1967; Carroll et al., 2006). Future research could examine the extent to which users feel that information presented by a mediating technology can be relied on, the degree to which users combine such information with additional information to create other aspects of awareness, and the extent to which users alter their practices to provide or impute activity information from tools ostensibly designed to provide presence or other awareness information.

In online communities research, the notion of social motivation losses has been used to explain the extent to which individual users contribute material and/or knowledge to a community (McLure-Wasko & Faraj, 2005; Butler 2001; Ling et al., 2005; Ludford, Cosley, Frankowski, & Terveen, 2004; Michinov & Primois, 2005, Yuqing, Kraut, & Kiesler, 2007). This study is unique in that it finds that social motivation can both drive contributions to a community (i.e., sharing one's status) and have social motivation effects on work that is not directly related to the community. For example, one might be following a company microblog on human resource practices, and find the tweets very useful and be impressed by the number and quality of contributions. However, one might not be an expert on human resources and thus feel like one has nothing to contribute. Instead, one might be motivated to contribute to the company wiki on a topic where one is able to provide some expertise.

References

Anantharaman, V., & Han, L. S. (2001). Hospital and emergency ambulance link: Using IT to enhance emergency pre-hospital care. *International Journal of Medical Informatics, 61,* 147–161.

Bal, R., Mastboom, F., Spiers, H. P., & Rutten, H. (2007). The product and process of referral optimizing general practitioner-medical specialist interaction through information technology. *International Journal of Medical Informatics, 765,* 528–534.

Bønes, E., Hasvold, P., Henriksen, E., & Strandenæs, T. (2007). Risk analysis of information security in a mobile instant messaging and presence system for healthcare. *International Journal of Medical Informatics, 76*(9), 677–687.

Butler, B. S. (2001). Membership size, communication activity, and sustainability: A resource-based model of online social structures. *Information Systems Research, 12*(4), 346–362. https://doi.org/10.1287/isre.12.4.346.9703.

Cameron, A. F., & Webster, J. (2005). Unintended consequences of emerging communication technologies: Instant messaging in the workplace. *Computers in Human Behavior, 21*(1), 85–103.

Carlson, N. (2013). How marissa mayer figured out work-at-home yahoos were slacking off. *Business Insider*. Retrieved September 15, 2015, from http://www.businessinsider.com/how-marissa-mayer-figured-out-work-at-home-yahoos-were-slacking-off-2013–3.

Carroll, J. M., Rosson, M. B., Convertino, G., & Ganoe, C. H. (2006). Awareness and teamwork in computer-supported collaboration. *Interacting with Computers, 18*(1), 21–46.

Chidambaram, L., & Tung, L. L. (2005). Is out of sight, out of mind? An empirical study of social loafing in technology-supported groups. *Information Systems Research, 16*(2), 149–168.

Chin, W. W. (1998). The partial least squares approach to structural equation modeling. In G. A. Marcoulides (Ed.), *Modern methods for business research* (pp. 295–336). Mahwah, NJ: Lawrence Erlbaum Assoicates.

Cooper, R. B., & Haines, R. (2008). The influence of workspace awareness on group intellective decision effectiveness. *European Journal of Information Systems, 17*(6), 631–648.

Dabbish, L., & Kraut, R. (2008). Research note—awareness displays and social motivation for coordinating communication. *Information Systems Research, 19*(2), 221–238.

Dourish, P., & Bellotti, V. (1992). Awareness and coordination in shared workspaces. In *CSCW '92: Proceedings of the 1992 ACM Conference on Computer-Supported Cooperative Work* (pp. 107–114). ACM Press. http://doi.acm.org/10.1145/143457.143468.

Erez, M., & Somech, A. (1996). Is group productivity loss the rule or the exception? Effects of culture and group-based motivation. *Academy of Management Journal, 39,* 1513–1537.

Garfinkel, H. (1967). *Studies in ethnomethodology*. Englewood Cliffs, NJ: Prentice-Hall Inc.

George, J. M. (1992). Extrinsic and intrinsic origins of perceived social loafing in organizations. *Academy of Management Journal, 35*(1), 191–202.

Goffman, E. (1961). Fun in games. *Encounters* (pp. 15–81). Indianapolis, IN: Bobbs-Merrill.

Greenberg, J., Ashton-James, C. E., & Ashkanasy, N. M. (2007). Social comparison processes in organizations. *Organizational Behavior and Human Decision Processes, 102*(1), 22–41. https://doi.org/10.1016/j.obhdp.2006.09.006.

Gross, T., Stary, C., & Totter, A. (2005). User-Centered awareness in computer-supported cooperative work-systems: Structured embedding of findings from social sciences. *International Journal of Human-Computer Interaction, 18*(3), 323–360.

Gutwin, C., & Greenberg, S. (1996). Workspace awareness for groupware. In *Proceedings of the Conference on Human Factors in Computing Systems* (pp. 208–209). Vancouver.

Gutwin, C., & Greenberg, S. (2002). A descriptive framework of workspace awareness for real time groupware. *Computer Supported Cooperative Work, 11,* 411–446.

Haines, R., & Riemer, K. (2011). The user-centered nature of awareness creation in computer-mediated communication. In *Proceedings of the Thirty Second International Conference on Information Systems* (p. 8).

Haines, R., Hough, J., Cao, L., & Haines, D. (2014). Anonymity in computer-mediated communication: More contrarian ideas with less influence. *Group Decision and Negotiation, 23*(4), 765.

Harper, R. R., Hughes, J. A., & Shapiro, D. Z. (1989). The functionality of flight strips in ATC work. The report for the civil aviation authority. In *Lancaster sociotechnics group, department of sociology, lancaster university january.*

Heath, C., & Luff, P. (1992). Collaboration and control: Crisis management and multimedia technology in London underground line control rooms. *Computer Supported Cooperative Work, 1*(1–2), 69–94.

Huber, G. P. (1990). A theory of the effects of advanced information technologies on organizational design, intelligence, and decision making. *Academy of Management Review, 15*(1), 47–71.

Jarvenpaa, S. L., & Leidner, D. E. (1999). Communication and trust in global virtual teams. *Organization Science, 10*(6), 791–815.

Jarvenpaa, S. L., Knoll, K., & Leidner, D. E. (1998). Is anybody out there? Antecedents of trust in global virtual teams. *Journal of Management Information Systems, 14*(4), 9–64.

Kahai, S. S., Sosik, J. J., & Avolio, B. J. (2003). Effects of leadership style, anonymity, and rewards on creativity-relevant processes and outcomes in an electronic meeting system context. *The Leadership Quarterly, 14*(4–5), 499–524.

Kekwaletswe, R. M., & Ngambi, D. (2006). Ubiquitous social presence: Context-Awareness in a mobile learning environment. In *IEEE International Conference on Sensor Networks, Ubiquitous, and Trustworthy Computing, 2006* (p. 2).

Kerr, N. L., & Hertel, G. (2011). The köhler group motivation gain: How to motivate the 'weak links' in a group. *Social and Personality Psychology Compass, 5*(1), 43–55. https://doi.org/10.1111/j.1751-9004.2010.00333.x.

Ling, K., Beenen, G., Ludford, P., Wang, X., Chang, K., Li, X., et al. (2005). Using social psychology to motivate contributions to online communities. *Journal of Computer-Mediated Communication, 10*(4), 00–00. https://doi.org/10.1111/j.1083-6101.2005.tb00273.x.

Ludford, P. J., Cosley, D., Frankowski, D., & Terveen, L. (2004). Think different: Increasing online community participation using uniqueness and group dissimilarity. In *Proceedings of the SIGCHI Conference on Human Factors in Computing Systems* (pp. 631–638). ACM. https://doi.org/10.1145/985692.985772.

Majchrzak, A., Malhotra, A., & John, R. (2005). Perceived individual collaboration know-how development through information technology-enabled contextualization: Evidence from distributed teams. *Information Systems Research, 16*(1), 9–27. https://doi.org/10.1287/isre.1050.0044.

Malone, T. W., & Crowston, K. (1994). The interdisciplinary study of coordination. *ACM Computing Surveys, 26,* 87–119. https://doi.org/10.1145/174666.174668.

McLeod, P. L., Baron, R. S., Marti, M. W., & Yoon, K. (1997). The eyes have it: Minority influence in face-to-face and computer-mediated group discussion. *Journal of Applied Psychology, 82*(5), 706–718.

McLure-Wasko, M., & Faraj, S. (2005). Why should I share? Examining social capital and knowledge contribution in electronic networks of practice. *MIS Quarterly, 29*(1), 35–57.

Michinov, N., & Primois, C. (2005). Improving productivity and creativity in online groups through social comparison process: New evidence for asynchronous electronic brainstorming. *Computers in Human Behavior, 21*(1), 11–28. https://doi.org/10.1016/j.chb.2004.02.004.

Ng, W. H., Wang, E., & Ng, I. (2007). Multimedia messaging service teleradiology in the provision of emergency neurosurgery services. *Surgical Neurology, 67,* 338–341.

Oemig, C., & Gross, T. (2007). Shifts in significance: How group dynamics improves group awareness. In *Mensch & computer 2007: 7. Fachübergreifende konferenz fuer interaktive und kooperative menien.*

Orlikowski, W.J. (2000). Using technology and constituting structures: A practice lens for studying technology in organizations. *Organization Science, 11,*(4), 404–428.

Parks, C. D., & Sanna, L. J. (1999). *Group performance and interaction.* Boulder, CO: Westview Press.

Piccoli, G., & Ives, B. (2003). Trust and the unintended effects of behavior control in virtual teams. *MIS Quarterly, 27*(3), 365–395.

Pinsonneault, A., Barki, H., Gallupe, R. B., & Hoppen, N. (1999). Electronic brainstorming: The illusion of productivity. *Information Systems Research, 10*(2), 110–133.

Riemer, K., Klein, S., & Frößler, F. (2007). Towards a practice understanding of the creation of awareness in distributed work. In *Proceedings of the Twenty-Eighth International Conference on Information Systems.*

Sarker, S., & Sahay, S. (2003). Understanding virtual team development: An interpretive study. *Journal of the Association for Information Systems, 4,* 1–38.

Shaw, B., Scheufele, D. A., & Catalano, S. (2007). The role of presence awareness in organizational communication: An exploratory field experiment. *Behaviour and Information Technology, 26*(5), 377–384.

Shepherd, M. M., Briggs, R. O., Reinig, B. A., Yen, J., & Nunamaker, J. F. (1996). Invoking social comparison to improve electronic brainstorming: Beyond anonymity. *Journal of Management Information Systems, 12*(3), 155–170.

Short, J., Williams, E., & Christie, B. (1976). *The social psychology of telecommunications.* New York, NY: Wiley.

Smale, S., & Greenberg, S. (2005). Broadcasting information via display names in instant messaging. In *Proceedings of the 2005 International ACM SIGGROUP Conference on Supporting Group Work* (pp. 89–98).

Steiner, I. D. (1972). *Group processes and productivity.* New York: Academic Press.

Watson-Manheim, M. B., & Bélanger, F. (2007). Communication media repertoires: Dealing with the multiplicity of media choices. *MIS quarterly, 31*(2), 267–293.

Yuqing, R., Kraut, R., & Kiesler, S. (2007). Applying common identity and bond theory to design of online communities. *Organization Studies, 28*(3), 377–408. https://doi.org/10.1177/0170840607076007.

Zajonc, R. B. (1965). Social facilitation. *Science, 149*(3681), 269–274.

Chapter 6
Discontinuities, Continuities, and Hidden Work in Virtual Collaboration

Mary Beth Watson-Manheim

Introduction

In this chapter, I argue that that there is significant hidden effort required to perform actual work activities in virtual collaboration. I employ the notions of *organizational discontinuity theory* (ODT) and *articulation work* to develop this proposition and explore potential consequences for virtual collaboration. Boundaries between individuals, such as time and geography, provide an effective starting point for investigating virtual collaboration. Boundaries are static but the effects of boundaries, or discontinuities, are dynamic. For example, time zone differences exist but are not always perceived as problematic in virtual collaboration. ODT suggests it is necessary to bring together discontinuous elements of virtuality into working configurations, i.e., continuities, in order for collaboration work to be most effectively performed. In other words, a new set of shared activities, or expected routine practices, emerge such that discontinuities are reduced or eliminated.

Articulation work is "work that enables other work to occur", i.e., unplanned aspects of work left out of rational work models, such as take up and learning of technology, organizing and sequencing of tasks, and aligning constituent actors to accomplish work. Using the lens of articulation work to examine evolving construction and reconstruction of routine practices surfaces unseen, and even unappreciated, work performed by virtual collaborators. When shared routine practices are developed, collaboration effort is reduced allowing individuals to focus on the content of their work such that collaboration can effectively occur. I hypothesize, however, that the hidden or invisible work of virtual collaboration remains and, while often perceived as unremarkable, increases the complexity of collaboration activities. I discuss potential consequences and future research directions.

M. B. Watson-Manheim (✉)
University of Illinois at Chicago, Chicago, USA
e-mail: mbwm@uic.edu

© Springer International Publishing AG, part of Springer Nature 2019
K. Riemer et al. (eds.), *Collaboration in the Digital Age*, Progress in IS,
https://doi.org/10.1007/978-3-319-94487-6_6

Virtual Collaboration

Virtual collaboration involves the performance of joint work activities by individuals who are in different geographic locations. For many years, beginning with telecommuting in the 1990s, employees have been using technologies to collaborate at a distance. As technology devices such as mobile phones and lap tops have become more sophisticated and access to Wi-Fi and broadband communications have become increasingly ubiquitous, virtual collaboration has become common and is viewed as a strategic necessity by many firms. In a recently reported survey of 1,700 knowledge workers, 79% reported working always or frequently in dispersed teams (Ferrazzi, 2014).

Moreover, to succeed in the global economy, firms are relying on far flung virtual teams to bring together employees with the best expertise and diverse knowledge and perspectives, and often lower cost talent, to address organizational challenges. These global virtual teams must navigate geographic boundaries as well as other boundaries such as time zone, language, and national culture making collaboration even more complex (Chudoba et al., 2005; Neeley, 2015). When teams consist of people from different backgrounds working at a distance, miscommunication is common and can lead to misunderstanding (Cramton, 2001) and conflict (Hinds & Mortensen, 2005) ultimately impairing global team performance (Neeley, 2015).

Despite the development of sophisticated information and communication technologies, including tools designed specifically to support virtual collaboration, adoption of these tools lags and significant challenges remain. In fact, based on a recent survey Ferrazzi, (2014) reports that nearly half of people communicating in a virtual environment admit to feeling confused and overwhelmed by collaboration technology. A recent literature review of virtual team research states that "most research finds that technology either impairs or has no effect" on performance (Gilson, Maynard, Jones, Varitiainen, & Hakonen, 2015). While there may be some debate as to how much of the research in this area has come to this conclusion, there is little debate that technology can be a facilitator as well as an inhibitor of effective communication among virtual collaborators (Watson-Manheim et al., 2012).

Thus, there is a long line of literature which has reached a clear consensus that virtual collaboration is challenging for many teams and often, but not always, results in communication and performance problems. On the other hand, many studies (over many years) have documented and championed work practices, managerial techniques, and strategies for employing ICT that are expected to enhance virtual team performance (e.g., Majchrzak et al., 2004; Ferrazzi, 2014; Neeley, 2015).

In this essay, I argue that we can gain additional understanding of the complexity of this work environment by a deeper in investigation of individual performance practices. I contend that there is significant unseen and unaccounted for effort required to perform actual work activities in virtual collaboration. I employ the notions of *organizational discontinuity theory* (ODT) and *articulation work* to develop this proposition and explore potential consequences for virtual collaboration.

Organizational Discontinuity Theory

As discussed in the previous section, many teams face significant challenges in virtual collaboration but other teams are able to perform successfully. Organizational Discontinuity Theory (ODT) takes an interactional perspective to examine this paradox (Watson-Manheim, Chudoba, & Crowston, 2012). The theory suggests that boundaries, e.g., time zones or national borders, are static and unchanging, but the effects of boundaries on the performance of virtual team members may differ and even change over time. To separate the effects of the boundary from the boundary itself, the authors introduce the notion of a *discontinuity* and it's corollary, a *continuity*.

The theory asserts that a boundary becomes problematic when an individual perceives a change in information and communication flows that requires conscious effort and attention to handle (Watson-Manheim, Chudoba, & Crowston, 2012). This disruption is termed a *discontinuity*. Joint behaviors must be adapted at the boundary to address the disruption. The resulting new practice routines are termed *continuities*. Alternatively, when individuals are jointly performing virtual work in an effective manner and the situation is perceived as normal, i.e., flows of communication and action are as expected by team members or require minimal attention and effort to manage, then a discontinuity is not present even though boundaries exist between team members.

Faced with a discontinuity, that is, with a disruption in the expected flow of communication, individuals will attempt to make sense of the disruption and address the problem. They may be motivated to consider alternative actions to deal with the discontinuity, leading to the emergence of new behaviors and expectations, i.e., the construction of continuities. These new action routines reduce or eliminate the attention and effort required to understand and manage the situation associated with problematic boundaries (i.e., discontinuities) (Dixon & Panteli, 2010; Watson-Manheim, Chudoba, & Crowston, 2012).

I was recently a member of a team with colleagues located in Australia, Germany and the US. The extreme difference in time zones across the 3 team members was initially difficult to manage. There was really no convenient synchronous time to meet. The option of working via email or discussion board in an asynchronous manner was not effective due to the complexity of the collaboration. After several failed meeting attempts, the German member volunteered to be a 'bridge team member'. He met in his morning with the Australian member (in that member's late night) and then met with me in the US in his afternoon and my morning. Our group was able to work effectively by creating a new routine for meetings that took into account time differences and allowed us to perform effectively. Thus, the boundaries of time, nationality and geography remained, but they were no longer perceived as problematic to performance.

ODT takes an interactional perspective on virtual collaboration suggesting that it is necessary to identify problematic elements of virtuality, i.e., discontinuities, and create new practices that reduce the difficulty of the situation, i.e., continuities, for collaboration work to be most effectively performed. In other words, a new set of shared activities, or expected routine practices, are generated such that problems are reduced or eliminated. While this theory helps us understand why boundaries may be problematic only under certain conditions, the underlying effort involved in the process of identifying discontinuities and in creating and maintaining continuities remains unexplored.

Articulation Work

Articulation work has been described as "work that enables other work to occur" (p. 1, Sawyer & Tapia, 2006). In other words, articulation work is comprised of unplanned aspects of work not accounted for in rational work models. Activities such as organizing and sequencing of tasks, and aligning constituent actors to accomplish work (Strauss, 1985) including the take up and learning of new technologies (e.g., Grinter, 1996; Sawyer & Tapia, 2006), are examples of articulation work.

I next briefly discuss the previous research on articulation work focusing on (1) ongoing or continuous articulation work that is essential to the performance of joint work activities, (2) event-based, or episodic, articulation work that is prompted by disruptions in the performance of joint work activities, and (3) cumulative and unmet needs articulation work as identified recently by Sawyer & Tapia, (2006).

Ongoing Articulation Work

Strauss, (1985) surfaced the importance of an interactional perspective in the performance of joint work activities. His conceptualization was based on intensive study of work taking place in hospitals where multiple clusters of work activities and combinations of collective activities, or projects, must take place to manage the care of patients. In addition, the care of the patient involves the performance of task clusters by different professional specialists, e.g., nurses, specialized physicians, and administrators. These different actors may work simultaneously or sequentially but the overall 'arc' of the work must be connected to accomplish the caring of the patient. The interleaving and connecting of tasks and task clusters does not happen automatically but must be negotiated and may be contested. These 'supra' work activities constitute articulation work as described by Strauss (p. 8):

> Articulation work amounts to the following: First, the meshing of the often numerous tasks, clusters of tasks, and segments of the total arc. Second, the meshing of efforts of various unit-workers (individuals, departments, etc.). Third, the meshing of actors with their various types of work and implicated tasks. (The term "coordination" is sometimes used to catch features of this articulation work, but the term has other connotations so it will not be used here.) All of this articulation work goes on within and usually among organizational units and sub-units.

Strauss, (1985) extended this concept to more generally address project work in organizations. He recognized that performing project work activities is separate from the larger organizational process of articulating the work, or joining work activities together to accomplish project work. Activities such as allocating resources to the project, persuading others of the importance of the project, and other organizational processes must be started and maintained for the project work to be satisfactorily performed and project goals to be met. Thus, the initial work on articulation focused on processes critical to accomplishing joint work activities, but which were not visible to "rationalized models of work" (Star, 1991: 275).

Early research in the CSCW community investigating the role of technologies in supporting collaborative work highlighted the importance of understanding the "nature and requirements of cooperative work" (p. 48, Schmidt & Bannon, 1992). As Sawyer & Tapia, (2006) observe, CSCW researchers viewed articulation work as primarily "overhead" activities which are the result of coordination of collaborative activities distributed across multiple actors.

This stream of research aimed to understand articulation work in order to design computer-based technologies that could manage these peripheral activities and allow individuals to focus their attention on the content work activities. The performance of joint work activities depends on the interweaving of clusters of activities distributed across individuals. Articulation work is all the coordinating and negotiating necessary to get the work at hand done" (Grinter, 1996, p. 451).

Event-Based Articulation Work

Regardless of the routineness of the project, contingencies will arise that may disrupt the course of the work and require rearrangement of processes to return to the proper course of action. Disruptions lead to misalignment of processes and the need for changes will become explicit to those involved (Strauss, 1985, 1988). For example, a project for a long-time customer may have clearly established resource needs and priority. However, new management in the customer organization may demand a shorter time frame for implementation than the usual process. Meeting this demand requires changes to the established procedures and responsibilities assigned to the project. Additional resources may need to be shifted to the project affecting other project priorities. Accordingly negotiating and implementing these changes will require significant problem solving and attention from affected stakeholders to meet the new goals.

Strauss, (1985) also highlights the possibility that the "intersection of workers and their [different] social worlds" (p. 11) will create disruption in the connecting of actors and tasks in the accomplishment of common goals. While differences in individual personalities may play a role in disruption, the languages and patterns of work in different occupational communities, e.g., nurse versus specialized physicians, arguably play a larger and often more complicated role. Contingencies or disruptions may also arise when a new member is added to a team that has worked together for a long time (Strauss, 1985). Such a team has developed a set of commonly understood practices and language about the work which will now have to be modified to bring the new team member on board.

Event-based articulation work can be thought of as the work that gets things back 'on track' in the face of the unexpected, and modifies action to accommodate unanticipated contingencies (Strauss, 1988). When processes have been adjusted to accommodate changes, the work returns to the normal course of action and the need for event-based articulation work disappears. It is important to note that event-based articulation work is also invisible to rationalized models of work (Star, 1991).

Unmet Needs and Cumulative Articulation Work

Sawyer & Tapia, (2006) investigate articulation work in technology adoption and implementation as individuals try learn to use the technology and integrate it into work practices. As they note, this work is often taken for granted and invisible. For example, resources for new technologies include the cost of purchasing the hardware and software and may include cost of installation and training. On the other hand, the time spent by the user learning to use the new technology and integrating the technology into work practices is critical to achieving expected benefits but is usually not accounted for by management or other decision makers.

The authors focus on articulation work arising from an implementation of ICT into organizational work activities through a field study of mobile device implementation for police officers. The new mobile devices and the secure mobile data network enabled the police officers to access secure information while in the field, such as driver's license records and a related picture database. The device also supported secure messaging, email, and reporting functions for users. The authors collected data through multiple methods in an intensive field study of the implementation of the mobile devices.

They identify two interrelated categories of articulation activities: *unmet needs* articulation and *cumulative* articulation. Unmet needs articulation is comprised of technology-based activities that were critical to officers performing work but were not addressed by the new system. For example, prior to the implementation of the new mobile device, the officers used applications on federal, state, and local systems that were not integrated and required separate authentication procedures and different levels of technical knowledge. The new system did not address this lack of integration. Thus, the police officers must continue to go through multiple log in procedures and make use of different systems to access information needed for their job as well as integrate the new mobile devices into their work activities.

Moreover, in addition to the concept of unmet needs articulation, the authors suggest that that computer-based articulation work is cumulative. Unmet needs which are not addressed by the new system remain and associated activities must be continue to be performed by the user. This work is usually invisible to the organization. In this case, the police officers need to log into the three different systems with very different technological designs was likely taken for granted and expected, and not accounted for in any assessment of the mobile device implementation. Thus, the new articulation work associated with the integration of the technology into an individual's work practices becomes routine. However, this new articulation work is accompanied by existing unmet needs articulation work. Each successive round of ICT implementation increases the articulation work taken on by the user in the organization.

> Implementing new ICT increases the articulation needs of the organization. However, we claim that many of these needs go unrecognized and unmet by the organization. A gap forms between the unmet articulation needs and the organizational efforts aimed at fulfilling those perceived needs. The organization does not return to its "normal" state in which all needs are met. A "new normal" is formed in which articulation issues either become invisible or are handled in some disruptive or destructive fashion. When the next new ICT is implemented, the organization does not start from zero level relative to articulation needs. This next round starts with existing, and unmet, needs (Sawyer & Tapia, 2006, p. 7).

Surfacing Hidden Effort in Virtual Collaboration

I next use the lens of articulation work to extend understanding of effort involved in collaboration across boundaries. Collaboration across boundaries involves the evolving construction and reconstruction of routine work practices, i.e., developing continuities, in response to disruptions encountered at boundaries, i.e., discontinuities. In this section, I aim to shed light on articulation in distributed collaboration identifying behaviors by actors that are critical to performance but are outside of the formalized work activities. In particular, my objective is to surface unseen, and even unappreciated, work performed by virtual collaborators. Building on Sawyer & Tapia, (2006), I suggest that it is useful to distinguish categories of articulation work in virtual collaboration work, especially differentiating articulation work that is eventually resolved and not cumulated from that which is enduring and cumulative.

Recognizing Discontinuities and Creating Continuities: Event-Based Articulation Work

ODT argues that discontinuities are perceived when individuals performing joint work at a boundary encounter unanticipated actions or information flows. Under normal conditions, distributed collaborators have developed routine practices such that their interactions and practices are expected and unremarkable. Routine and expected joint behaviors simplify the work environment and allow collaborators to focus on the content of their work. When action responses are unexpected, the individual must focus attention on the process of the joint work, moving attention away from the content of the work. The following vignette, from Watson-Manheim et al., (2012, p. 39), illustrates perception of a discontinuity and the team leader's reaction.

> Consider a distributed team that adds a person whose first language is different from current members. An existing practice had the team leader send a short email summary of the meeting to participants listing decisions made and specific actions plans. Such a message might be too terse for a non-native speaker who had trouble following the discussion during the meeting, leading to misunderstandings and missed assignments. In response, the team leader could try a new practice of sending a more extensive email message documenting specific agreements and actions.
>
> In this case, the trigger for the team leader to change her established pattern of behavior was a discrepancy in the behavior she expected of team members. When she recognized the discrepancy, the leader focused attention on the situation and surmised that the difficulty in the team's performance was due to misunderstanding by the new member. She then varies her usual practice and observes the results of this change. (p. 40)

In this example, the team leader noticed that the new team member was not responding as expected and that this was impacting individual and ultimately team performance. Building on the concept of 'cognitive switching' (Louis & Sutton, 1991), Watson-Manheim et al., (2012) argue that three conditions trigger this movement from routine practices to a more attentive state, i.e., discrepancy, novelty, and deliberate initiative. In all three conditions, interactional processes of joint work, or articulation work as defined by Strauss, (1988), are moved to the forefront of the individual's consideration. In our example, the team leader is motivated to return team interactions to a normal state. Thus, her attention will be focused on making sense of the discrepant situation. Based on her observations and experience, she attempts behavioral adjustments to remediate the communication difficulties faced by the team.

In this example, the team leader may vary actions in an effort to alleviate the difficulty of the situation. This action response is the beginning of the creation of continuities, or action routines, that are better aligned with the changed situation.

> [Continuing] our example above, if the team leader perceives her action to have mitigated the difficulty, if this new practice enabled the new member to integrate well into the team and interactions and performance improved, then the leader would be motivated to continue the new practice. Over time, as she repeats this action under similar circumstances, she and the team members change their understanding of expected behavior in this situation.

In this example, one action was to provide more detailed action plans and observe resulting consequences. Only if the team leader observes that the additional details increase the overall team performance, will the leader adopt this change as an ongoing practice. Changes in the team performance are due to their use of the more detailed minutes to guide behavior. Thus, while the discrepancy may lead to new behaviors, a continuity, or new behavioral routine, is established only when changes are adapted and repeated.

Over time, repeated and successful actions lead to a change in understanding of the normal and expected work practices (Feldman & Pentland, 2003). Thus, the articulation work of aligning joint work practices to allow collaborators to move to a more automatic state in the conduct of their interactions is completed. We consider this as *event-based articulation*. Articulation needs stemming from the introduction of a new boundary have been resolved and collaborators return to a normal state of interactions.

Maintaining Continuities: Enduring Hidden Work in Virtual Collaboration

While the articulation work of recognizing discontinuities and creating continuities can be categorized as an event-based articulation work, the work of maintaining continuities remains. When shared routine practices are developed, collaboration effort is reduced allowing individuals to focus on the content of their work such that collaboration can effectively occur. Following our example.

> Team members may now come to expect a more extensive email from their leader after each meeting and find that the more comprehensive documentation reduces the chance for misunderstanding. With this new practice, accommodating the new member now requires little extra attention by members or the team leader; they have developed a continuity that enables activities at the boundary to occur in an expected and ordinary fashion. Members of the team develop revised expectations about behavior in the situation and are able to function in a relatively automatic mode because of the emergent continuity, allowing them to focus on the content of the work rather than the process.

While this work may be expected and ordinary, even perceived as unremarkable, it still exists. However the fact that these behaviors are considered expected and commonplace may also that the work activities are not recognized and may be hidden, even to the actor performing the work.[1] The work will likely not be obvious to an outside observer, e.g., senior management or other team leaders. Additionally, due to being an assumed and necessary activity, the work associated with developing more extensive meeting minutes may also be concealed from the actor performing it. In this case, providing longer and more detailed minutes of meetings takes the team leader longer but this has now become a routine practice. The team leader expects to perform this work and does not find it burdensome. However, the additional work still exists. While the team has returned to its previous state of interacting and the number of misunderstandings has been reduced, a 'new normal' of work activities has been created for the team leader.

I adapt the notion of cumulative work as argued by Sawyer & Tapia, (2006) to conceptualize the effects of ongoing hidden work emerging from the construction of continuities. The authors argue that articulation work in the face of ICT implementation is cumulative in that new technologies may only partially meet the needs of users leading to frustration and new articulation work is created as the users learn to use the ICT and create practices around what meets their needs as well as what does not. This hidden collaborative work and its cumulative effect emerge precisely because the frustration of navigating the challenges introduced by the boundary is

---

[1] I would like to acknowledge helpful discussion with my colleague Catherine Cramton in developing these ideas.

removed and the new practices have become routinized. These practices are now unexceptional and expected to all actors.

The new practice has been developed such that joint team activities can be effectively performed. However, the team leader has taken on a new work activity that did not exist before the practice was developed. This new work activity must continue to exist as expected by all team members to insure effective performance. As Sawyer & Tapia, (2006) point out, the team does not return to its 'normal' state after the continuity is developed. A 'new normal' of practice routines is formed with increased articulation work.

The Effect of Unmet Needs in Virtual Collaboration

I have focused on the creation of continuities by collaborators when faced by discontinuities. However, not all discontinuities are successfully addressed by collaborators. While the disruption created by a discontinuity may lead to new behaviors, a continuity, or new behavioral routine, is established only when changes are adapted and repeated. As Watson-Manheim et al., (2012, p. 40) state:

> First, the new behaviors may not be perceived to mitigate the problem, rightly or wrongly. While the experiment might in fact not work, it is also the case that people can 'rationalize discrepancies to the point where they are actually seen as supporting one's expectations' [George & Jones, 2001]. A person who may be skeptical about working virtually may rationalize a problem as being inherent in this environment, and problems he encounters reinforce his expectations, thus discouraging attempts to address the problem. Second, because established structures are resistant to change, behavioral changes may be resisted and not repeated. Finally, individuals will not continue to try new behaviors indefinitely. Over time, if the behavioral trials are not successful in addressing the discontinuity, other more pressing matters may take precedence [George & Jones, 2001]. For a variety of reasons, individuals may be dissatisfied with responses to a behavioral trial and choose not to repeat it, failing to create a continuity to support virtual work and leaving the discontinuity unsuccessfully addressed. (p. 40)

Returning to our example of the global team with the new member with a different first language, if the team leader was not able to develop a continuity to enable the team to return to effective communication patterns, the entire team is likely to experience an increase in articulation work. The difficulties in joint performance are experienced by the entire team. Each member must make sense of misunderstandings, missed assignments and other consequences of the discontinuity. While dealing with these misunderstandings may become a routine practice as the team member may have unique expertise that is critical to the team, but the articulation work remains.

I characterize this work as unmet needs articulation work. Unmet needs articulation work is also likely to be cumulative in virtual collaboration potentially leading to dissatisfaction among team members and poor overall team performance. On the other hand, team members may work to individually overcome the problems and create a successful team outcome, e.g., new product design, but at the cost of significant individual frustration and even burnout as they struggle to perform the associated level of increased articulation work.

Conclusion

In this chapter, I have attempted to develop deeper insight into virtual collaboration from a practice perspective. I use the notions of *organizational discontinuity theory* (ODT) and *articulation work* to argue that virtual collaboration involves significant unseen and hidden work that increases the complexity and effort involved. This hidden work is often perceived as unremarkable and may not be recognized even to the involved actors.

Integrating the ODT and articulation work perspectives provides a basis for examining additional questions. For example, surfacing and acknowledging hidden work in virtual collaboration may shed light on the continued resistance of many teams to the adoption of new collaboration technologies. Adopting new technologies means that distributed collaborators must learn to use new technology and integrate use into individual as well as team practices. The adoption of the technology will lead to new significant new articulation work for individuals. Moreover, the technology will not facilitate the performance of the team unless common practices are developed by collaborators. Thus, it is not surprising that sophisticated collaboration tools continue to be resisted by virtual teams.

Moreover, much of the articulation work in virtual collaboration is perceived as expected and unremarkable even to the actor herself. This has implications for the effective design of new collaboration tools. If the hidden work is not surfaced or understood, new technologies cannot be designed to mitigate the underlying effort involved in the collaboration process.

References

Barley, S. R., & Kunda, G. (2001). Bringing work back in. *Organization Science, 12*(1), 76–95.

Chudoba, K. M., Wynn, E., Lu, M., & Watson-Manheim, M. B. (2005). How virtual are we? Measuring virtuality and understanding its impact in a global organization. *Information Systems Journal, 15*(4), 279–306.

Cramton, C. D. (2001). The mutual knowledge problem and its consequences for dispersed collaboration. *Organization Science, 12*(3), 346–371.

Dixon, K. R., & Panteli, N. (2010). From virtual teams to virtuality in teams. *Human Relations, 63*(8), 1177–1197.

Ferrazzi, K. (2014). Getting virtual teams right. *Harvard Business Review, 92*(12), 120–123.

Feldman, M. S., & Pentland, B. T. (2003). Reconceptualizing organizational routines as a source of flexibility and change. *Administrative Science Quarterly, 48*(1), 94–118.

George, J. M., & Jones, G. R. (2001). Towards a process model of individual change in organizations. *Human Relations, 54*(4), 419–444.

Gilson, L. L., Maynard, M. T., Jones Young, N. C., Vartiainen, M., & Hakonen, M. (2015). Virtual teams research: 10 years, 10 themes, and 10 opportunities. *Journal of Management, 41*(5), 1313–1337.

Grinter, R. E. (1996). Supporting articulation work using software configuration management systems. *Computer Supported Cooperative Work (CSCW), 5*(4), 447–465.

Hinds, P. J., & Mortensen, M. (2005). Understanding conflict in geographically distributed teams: The moderating effects of shared identity, shared context, and spontaneous communication. *Organization Science, 16*(3), 290–307.

Louis, M. R., & Sutton, R. I. (1991). Switching cognitive gears: From habits of mind to active thinking. *Human Relations, 44*(1), 55–76.

Majchrzak, A., Malhotra, A., Stamps, J., & Lipnack, J. (2004). Can absence make a team grow stronger? *Harvard Business Review, 82*(5), 131–137.

Neeley, T. (2015). Global teams that work. *Harvard Business Review, 93*(10), 74–81.

Rice, D. J., Davidson, B. D., Dannenhoffer, J. F., & Gay, G. K. (2007). Improving the effectiveness of virtual teams by adapting team processes. *Computer Supported Cooperative Work, 16,* 567–594.

Sawyer, S., & Tapia, A. (2006). Always articulating: theorizing on mobile and wireless technologies. *The Information Society, 22,* 1–13.

Schmidt, K., & Bannon, L. (1992). Taking CSCW seriously. *Computer Supported Cooperative Work (CSCW), 1*(1–2), 7–40.

Star, S. L. (1991). The sociology of the invisible: The primacy of work in the writings of Anselm Strauss. *Social organization and social process: Essays in honor of Anselm Strauss* (pp. 265–283).

Strauss, A. (1985). Work and the division of labor. *The Sociological Quarterly, 26*(1), 1–19.

Strauss, A. (1988). The articulation of project work: An organizational process. *The Sociological Quarterly, 29*(2), 163–178.

Watson-Manheim, M. B., Chudoba, K. M., & Crowston, K. (2012). Perceived discontinuities and constructed continuities in virtual work. *Information Systems Journal, 22*(1), 29–52.

Chapter 7
A Coaching Style of Management and the Affective Structuration of Workplace Relations

Camilla Noonan, Séamas Kelly and Geoff Pelham

Introduction

This paper describes an effort by a medium-sized organisation in the UK's social housing sector to make sustained and long-term investments in coaching training, with a view to broadly developing the skill-sets of their managers. These efforts resulted in the emergence and institutionalisation of a distinctive kind of management style—described here as a *coaching style of management*—which has had important implications for workplace relationships, and associated forms of affectivity/moods.

In what follows, we begin by briefly describing coaching and the associated philosophy underpinning the practice, before going on to provide an account of the introduction and institutionalisation of coaching practices at THG. In particular, we focus on their role in the emergence of distinctive new kinds of management practices, and of the 'felt' effects of these around the organisation. We conclude by offering a theoretical reflection on the significance of these changes by considering the performative effects of such practices; specifically the modes of relating and feeling that they produce.

Overall, we argue that the notion of a *coaching style of management* deserves more sustained empirical and theoretical attention, not least because of the sharp contrasts that can be drawn between it and more conventional *directive* approaches to the practice of management. In particular, a coaching style is marked by an emphasis

C. Noonan (✉) · S. Kelly
University College Dublin, Dublin, Ireland
e-mail: camilla.noonan@ucd.ie

S. Kelly
e-mail: seamas.kelly@ucd.ie

G. Pelham
Leeds, UK
e-mail: g.pelham@yahoo.com

© Springer International Publishing AG, part of Springer Nature 2019
K. Riemer et al. (eds.), *Collaboration in the Digital Age*, Progress in IS,
https://doi.org/10.1007/978-3-319-94487-6_7

on a *collaborative mode of problem solving*, as manager/coach and report/coachee engage in practices of collaborative inquiry that are oriented to promoting new forms of awareness and development. As such, these kinds of coaching relationships are promising subjects for studies of emergent forms of collaborative organisation in our contemporary digital age.

Coaching, Practice, Style, and Performativity

> Coaching sometimes seems like Keats' rainbow - the more we try to define it, dissect it, classify it and demystify it, the more we diminish it and lose its essence. (Clutterbuck & Megginson, 2011)

In recent years, coaching has come to be seen as an important employee development practice in many organisations. Although definitions of coaching vary, it is generally understood as a collaborative relationship that forms between a coach and coachee for the purpose of attaining professional or personal development outcomes (Grant et al., 2010). Whilst traditionally associated with sports, the notion that coaching could be adopted as a management practice in organisations is not a new idea (for an overview of the early appearances of 'coaching' in management contexts, see (Athanasopoulou & Dopson, 2018)). Following influential developments in humanistic psychology (Maslow, 1943; Rogers, 1951, 1957), scholars increasingly argued that managers had much to gain by adopting more supportive or developmental approaches (Hague, 1978; Kanter, 1984) and, throughout the 1980s, coaching came to be understood as an important set of skills that could assist in the correction of lacklustre performance in the organisation. Since performance related issues were usually dealt with as part of the formal performance review process, this is typically where coaching was homed. Oftentimes, what tended to play out in practice was a rather directive style of coaching/mentoring, which was typically enacted in ways that reinforced the superior/subordinate relationship and command-and-control type thinking. These 'coaching' engagements often took place against a backdrop of a potential threat of employment termination (Evered & Selman, 1989). The limitations of these early organisational enactments of coaching were very apparent and in the intervening period, scholars and practitioners have made great strides in their efforts to develop deeper understandings of coaching enactments in organisational settings (for reviews of executive and workplace coaching theory and practice see (Feldman & Lankau, 2005; Grant et al., 2010; Passmore & Fillery-Travis, 2011; Athanasopoulou & Dopson, 2018)). Recently, attention has turned toward the possibility of broadening and institutionalising these practices within organisations or, in other words, developing 'coaching cultures' (Clutterbuck & Megginson, 2005; Crane & Patrick, 2014; Gormley & van Nieuwerburgh, 2014; Clutterbuck et al., 2016)

While much has been written about the virtues and potential power of coaching in the practitioner literatures—see for example (Garvey et al., 2017)—attention has been drawn to the high degree of variation in actual coaching practice (Kampa-Kokesch & Anderson, 2001). This variation is associated with practitioner education and the array of theoretical/conceptual approaches drawn from in the delivery of coaching in organisational settings. For the purposes of this study, our intention is not to review these varying approaches but to report on an empirical case study of an organisation that became socialised into a set of practices associated with the humanistic/person-centred approach to coaching. In the following section, we briefly outline the core principles of this orientation.

Coaching—The Humanistic, Person-Centered Approach

Core to the humanistic approach to coaching is the notion that development and change can be produced by means of a *facilitated* collaborative learning process involving coach and coachee. In contrast to the early conceptualisations and applications of coaching to management, Bluckert (2006) reminds us that coaching is not about instructing or giving direction from the exalted position of a superior positioning in some hierarchy. A central premise of coaching is non-directive engagement—people often know more than they think; and, with help, are capable of accessing deeper understanding and resolving issues and moving forward in their lives (p. 4). In other words, according to this approach, the biggest obstacles to an individual's performance are regarded as being 'internal' (not 'external' (Gallwey, 1972)) and it is the coach's job to help the coachee identify and address these obstacles. This takes place within the context of a safe and non-judgemental coaching relationship. Facilitating learning via non-directive engagement goes to the heart of effective coaching practice, and actively listening to what is being said (and not said) is an important element of this practice. A second important principle of coaching is focusing on current performance but also on future potential performance that can be unlocked. Following on from this is the importance of developing self-belief. Here, the focus turns to coachee self-confidence and how growth can be enabled by helping the coachee to attribute successes, however small, to their own work or effort. Finally, building self-awareness and responsibility are key goals of coaching. Humanistic approaches to coaching are rooted in the believe that an individual's willingness to embrace change increases when there is greater awareness of the assumptions, belief systems, behaviours etc. that govern action. Once these background assumptions are surfaced, people can "move[s] into a position of choice—to stay with them or to change… the responsibility for this choice is with [them]" (p. 5). While awareness is no guarantee of change, it is treated as an important precursor because it urges one to take charge and assume ownership of the consequences of one's actions. These broad principles of coaching are outlined in Table 7.2 in the appendix.

The idea that these principles (and associated practices) could be popularised and institutionalised within an organisational context goes to the heart of what is understood by the term 'coaching culture'. While increasingly promoted as desirable, there is a noticeable dearth of empirical studies that examine the introduction and institutionalisation of the kinds of practices that might constitute a coaching culture. In the study that follows, we seek to redress this. We investigate what coaching looks and feels like in practice in a specific organisational setting and, in addition to examining what effect these practices had, we explore the process of institutionalising them over time. To facilitate this project, we synthesise a performative, practice-based approach to theorising coaching as an on-going accomplishment that enacts, or discloses, the world in distinctive ways. We suggest that this theoretical approach helps us unpack coaching in a way that helps us appreciate its power without *"diminishing it or losing its essence"* (Clutterbuck & Megginson, 2011). It is to this task that we now turn.

Coaching as a Performative Practice

In this study, we understand practice to be the basic unit of social analysis. Practices are ontological—they are world disclosive—shaping how we find ourselves in the world. They may be taken to be comprised of several interconnected elements—bodily activities; forms of mental activities; 'things' and their use; and background knowledge in the form of understanding, know-how, states of emotion and motivational knowledge (Reckwitz, 2002). While each of these elements is considered necessary to the enactment of a practice, it is important to note that they do not exist as separate, isolatable, atomistic components that precede their relations with one another, and a practice cannot be reduced to any single one of them. We suggest that different management styles can be helpfully understood as distinctive practices—they involve much more than mere doings and the ways in which we skilfully accomplishment such practices opens up the world to us in very specific ways. In other words, management practices enact a distinctive *way of being-in-the world-with-others*—this is what the doing *does* (Spinosa et al., 1999).

Mostly, the background knowledge that forms the basis of our skilled practice goes unnoticed. We become socialised into certain ways of being and the assumptions and understandings that underpin our patterns of behaviour frequently fade into the background and to the realm of the taken for granted. Things show up for us in terms of our familiar practices for dealing with them and, over time, we develop skilled responses that become deeply institutionalised. Management has come to be understood as a practice that is predominantly shaped by notions of explicit intention and calculative technique. These conceptualisations, propagated by mainstream business education and deeply institutionalised in the Western world, see management as being mostly about analysis, systematic decision-making and the formulation of deliberate strategies. The main task of managers is to solve, direct, control or, put differently, to domesticate what is seen as a very unruly world. Managers are often depicted as autonomous individuals of great strength, always in control, always in command of an understanding of what needs to be done to bring about certain outcomes (Mintzberg, 2009). When socialised into this way of being, managers respond to the world in ways that serve to reproduce these understandings.

Each skilled practice embodies a distinctive *style*. In other words, practices can be performed in different ways and different performances or styles illuminate how certain kinds of actions and things matter. Spinosa et al., (1999) explain the importance of style by asking us to consider the different ways in which children are reared in Japan versus the USA (Spinosa et al., 1999, pp. 20–21). Different ways of tending to babies socialises different ways of being in the world. For example, Japanese mothers tend to place babies on their backs so that the babies will lie still and be quieted by whatever they see. They tend to promote 'relative passivity and sensitivity to harmony' in the action of their babies; they are soothing and pacifying. In contrast, American babies are typically placed on their stomachs, which encourages movement. Their mothers tend to encourage animated gesturing and vocalising, which 'promotes active and aggressive styles'. The 'style' socialises the child into a particular way of being in the world because in their *doing*, the practices reveal how certain kinds of things, and ways of doings things, matter and are worthy of our notice and attention.

In a similar way, management practices embody certain styles, which, in communicating what one ought to care about, socialise organisational communities into very particular ways of being. These practices/styles are thus implicated in the production of very specific kinds of subject positions and in the affective structuration of workplace relations.

In this study we draw on these ideas to help us make sense of an organisational innovation that is on-going in a medium-sized, UK-based organisation in the social sector. The innovation involved the integration of coaching practices within the context of broader management activities. We suggest that this has resulted in the emergence of a distinctive management style—a coaching style of management—and our aim here is to explore its performative effects. We focus attention on the key skills required to master a coaching style of management (asking, listening, encouraging, challenging, giving feedback, supporting, etc.), and explore what increasing mastery of these skills produces.

Research Approach

This study reports on some preliminary findings from an on-going research project that began in October 2015. The context of our empirical work is The Housing Group (THG), which is a UK housing association that was established in 2000. At this time, and with the support of his executive team, David (CEO) decided to invest significantly in in-house executive coaching training. Before stepping into the position of CEO of this organisation, David had worked with an executive coach and was deeply influenced by this experience. Such was the power of his exposure to coaching that he wanted others to experience it too—he had a hunch that coaching could greatly benefit the management team of this newly formed organisation.

To date, we have carried out five field visits to THG—two before a major restructuring of the organisation and three afterwards—spanning a period of more than two years. We have completed approximately 31 semi-structured interviews with people working at different levels and across different areas within this organisation.

Anonymity was assured and so all names and full positions within the organisation are therefore unreported (see Table 7.3, appendix).

Research notes were created to capture our reflections during/after interviews, and we ritually discussed our impressions and developing understandings at the conclusion of each day. During this fieldwork, we were also permitted to observe employees in this workplace and to shadow a number of employees as they went about their daily activities. These exercises proved very insightful for us and helped us to gain a deeper understanding of this context—the nature of the work and the kind of services provided within the local communities.

We held a number of feedback sessions with members of the executive team and also presented some of our early observations to the Board in September 2016. We find these kinds of exercises a very helpful means of developing our interpretations and opening them up to the critical scrutiny of others.

The Housing Group (THG)

The Housing Group (THG) describes itself as a social business. It is based in the UK and, with a portfolio of approximately 20,000 houses, is one of the area's largest registered providers of social housing.[1] It was established in 2000 and employs 900 people. The group comprises three housing companies, as well as a building company, and a homeless charity. It also sponsors an Education Trust and has developed partnerships with a local newspaper, theatre, and radio station. In July 2017, THG announced a merger with another housing association (Home Group) and together, these two groups will manage approximately 33,000 homes.

David was the Director of Housing at a large UK metropolitan council in 1992—a time when the public housing stock was suffering from serious under investment. Operating within the UK public sector, David found this environment very difficult:

> I felt I couldn't be effective… I felt completely impotent; I had no sense of being valued…
> I was a buffer between the political leadership and my people. I saw my job as having to soak up all the difficulty and try not to pass it on; I was being constantly criticised, I was uncomfortable in my own skin… uncertain of my own abilities and every unclear about my own sense of self-worth.

Former employees of the Council described this work environment as characterised by a managerial need for control and ambiguity reduction, with an emphasis on bureaucratic rules and impersonal and impatient interactions with subordinates. In turn, these kinds of cultural practices produced a conservatism and risk-aversion;

---

[1] In the UK, housing associations are private, not for profit organisations that provide affordable or low cost social housing. Their genesis follows the Thatcher government's "Right to Buy" scheme, whereby allowed tenants to buy their council houses at a discounted price. Councils were prohibited from investing these proceeds into new housing, which led to a large contraction in the availability of council housing across the UK. The Housing Acts of 1985 and 1989 attempted to address this by enabling the transfer of council housing to not for profit housing associations.

a preoccupation with secrecy, or hiding, and spinning; and a strong deference to authority:

> People used to be in boxes and management was very hierarchical… it was extremely bureaucratic and you were really restricted in what you could say and do. There were rules for everything. (Evan, Business Development)

In 2000, and against the backdrop of changes to the UK's social housing policies, David led the transfer of the Council's housing stock to a new organisational entity (THG) and became its CEO. At the time, this was the UK's largest voluntary stock transfer. Following 20 years of under-investment in the local housing stock, THG began life with many challenges—1290 empty properties; £33 m in outstanding housing repairs; a deluge of tenant complaints; a toxic organisational culture; and a very unhappy and ineffective staff.

For David, taking up the position of CEO at the newly formed THG was daunting:

> … I was sort of waiting for people to come in and tell me what to do… it was like, 'shit, what do I do now?' The Council put on a leadership course, with gave me some insights but then a colleague of mine suggested coaching and it really worked for me… it's all about self-awareness… it opened up a whole new way of thinking about management… I was Bluckert'ed).[2]

He explained how he started to develop a picture of what THG might look like:

> I started to develop a growing sense of the value of coaching and started to develop a picture of the organisation 'as coachee'… I started to see coaching principles as a model for organising. It starts with listening to the customers. Their journey is our journey. They want clean, safe and well-managed homes and communities. They do not want anti-social behaviour in their areas and so the logic is that if we can help solve the various issues experienced by these families, then we will get the rent… We place a large emphasis on listening to customers. (CEO, 25th October 2015)

Further, managers would be encouraged to live coaching principles and for cultivating coaching practices—not just within their immediate domain of official responsibility, but across the entire organisation:

> People need to feel like they are part of the whole organisation. (David)

Indeed, following his exposure to coaching, David's own management style seemed to change dramatically:

> In the past, we would say 'David just issued a JFDI' and the idea was that if he shouted loud enough, somebody would do it… it was like, 'I'm not the problem, you are!'… the assertive approach to management is there when it's needed but, unlike in the past, when David is under a lot of pressure he does not react. Now, he is different - he reflects. The toys don't come out of the pram. (Evan, Business Development Manager, 16th March 2016)

In an effort to achieve "critical mass", each member of the executive team worked with an external coach and some went on to formally train as executive coaches.

---

[2]Peter Bluckert is an executive coach and author of the 2006 book titled "Psychological dimensions of Executive Coaching", Open University Press, Oxford.

Further, team coaching for the senior management team was also put in place. This early emphasis on, and investment in, coaching was considered to be quite a risky move and it was not without its dissenters:

> We took coaching on when we were very young as an organisation and there were many sceptics. The investment in coaching was a big bet. It was a risky thing to do - 'all that coaching malarkey!'. Some areas of the business still see it as a lot of namby-pamby. (Evan, Manager March 2016)

While coaching was available to executive/senior and middle-level managers, it was mostly the more senior people who availed of it in the early years:

> When I arrived (in 2006), only the top team availed of coaching. Elsewhere in the organisation coaching was recommended to people with performance problems, and so it had become stigmatised. We went through a long process of trying to communicate that coaching was not punitive. We would say, 'look at David - from 2000 until now he has a coach', and that has helped to dispel the association. (Jackie, Director of Organisational Transformation, October 2015)

The focus turned to continuous training and, from 2006 onwards, an external coaching consultancy was hired to facilitate this training as part of their broader talent development agenda. The programmes offered varied from three to five days over a period of four months and, on completion, each manager was expected to be available to provide coaching to members of his/her own team or to employees elsewhere in the organisation. To date, approximately 120 employees across all areas of THG have participated in these coaching programmes.

After 17 years of promoting and supporting coaching at THG, the senior team were confident that, while it may not have taken hold in equal measure across the entire organisation, there was considerable evidence to suggest that THG was a successful organisation and that coaching had played no small part in enabling such performance outcomes (see Table 7.1).[3]

In terms of tracking more granular rates of return on their coaching investments, David was keenly aware of the difficulties and limitation of such exercises:

> The general consensus at board-level was that there was not a huge need for this; coming up with a rate of return for everything is bloody tedious... it is just so boring, isn't it? (CEO, June 27th, 2016)

Nonetheless, the senior team expressed some concerns about the extent to which coaching was taking hold across the organisation while others, against the backdrop of recent redundancies[4] and rumours of a merger with another housing association, reinforced the felt need to point to tangible returns on THG's coaching investments:

---

[3]It is perhaps important to note that many employees of THG have given a long number of years service to the organisation and it was not unusual for us to meet with people who had worked at THG since its establishment. Thus, a considerable number of THG employees had been socialized into coaching practices over an extended period of time.

[4]In 2015, the UK Government imposed a one per cent reduction in social housing rents. This impacted THG's revenue model and forced the organisation to introduce a redundancy programme.

Table 7.1 Performance indicators—THG

Key performance indicator	2000	2017
Property turnaround times	32 days	23.6 days
Outstanding repairs	£3 m	£0
Customer satisfaction (%)	57	90
Turnover (m)	£40	£100
Completion and cost of repairs	Data not available	Upper quartile
People (employee satisfaction)	52%	In Sunday Times top 100 employer over nine years. Ranked within the top 20 for seven years running

Source THG reports and documentation

> It's fantastic, it changed my life; but is it of benefit to the business? There is no corporate requirement to record the benefit. The problem is that when there is a lot of enthusiasm around coaching, it doesn't get questioned. People say it's great, but what has changed? What does it actually contribute?… What if Sandra or David leave? In the context of a merger, what would happen to the coaching programme? (Neil, Strategic Organisational Development Consultant, March 15th, 2016)

The Exposure to, and Experience of, Coaching at THG

There are three main ways in which employees of THG encounter coaching. The first is through their participation on a coaching programme.[5] As noted above, since 2006 THG have provided coaching training, on a voluntary basis, for all managers. The second is by engaging with a coach (i.e. one-on-one coaching). On completion of internal coaching training, managers join a list of people who are available to coach. Any employee in the organisation can register with one of these coaches. The third way of experiencing coaching at THG is through the daily interactions that employees have with their managers and co-workers in and around the organisation.

In what follows, we offer four vignettes that are illustrative of what we heard and saw while undertaking fieldwork in this organisation. In the first two instances, we introduce Mary and Thomas, both of whom are managers at THG. The third and fourth vignettes focus on Anne and Kevin, respectively, both of whom are more junior employees who are in direct customer-facing roles.

---

[5] While the majority of managers that we spoke with first encountered coaching through the internally provided training programmes; some had undertaken coaching training prior to joining THG (e.g. Mary in vignette 1).

Vignette 1: Mary

Prior to joining THG in 2010, Mary worked at two other UK housing associations and had earned a diploma in coaching. She leads the Customer Service Group and sits in the middle of a large open plan office that is occupied by a team of people wearing headphones and working at computers. Although thirty advisors and two team leaders report to her, she explained that she does not see herself "as managing thirty-two people". Rather, she sees her job as "*empowering*" her two-team leaders to get on with the job:

> You know, if you asked me ten years ago, I would have said management was all about decision-making… oftentimes in meetings, managers feel compelled to be the ones standing and in front of the flipchart, but I have come to realise that the other people sitting around the table should be given the floor. So I sit back and let them be the boss… When trying to solve a problem it is not always about me being in control. (March 15, 2016)

Mary explained that she started to realise this some years ago when she had an opportunity to study for a diploma in business coaching and, subsequently, work with a coach. She recalled her "light bulb moment" when, while managing a project that relied on a key deliverable from a group of engineers, she started to adopt a coaching style in her interactions. There were many delays and frustrations with this project, but rather than engage with the engineers in the combative style to which she was well accustomed, she decided to change tack:

> I arranged to meet the head guy for a coffee - had some small chat with him and then showed him a drawing - my interpretation of what needed to happen - and explained where we needed to get to as an organisation and I ask him what he thought and what his views were on getting everybody to that point. (March 15, 2016)

She was very taken by how this different approach influenced project relations and outcomes. The focus was put on the work and the collective effort that was needed move forward, rather than personalising the difficulties that had beset the project up to that point.

Reflecting on her time in her previous employment, she remarked:

> There was a focus on coaching at [name of previous employer] but it did not compare to here - they were very early on in their journey and the leadership team was not as strong as here… I think the key difference between THG and other places I have worked is that values and beliefs are lived here. They don't just talk about being a listening organisation… What is different here are behaviours. (March 15, 2016)

Mary explained that she has come to appreciate how small things can make a difference when leading a team:

> Good management is about bringing people to a place where they really want to be at work. (March 15, 2016)

Mary talked about how she makes time to send cards to new people joining the team, or sometimes buys them small tokens (e.g. notebooks) to welcome them to THG. She said that when things go wrong the focus is never on blame, but on collectively finding solutions—above all, there is an ethos of care throughout THG. She recalled how busy they all were the previous day—recent staff cuts were really felt, as 48% of calls went unanswered in the centre. She said that John (a Team Leader) was really concerned about the performance. Mary seemed to be impressed by the fact that a very junior employee, whose job it is to simply report the statistics in real time, was also very anxious about the dip in performance.

She talked about the importance of managers demonstrating that they care about their people and went into some detail about how the manner in which the senior team managed the recent redundancies reflected this care. She also recalled a recent situation that illustrated how oftentimes small, and ostensibly trivial, gestures can mean a lot—a few weeks previously, inclement weather resulted in a number of the Customer Service team arriving late to work. Unannounced, and very unexpectedly, David (CEO) arrived into the office and asked if people were OK or needed to go home early. She said that his concern for the front line people was "an example of why [she] work[s] in THG."

Vignette 2: Thomas

Thomas joined THG in 2008 and, in his current management role, he is responsible for eight direct reports (three administrators, three Team Leaders, and two technical liaisons). He still remembers being "*stunned rigid by the feel of the place*" when he first arrived, and how it took him quite some time to get used to how THG worked. In contrast to his previous workplace ("*where people are left to fail, where there are often high consequences associated with failure, and where those who do fail are typically left hang out to dry*"), he explained that, for him, it was "*like a breath of fresh air to come into such an open and honest culture, where it's ok to say what you think*."

Prior to joining THG, he had no knowledge of business coaching. During his first year, he participated on one of the coaching programmes, which he found really helpful because he "*learned a lot about [him] self*". Some members of the executive team participated on this programme, and he was particularly impressed by how they engaged with the other (more junior) participants:

> David and Sandra are huge role models. On the coaching programme, Sandra was particularly good at interacting with people. I have also heard that at senior management team meetings, they regularly check-in and check-out at beginning and end of the meetings. This is a really good practice.[6]

---

[6]'Checking-in' is a common activity in coaching, whereby a group of people take it in turns to notice, and share with others, how they are feeling about a particular issue, or in general. The practice is designed to help bring people's attention to what's going on for them and others, to enable them to 'arrive' properly and 'leave outside the door' whatever may be a distraction from being fully present in the meeting.

Thomas decided to continue to further develop his skills by working with an external coach and by registering for some additional leadership/coaching training at THG:

> My approach to managing has been really shaped by this. The key things are helping people to work through issues themselves and helping them to see a broader picture… It taught me to listen more than talk, and for me, this was a big breakthrough.

He talked about how he has been trying to encourage these kinds of practices within his team. He recounted a situation where one of his team leaders wanted to reprimand a member of his team for what he considered sub-standard work. Thomas explored possible ways of handling this situation with him, encouraging him to think through the longer-term implications of the various potential interventions. After some discussion, the team leader decided to engage with the junior and help him appreciate why the work was not up to scratch and to support him as he tried to improve.

Since Thomas has been exposed to a coaching style of engagement, he explained how he has become a lot more attuned to recognising this style of engagement in others:

> My current stand-in Director is also very coaching oriented - he's stretching me even more. My interactions with him feel like coaching, although it's never explicitly pitched as such. From David and Sandra right down to the managers, there is a coaching culture and these practices are really appreciated.

Vignette 3: Anne

Anne joined THG in 2011. Working in a customer advisory role, her daily duties involve dealing with tenant complaints. She spoke enthusiastically about her work:

> I am really passionate about what I do. Everybody seems to see it as mattering. It's not just a job. Nobody ever plans to work in housing, but they arrive in here and they end up being passionate about it. (March 14th, 2016)

Since joining THG, she has had two internal coaches who helped her to cope with some of the day-to-day issues that she encountered with her work. Moreover, this experience of coaching helped her recognise the power of a distinctive style of engagement that she has attempted to incorporate into her own way of interacting with others:

> I picked it up from the coaching sessions. It is all about coming to a solution yourself instead of being shown a solution; It is about how you interact with colleagues… I try to copy how people have dealt with me… it is just how we do it around here… People who do not take a coaching approach stand out a lot more. They come across as being very blunt.

She explained that because the coaching style of engagement can oftentimes be *"very subtle"*, it is not always easy to point to tangible examples. She pointed to her manager, however, as someone who exemplifies this style of engagement:

> She gets me to come up with my own solutions. And when she does this, I realise it and think, 'hey, you've just done that to me again' [laughs]

Anne spoke about the confidence that her manager seems to have in her and the trust that has built up between them over time:

> We have conversations about what needs to be done. She stays involved but sometimes she'll say 'sorry, I'm getting too involved in that…' I feel like she has great confidence in me. She says, unless it is a really big decision, I should just go ahead myself. If it goes wrong, she says it'll be her fault… Trust builds and I feel very comfortable talking to her… She never rushes and she takes the time to listen. (March 14th, 2016)

Anne also noticed how she has come to incorporate these kinds of practices into her interactions in her personal life:

> I was talking with my friend recently and she accused me of doing therapy on her! [laughs]

Vignette 4: Kevin

Kevin has been with THG for 13 years. Although he has had a number of different roles during this time, he currently works in customer service, where, similar to Anne, he handles complaints, inquiries and offers advice to people about housing. He recalled his first encounter with coaching:

> About a year ago, I went for a new job and was not successful. I was really deflated and the idea of getting a coach came up in one of my performance reviews. I said that it was not for me, but I have been doing it for over a year now. My manager's manager is my coach. (March 14th, 2016)

He described himself as being "predominantly negative" and so for him, coaching was helpful because it focused on bringing out the positive from situations in which he found himself:

> THG has always been about bringing people on and, oftentimes, coaching and mentoring melt into one.

He recounted a recent situation where his direct manager helped him to recover from a setback by helping him to reframe his experience:

> Last week I didn't get a job that I went for, but my manager tried to frame it in a positive way - I had put myself out there, and that was a positive thing. This opened my eyes to a different world. He told me that the same thing happened to him in the past and I found that very helpful to hear; him showing vulnerability has really changed me… It's not about giving you something, it is about helping you to recognise what is already there.

He explained how these experiences have shaped his engagements with people outside of THG. He is a volunteer at the local unit of an international humanitarian organisation, and explained how recently he has become involved with the new recruits:

> Informally, I take on the role of coach and mentor for the trainees. It's about sharing my experience with them… telling them that I did the same thing that you did; and helping them to see another way of doing it. I would not have done this in the past. It is about having the confidence to do it.

He explained that having had a coach, he is now able to recognise the influence of coaching in other people's interactions with him:

> They ask how you are doing, whether there are any problems, and coaching always creeps in. It's always there - asking how can they help - small things… All the managers seem to engage in the same way; you see it all the way up.

A Perspective on Management Styles and Performativity at THG

In this section, we reflect upon the vignettes just outlined and supplement these with some additional field data, in an attempt to draw out some important insights about the institutionalisation of these new management practices at THG and their implications for the affective structuration of workplace relations.

Introducing and Institutionalising the New Style of Management at THG

> It's all very well to talk about coaching but you don't really get it unless you experience it. (Alison, March 15th, 2016)

As noted above, the reconfiguration of management practices at THG began when David (the CEO) experienced coaching first-hand and then, following a hunch that these practices may prove helpful to his senior management team, began to promote coaching more widely. In an effort to appreciate how these new practices started to spread and become institutionalised at THG, we draw attention to two important aspects—the provision of effective coaching training for senior (and eventually mid-level) management, and the role of influential articulators who began to model this style of management for others in their daily engagements.

Similar to many other organisations, both in the social housing sector and beyond, THG has been actively trying to introduce a coaching ethos over a number of years. What is striking about THG, however, is the extent of the understanding and buy-in at senior levels. Employees explained that they had worked in other organisations where coaching had one, sometimes two, sponsors; but at NHG, there was widespread support within the top team. David encouraged his senior management team to work individually and collectively with coaches and to experience it for themselves, and this created a critical mass of senior people who continue to champion these practices:

> … in other places it is seen as remedial; in THG coaching is like a badge of honour. (Emma, Strategic Organisational Development Consultant, March 14th 2016)

Following the introduction of coaching at senior management level, training programmes were introduced for mid-level managers. Importantly, because of the experiential nature of coaching training, participants are able to experience the power of the practices first-hand. Training exercises typically require each participant to alternate between being the 'coach' (i.e. helping somebody to work through a particular issue with which they are struggling) and being 'coachee' (i.e. receiving help from another to work through their own particular issue). Actively participating in these kinds of exercises afforded managers the opportunity to experiment with these ways of engaging with others and to experience the felt effects of such practices at first-hand. For example, Patrick (MD of the Building Division) described the importance of a very positive, and lasting, emotional impact from working with his coach:

> How she made me feel as a coachee is what I remember when people come to my door to discuss some issue or problem.

Managers that had participated on these programmes summarised their experiences with comments such as: "I really learnt a lot about myself"; that it was the "first time that [they] felt really developed on a training programme"; and how "life changing" the whole experience had been for them. One respondent (Jamie, Head of Business Solutions) explained how after the training he realised the different between "being a manager who is good at his job, and being a good manager".

A number of people (both senior and mid-level managers) seemed to stand out as very influential carriers of these practices. People referred to particular individuals (e.g. David, Sandra, or their direct managers) as "huge role models" and examples of individuals who communicate what matters by the ways in which they engage with others. We have seen, for example, the impact of members of the senior management team getting involved in the delivery of the coaching training at THG. As they shared their personal experiences of coaching and their on-going development as senior managers, they seemed to establish important connections with others across the organisation.

It is clear that experiencing these practices and styles of managing have helped to nurture quite a unique work environment at THG. Moreover, the influential power of these practices extends beyond the immediate manager-subordinate relationship in two important ways. First, the influence of these practices can be seen in the ways that THG employees reproduce the practices when dealing with tenant complaints and engaging with tenants in their communities. We experienced employee engagement with tenants first-hand through our shadowing activities and were struck by the coaching styles of engagement that were adopted. Second, in the ways that people begin to draw on these practices in their private lives. In terms of the latter, we recall Kevin's work as a volunteer (vignette 4) or Anne jokingly being accused of "doing therapy" on her friend (vignette number 3). To this, we add another employee's account of finding herself adopting a coaching approach with her husband—"*it seeped in without my realising it*" and another's description of how these practices have spilled over into his private life and how his home life with his partner is benefitting:

> [I] hold back on saying things in certain situations - I check myself and bite my tongue and this reduces conflict… Now I notice more how I am with people… Maybe not making the changes I should be, but at least I'm noticing anyway! (Noel, Team Leader, March 15th, 2016)

This is not to say that this coaching style of management has spread evenly across the organisation. Although, they were in the minority, there were some parts of THG where these practices did not seem to take hold. The kinds of reasons offered to explain this included time and resource constraints, the 'uncoachability' of some, or a sense that in some areas there was a lack of understanding about its role and value. Whatever the reason, and as noted earlier by Anne in vignette 3, the alternative style(s) of management really seem to stand out by comparison:

> I don't think [my manager] has had any management training. I am pretty much left to get on with the job. I have an annual performance review but it's like a school report. I just sign off on whatever my manager writes. It's usually hard to get hold of him. I am here today for a meeting with him but he did not turn up. (Will, Health and Safety, 16th March, 2016)

The Coaching Style of Managing and the Affective Structuration of Workplace Relations

> When I started working at THG initially, I was stunned rigid by the feel of the place. (Thomas)

> When I joined THG in 2015, levels of trust were unbelievable. (Emma)

> … there is much more awareness and care here. (Noel)

In this section, we draw out some of the distinctive micro-practices associated with this coaching style of management at THG and reflect upon their 'felt' effects. In other words, we focus on the role of such practices in the production of specific kinds of subject positions and the associated affective structuration of workplace relations—or, how such practices configured people's disposedness to one another, and to their work, in distinctive ways. The quotations above bear testament to the fact that employees noticed a distinctive 'feel' to the working environment that had been fostered at THG. In what follows, we identify four practices—constitutive of a broader coaching style of management— that contributed to the production of this 'feel'. These are (i) **connecting** (ii) **presencing**, (iii) **nurturing**, and (iv) **committing**. Moreover, we try to be more explicit about identifying the moods—**trust, openness, empathy, solidarity, hope** and **commitment** (i.e. an emotional investment in THG's collective project)—that were produced by such practices and constitutive of the 'feel' of the working environment.

(i)   *Connecting*

Coaching places a big emphasis on the quality of the contact between coach and coachee that is produced in any given coaching conversation. Coaches need to master a set of skills for contributing to producing an 'authentic contact'. One respondent recounted his experience with his external coach:

> I don't really know her. She has a skill and she opens me up. I am quite emotional. She relaxes me… its ok to be honest and open. You feel you don't have to bullshit.

Noel (Team Leader in Client Services) recounted his experiences of working with his manager—Mary, (whose testimony is reported in vignette 1 above). He talked about how she has regular one-to-ones with her people (every 4–6 weeks, or more informally when necessary); how she "*values honest conversations and openness*"; how she typically "*challenges* [*him*] *to solve problems for* [*himself*] *rather than telling him what to do*". Others also referred to these kinds of practices when they talked about their direct managers. Addressing senior managements concerns that these conversations may be too gentle and overly forgiving around performance, Noel was clear to point out that sometimes, these conversations are "*not very comfortable*", but "*they are great for learning*".

Important skills here include deep listening, empathy, a non-judgemental attitude, and a sense of care for the coachee and their plight. A number of people described how they felt, as stronger and more authentic connections began to take shape with their managers and colleagues in THG. One person described these connections as "*bonds of appreciation*" (Greg, Assistant Director) that develop between coach/coachee or manager and team member over time. Managers who had received coaching training described how vital this training experience was in giving them the confidence to engage in qualitatively different kinds of conversations with their teams and their colleagues. Conversations became more non-directive, developmental (see vignette 1), and managers felt more confident to discuss difficult issues (that they might previously have avoided) in a more open way:

> … rather than keeping my cards to my chest, which was my old way of doing things, I have become more open, honest and transparent. (Patrick, Director of one of the three companies in the THG group)

Overall, these ways of connecting seem to produce better quality engagements and professional relationships between people.

(ii) *Presencing—Being present (noticing and supporting)*

In coaching, a key aspect of the practice is self-awareness and of understanding what one's presence evokes in others:

> Our presence contributes to whether we attract and interest others; it also can be a factor in distancing or putting them off. It is the source of our capacity to influence and equally it can explain our lack of impact…The individual who has yet to learn how to use different aspects of self—soft and hard, loud and quiet, strong and mild—is not yet a finely tuned instrument of change (Bluckert, 2016, p. 1).

In an organisational setting, presencing can be understood as the manner in which managers make themselves available to their teams. Skilled and effective managers know what different situations call for, and they draw on appropriate aspects of self to respond with skill and tact. They know when to be assertive, when to increase their involvement, but also when to pull back:

> She stays involved but sometimes she'll say 'sorry, I'm getting too involved in that…' (Anne, describing her manager)

An important aspect of effective presencing is noticing. Skilled and effective managers take the time to develop self-awareness and to get to know their people. With time, they learn how to be present in ways that solicit them to notice and intervene tactfully, and with generosity, (*"she never rushes, she takes the time to listen"* Anne); to know what they are doing and what they are struggling with (*"They know the stuff that's going on… sometimes I wished they didn't [laughs]"*—Will); and to encourage them to see that they are not alone and have a supportive team behind them. They get to know their subordinates and teams as people (adopt a holistic approach) and irrespective of rank or profile, treat them with respect. They clarify tasks and performance expectations (*"are assertive when needs be"* Evan) but focus on enabling people to get on with their work.

(iii)   *Nurturing—developmental orientation towards the other—building trust and self-reliance*

Coaching practices place great value on developing people and unlocking their potential and managers who practice a coaching style of managing are always attentive to each individual's future potential as well as their current performance. Managers enter into developmental dialogues with the goal of seeking to challenge and stretch their people, and remove all interference, in an effort to help them to achieve ("THG wants people to do well"). To be effective in this regard, it is crucial that managers develop and perfect certain skills—such as asking good questions (as opposed to telling subordinates what to do); learning how to mostly listen (as opposed to mostly talk *"I no longer jump in and there is a greater calmness to our interactions"*); providing timely feedback and soliciting feedback from others; developing self-awareness and the ability to self-regulate their behaviours; giving people permission to find their own solutions and not blaming them when (good) mistakes are made; developing their empathy and their ability to genuinely care about the livelihoods of subordinates:

> … coaching opened my eyes to stuff. I was blinded to it before. I notice when colleagues are below par… God, I'm starting to sound all sensitive now. [laughs] (Jamie)

Above all, these managers become very skilled at mobilising collective action and building relationships by facilitating *conversations that matter.*

Further, these managers are sensitive to feelings and mood; they strike the right balance between challenging and supporting, and these practices foster a pronounced sense of benevolence and care within the organisation ("An ethos that has been developed here over the years has got us through the difficult times." (Mary, March 15, 2016)). People seem to have a tangible sense that THG wants them to do well ("THG has always been about bringing people on") and employees are made to feel that the work that they do "matters". The style of management at THG, and the experience of coaching, makes people feel valued, supported and part of a collective. One respondent recounted his experiences of being promoted within THG, which required him to work alongside a very challenging colleague. He felt constantly undermined.

He told us about how coaching made him feel that he was being supported by the company—it gave him an:

> inner confidence that the company is behind [me]... I was getting extra money in the new job but the stress and extra responsibility wasn't worth it. I have a lot to do, and in an environment where you feel people are against you, it's really difficult.

Confidence frequently emerged as an important theme for many of the people with whom we spoke. Managers talked about the important role that coaching played in helping them to develop the kind of confidence required to do their work—to engage in particular kinds of conversations with their subordinates and to work independently of their managers. For example, Patrick (Director of one of THG's three companies) explained how, following his coaching training, he was very attuned to the importance of nurturing independence and responsibility:

> ... our old gaffer used to have us on very tight leads and if we challenged him, he'd shout at us. [When I became director] I unclipped everybody and told them to go and do your job.

This principle of subsidiarity (recall Anne, vignette 3 "*she gets me to come up with my own solutions*") helps to nurture greater self-confidence and more trustful relationships as employees are empowered to work through challenges and find solutions independently, all the while secure in the knowledge that others are there to support them.

An influential practice in the effort to nurture confidence amongst team members seems to have been managers' preparedness to show or admit vulnerability. This was evident in situations described to us where managers got getting visibly upset when delivering bad news; were prepared to share past failures or openly admit that they did not have all the answers, etc. This is of course intimately linked to "presencing" but what is perhaps most important to appreciate here is what these kinds of 'doings' do in THG - they have lasting effects on the people working there—"*him showing vulnerability really changed me*" Kevin (vignette 4).

It is clear that experiencing these practices and styles of managing have helped to nurture quite a unique work environment at THG:

> it makes for a better atmosphere around the place and people are more willing to express their opinions.

Moreover, the influential power of these practices extends beyond the immediate manager-subordinate relationship in two important ways. First, in the ways that people begin to draw on these practices in their private lives (as highlighted on page 17) and second, in the manner in which THG employees routinely handle tenant complaints and engage with tenants in their communities. We experienced employee engagement with tenants first-hand through our shadowing activities and were struck by the coaching styles of engagement that were adopted.

(iv) *Committing—building awareness and responsibility for the broader collective project*

In contrast to coachee development within a conventional coaching relationship (whereby the emphasis is placed on the individual's personal project), in an organisational context there are typically broader issues at stake. Developing self-awareness is key, but this is situated in the context of the work—it is intimately related to how one understands one's place within a broader team/organisational project. Consequently, we might understand there being two important foci for the coaching manager—first, developing individuals and, second, developing the broader organisational community.

In the case of THG, this resulted in people being emotionally invested in, and committed to, the organisation and to the broader project of developing good social housing and communities. Employees seem to feel a very strong connection with THG 's mission, and seem very grateful for what they have experienced and contributed through their work there. This was borne out by the testimonies in the above vignettes, but also by those of others in THG:

> I got other job offers while I was here - better money, you know. But working here, it's not even about the salary, the holidays, the pension. At THG it's always been about doing the right thing for tenants, for communities... the radio station, the education... it's the right thing to do. (Jamie)

> I love my job, love working with [his manager], love the environment, love the organisation – I'm a big THG fan. (Noel)

Working for THG was viewed by many as much more than a job—people were invested in the larger project and an overall mood of commitment was very palpable around the organisation.

Conclusion

> Coaching has changed me personally and professionally over the years and these ideas and approaches just became part of the day-to-day way of doing stuff around here. (Andrew, Director, March 15th 2016)

> Sometimes you mirror the culture you're in. It helps me being in this kind of culture... I have seen the changes in myself as a manager, and as a person. (Noel, Team Leader, March 15th, 2016)

This paper presents rare empirical evidence of sustained attempts to promote the use of coaching practices as a means of managing and engaging with others in a medium-sized, UK-based, social-sector organisation. Although there has been much speculative writing about the potential for the broader incorporation of coaching skills within organisational life—often with a view to fostering so-called *coaching cultures*—there has been a noticeable dearth of in-depth empirical studies in the area that examine how these ideas might work in practice. As well as addressing this empirical lacuna, we have also attempted to make a conceptual contribution, by synthesising a performative, praxeological approach to understanding coaching practices and the role that these may play in the enactment of particular kinds of subjectivities and associated moods.

Our paper, therefore, drew on the empirical and theoretical materials presented, to offer an account of how a specific set of management practices—which, taken together, we label a *coaching style of management*—became institutionalised at THG over time. Moreover, we also examined what made these practices so distinctive in terms of their performative effects (what their doing does)—i.e. the kinds of organisational relationships and associated moods that they produced.

With respect to the institutionalisation of the practices associated with this coaching style of management, the testimony presented points to how the power and significance of these practices was recognised and understood through their experiential felt affect. It was only after experiencing them at first hand (e.g. the experience of being listened to by managers or of being trusted by managers to find their own solutions) that people realised how impactful they were. Thus, we see this affective power (i.e. related to how one is made to feel, or affectively configured, by a practice) as a key feature that explains how these practices moved and were institutionalised at THG. This points to the importance of both the set-piece coaching training programmes and the active modelling of such practices in the workplace interactions. Moreover, our analysis emphasises the importance of taking the affective seriously in theories of cultural persistence and change—modelling practices is not merely about symbolic acts (as emphasised by literatures on organisational culture that draw on symbolic anthropology), but about what these acts do to impact and configure people affectively.

Our analysis pointed to how coaching practices were adapted to work in a broader management context. Specifically, we named four important practices that were constitutive of a coaching style of management—connecting, presencing, nurturing and committing—and reflected upon the ways that these were adapted from a one-to-one coaching (walking alongside) to a broader management (reporting relationship) context. The different power relations that are at play in these two contexts is a topic that deserves greater scrutiny.

Further, we suggested that the key to explaining the appeal of these practices is the kinds of moods that are produced through their doing. Moreover we named some of the moods that these appeared to produce—trust, openness, empathy, solidarity, hope, and commitment—which stood in marked contrast to descriptions of the "low morale" that characterised the organisation in earlier years. This, again, emphasises the importance of attending to what the doing of particular practices does, in terms of producing distinctive and consequential kinds of affective social structurations.

We do not wish to suggest that these coaching practices or the coaching style of management swept all practices before them and that the inherited hierarchical, detached and distant style of management was completely displaced. Clearly, the coaching sensibility did not reach all areas of THG and many people still struggle to experience and appreciate the powerful effects of this other style of management. We continue to explore these issues.

Appendix

See Tables 7.2 and 7.3.

Table 7.2 Coaching principles—coaching practices—coaching moods

Principles (cognitive)	Practices (embodied)	Micro practices	Moods
Focus on non-directive engagement	**Connecting**—opening up a neutral, safe space; creating a clearing, in which understanding can be produced	Non-judgemental listening Empathising Attending Caring Reframing Noticing Sensing Intuiting Encouraging Supporting Acknowledging Being compassionate Asking good questions Challenging	Trust Openness Empathy Solidarity Hope Commitment
Focus on the performance of the individual	**Presencing**—being in the moment with the other and knowing what is needed of oneself in the situation		
Focus on building self-belief	**Nurturing**—developing the other's confidence; helping the other to see how they can produce change through their actions		
Focus on awareness and responsibility	**Committing**—promoting the development of self-awareness and responsibility for the broader organisational project		

Table 7.3 Data collection

Pseudonym	Position	Duration (min)	Date
Initial project scope meeting			
Sandra	Deputy executive officer	90	21.10.15
David	Group chief executive officer		
Interviews			
Anne	Client services	120	14.03.16
Winston	Manager	30	28.09.16
Mary	Manager	60	15.03.16
Jackie	Director of organisational transformation	60	15.03.16
Evan	Manager strategic organisational development	60	16.03.16
Neil	Consultant	60	15.03.16
Kevin	Client service strategic organisational development	60	14.03.16
Emma	Consultant	90	14.03.16
Thomas	Manager	75	15.03.16
Ivan	Team leader	60	16.03.16
Adeena	Services manager	35	28.09.16
Nadia	Officer	70	28.09.16
Will	Health and safety	60	16.03.16
Noel	Team leader	75	6.11.16
Andrew	Director	60	15.03.16
Alison	Deputy solicitor	45	15.03.17
Alex	Project manager	50	13.11.17
Sandra	Deputy executive officer	60	13.11.17
Evan	Manager	60	13.11.17
Jackie	Director of people and risk	60	14.11.17
Patrick	MD, building company	90	14.11.17
Maurice	Group head of risk and governance	50	14.11.17
Greg	Assistant director, people	70	14.11.17
Jamie	Head of business solutions	60	15.11.17
David	Group chief executive officer	60	15.11.17
Adam	Officer	30	14.11.17
Shadowing			
Sally	Manager	120	16.03.16
Niall	Manager	90	16.03.16
Brian	Surveyor	90	15.03.16
Feedback session			
David and Sandra		100	27.06.16
Board of NHG		60	30.09.16

References

Athanasopoulou, A., & Dopson, S. (2018). A systematic review of executive coaching outcomes: Is it the journey or the destination that matters the most? *The Leadership Quarterly*.

Bluckert, P. (2006). *Psychological dimensions of executive coaching*. UK: McGraw-Hill Education.

Bluckert, P. (2016). *Presence and the intentional use of self as instrument of change*. UK: Peter Bluckert Consulting.

Clutterbuck, D., & Megginson, D. (2005). *Making coaching work: Creating a coaching culture*. CIPD Publishing.

Clutterbuck, D., & Megginson, D. (2011). Coach maturity: An emerging concept. *The handbook of knowledge-based coaching: From theory to practice*. London: Wiley.

Clutterbuck, D., et al. (2016). *Building and sustaining a coaching culture*. London: Chartered Institute of Personnel and Development.

Crane, T. G., & Patrick, L. N. (2014). *The heart of coaching: Using transformational coaching to create a high-performance coaching culture*. FTA press.

Evered, R. D., & Selman, J. C. (1989). Coaching and the art of management. *Organizational Dynamics, 18*(2), 16–32.

Feldman, D. C., & Lankau, M. J. (2005). Executive coaching: A review and agenda for future research. *Journal of Management, 31*(6), 829–848.

Gallwey, W. T. (1972). *The inner game of tennis: The classic guide to the mental side of peak performance*. Macmillan.

Garvey, B., Garvey, R., Stokes, P., & Megginson, D. (2017). *Coaching and mentoring: Theory and practice*. London: Sage.

Gormley, H., & van Nieuwerburgh, C. (2014). Developing coaching cultures: A review of the literature. *Coaching: An International Journal of Theory, Research and Practice, 7*(2), 90–101.

Grant, A. M., Passmore, J., Cavanagh, M. J., & Parker, H. M. (2010). 4 The state of play in coaching today: A comprehensive review of the Field. *International review of industrial and organizational psychology, 25*(1), 125–167.

Hague, H. (1978). *The organic organisation and how to manage it*. Wiley.

Kampa-Kokesch, S., & Anderson, M. Z. (2001). Executive coaching: A comprehensive review of the literature. *Consulting Psychology Journal: Practice and Research, 53*(4), 205.

Kanter, R. M. (1984). *Change masters*. Simon and Schuster.

Maslow, A. H. (1943). A theory of human motivation. *Psychological Review, 50*(4), 370.

Mintzberg, H. (2009). *Managing*. Berrett-Koehler Publishers.

Passmore, J., & Fillery-Travis, A. (2011). A critical review of executive coaching research: A decade of progress and what's to come. *Coaching: An International Journal of Theory, Research and Practice, 4*(2), 70–88.

Reckwitz, A. (2002). Toward a theory of social practices: A development in culturalist theorizing. *European Journal of Social Theory, 5*(2), 243–263.

Rogers, C. R. (1951). *Client-centered therapy: Its current practice, implications, and theory*. Houghton Mifflin.

Rogers, C. R. (1957). The necessary and sufficient conditions of therapeutic personality change. *Journal of Consulting Psychology, 21*(2), 95.

Spinosa, C., Flores, F., & Dreyfus H. L. (1999). *Disclosing new worlds: Entrepreneurship, democratic action, and the cultivation of solidarity*. Cambridge MA: MIT Press.

Part II
Digital Networks and Inter-Organisational Collaboration

Chapter 8
Citizens' Cooperation in the Reuse of Their Personal Data: The Case of Data Cooperatives in Healthcare

Joan Rodon Mòdol

Introduction

Over the last few decades, healthcare public agencies, public and private insurers, and care providers have heavily invested in digital infrastructures to integrate existing data silos and support the administrative and clinical processes for the delivery of health services (Aanestad, Grisot, Hanseth, & Vassilakopoulou, 2017). The advent of big data analytics however, has created new opportunities for the repurposing and reuse of the data stored in those infrastructures that are socially and economically desirable (Geissbuhler et al., 2013). Big data analytics is expected to have a transformative effect on how healthcare is delivered and consumed, on the management of health services, and on how health research is conducted (Raghupathi & Raghupathi, 2014). Realizing these outcomes requires the collaboration among stakeholders in the health data ecosystem (Vayena, Dzenowagis, & Langfeld, 2016) in order to liberate and share the data beyond the organizational boundaries.

Although these data-sharing agreements have a great potential, several cases have been controversial, faced serious opposition, and failed to win the public's trust. For instance, on May 2017 a leaked letter from the National Data Guardian at the UK Department of Health revealed that DeepMind, Google's artificial intelligence company, obtained the personal medical records of 1.6 million patients on an inappropriate legal basis, meaning that the patient record transfer was not for direct care (Martin, 2017). The Royal Free Hospital Trust in London had shared those patient records with DeepMind in order to test Streams, a mobile app to help clinicians manage acute kidney injury that both organizations were working on. Yet it seems difficult to sustain that the data was shared for direct care since a sizable chunk of the data being shared belonged to patients who were never treated for kidney injury (Powles & Hodson, 2017). On July 2017, the Information Commissioner's Office

J. R. Mòdol (✉)
ESADE Business School, Barcelona, Spain
e-mail: joan.rodon@esade.edu

© Springer International Publishing AG, part of Springer Nature 2019   159
K. Riemer et al. (eds.), *Collaboration in the Digital Age*, Progress in IS,
https://doi.org/10.1007/978-3-319-94487-6_8

clarified that the Royal Free Hospital failed to comply with the Data Protection Act when it provided patient details to DeepMind (Hern, 2017). The transfer of data was made without patients being adequately informed and in the absence of their explicit consent.

This incident resonates with the logic of surveillance capitalism (Zuboff, 2015) in which public and private organizations extract and accumulate citizens' personal data and control the means of analyzing and deriving value from it, sometimes invisibly. Zuboff further warns that those data-driven organizations become increasingly disentangled from the data subjects they profess to serve. Overall, surveillance capitalism describes a world "in which those who have a right to privacy – individuals – do not have it while those who should be transparent – corporations and democratic governments – do" (Balkan, 2017). That is, the rights about the access and reuse of personal data are unevenly distributed among three main stakeholders: organizations that collect and store data to deliver healthcare services, organizations that reuse the data for research and/or commercial purposes, and the subjects of data. In particular, data subjects have little control over the access of their personal data by third-party organizations and the appropriation of the value from data reuse.

This chapter advocates for the search of new forms of organizing the sharing and reuse of personal data that guarantee that data subjects have a say over how their personal data is reused. One of those forms is data cooperatives (DC). DCs represent a new logic of cooperation between citizens (the member of the cooperative) who voluntary pool their personal data and organize to release it to third parties who will generate value from reusing that data. Members of the DC also have a say in the type of services developed and analysis done with their data, and keep some of the value that is created from reusing their data. So DCs is about shared and collaborative governance of personal data reuse. This chapter studies the working of DCs by addressing the following research questions: What problems do DCs solve? How do DCs function? What are the challenges of DCs?. We address these questions with a revelatory case study (Yin 2009) about MiData.coop, a healthcare DC in Switzerland. Our findings show how DCs are a new model of shared governance that balances the power relationship between those who consume personal data and the subjects of that data, and creates new forms of reciprocity between both sides.

In the next section, we present the central concepts, the main theoretical perspectives, and propose a framework to study DCs. Next, we introduce our research setting and overall research approach. Section 4 presents the findings of the case study. Finally, we discuss the implications of our findings for the literature.

Conceptual Background

Reusing Personal Health Data

Under the current EU regulation (GDPR, 2016) the notion of personal health data (PHD) "means any information relating to an identified or identifiable natural person ('data subject')"[1] (Art 4 (1)) that relates to "the physical or mental health of a natural person, including the provision of health care services, which reveal information about his or her health status" (Art 5 (15)). In the face of the developments of big data technologies, this definition of PHD is all-encompassing, leaving us to conclude that apparently non-personal data (e.g., data such as an address that apparently does not identify an individual) and non-health data (e.g., socio-economic data of an individual) can be re-identified by assembling disparate sets of data and hence, turn out to be PHD (Purtova, 2017; Vayena et al., 2016).

We must distinguish two purposes of PHD reuse: primary and secondary. When the PHD comes into the health system from the citizen or from other sources on the citizen's behalf for direct health care delivery, then we speak of 'primary uses of data'. These include: (1) clinician-reported data (generated from clinical encounters) which is stored in hospital, regional and national IT systems; and (2) citizen-reported data through wearables, smart-sensing and biometric devices (automated data), and through mobile apps and social media (volunteered data) that can be stored in a device owned by the citizen and/or stored by the health service provider. 'Secondary use of PHD' refers to the use of PHD for purposes other than direct care—e.g., research, quality and safety measurement, performance monitoring, public health, commercial activities. We use the term PHD reuse to refer to the secondary use of data.[2]

From an economic perspective (Frischmann, 2005), PHD shares key attributes with infrastructural resources and that qualifies PHD for special management in the public interest. PHD satisfies the three criteria of infrastructural resources: non-rivalrous good, intermediary good and general-purpose input (Frischmann, 2005). First, PHD is a resource that may be consumed non-rivalrously or partially non-rivalrously; that is, it can be consumed by multiple users and an unlimited number of times. Non-rivalrous consumption describes the degree to which the consumption of a resource affects (or does not affect) the potential of the resource to meet the demands of others. It thus reflects the marginal cost of allowing an additional consumer of the good. Second, PHD is an intermediary good (i.e., a good that is used as input to produce other goods) that creates social value when used productively downstream (i.e., PHD is used as an input resource by downstream activities such health research,

---

[1] "An identifiable natural person is one who can be identified, directly or indirectly, in particular by reference to an identifier such as a name, an identification number, location data, an online identifier or to one or more factors specific to the physical, physiological, genetic, mental, economic, cultural or social identity of that natural person" (Article 4 (1)).

[2] For a taxonomy of data reuse see Custers and Ursic (2016).

personalized medicine,[3] other health innovations), particularly in its aggregated form (e.g., to do predictive analytics at the population level). Third, PHD may be used as an input into a wide range of goods and services, including private goods, public goods and/or non–market goods, many of which cannot be devised during the generation of the PHD.

Frischmann (2005) claims that it is desirable to manage and sustain an infrastructural resource (in our case PHD) based on a non-restrictive open access regime; that is, the "resource is openly accessible to all within a community regardless of the entity's identity or intended use" (p. 921). Doing so can harness a wide range of innovations (OECD, 2015). In that vein, sharing PHD in order to reuse it is desirable because it can be economically and socially beneficial. Achieving those benefits is contingent on a number of aspects. This paper studies two important particular aspects: considerations bearing on the nature of the resource, and the way PHD reuse is organized. With regard to the nature of the resource, the reuse of personal data to advance research or the management of healthcare services requires huge amounts of data be linked and jointly analyzed. In particular, the value of PHD lies in its aggregation (i.e., having access to data from multiple individuals) and linkage[4] (i.e., combining and interlinking multiple data streams of each individual). The higher the degree of aggregation and linkage, the greater the value of PHD reuse. Next section develops the second aspect: the way PHD reuse is organized.

Organizing the Reuse of PHD

The reuse of PHD involves at least three main groups of actors. First, there are the data holders who manage and own the infrastructures that store the PHD. Data holders are also responsible for the security measures to protect the PHD. Second, there are the data subjects who are the persons on whom PHD is collected, held or processed. Data subjects sometimes also act as data holders when for instance they collect data through wearables and store that data in their own devices. Third, there are the data consumers who are interested in having access to the data and use it as an input for a variety of purposes.

In the literature we identify three main approaches for organizing PHD reuse (see Table 8.1 for a summary of the three approaches). Next we compare and present these approaches based on (1) who is the data holder and the data consumer; (2) who decides about the rules of access and use (which subsets of PHD can be accessed

---

[3]The Council of the EU defines personalized medicine as "a medical model using characterization of individuals' phenotypes and genotypes (e.g. molecular profiling, medical imaging, lifestyle data) for tailoring the right therapeutic strategy for the right person at the right time, and/or to determine the predisposition to disease and/or to deliver timely and targeted prevention." (EU 2017). Related terms that are also used: precision, stratified, or individualized medicine.

[4]Günther et al. (2017) use the term interconnectivity to refer to "the possibility to synthesize data" from various data streams. Given the technological connotation of the term interconnectivity we choose the term linkage.

Table 8.1 Summary of the three approaches to PHD reuse

	Healthcare system-centric approach	For-profit data-driven approach	Individual-centric approach
Data holder	Public agency, health provider	For-profit data-driven company	Private business, public agency, the same individual (data subject)
Data consumer	Public agency, health provider, research institution (usually for non-commercial purposes)	For-profit data-driven company, or other consumers (mainly for commercial purposes)	Public agency and research institution, for-profit data-driven company (for commercial and non-commercial purposes)
Control over the rules of access and use of PHD	Data holder (implied consent from data subjects when reuse for care purposes)	Data holder (the consent of data subjects is neglected or forced)	Data subject and data holder (depending on conditions of the contract between data holder and data subject). Individual granular consent
Control over the appropriation of the outcomes of PHD reuse	Data holder, data consumer	Data consumer	Data subject and data consumer (depending on conditions of the contract between data consumer and data subject)
Aggregation	High (depending on the scale of operations of the public agency or health provider)	High (depending on the scale of operations of data-driven company)	Low/Medium (difficult to mobilize a critical mass of data subjects to share their PHD)
Linkage	Medium (limited to medical data)	Medium (limited to the personal data that controls the for-profit data-driven company)	High (the data subject is the only one who has all her/his data and hence s/he becomes the integration point)

and reused, who can reuse PHD, under what conditions, and for what purposes); (3) who controls the appropriation of the outcomes of PHD reuse[5]; and (4) the degree of aggregation and linkage of PHD.

We identify a first approach in the context of national healthcare in Australia (Pearce & Bainbridge, 2014), Canada (Gagnon et al., 2016), Europe (Aanestad et al., 2017), and US (Shapiro, Mostashari, Hripcsak, Soulakis, & Kuperman, 2011) where

---

[5]We distinguish two types of outcomes of PHD reuse: knowledge outcomes (e.g., findings from the research), and economic outcomes (e.g., generated by data consumers).

public agencies and health providers have traditionally acted as data holders and data consumers operating at local, regional, state or national scales. These organizations independently or collaboratively have built digital infrastructures to gather and store PHD[6] and share it among healthcare professionals to coordinate the provision of care. Later, the PHD stored in those infrastructures is also used for analytical purposes to improve the management of healthcare at the individual and population levels and for research purposes (Kostkova et al., 2016). This approach has some limitations. For instance, as argued in the section above, the boundaries of PHD are not clear since non-health data can become relevant for health research. Therefore, this approach seems insufficient because those infrastructures are designed to gather and store mainly medical data, while other kind of personal data (e.g., genomic, nutrition, sleep data, socioeconomic) remains under the control of other organizations. Second, data subjects are considered to have given their consent (implied consent) when the PHD is shared for the purpose of direct care. Hence, data subjects are not usually engaged in and aware of the reuse of their PHD. Third, because data curation and analysis have a significant cost and require skills that are scarce, public agencies have increasingly outsourced those data services to for-profit data-driven organizations on a competitive basis. When that happens, a for-profit organization which usually does not provide a health service has access to the PHD. In short, although public agencies are supposed to act as reliable trustees of citizens' PHD, these public-private deals are claimed to pose a threat to citizens' privacy, promote private interests and facilitate the privatization of public services (Aitken et al., 2016; Kostkova et al., 2016).

In the second approach to PHD reuse, the data holder is a for-profit data-driven company that either provides some (either health or non-health related) direct service to data subjects (citizens) in exchange of generating and collecting their personal data[7] or gets the data from third-parties (e.g., hospital, pharmacists) that provide health-related services to the data subjects—what Tanner (2016) calls data brokers.[8] Then the same data holder processes the collected data to enrich, cleanse and consume it, or bundle and sell it to another data consumer. This approach is problematic in three main ways. First, this approach exhibits limited linkage as these organizations extract and have access to a specific subset of the data subjects' personal data.[9] That is, all the personal data of an individual is scattered and fragmented across multiple data-driven companies. Moreover, since a great deal of the business model of these companies relies on extraction and analysis of personal data, they have no interest in sharing it with other data consumers—in fact, quite the opposite since companies compete for control over personal data (Srnicek, 2016). Accordingly, in this PHD reuse approach, personal data can turn into a rivalrous, excludable

---

[6]Those infrastructures adopt either a centralized (i.e., a single, shared repository for the data) or a federated (i.e., data is distributed, remaining at their source, and is accessed on demand when needed) model.

[7]e.g., 23andMe, FitBit, Microsoft HealthVault, Google, Apple.

[8]e.g., IQVia, Symphony Health.

[9]Each data-driven organization extracts and controls PHD around the service it provides, but does not have access to other subsets of PHD tied to services provided by other data-driven organizations.

resource. Once a data-driven organization has control over a personal data set, it has the power to exclude other data-driven organizations from using that data set. Hence, different data-driven organizations do not have the same freedom to access vis-à-vis the data set. This restrictive access regime undermines the potential of PHD reuse. Second, data extraction is characterized by the absence of reciprocity between data consumers and data subjects (Zuboff, 2015). Data holders and data consumers treat data subjects as passive agents whose consent is either neglected or forced with no opt-out clauses, and who do not benefit from the outcomes of reusing their personal data (Tanner, 2016). Third, certain uses of big data technologies are subject to negative externalities, for instance, to re-identify anonymized data of individuals thereby eroding their privacy, to link unrelated data from different subjects and know more about a subject for which data was not directly gathered (Tanner, 2017). These negative externalities undermine data subjects' trust in those for-profit data-driven companies. Although these negative externalities can also be present in the healthcare system-centric approach, we consider that it becomes more relevant in the for-profit data-driven approach because the business model of these companies is built around the exploitation of personal data.

Overall, in these two PHD reuse approaches, the allocation of power to decide who has access to the PHD and who can appropriate the outcomes of PHD reuse is asymmetric. Data subjects have little control over the access to their PHD by down-stream activities (e.g., research, innovation in new services), and the appropriation of the outcomes of those activities is unbalanced in favor of data consumers rather than data subjects. Therefore, a way to counteract these asymmetries would be to give data subjects greater control over their PHD. Against this backdrop, and aiming to protect citizens' privacy and hence, break the power imbalance between citizens (as data subjects) on the one hand and data holders and consumers on the other hand, the EU General Data Protection Regulation (GDPR, 2016), which comes into force in May 2018, provides citizens with certain rights:

- Right to access one's own personal data (Article 15).
- Right to data portability/to transfer one's data from one data holder to another. The "data subject shall have the right to receive the personal data concerning him or her, which he or she has provided to a controller, in a structured, commonly-used and machine-readable format and have the right to transmit those data to another controller without hindrance from the controller to which the personal data have been provided." (Article 20).
- Right to be forgotten, that is, to have one's data erased (Article 17).
- Right to be informed/transparency. Data holders have to provide some information in a concise, transparent, intelligible and easily accessible form, using clear and plain language (Article 13 and 14).
- Right to consent. Consent "should be given by a clear affirmative act establishing a freely given, specific, informed and unambiguous consent indication of the data subject's agreement to processing of personal data relating to him or her, such as by

a written statement, including by electronic means, or an oral statement" (Recital 32). Silence or inactivity (e.g., a pre-ticketed check box in a form) cannot be considered as consent. Data subjects can always withdraw their consent (Article 7).

A first straight implementation of this EU regulation leads to an approach to PHD reuse in which citizens themselves have a say over the reuse of their PHD on an individual basis[10] (Abiteboul, André, & Kaplan, 2015; Haug, 2017; Simonite, 2014). This approach adopts a "you are on your own" scheme based on individual rights with individual control and management over PHD. In this approach, PHD reuse relies on a granular individual consent of data subjects. We distinguish two different architectures of this individual-centric approach (Sjöberg et al., 2017). A first architecture focuses on storage, meaning that all the personal data of a subject is centralized in a single repository. In the second architecture, the data subject's personal data remains scattered in different sources which are federated; the system then manages the flows of personal data between those scattered sources and the data consumers. Although this individual-centric approach enables data subjects to take back control over their PHD by turning them into integration points, and increase their awareness, we consider it has two major constraints. First, it seems a daunting task to manage and exercise those rights on an individual basis; for instance, an average person may be unable to understand the content of consent forms, which are often designed to shield organizations from liability instead of truly informing individuals, or to comprehend the terms and implications of data reuse. Second, dispersion of individuals using diverse technological solutions to store their PHD sometimes using different meta-data makes it complex and expensive for data consumers to reach and mobilize a sufficient amount of individual data subjects to release their PHD. Therefore, the individual-centric approach to PHD reuse undermines the quality of data available for data consumers. In short, the individual-centric approach addresses the problem of the asymmetric power relationship between data consumers and data subjects by giving the latter more control over their data—i.e., the data subject is the major locus of control for disclosing personal data. Yet, the individual-centric approach to PHD reuse can be worthless for data consumers and research in general due to the complexity of mobilizing a critical mass of individuals to share their PHD (limited aggregation).

To sum up, the first two approaches to PHD reuse are governed in a centralized form, and structure the role of data subjects as highly passive. This happens as the control over data subjects' PHD and the means of collecting, analyzing and deriving value from it are in the hands of organizations that are not always accountable to the data subjects and whose objectives sometimes clash with the interests of data subjects. Moreover, when PHD reuse is governed by for-profit data-driven companies it is likely that other organizations will be excluded, and that in turn, will limit the potential of downstream activities using that PHD—because of the limited linkage. On the other hand, when PHD reuse is controlled in a decentralized form by the

---

[10]e.g., Digi.me (www.digi.me), Blue Button (bluebuttonconnector.healthit.gov), Datacoup (www.datacoup.com), CitizenMe (www.citizenme.com), Meeco (www.meeco.me), and Dime (www.dataisme.com).

same data subjects on an individual basis (individual-centric approach), what is put at risk is the reliability of PHD reuse due to the limited aggregation and hence the value of the downstream activities using the PHD. Therefore, the challenge is how to guarantee that data subjects have a real say over how their PHD is reused while at the same time ensuring high aggregation (that is to say, that data consumers see value in reusing that PHD as an input to other activities). An emergent approach of PHD reuse that addresses this challenge is that of data cooperatives (Evans, 2017; Hafen, Kossmann, & Brand, 2014; Vayena & Gasser, 2016).

Data Cooperatives

The International Co-operative Alliance defines a cooperative as "an autonomous association of persons united voluntarily to meet their common economic, social, and cultural needs and aspirations through a jointly owned and democratically-controlled enterprise" (ICA, 2017). According to the ICA (2017) cooperatives operate according to seven principles: voluntary and open membership; democratic member control; members' economic participation; autonomy and independence; education, training and information; cooperation among cooperatives; and concern for community.

Data cooperatives (DCs) have emerged alongside the platform cooperativism movement (Scholz & Schneider, 2016) in response to private, for-profit digital platforms with the pretext of providing services at no cost to users, they have unrestricted access and monetize those same users' personal data (Srnicek, 2016).[11] Platform cooperativism sustains that "the digital 'means of production', the platform, should be owned by, governed by and should enrich the participating value creators" (PlatformCoop, 2017). In that respect, DCs emerge to "rebalance the relationship between those that create data and those that seek to exploit it whilst also creating the environment for fair and consensual exchange" (DataCoop, 2017). This is expected to empower data subjects by engaging them in decisions about the reuse of their personal data, and at the same time to diminish the power of exclusion by for-profit data consumers of the data against other data consumers.

Accordingly, we define an DC as a digital platform centered on data subjects who pool their PHD, designed for secondary use of their PHD, and sustained by cooperative governance. As a digital platform (Parker, Van Alstyne, & Choudary, 2016; Srnicek, 2016), an DC enables two or more groups (or sides) of users to interact: at least, data subjects who populate the DC with personal data on the one hand, and data consumers who offer services for data subjects and generate funds on the other hand. Moreover, DCs rely on network effects—e.g., the more data subjects pool their personal data in the DC, the more attractive the DC becomes for data consumers. Literature suggests that the study of the working of digital platform ecosystems requires bearing in mind two mutually reinforcing elements, the technological architecture

---

[11]Of course this paper does not presuppose that all for-profit digital platforms are extractive.

and governance: "the architecture of a platform is inseparable from how it ought to be governed" (Tiwana, 2014, p. xv).

Architecture refers to the description of the technical components, their function (i.e., what they do), and how they are arranged and interact to provide the overall functionality of the DC (Tiwana, 2014). The architecture of a DC is not a clone of the architecture of infrastructures under the healthcare system-centric, for-profit data-driven, or citizen-centric approaches. It entails differences in the design of at least, four core groups of functionalities: capture (ingest), storage, management & access, and analysis. Hafen et al. (2014) suggest that to support these functionalities DCs have three central architectural components. First, a 'core database' that allows to capture and integrate data from multiple sources, store it in different formats, and manage its access. Second, an "app store to provide applications and visualizations for citizens of their data" (p. 3). To integrate and visualize data from different sources, each record is associated with an app that defines the structure, visualization and mapping of data items. Third, big data analytics components to carry large-scale analytics on all the data stored in the database.

Governance broadly refers to the set of rules, structures and mechanisms that drive how the authority and responsibility for DC decisions are divided between the different sides (Tiwana, 2014). Considering that we study the governance of DCs (as an approach to personal data reuse), we focus on the following decisions: who can reuse data, under what conditions, and for what purposes, and who can appropriate the outcomes of reuse. Moreover, since the governance of DCs involves the cooperation of their members, we draw upon ideas from commons literature (Benkler, 2003; Frischmann, Madison, & Strandburg, 2014; Hess & Ostrom, 2007). Commons broadly refers to "a particular type of institutional arrangement for governing the use and disposition of resources. Their salient characteristic, which defines them in contradistinction to property, is that no single person has exclusive control over the use and disposition of any particular resource. Instead, resources governed by commons may be used or disposed of by anyone among some (more or less well defined) number of persons, under rules that may range from 'anything goes' to quite crisply articulated formal rules that are effectively enforced." (Benkler, 2003; p. 6). The hallmark of commons is "freedom-to-operate under symmetric constraints, available to an open, or undefined, class of users" (Benkler, 2014; p. 71).

Hess and Ostrom (2007) point out that "self-organized commons require strong collective-action and self-governing mechanisms, as well as high degree of social capital on the part of stakeholders" (p. 5). Collective-action means that the functioning of the commons demands the voluntary participation of all its members to achieve a shared goal. Self-governance means that the collective action requires knowledge and will of members and at the same time a consistent institutional arrangement. Finally, social capital refers to the existence of norms of reciprocity between the members of the commons. Frischmann et al. (2014) propose a framework to study the institutional details and the governance mechanisms of knowledge commons that involves a set of interlinked components such as a resource or set of resources, the community of actors that produces and shares the set of resources, the structures and rules that govern the community interactions, and the outcomes resulting from those interactions that feedback to the resource.

To study the functioning of DCs we propose to focus on the interplay among architecture, governance structures (institutional setting, legal structures, mechanisms), and the rules and norms that regulate the interactions between members of the DC.

Research Method

We conducted a revelatory case study (Yin, 2009) about MiData.coop, a DC in Switzerland. Yin recommends this type of case study when it involves a novel situation and there are no theories to explain the phenomenon under research; hence our decision to adopt it for studying an DC such as MiData.coop. We briefly overview the research site before describing the data collection and analysis in the following section.

Site

The Data and Health[12] association was founded on July 2012 to analyze and discuss the scientific, ethical, societal, legal and political aspects of the use of personal health data for personal health and medical research in Switzerland, and at promoting the creation of a Swiss Health Data repository, which ended up as the MiData cooperative (MiData.coop) in 2015. MiData was founded as a cooperative because it allowed the value of exploiting PHD to be returned to data subjects and the community. As Ernst Hafen[13] notes, "This asset [PHD] should be back to society and that's why we came up with a cooperative model" [AVSrc6]. Moreover, Switzerland has a high penetration of cooperatives in terms of membership and employment[14] relative to the overall population (UN-Coops, 2014). Cooperative legislation can be found in specific chapters of The Civil Code.

MiData cooperative's mission is to enable "citizens to securely store, manage and control access to their health-related personal data by helping them to establish and own national/regional not-for-profit MIDATA cooperatives" (MiData.coop, 2017). MiData cooperative provides a citizen-centered data storage system with the idea of bringing PHD into one location and giving back the control of PHD to data subjects: "If users have a copy of their data, they will have the power. If this space is not occupied as a commons it will be privatized" [AVSrc6]. In that respect, on

---

[12]http://www.datenundgesundheit.ch/?lang=en.

[13]Ernst Hafen is the co-founder and president of the Board of MiData.coop, co-founder of the Data and Health association.

[14]Cooperatives are the largest private employer in Switzerland. Particularly, the two largest consumer co-operatives (Migros and Coop) are responsible for 8% of Switzerland's GDP (ICA, 2017).

the one hand, MiData promotes the digital self-determination[15] of the population by enabling citizens to use their PHD as self-determining agents and according to their wishes, in particular to support research purposes. On the other hand, MiData also promotes the collective interests of citizens and it enables the utilization of PHD as a common resource: "MiData's move is essentially to build the commons. Not only do we aggregate our data together but the for-profit companies licensing our data will be forced to return the product of their studies into the commons" [AVSrc6]. In short, MiData is about data subjects (users of MiData) taking control over their personal data and using it for their own benefit and for the benefit of the community and society as a whole.

Data Collection and Analysis

We collected qualitative data over 5 months: April–September 2017. We gathered these data from several sources (see Appendix 1): semi-structured interviews, internal documents, research articles about MiData (Hafen et al., 2014; Riso et al., 2017), videos, podcasts, and tweets. We used Twitter to obtain and analyze the events around MiData.coop. We followed the accounts of Midata.coop (@midata_coop) and some of its management (e.g., @ehafen, @SBignens, @UlrichGenick, @golliez), and searched for all the tweets that refer to those accounts. We studied MiData.coop covering the period 2014–September 2017.

We started analyzing all the data gathered and organized it chronologically. Next, we analyzed the data using the three elements of our framework: governance structures, rules and norms, and architecture. In order to identify and code each element in the data we used the operationalization presented in Table 8.2. The fact that we had started with a chronological analysis of events was useful at this stage of the analysis as it helped us understand the evolution of the governance structures, rules and architecture, and the challenges ahead (which are outlined in the discussion). Finally, we structured a narrative of the research findings around the elements in Table 8.2.

Research Findings

Overview of the DC

MiData involves several sides or types of roles (see Fig. 8.1). First, there are the account holders. MiData is available (open) to individuals domiciled in Switzerland who wish to become account holders. Registration and use of the platform is free of

---

[15]Digital self-determination broadly refers to the ability to shape who we are and protect our own identity (by for instance, controlling our personal data) in the digital world.

Table 8.2 Operationalization of the elements of the DC

General overview of the DC

- Who are the data holders, data subjects and data consumers of the DC?
- Who can become a data subject and data consumer of the DC? How (process, cost, etc.)?
- What is the core resource of the DC?
- Who can access and use the PHD? Under what conditions?
- Who are the developers of the DC?
- Who can contribute to the code/software?
- What are the data, service and financial flows of the DC?
- How do those flows interact?

Governance structures

- What structures has the DC in place?
- What is the role of each structure? What is being decided at each structure?
- Who is involved in each structure and in those decisions? (Who are the decision-makers and how they are selected?)
- What is the legal form of DC? What legal structures govern the DC?

Governance—rules and norms

- What are the membership rules? Does the DC have any code of conduct for data consumers, data subjects, developers?
- Does the DC have any mechanism of dispute/conflict resolution?
- What are the sanctions for rule violation?
- What is the relationship between developers and workers, developers and user subjects, developers and data consumers?
- What legal rules apply to what and informal norms govern the DC?
- How do non-members interact with the DC?

Architecture—functionalities

- How is PHD captured (ingested)?
- How is PHD stored? How are the databases of the DC structured? Where is PHD stored?
- How is PHD managed (authorization, access, and consent)? At what level is PHD managed?
- How is PHD analyzed?
- Which architectural components reflect/embed the governance structures, rules and norms?

Architecture—security

- How are PHD and other resources secured/protected?
- How is PHD anonymized?
- How is the privacy of citizens guaranteed?

Architecture—interfaces

- How does the DC interact with external (3rd-party) applications?
- Which APIs have been implemented? How have they evolved? Which APIs are planned in the future?
- Which data analytical technologies are used?

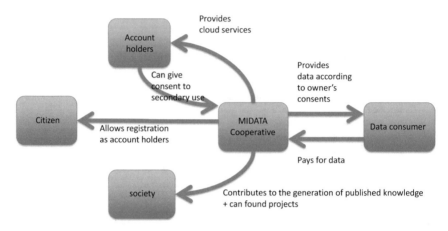

Fig. 8.1 MiData's flows (*Source* MiData)

charge for account holders. If an account holder wants to become a member, he/she has to subscribe for and buy one share certificate with a nominal value of CHF 40. Second, there is the MiData cooperative that gathers personal data from account holders and provides them with services developed on the platform (for instance tools for analyzing, visualizing and interpreting personal data). The cooperative acts as fiduciary of its members' PHD. Third, there are the data consumers (e.g., research organizations, healthcare providers) who receive the personal data from MiData once it gets the explicit consent from account holders. Moreover, the MiData cooperative decides whether a data consumer has to pay for the PHD, and whether that data consumer has to give back the results from reusing that PHD; accordingly, those results can then be given back to the community (for example in the form of new knowledge).

Another side is those who develop the core and interfaces of the platform. A team led by Donald Kossmann (from ETH Zurich Systems Group) started the design of the architecture and the basic development of the MiData platform in 2014. Later in 2015, a team led by Serge Bignens (from the Bern University of Applied Sciences) carried out a functional development and a GUI redesign. The first pilot project on the MiData platform started on May 2016. From then and until June 2017, MiData piloted over 14 uses cases (e.g., mobility and outcome measure after bariatric surgery; tests for the capabilities of multiple sclerosis patients; drug rehab program; recovery between chemotherapies; physiotherapy exercise monitoring; hypertension prevalence in low income countries; secure communication between patient and physician; citizen science for base line measure of personal glycemic Index; self-monitoring of lungs function for COPD Patient; or pain self-monitoring). MiData has gone live in the third quarter of 2017. The development of those use cases involved third-party developers who are part of the data consumers. A third-party developer needs an account at MiData in order to register new plugins or mobile apps and manage them [WSrc14].

The core resource of MiData.coop is the personal data of account holders. Since all citizens have personal data (e.g., we all have the same amount of genomic data), they all can contribute equitably to the commons. Personal data of an account holder is accessible to anyone to whom the account holder grants access. Account holders decide individually about sharing their PHD (or specific subsets of their PHD) with other account holders, MiData, or third parties (for scientific research or personalized services). Therefore, the access to an account holder's PHD requires the explicit and informed consent of the latter [WSrc12].

Another important resource of the platform is its code. The code is open-source software and is available at open-source platform GitHub.[16] The reasons for being open-source are transparency and replicability. On the one hand, people need to trust the software, so there is a need to be transparent about how it works. On the other hand, open-source also enables growth and replicability of MiData. MiData aims to foster the development of an ecosystem in which third parties can offer data-based services to account holders, and open-source is expected to help this ecosystem grow—i.e., to help 3rd-parties develop apps for MiData. Growth can also come from the replication of MiData in other national contexts. This relates to another of MiData's objectives that is to support cooperatives of equal purpose and to form a federation of cooperatives.[17] For this purpose, the code is released open-source and licensed for-free to other DCs having the same mission. The corresponding license is not exclusive, non-transferable and revocable at any time. Any interference with the source code of the platform, any decompilation and/or modification of the software as well as any commercial use is forbidden [WSrc13].

Governance

Structures

MiData structure comprises four governing bodies [WSrc11]: General Assembly, Board of Directors, the Data Ethics Review Board, and the Auditors. The General Assembly is the supreme body of the Cooperative, and has the legal powers to: determine and change the articles of association; elect and release the members of the Board of Directors and Auditors; approve annual financial statements and associated management reports, and to pass resolutions on the use of the net profit; grant discharge to the members of the Board of Directors; decide the dissolution or merger of the cooperative; and decide about the appeal of expelled members. Every member has one vote in the General Assembly.

---

[16]The prototype source course is available at https://github.com/amarfurt/hdc, https://github.com/i4mi/midata.js, https://github.com/SebastianHaag/midata.coop.

[17]In 2017 MiData was working with partners in Germany (Charité and Berlin Institute of Health), the Netherlands (Medical Delta, TNO) and in collaboration with INDEPTH-Network.org in Ethiopia and Vietnam.

The Board of Directors has the following powers: supervision of management (in particular regarding its compliance with laws, the articles of association and relevant regulations) and leadership of the Cooperative; determination of the organization of the Cooperative; determination regarding the conditions of value creation by secondary use of the data of the account holders; exclusion of members and update of the member register; and resolution on recommendations by the Data Ethics Review Board.

Finally, the Data Ethics Review Board has two main functions: (1) to review the ethical quality of the services (e.g., 3rd-party apps) and research projects and make recommendations to the Board of Directors based on this review; (2) to review the ethical quality of the consent agreement template documents associated with the services and research projects and to make recommendations to the Board of Directors based on this review. Resolutions of the Data Ethics Review Board have to be passed by an absolute majority.

Rules and Norms

Account holders can export their PHD from MiData in a documented data format, delete all their PHD from MiData, and delete their account [WSrc12]. In order to avoid individual financial incentives, MiData does not provide services that allow account holders to individually sell access to their PHD to third parties and individuals discounts based on the account holders' data sharing behavior are forbidden [WSrc11].

MIDATA pursues a not-for-profit business model that neither provides financial incentives for data sharing nor pays dividends to its members. "Those companies who do seek out the information held by MiData cooperative will serve as the cooperative's source of funding, paying a fee to use the data in their research. Revenues collected will be used to pay for administrative overhead, and any leftover profits will be invested under the guiding hand of the cooperative's General Assembly made up of its members" [AVSrc6]. According to MiData's bylaws, the profits from the "sale" of the PHD cannot be redistributed to the stakeholders in the form of dividend but "revenues will be reinvested into services on the platform and into research projects for the benefit of society" (MiData.coop, 2017). Accordingly, the benefit is achieved for the collective.

Regarding the legal rules, MiData and its users[18] are subject to the Swiss Data Protection Act. Moreover, the Data and Health association [WSrc1][19] has been working to include the 'right to a copy' (which refers to "each person having the right to receive a digital copy of their personal data in an adequate form… The person itself can decide about any further user of his/her data (secondary use)") as a constitutional right in Switzerland. Accordingly, the 'right to a copy' is not about the government protecting user personal data but about giving the individuals freedom to access their

---

[18]User must comply with the Swiss Data Protection Act with regard to data from other users.

[19]Newsletter #5, February 2 2017.

personal data, give it to a cooperative such as MiData that provides an ecosystem to use that data, and become a member and participate of the governance of that cooperative.

Architecture

The design and management of the platform followed four principles. First, transparency in the sense that the core and the apps for visualization and analysis are open-source. Second, portability as the components of the platform are distributed under a public license making the platform easy to clone (https://libraries.io/github/amarfurt/hdc). Third, anyone can contribute with new apps and visualization tools. Fourth, the platform runs in the cloud and the maintenance and operation of the hardware platform is outsourced. As Donald Kossmann notes, "it only makes sense to operate in the cloud because the data volumes are just too big… [particularly] if you have genome data" [AVSrc7].

The general architecture of MiData platform (see Fig. 8.2) separates the core of the platform comprising the functionalities of storage, access and consent management from the periphery where there are the applications. Data is generated in and captured from mobile apps (e.g., EVOLI, MIWADO 2.0, GlucoMan, MIMOTI, eMMA), the patient and health professional portal, and external data servers (e.g. EHR of a provider). Mobile and external apps interact with MiData through a version of the FHIR API[20] and/or the MIDATA API. Developers can also create plug-ins that run in the browser and have read and write access to a set of records.

With regard to storage, MiData uses a flat database based on records of any kind of data.[21] The core of the system understands very little about the semantics of the data; the data is managed with very few meta-data (e.g., timestamp, app that generated the record, version of that app, user, and some other technical information). Initially designers considered adopting standards such as HL7[22] as a format for the data to be stored at MiData. Yet finally they decided to accept any data format (with some minimal meta-data) and let users and app developers decide which data they want to support. The core of the system provides an API so 3rd-parties can create new data source plug-ins. The idea is that the core handles the data storage and access controls, while applications run on top of the core to interpret the semantics of data (e.g., MIMOTI to assist patients after bariatric surgery, EVOLI to follow-up patients with

---

[20]FHIR API stands for Fast Healthcare Interoperability Resources API and is an API for exchanging electronic Health records. https://test.midata.coop/fhir.

[21]This includes many data types—for instance, the data types used in the use cases are: steps, weight, well-being, diary notes, cognition tests, hand-eye coordination, blood lab results, glycemic index, patient/physician communication, anxiety level, craving scale, therapies, lungs functions, glucose level, stress level, electro dermal activity, citizen self-reported drug consumption, genome genotyping, sensory perception, food intake, nutrition, metabolomics, sleep behavior and electrophysiology, and patient feedback.

[22]Health Level Seven International.

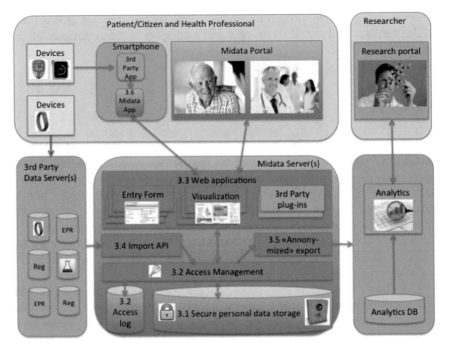

Fig. 8.2 Overall architecture (*Source* MiData)

leukemia, MIWADO to enable and record the patient-physician communication).
MiData management expects that by having a flat database that aggregates all sorts
of data streams and letting the applications interpret those data, they can build an app
marketplace where new applications (services) that combine different data streams
are developed. As Hafen notes, "What you will generate here is an entirely new
economy because you will now have start-ups that can develop apps that integrate
your shopping data with your genome and your fitness data… So you create new
data services on this personal data platform" [AVSrc6].

MiData platform also has a consent management functionality for the secondary
use of PHD, and functionalities to anonymize, aggregate and export for data analysis (see Fig. 8.2). Data is displayed through viewers specific for each data type.
Dashboards are made available with faceted views about for instance news, data,
coaching, running studies.

With regard to data security (see Fig. 8.3), records are stored without any refer-
ences to the data subject (i.e., the data that is stored has a minimum identification
of the data subject) and are encrypted. Those record encryption keys are stored in
access permission sets (another database) accessible only to account holders who
in turn, can share their access permissions sets with third parties. Therefore, no one

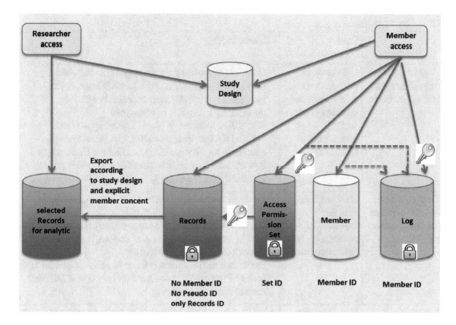

Fig. 8.3 Data storage and security (*Source* MiData)

can access and decrypt an account holder's PHD unless explicitly authorized by the account holder to do so. PHD is shared with third parties in an anonymized form.[23]

Discussion

The Functioning and Challenges of DCs

This paper empirically shows how in DCs data subjects pool their PHD and participate in decisions about the reuse of their PHD. In line with digital platforms literature (Tiwana 2014), we have shown that the functioning of DCs can be understood by looking at the interplay between architecture and governance (See Table 8.3). For instance, the capture and storage functionalities linked to the set of APIs that support the connection of 3rd-party apps, the centralized flat database that accepts many types and streams of data, the 'right to copy' that gives data subjects freedom to access their personal data, and the Board of Directors of MiData that determines the conditions of value creation of data consumers. Together, these elements support the aggregation of personal data from multiple subjects, and the linkage of different data

---

[23]Anonymized form refers to data that cannot without disproportionate effort, be traced to specific person [WSrc11].

Table 8.3 Case observations

	Data cooperatives	MiData findings
Control over the rules of access and use of PHD	Data subjects (either on an individual basis or through some sort of community structure)	• Data subjects when data sharing takes place on an individual basis; that is, each account holder gives individual consent to other account, health professionals, friends, relatives, etc. • When data is shared with and reused by research projects first the Board of Directors determines the conditions of value creation, second the Ethics Data Review which reviews the quality of research projects, and finally data subjects give their consent
Control over the appropriation of the outcomes of PHD reuse	Data subjects who are members of the cooperative (at a collective level)	• Partly at the Board of Directors when determines the conditions of value creation of data reuse, and at the General Assembly where each member has one vote to decides about the allocation of economic surplus (generated in research projects) • In the case of the citizen science initiative, there are new forms of reciprocity between data consumers and data subjects (account holders)
Aggregation	High/Medium (depending on the scale of operations of the cooperative)	• FHIR API and MIDATA API to boost an app ecosystem (apps use MiData as a repository) • Flat database • 'right to copy' • Open-source software (to enable growth through replicability) • Federation of MiData cooperatives
Linkage	High/Medium	• FHIR API and MIDATA API (the data subject being the integration point) • Flat database • 'right to copy'

streams (e.g., genome data, with physical activity, with medical records) of those data subjects.

Until now it seems MiData has been able to attract a critical mass of users on both sides (account holders on the one hand, and researchers on the other hand) and facilitate their interactions (Parker et al., 2016). This has happened by prioritizing applications for direct benefit of both groups of users. As Hafen notes, "the way we started is with specific applications targeted for people that give patients a direct benefit" [AVSrc6]. This is reflected in the 14 uses cases that have being piloted, in which MiData has been able to persuade healthcare providers and research organizations in order to develop applications that lead their patients to become account holders of MiData. With each new application, a new user community has enrolled MiData. Another example is the 'citizen science' initiative that provided a fun space for user engagement. As Ulrich Genick[24] notes, "One of the citizen science projects in which we are trying to use MiData is a project on the relationship between your genetics and your sensory perception. The idea is to get people involved in a fun way, so the data they have of themselves can be used in science and can really lead to new discoveries." [AVSrc6].

On the other hand, as noted in the case analysis, the design and operation of MiData has the following characteristics reflected in the governance structures and the architecture: transparency, participation, openness, and modularity. Although these characteristics are expected to encourage growth and scalability of MiData (Parker et al., 2016; Tiwana, 2014), they also pose some challenges that will require extending the existing governance structures, rules and architecture.

A first challenge refers to the tension between aggregation and linkage related to the choice of a flat database. The fact that MiData has a flat database avoids MiData designers having to work much on the semantics of data. Rather, it is the applications that store and retrieve the data the ones that define and interpret its format and meaning. In other words, MiData management opted for a design strategy in which there is a small common metadata at the core while allowing a wide variety of metadata at the user communities (Ure et al., 2009). This strategy accommodates the preferences of user communities and the speed of change thus favoring the aggregation of personal data. Yet, it also creates a situation in which the same data type has multiple formats (e.g., different apps can code blood pressure differently) and this limits the degree of linkage of PHD and hence future reuses of that data.

Another challenge refers to the interoperability across MiData cooperatives. MiData does not pretend to be a global aggregator rather it operates at the regional or national level. Geographical expansion will come through a federation of those regional/national cooperatives that will have a common technical infrastructure sponsored by MiData Switzerland. The idea then is that those regional/national cooperatives are going be interconnected and that will enable them to reach global issues (e.g., global research projects): "The MIDATA model enables the construction of regional/national cooperatives which, by a set of common rules, permit global research projects to be set up and carried out in a fair and democratic manner" (MiData.coop, 2017). However, that interconnection will require a kind of data exchange platform (or standard) which has not been conceived yet.

A third challenge is how to replicate the functioning of the governance structure of MiData Switzerland in other regional/national cooperatives operating in different institutional settings (with different regulatory framework, healthcare system, ethics, etc.), and how to create a new level of governance of the federation of cooperatives. Such a federation of cooperatives will involve new centers of decision-making which in turn, will require a new overarching set of rules (not already defined) to operate—e.g., participation, mutual monitoring, dispute resolution.

---

[24]Ulrich Genick is responsible for citizen science and a founding member of MiData.

DCs as an Alternative to PHD Reuse

This paper contends that DCs can be an alternative to the three dominant approaches to organizing PHD reuse found today (healthcare system-centric, for-profit data-driven, and individual-centric; see Table 8.1).[25] DCs have emerged to rebalance the existing asymmetric power relationships between those who consume personal data and the subjects of that data. These asymmetries are reflected in two aspects of the control over the organization of PHD reuse: who decides the rules of access and use (which subsets of PHD can be accessed and reused, by whom, under what conditions, and for what purposes), and control over the appropriation of the outcomes of PHD reuse (See Table 8.3).

We have argued that in the healthcare system-centric and for-profit data-driven approaches to PHD reuse there is a monocentric control that denies data subjects a voice. While decisions on the rules of access and use are made by data holders, data consumers control the appropriation of the outcomes of PHD reuse. In contrast, in DCs no single individual or organization has exclusive control over the use and disposition of all the PHD; rather control is spread among various actors and across levels. MiData is not governed by an influential state or non-state actors—which is the case of healthcare system-centric or for-profit data-driven approaches; rather there is a combination of governance modes (Provan & Kevin, 2008). For instance, the rules of access and use of PHD are first centrally decided by the Board of Directors and the Data Ethics Review, and next data subjects self-govern in a decentralized way—each account holder of MiData decides whether she gives consent for the reuse of her PHD. On the other hand, the decisions about the appropriation of the value of PHD reuse are made collectively by members at the General Assembly. In that respect, DCs place the locus of decision-making where it is more likely to be effective for the reuse of PHD and at the same time acceptable to data subjects.

Moreover, unlike the for-profit data-driven approach, DCs open the door to creating new forms of reciprocity between data consumers and data subjects (Zuboff, 2015). This is for instance the case of the 'citizen science' initiative, which shows a change in the conditions of doing research as citizens become active participants in research projects. Yet in practice, this active participation of individuals in approving policies, making decisions, or becoming involved in research requires that they assume new responsibilities and a significant amount of work. The question is whether this extra-work related to the engagement of individuals will be sustainable over time. Therefore, a line of future research is the design of incentive systems that sustain the engagement and participation of data subjects over time.

On the other hand, unlike the individual-centric approach to PHD reuse (Table 8.1) that balances the asymmetries between data consumers and data subjects by appealing primarily to self-interest, DCs do so through the cooperation of data subjects. Moreover, because in DCs there is higher goal consensus than in the individual-centric approach, data subjects are more likely to be more committed to contribute

---

[25]We do not foresee that DCs will substitute existing PHD reuse approaches, particularly the health-care system-centric and for-profit data-driven approaches; rather, DCs will co-exist with them.

to the community (Provan & Kevin, 2008). Ernst Hafen, president of the Board of MiData.coop, notes, "[a]s a member you have not only the agency of controlling your data sets but you also have the agency of governing the value of the data set in the community". Therefore, MiData not only harnesses the agency of individuals but also the agency of the community (e.g., the decisions on where to invest profits, the selection the Board of Directors, changes in the articles of association). However, some of those community decisions have to be confirmed at the individual level afterwards. For instance, the Board of Directions and the Data Ethics Review Board approve the new research projects that will reuse PHD and which data they will have access, but afterwards account holders have to give consent for the reuse of their PHD on a granular individual basis. So at the end of the day, it is still individual account holders who choose whether to give consent or not. This means that if there are not enough account holders willing to give consent, the value for data consumers will be constrained (because of limited aggregation). One way to address this challenge would be to move gradually from individual to community consent. For instance, explore which subsets of PHD for each research project can be approached as "our data" instead of "my data". Then for those subsets of PHD, individuals would delegate their consent to the community.

Conclusions

Healthcare—like other sectors of the economy– is in a race to collect and reuse personal data. We have argued that the way the reuse of personal data is organized has broad implications on how the outcomes of personal data reuse are distributed. We have shown that approaches to personal data reuse reported in the literature, particularly, healthcare system-centric and for-profit data-driven approaches, are monocentric; i.e., they tend to involve a single organization that controls the data, thus creating power asymmetries between this organization and data subjects. An alternative emergent approach to personal data reuse that minimizes these asymmetries is data cooperatives (DCs). DCs create a data commons that empower data subjects, giving them greater control over their personal data, creating value for themselves and their communities, and for those same data subjects to have more of a say in the agenda of health research and the health services. The MiData.coop case study gives a line of empirical evidence showing how citizens can effectively govern the reuse of personal data.

Appendix 1: List of Data Sources

Videos, interviews and podcasts

[AVSrc7] Interviews with Donald Kossmann who was involved in the design of the architecture of MiData, July 2017.

[AVSrc6] Interview to Ernst Hafen and Ulrich Genick, "Do you want to learn more about health-data cooperatives? Listen to this podcast about Midata.coop", March 2017, https://platform.coop/stories/do-you-w ant-to-learn-more-about-health-data-cooperatives-listen-to-this-podcast-about-midata-coop

[AVSrc5] André Golliez, "MiData.coop – My Data, our Health", MyData 2016 Helsinki, August 2016, https://www.youtube.com/watch?v=ZZIGYn5I3yk&list=PL6_IssKYHuPReO0Sr7_7GRbUtRkRqnm6m&in dex=54

[AVSrc4] Serge Bignens, "MiData Ecosystem", MyData 2016 Helsinki, August 2016, https://www.youtube.c om/watch?v=ngMo03dYrAI&list=PL6_IssKYHuPReO0Sr7_7GRbUtRkRqnm6m&index=51

[AVSrc3] Ulrich Genick, "Personal Data Cooperatives", 2016 Platform Co-op Showcase 14 – MIDATA, https://livestream.com/internetsociety/platformcoop2016/videos/141725493

[AVSrc2] Ernst Hafen on "Personalisierte Daten", March 2016, https://www.youtube.com/watch?v=nORuA2 ydp80

[AVSrc1] Andre Golliez, "Citizen-Controlled Reuse of Personal Data", 2015, https://www.youtube.com/watc h?v=mAbyLDk1EK0

Written documents and presentations

[WSrc15] "Forschen mit Gesundheitsdaten unter Kontrolle der Bürger", 13/09/2017, http://www.netzwoche. ch/news/2017-09-13/forschen-mit-gesundheitsdaten-unter-kontrolle-der-buerger

[WSrc14] "Developer's guide", https://test.midata.coop/#/developer/guide

[WSrc13] "Terms of use", https://test.midata.coop/#/portal/terms/midata-terms-of-use

[WSrc12] "Privacy Policy", https://test.midata.coop/#/portal/terms/midata-privacy-policy

[WSrc11] "MiData Articles of Association", https://midata.coop/docs/MIDATA_Statuten_20170403_Englis h.pdf

[WSrc10] Dominik Steiger, "MyData, Our Health", MyData Switzerland Workshop, HSLU Luzern, June 2017, https://www.swissdataalliance.ch/s/MIDATAcoop.pdf

[WSrc9] Ernst Hafen, "Personal Data Economy – A cooperative approach", Inspire2live, Amsterdam, February 2017, http://inspire2live.org/wp-content/uploads/10.-Ernst-Hafen-Personal-Data-Economy-a-coope rative-approach.pdf

[WSrc8] Ernst Hafen "What is the trade-off between opportunities and privacy in the health business?", Mastering the Challenges of our Digital Society, Nov 2016, https://www.sg.ethz.ch/media/medialibrary/201 6/11/Ernst_Hafen.pdf

[WSrc7] Ernst Hafen "Citizen-Controller Personal Data is Essential for Personalised Medicine", Personalized Medicine Conference, June 2016, https://ec.europa.eu/research/conferences/2016/permed2016/ pdf/presentations/e_hafen.pdf

[WSrc6] Ernst Hafen "MIDATA.coop – Enabling efficient linkage of health data by citizen-controlled data access", Digital Enlightenment Forum - Trusted Data Management in Health Care, June 2016, https://digitale nlightenment.org/sites/default/files/users/14/20160607_MIDATA_Dig_Enlight.pdf

[WSrc5] Ernst Hafen "MIDATA.COOPs – Personal Health Data Cooperatives – Democratizing the Personal Data Economy", 2015, http://healthcoopscanada.coop/wp-content/uploads/2015/10/Best-Prac-MIDATA.pdf

[WSrc4] Ernst Hafen "Personal (Health) Data Cooperatives – Placing the Citizen at the Center of Personalized *[WSrc3]* Health and the Democratization of the Personal Economy", Gastein, October 2014, http://www.ehfg.org/intranet/app/webroot/uploads/presentations/files/uploads/d0bcdaa974556eba4c7e1f71d e52f5.pdf

[WSrc2] Ernst Hafen "Health Data Cooperatives – Citizen-Controlled Health Data Repositories as a Basis for Big Data Analytics in Health", Athens, May 2014, http://www.ehealth2014.org/presentations/big-data-fo r-healthcare-reform

[WSrc1] Newsletter of the "Data and Health" association, www.datenundgesundheit.ch

---

References

Aanestad, M., Grisot, M., Hanseth, O., & Vassilakopoulou, P. (2017). *Information infrastructures within European health care: Working with the installed base.* Springer.

Abiteboul, S., André, B., & Kaplan, D. (2015). Managing your digital life. *Communications of the ACM, 58*(5), 32–35.

Aitken, M., de St. Jorre, J., Pagliari, C., Jepson, R., & Cunningham-Burley, S. (2016). Public responses to the sharing and linkage of health data for research purposes: A systematic review and thematic synthesis of qualitative studies. *BMC Medical Ethics, 17*(1).

Balkan, A. (2017). *The nature of the self in the digital age.* https://ec.europa.eu/futurium/en/conte nt/nature-self-digital-age.

Benkler, Y. (2003). The political economy of commons. *Upgrade, IV*(3), 6–9.

Benkler, Y. (2014). Between Spanish Huertas and the Open Road: A tale of two commons? In B. M. Frischmann, M. J. Madison, & K. J. Strandburg (Eds.), *Governing knowledge commons* (pp. 69–98). Oxford University Press.

Custers, B., & Ursic, H. (2016). Big data and data reuse: A taxonomy of data reuse for balancing big data benefits and personal data protection. *International Data Privacy Law, 6*(1), 4–15.

DataCoop. (2017). Retrieved June 22, 2017, from http://wiki.p2pfoundation.net/Data_Cooperativ es.

EU. (2017). Conclusions on personalised medicine for patients. Retrieved August 27, 2017, from http://eur-lex.europa.eu/legal-content/EN/TXT/?uri=uriserv:OJ.C_.2015.421.01.0002.01. ENG&toc=OJ:C:2015:421:FULL.

Evans, B. J. (2017). Barbarians at the gate: Consumer-driven health data commons and the transformation of citizen science. *American Journal of Law and Medicine, 42*(4), 651–685.

Frischmann, B. M. (2005). An economic theory of infrastructure and commons management. *Minnesota Law Review, 89,* 917–1030.

Frischmann, B. M., Madison, M. J., & Strandburg, K. J. (2014). *Governing knowledge commons.* Oxford University Press.

Gagnon, M.-P., Payne-Gagnon, J., Breton, E., Fortin, J.-P., Khoury, L., Dolovich, L., et al. (2016). Adoption of electronic personal health records in Canada: Perceptions of stakeholders. *International Journal of Health Policy and Management, 5*(7), 425–433.

GDPR. (2016). General data protection regulation. *Official Journal of the European Union, L 119.* http://eur-lex.europa.eu/legal-content/EN/TXT/?uri=OJ%3AL%3A2016%3A119%3ATOC.

Geissbuhler, C., Safran, I., Buchan, R., Bellazzi, S., Labkoff, K., Eilenberg, A., et al. (2013). Trustworthy reuse of health data: A transnational perspective. *International Journal of Medical Informatics, 82*(1), 1–9.

Günther, W. A., Rezazade Mehrizi, M. H., Huysman, M., & Feldberg, F. (2017). Debating big data: A literature review on realizing value from big data. *The Journal of Strategic Information Systems, 26*(3), 191–209.

Hafen, E., Kossmann, D., & Brand, A. (2014). Health data cooperatives: Citizen empowerment. *Methods of Information in Medicine, 53*(2), 82–86.

Haug, C. J. (2017). Whose data are they anyway? Can a patient perspective advance the data-sharing debate? *The New England Journal of Medicine, 376,* 2203–2205.

Hern, A. (2017). Royal Free breached UK data law in 1.6 m patient deal with Google's Deep-Mind. https://www.theguardian.com/technology/2017/jul/03/google-deepmind-16m-patient-roy al-free-deal-data-protection-act.

Hess, C., & Ostrom, E. (2007). An overview of knowledge commons. In C. Hess & E. Ostrom (Eds.), *Understanding knowledge as commons.* Cambridge, MA: MIT Press.

ICA. (2017). Retrieved August 22, 2017, from https://ica.coop/en/whats-co-op/co-operative-identi ty-values-principles.

Kostkova, P., Brewer, H., de Lusignan, S., Fottrell, E., Goldacre, B., Hart, G., et al. (2016). Who owns the data? Open data for healthcare. *Frontiers in Public Health, 4*(7), 1–6.

Martin, A. L. (2017). Google received 1.6 million NHS patients' data on an 'inappropriate legal basis'. http://news.sky.com/story/google-received-16-million-nhs-patients-data-on-an-inappropriate-legal-basis-10879142.

MiData_Coop. (2017). Retrieved June 22, 2017, from http://www.midata.coop.

OECD. (2015). *Data-driven innovation: Big data for growth and well-being*. Paris: OECD Publishing.

Parker, G., Van Alstyne, M., & Choudary, S. (2016). *Platform revolution: How networked markets are transforming the economy and how to make them work for you*. New York: W. W. Norton & Company.

Pearce, C., & Bainbridge, M. (2014). A personally controlled electronic health record for Australia. *Journal of the American Medical Informatics Association, 21*(4), 707–713.

PlatformCoop. (2017). Retrieved July 26, 2017, from https://platform.coop/stories/protocol-cooperativism.

Powles, J., & Hodson, H. (2017). Google DeepMind and healthcare in an age of algorithms. *Health and Technology*, 1–17.

Provan, K. G., & Kevin, P. (2008). Modes of network governance: Structure, management, and effectiveness. *Journal of Public Administration Research and Theory, 18*(2), 229–252.

Purtova, N. (2017). Health data for common good: Defining the boundaries and social dilemmas of data commons. In S. Adams, N. Purtova, & R. Leenes, (Eds.), *Under observation: The interplay between eHealth and surveillance* (pp. 177–210). Springer.

Raghupathi, W., & Raghupathi, V. (2014). Big data analytics in healthcare: promise and potential. *Health Information Science and Systems, 2*(3), 1–10.

Riso, B., Tupasela, A., Vears, D. F., Felzmann, H., Cockbain, J., Loi, M., et al. (2017). Ethical sharing of health data in online platforms—Which values should be considered? *Life Sciences, Society and Policy, 13*(12), 1–27.

Scholz, T., & Schneider, N. (2016). *Ours to Hack and to Own: The rise of platform cooperativism, a new vision for the future of work and a fairer Internet*. New York: OR Books.

Shapiro, J. S., Mostashari, F., Hripcsak, G., Soulakis, N., & Kuperman, G. (2011). Using health information exchange to improve public health. *American Journal of Public Health, 101*(4), 616–623.

Simonite, T. (2014). Sell your personal data for $8 a month. *MIT Technology Review, 117*(3), 20–20.

Sjöberg, M., et al. (2017). Digital me: Controlling and making sense of my digital footprint. In L. Gamberini, A. Spagnolli, G. Jacucci, B. Blankertz, & J. Freeman (Eds.), *Symbiotic interaction. Symbiotic 2016*. Lecture Notes in Computer Science (Vol. 9961). Cham: Springer.

Srnicek, N. (2016). *Platform capitalism (Theory Redux)*. Polity Press.

Tanner, A. (2016). How data brokers make money off your medical records. *Scientific American*. https://www.scientificamerican.com/article/how-data-brokers-make-money-off-your-medical-records/.

Tanner, A. (2017). *Our bodies, our data: How companies make billions selling our medical records*. Beacon Press.

Tiwana, A. (2014). *Platform ecosystems: Aligning architecture, governance, and strategy*. Waltham, MA: Morgan Kaufmann.

UN-Coops. (2014). Measuring the size and scope of the cooperative economy: Results of the 2014 global census on co-operatives. Dave Grace and Associates, Commissioned by the United Nations Department for Economic and Social Affairs. http://www.un.org/esa/socdev/documents/2014/coopsegm/grace.pdf.

Ure, J., Procter, R., Lin, Y.-W., Hartswood, M., Anderson, S., Lloyd, S., et al. (2009). The development of data infrastructures for eHealth: A socio-technical perspective. *Journal of the Association for Information Systems, 10*(5), 415–429.

Vayena, E., & Gasser, U. (2016). Between openness and privacy in genomics. *PLoS Med, 13*(1), e1001937.

Vayena, E., Dzenowagis, J., & Langfeld, M. (2016). *Evolving health data ecosystem*. World Health Organization, http://www.who.int/ehealth/resources/ecosystem/en/.

Yin, R. K. (2009). *Case study research: Design and methods*. Thousand Oaks, CA: Sage.
Zuboff, S. (2015). Big other: Surveillance capitalism and the prospects of an information civilization. *Journal of Information Technology, 30*(1), 75–89.

Chapter 9
Cooperatives in the Age of Sharing

Theresia Theurl and Eric Meyer

Introduction

The sharing economy has been hyped up recently and many "new" business models like Uber or Airbnb have evolved, which allow people to share their cars or flats. A different perspective would interpret these new offers as a kind of supply of mobility and housing solutions, i.e. new supply in traditional markets. Other applications of the sharing principle can be found in numerous markets like cloud computing, the joint use of goods and machines and especially in sharing information goods. These new applications should not blur the fact, that sharing is not a really new idea and is having a long tradition. Centuries ago farmers jointly bought and shared agricultural machines to cultivate their land, because they could not afford to own these machines individually. Every kind of renting goods is a kind of sharing, which is frequently offered by professional companies like car rental firms. So the idea of sharing is not new, but part of the economic life for a long time. Therefore, it is important to identify the economic core of the sharing economy, which distinguishes the sharing economy from traditional parts of the economy.

In the section "Defining and Characterizing the Sharing Economy" we will define the sharing economy and we will give an economic characterization of the sharing economy. It will turn out, that the platforms that connect supply and demand in the sharing economy constitute a significant governance challenge. A cooperative ownership structure could mitigate the problems originating from this platform. Thus, the section "Basic Economic Characteristics of Cooperatives" will explain the characteristics of a cooperative. Finally, the section "Conclusion and Practical Implications"

T. Theurl (✉) · E. Meyer
WWU - University of Muenster, Münster, Germany
e-mail: theresia.theurl@uni-muenster.de

E. Meyer
e-mail: eric.meyer@wiwi.uni-muenster.de

© Springer International Publishing AG, part of Springer Nature 2019
K. Riemer et al. (eds.), *Collaboration in the Digital Age*, Progress in IS,
https://doi.org/10.1007/978-3-319-94487-6_9

will show how a platform in the form of a cooperative could improve the functioning and the economic welfare of these markets and will also present the limits of this model.

Defining and Characterizing the Sharing Economy

Definition and Delineation

The "Sharing Economy" is frequently ideologically overrated by declaring it an alternative to the capitalist economy. This type of reasoning claims that in the future the *use* of goods will dominate, instead of *owning* them overlooking that even if people just use goods there will still be an ultimate owner of these goods. Just using goods is therefore not an alternative to ownership, but at most an alternative application of ownership. Even worse sometimes sharing of goods is interpreted as "collaborative consumption" in contrast to the common individualistic consumption and because the collaborative consumption is striving for social coherence and community it is morally superior to the ordinary consumption that simply pursues profit maximization. These ideas and interpretations are lacking a solid foundation and (intentionally?) leave out a precise economic definition and delineation of the sharing economy. Defining the term "sharing economy" is difficult, since it has been extended to various areas, although some of these are hardly connectable to the sharing idea. Ride-hailing business (e.g. Uber, Lyft, BlaBlaCar) or renting out rooms (e.g. Airbnb, Wimdo, InstantOffices) are some activities that are mostly considered to be part of the sharing economy. Renting other goods on platforms like Frents or Leihdirwas.de could also be considered to be part of the sharing economy. Sometimes social networking platforms (like Facebook, Instagram) are also assigned to the sharing economy, because people exchange information or pictures that can be used by other participants in these networks. What makes this sharing different is the digital nature of the shared information. Sharing these "information goods" does not prevent the use of the shared information by the owner. On the other hand some sources extend the scope of the sharing economy to more businesses like crowd-working (e.g. Upwork, Clickworker), peer-to-peer-lending (e.g. Auxmoney, Kickstarter) or streaming services (e.g. Netflix).[1] But which of these businesses are to be considered to be part of the sharing economy and which are not? In order to delineate and later on to define the sharing economy we suggest three questions that will help us to carve out the economic characteristics of businesses belonging to the sharing economy:

- Which are the goods that are shared between the individuals?
- Who shares these goods (individuals or professional suppliers, i.e. companies)?
- Are the participants connected by a platform, i.e. how does demand meet supply?

---

[1]For this extended view see for example PwC (2016), p. 3.

The first question refers to *the objects of sharing* i.e. the type of exchange. For the ride-hailing business a combination of sharing a good (here: car) and a service (driving the car) can be observed. Because the ride-hailing includes the sharing of the car, it is part of the sharing economy. In contrast crowd-working does not meet the criterion of exchanging goods. People "share" their work capacity or provide services, which is the usual way of earning money. The difference is that people are not employed with long-term contracts, but on the basis of small bits of work for which they apply on a platform. So crowd-working meets the third criterion but not the first one. In a similar way the sharing of capital in peer-to-peer lending does not include the provision of goods and therefore it is not part of the sharing economy. The exclusion of crowd-working and peer-to-peer-lending is based on the same reason, that providing capital (human capital and monetary capital, respectively) is not characterising the sharing economy.

The goods that are available for sharing can be further differentiated. Non-durable consumer goods (like chocolate) are ill-suited for sharing, because they are used up during the process of consumption. Durable consumer goods, that are used in consumption (like cars) are the goods that are available for sharing. This does not preclude the degradation of these durable consumer goods, while they are used. For example a car needs more maintenance if it is used more intensively in order to minimize the degradation effects of the use. In some rare cases the degradation effect is close to zero and therefore sharing these goods comes with very little additional costs for the suppliers of these goods. Computing power is an example for a good, where additional use causes almost no degradation.[2] Similarly, sharing information in social networking platforms results in no losses due to the digital nature of the goods (e.g. photos). The use of durable consumer goods in for-profit activities of the sharing economy turns them—temporarily—to capital goods. That means that the nature of a good is determined by the purpose of its use. If it is used in private, it remains a consumer good, but employing the same good by offering it to other individuals makes it an investment good due to the for-profit intention of the sharing activity.

The object of sharing is usually not part of the efforts to define the sharing economy. Peitz and Schwalbe (2016) mention, that a durable good must be object of the sharing activity.[3] In contrast Miller (2016) extends sharing also to "services, space and money."[4] Sundararajan (2014) also includes the provision of labour to the sharing economy.[5]

The sharing of goods can be carried out in different ways. The most common way to share a good is the offering of the good by one individual who owns the good to another individual to use the good for a specified time. In this case sharing means that the individuals sequentially or jointly use goods, which are owned by

---

[2]This only refers to the CPU use, for which it makes no difference whether the processor is running idle or is actually computing.

[3]Peitz and Schwalbe (2016), p. 233.

[4]Miller (2016), p. 150.

[5]Sundararajan (2014).

one individual. Sometimes the provision of the goods is part of the problem, i.e. the number of available goods is insufficient. In this case another type of sharing could be applied. The individuals could jointly own the goods and then use the goods from the pool of goods according to pre-specified rules. For example the individuals could jointly own a pool of cars, which they use if needed, which will reduce the ownership costs for the individuals.[6]

The second question refers to the *acting subjects* of the sharing economy, which are individuals. Therefore, Netflix or other streaming services are not part of the sharing economy, because the supplier of the movies (and owner of the copyrights) is a firm. The idea, that streaming could be a sharing activity, stems from the comparison of the previous activities. People bought DVDs to watch a movie or CDs to listen to music. By the same token we have to exclude other professional providers from the traditional economy. Renting cars or holiday flats is part of the traditional economy. The agents of the sharing economy are implicitly part of some definition attempts, because they emphasize the peer-to-peer characteristic of the sharing economy.[7]

The third question refers to the *way of connecting individuals* in the sharing economy. The path-breaking innovation, that allows the connection of individuals at low costs, is the creation of platforms in the internet. The platform-connection characterizes all of the examples above, and is a distinguishing characteristic, which delineates the sharing economy from traditional rental services. Platforms are part of almost all definition attempts and are the origin of the governance challenges that we will observe later on, but not all platforms are part of the sharing economy.[8] Thus, platforms are a necessary, but not a sufficient requirement for the sharing economy.

From the description above we derive a tentative definition of the sharing economy. We define as the sharing economy all activities, which

- are carried out by individuals on a peer-to-peer basis,
- by using a connecting platform in the internet
- for sharing (physical) goods with each other.

We consider this definition well-suited in order to focus on the substantial features of the sharing economy and to set aside activities that mainly have the platform characteristic. Admittedly, the definition is quite narrow but will allow for more stringency in considering the phenomenon of the sharing economy.

These characteristics will be further analysed in the following subsections. We will have to explain, what determines the individuals' ownership decision, what peer-to-peer activities imply for markets and which economic effects platforms will have.

---

[6]This differentiation follows Demary (2015) or Rauch and Schneider (2015), p. 11, who discriminate between peer-to-peer sharing and asset hubs.

[7]See for example Katz (2015), p. 1073 explicitly mentioning the peer-to-peer characteristic.

[8]See for example Dittmann and Kuchinke (2015), p. 245, Peitz and Schwalbe (2016), p. 235, Fraiberger and Sundararajan (2015), Katz (2015), p. 1070.

Determinants of Ownership

If people deliberately choose a sharing arrangement to use goods instead of buying them, they have to base their decision on cost-benefit considerations that guide
them to the decision of sharing the goods, i.e. it must be beneficial for them to only
temporarily possess the good. Surprisingly, this question has not been part of economic analysis up to now. This could be explained by the limited decision making
options for individuals in traditional markets. With the recent establishing of peer-
to-peer markets renting and renting out goods becomes a relevant decision option for
individuals that requires a closer economic introspection.[9] The buy-or-rent decision
resembles the make-or-buy problem that firms have to solve and for which extensive
research exists.[10] We use this line of research to transfer and adapt the results to the
problem of sharing or owning faced by individuals. There are five main determinants
for the individual's decision to own or to share a good:

- *Frequency of use*: The more often people use a good, the more they will be inclined
  to buy and own a good. For instance a mobile phone, that is used every day or
  every minute, is probably ill-suited as a device that could be used by sharing it.
  The reason is the size of transaction costs. Although modern platform technologies
  lower these costs, they have to be incurred for every transaction, i.e. for every use
  of the mobile phone. For every transaction a sharing partner has to be found, the
  good has to be supplied, and—at least for more complex products—it has to be
  ensured, that the good is of sufficient quality. Buying a good and then frequently
  using it drastically reduces the costs per use for the good. An example of different
  transaction types for the same good could be a car. If you use your car very often
  (for example for professional purposes), you will probably prefer to own the car
  instead of going through the (costly) process of finding an appropriate vehicle
  every day. If you need a car just once in a while, you will probably prefer a sharing
  solution. Closely related to the frequency of use is the problem of availability (see
  below). When using a good frequently by sharing arrangements the likelihood of
  unavailability of the good increases with the number of uses, that means you are
  not able to use the good or have to accept delays in the use. This results in waiting
  costs or search costs for other options.
- *Availability/option benefits*: Ownership of a good ensures that the good can be
  used any time. Consequently, the user of the good is not dependent on other market
  participants to provide the good. This is a particular problem in peak times, i.e.
  when demand for the good is temporarily very high. This does not immediately
  result in unavailability but in price surges which make the market solution more
  expensive. Sometimes, the immediate use of a good is not the primary objective

---

[9]Horton and Zeckhauser (2016) is one of the rare papers discussing the ownership-rental decision
in an economic model, but is not taking into account the criteria listed below.

[10]This research is based on the pathbreaking contributions by Coase (1937), Williamson (1985) for
a transaction cost perspective and Hart (1995) for a property rights view. A textbook presentation
extending the number of criteria can be found in Picot, Dietl, Franck, Fiedler, and Royer (2015),
p. 70.

of owning the good. People may derive an option benefit from the good, i.e. they derive utility from the fact, that the good is available for them, when they decide to use it.

- *Avoiding dependencies*: Ownership of goods reduces the dependencies on others. When using platforms of the sharing economy the consumer of the goods depends on the supply of the good by another individual. This is exactly the problem markets are supposed to solve. Therefore, the participants of a sharing platform crucially depend on the functioning of this platform. If there is a sufficient number of suppliers in the market, the dependencies and the costs associated with these dependencies are low. Thus, the better these markets work, the lower the dependency costs for the participants will be. Nevertheless, the dependency costs of the sharing platforms will always be higher than the costs of ownership, where these costs are zero due the independence created by the ownership.
- *Avoiding uncertainties*: Owning a good gives complete control over the good to the user. This especially relates to the quality of the good. Since the owner of the good knows what he has done with good in the past, he is able to assess the quality of the good. By using goods supplied by sharing platforms uncertainty concerning the quality of the good arises. In response to this information asymmetry the platforms of the sharing economy try to implement instruments that reduce these asymmetries. Typically, the platforms establish rating systems where users have to evaluate each other and users share their experience with the other suppliers (and consumers) of goods. Other signalling options are photos or films that try to appropriately describe the state und the quality of the good.
- *Costs of the good*: The advantages of ownership are subject to costs of acquiring the goods. Of course it would be highly appreciable to own a holiday flat in numerous locations, because the flats would be available at any time and at the exact quality the user wishes to have. Unfortunately, this extensive ownership is subject to a budget constraint for most people. Therefore, renting a holiday flat is usual way to use a holiday flat.

The items above mainly focus on the demand for goods provided by sharing platforms. On the other hand we also have to explain, what determines the owners' willingness to give away their property by sharing it with other people. Unsurprisingly, similar reasons apply. The main driver to supply goods is of course the additional income that could be created by sharing the good. Existing capacities could be better utilized and would generate profits for the suppliers. Concerning the frequency of use, the suppliers of goods will be more inclined to share those goods that they do not use frequently, because these goods are more readily available for other people's use.[11] Handing over one's property to another person is subject to similar information asymmetries as for the demand side. When renting out a room, the supplier wants to be sure, that the room will not be destroyed after the guests have left the room. Therefore, the rating systems of the platform can also be used to assess and rate the consumers of goods.

---

[11]One exception is the joint use of products like for BlaBlaCar, where the supply od the service can only be offered if the owner uses the good (in the case of BlaBlaCar the car).

Now, that we know the main influencing forces for deciding whether to own or to rent a good, we can answer the question, which developments have changed the relative costs and therefore helped to create the sharing economy, i.e. a movement from owning goods to not owning and (only) using these goods. This observation resembles a similar line of research in the theory of the firm, which explains that new information technologies and the connection of people via the internet reduces the transaction costs of market transactions and therefore transactions are no longer carried out within the boundaries of the firm but are turned into market transactions (Move-to-the-market hypothesis).[12] The same idea also applies to the sharing economy, where the acting subjects are individuals instead of firms. Information technologies and the internet are able to significantly change some of the costs for owning or renting a good. The platforms, which have been identified to be constitutive for the sharing economy, reduce the information asymmetries between suppliers and consumers and reduce the threats of unavailability of goods. Providing information about a good and researching information about it has become much simpler with the use of the internet. Thus, because of the reduced information asymmetries more people are willing to provide goods on these platforms and on the other hand more people are also willing to rent goods temporarily, since the platforms reduce the probability of receiving a bad quality product. Moreover, because more people are willing to provide their property to other people via the sharing platform, the availability of goods for rent on these platforms increases. Therefore, it becomes less likely that a good will be unavailable shrinking the costs associated with unavailability.

In consequence, the internet and the creation of platforms which reduce information costs and connect individuals have a similar effect for the decision between owning and renting a good as it can be observed for the make-or-buy decision of firms. Therefore, it is necessary to analyse the economic characteristics of these platforms and whether they may come along with new costs for the individuals.

The Economic Characteristics of Platforms

The platforms of the sharing economy, which connect the individuals supplying and demanding goods, exhibit the characteristics of two-sided markets. The term "two-sided market" may sound tautological, since every market has two sides, demand and supply. However, the analysis of two-sided markets considers the establishing of such markets as a separate entrepreneurial effort and analyses factors that influence the creation of these markets.[13]

An essential feature of two-sided markets is the existence of network externalities. When joining a network an individual benefits from the connections in this network.

---

[12]Cf. Malone, Yates, and Benjamin (1987) and Malone (2004). Clemons, Reddi, and Row (1993) provide are more detailed analysis of transaction cost in make-or buy decisions of the firm.

[13]The characteristics of two-sided markets have been analyzed extensively in Armstrong (2006) and Rochet and Tirole (2006).

In addition to this benefit all other existing members of the network gain from the further network member, because they receive one additional potential partner for exchange within the network. These gains of the other network members are not internalized by the newly joining member and require compensation schemes for achieving an optimum network size. For two-sided markets these network effects are more complicated, because they take the shape of indirect network externalities.[14] This indirect effect refers to the observation that the externalities occur on the other side of the two-sided market. For instance, if a new consumer joins the platform, this will be a benefit for the suppliers on the other side of the market, because they have one additional (prospective) customer to serve, and if a new supplier is joining the network, this exhibits positive effects for the consumers, because this increases their choices. This mutual relationship can turn into a virtuous circle for the platform, because new customers attract new suppliers to the platform and new suppliers will attract new customers, which results in an upwards spiralling growth of the platform. Of course this spiralling effect may also work in the opposite direction. If there are only a few suppliers, the platform is unattractive for consumers, who will leave the platform, which will again turn the platform less attractive for suppliers and so on. These indirect network externalities are crucial for the working of the platform. Notice, that a new consumer joining the platform also creates negative effects for all other consumers, because it is an additional competitor competing for the same supply. Thus, it is necessary, that the consumers as a whole benefit from the indirect externalities on the other side of the market, which increases the supply due the more attractive demand base of the platform.

These two-sided markets are not new and we find them not only in the internet. Examples of two-sided markets are credit cards (cardholders and merchants), for-free newspapers (readers and advertisement customers) or in the internet e.g. Ebay (customers and suppliers). The art of creating a platform is the balancing of the demand and supply side in order to maintain the virtuous circle and to prevent it tilting into a vicious circle. These indirect network effects and as a consequence the virtuous circle of the spiralling growth imply economies of scale for the operation of the platform. The bigger a platform is, i.e. the more consumers and suppliers can be reached on the platform, the more attractive it is for new platform members. Even if there were competing platforms, the bigger platform would attract more and more members from other platforms due to its larger benefits it can offer created by its bigger size.[15] Thus, these platforms show a tendency to end up in a monopoly or at least an oligopoly. However, a monopoly platform creates new dependencies for the platform members and may increase the costs of using the platform for the platform members. As long as there is a sufficient number of suppliers und buyers using the platform, the owner of the platform will be able to appropriate the monopoly rents and will create the new dependencies mentioned above. This fact has to be distinguished from the platform's price setting behaviour in order in initiate the

---

[14]For a more detailed differentiation of indirect network externalities see Peitz (2006).

[15]Rare exemptions are smaller platforms that create additional value for their members like a certain specialization, which over-compensates the size benefits of larger platforms.

virtuous circle to balance the number of suppliers and buyers on the platform to increase the platform's attractiveness for both sides of the market. This price-setting scheme has distributional consequences between buyers and suppliers but should not be confused with the monopoly rent extracted by the platform owner.

The burden of a monopoly platform would be less harmful, if the platform market (i.e. the competition between platforms) was contestable. In a contestable market the market power of a monopoly cannot be applied to increase prices because increasing prices would immediately attract new competitors entering the market and thus lowering the prices. Unfortunately, the very nature of the platforms are the economies of scale due to the indirect network externalities. Therefore, new contesting competitors that start as a small platform are lacking the size which is a necessary production factor to become a new competitor in the market. Consequently, platform markets are mostly not contestable which increases the risks of exploitation by a monopoly platform. Moreover, switching to another platform can be further impeded by platform specific investments that have been made by platform members in the past. Such specificities are for example the ratings that a platform member gets for his supplies. A good rating allows platform members to charge higher prices. Such ratings usually cannot be transferred to a competing platform. Thus, if a member changed the platform, he would start without his reputation capital, which results in lower prices he could charge for his products and which will deter him from changing the platform. Another mechanism that could slightly reduce the exploitation risk is multi-homing. If more than one, similar sized platforms have evolved over time, consumers and suppliers may use all the platforms for their operations, i.e. they are homing their supply or demand on all platforms. Evidently this only works, if the homing costs of a platform are relatively low. In such an oligopoly the prices of the platforms are contained by the few remaining competitors. The disadvantages of separate ratings for each of the platforms remain and are another disadvantage for the multi-homing platform members.[16]

Peer-to-Peer Relationships and Power Law Effects

Closely related to the electronic platforms are so-called power law effects. These power law effects describe for example the distribution of supplies in a market. Typically, such supply distribution takes the shape of a hyperbola. An example is shown in Fig. 9.1. Let us assume that we would like to describe the room capacities of a city and we are sorting the capacities offered according to the size of the room suppliers. We start on the left with the largest hotels in town and then move downwards to smaller hotels, boarding houses and B&B-offers. At the end of the sorting we will find single room offerings that can be supplied by individuals. Without internet platforms, which facilitate the search for rooms, the supply of single rooms by individuals would be inconceivable and they would therefore stay out of the market.

[16]See Monopolkommission (2016), no. 1233 on the impediments of switching platforms.

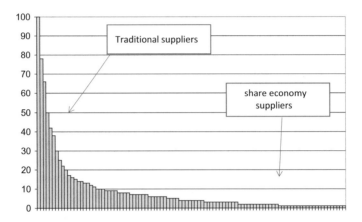

Fig. 9.1 Power law effects in the sharing economy

In order to bring their offerings to the market significant marketing expenditures would be necessary, which could not be recouped by renting out just one room. The platforms of the sharing economy have reduced information cost (here: signalling costs of suppliers). Therefore, the entry barriers to these markets have been lowered allowing more suppliers to participate in these markets. These new market participants are (private) individuals bringing their goods to the market and increase the supply in these markets. Consequently prices in these markets will fall, which allows new consumers to use these goods. Since these long tails of the distribution may accumulate a large number of new products, the available capacities may increase significantly having considerable effects on prices.[17]

Traditional markets are marked by their B2B or B2C characteristic, i.e. at least one exchange partner is classified as "business", which means a professional company that provides goods to the market. The distinctive feature of the sharing economy platforms is the inclusion of (private) individuals as suppliers in the markets. They are creating C2C markets, where some consumers temporarily put on the hat of business and offer their products to other people and in the next period they put on their hat as a consumer and use the product they own themselves. These (supplying) consumers turn themselves into hybrids acting on different sides of the markets and become "prosumers", a combination of producers and consumers. The new "prosumer" characteristic of individuals is one of the main challenges for regulation in markets. As prosumers the individuals take temporarily the role of a supplier, but evade many regulations that apply to their professional competitors.

Thus, the sharing economy is not creating new markets, but it is bringing new participants to existing markets. Similar developments have been observed for other (internet) platforms. Ebay was a platform that addressed the long tails of markets, for which it has been economically unattractive to offer their goods before. For the first time individuals received a marketing and sales platform that allowed them to

---

[17]These power law or long-tail effects have been initially described by Anderson (2006).

offer their products at low transaction costs. Interestingly, the platform has developed over time and today individuals share the platform with smaller professional shops. Similar developments could also be expected for some platforms of the sharing economy.

Interim Conclusion

The sections above described how new information technologies and especially platforms have changed the transaction costs for individuals and that consequently the boundary between ownership and renting has shifted towards renting. The basic economic characteristics of the sharing economy have been carved out. It has been shown that the platforms that enable the sharing economy have a tendency towards a monopoly. Thus, the positive effects of integrating more people to the market and allocating existing capacities more efficiently is accompanied by the detrimental creation of a monopoly, which will acquire parts of the rents created in the platform by the participants of the platform. Since the participants of the platform are individuals there will be no countervailing power to contain the platform monopoly.

One way to counter these monopolies would be the application of the usual regulations against the abuse of market power, which will take a long time that the platform may use to extend its reach. In the following section we will present a different solution for the problem of the structural monopolization of the platform. The problem of a platform monopoly could be easily resolved, if the users own their platform. Therefore, a platform taking the shape of a cooperative will be analysed.

Basic Economic Characteristics of Cooperatives

Cooperatives have been invented and developed in Germany in the 19th century and are usually not associated to be part of innovative business models of the information technology sector. This should not blur the fact that cooperatives have been a business innovation themselves and were a necessary basis for a blossoming German economy in the 19th century and still are the backbone of the German economy's SMEs.

The distinctive mark of cooperatives is the unification of owner and customer.[18] The owners of the cooperative are at the same time customers of the cooperative, which is in contrast to other corporations, where owners and customers are separate and follow different interests. In these corporations the customers are a vehicle to generate profits for the owners providing the capital to the firm. While the owners are interested in higher profits, for example by increasing prices, the customers usually favour lower prices. Thus, the owners' and the customers' expectation of the value for

---

[18]In cooperatives demand or supply can be bundled. In the following we will confine ourselves to the demand side. Nevertheless, all arguments also apply to supply-side cooperatives.

money go into opposite directions. In a market economy this conflict of interests is contained by market forces. Exploiting a more powerful position as a firm by raising prices will attract new suppliers, which will lower the prices again and if prices are too low additional customers will drive up prices again. Problems arise if there are market failures, i.e. if market forces fail to contain the contradicting interests. Here cooperatives come into play and could provide a solution. Because in a cooperative all customers are at the same time owners, the conflict is resolved. In a cooperative the owners (which are customers), generate their profits with the customers (which are owners) or—to put it differently—at worst they are exploiting themselves by increasing or decreasing prices or the efforts they spend. Therefore, cooperatives provide a solution in situations when markets fail. These failures could take different forms:

- Providing products to consumers is unattractive for companies and no supply of products is available for consumers. Therefore, consumers could organize the supply themselves by founding a cooperative which produces the products.
- Due to production technology there are no competitors and monopolies occur. This is a well-known situation in the agricultural sector, where local farmers depend on a local dairy company or a local supplier of seeds. Thus, a most common governance form for these transactions is a cooperative. Here the customers prevent the exploitation by the monopolist by owning the monopolist themselves.

Because cooperatives have two different relationships (provision of capital as owners and buying goods provided for them by the cooperative), the governance of these relationships is more complicated than the one-dimensional relations in other companies. Cooperatives provide a member value to their members, which consists of three different elements. First, the component of the direct member value refers to the founding reason of the cooperative, the products or services that the members want to acquire but for which market failures exist. This part of the member value is linked to the customer relationship that members have with their cooperative. Second, the indirect member value addresses the members' role as owners of the cooperative which provide capital to their joint venture. Because they provide capital to the cooperative, they are entitled to receive a dividend on this capital. Third, the sustainable member value is associated with the dynamics of a cooperative. Since substitutive providers are not available, the cooperative's members have a special interest in the sustainability of the cooperative's business. If the cooperative cedes to exist, they would lose their access to the products that are provided by the cooperative and which have been the founding reason. Consequently, they are willing to forgo some profits and leave some money in the cooperative. Due to these three types of member value the members have to decide how they weigh the components, i.e. the cooperative's profit is split into three parts and the ratios for the split have to be decided by the members.

The double relationship that the members have with their cooperative leads to another governance challenge. In other (one dimensional) corporations voting rights are allocated according to the capital that shareholders provide to the corporation. Applying this rule to a cooperative would ignore the twofold relation that members have with the cooperative. Moreover, such rule would not take into account that the economic relationship is the pivotal driver of a cooperative and these interests have to be reflected in the voting rights. Thus, most cooperatives allocate their voting rights on a per head basis, i.e. one man, one vote. Some exemptions are made for those cooperatives whose members are legal and not natural persons. This voting scheme guarantees that the owner relationship (providing capital) will not dominate the customer relationship (buying products).

While cooperatives are well-suited to respond to monopoly power or lacking supply of goods, they also show some challenges in their governance. Because the customers of the cooperative are also their owners, the communication between customers and owners is more complex than in other corporations, since they have to decide on the implementation of the three components of the member value. This is a minor problem as long as the members are homogeneous in their preferences. If their preferences are similar, they will have similar needs and therefore will come to similar conclusions for the provision of goods by the cooperative. As soon as the members become more heterogeneous the decision-making costs will increase, because longer discussions and intensified negotiations are to be expected. Moreover, in the case of heterogeneous members it will be more likely that the members come up with a decision that is against the preferences of some members and these members then have to bear these external costs of being outvoted. The probability of heterogeneous members will increase with the number of members of the cooperative. In order to manage this heterogeneity and to contain the costs of heterogeneity the cooperative should implement distinct rules on the topics and procedures of voting. When evaluating these governance costs of cooperatives, the correct reference has to be identified and sometimes a market solution is taken as a reference. This ignores the unavailability of a market solution, which was the starting point for establishing a cooperative. An appropriate comparison has to take into account the solutions that can be implemented subject to the production technology and market determinants. Since the cooperative is a reaction to a market failure, the relevant alternative is a monopoly associated with much higher costs for the individuals or the non-supply of goods with the costs of non-availability for the individuals.

The cooperative is financed by its members who contribute the capital by taking their function as owners of the cooperative. This works fine as the size of the cooperative is in proportion to its members' needs and may grow with number of members. However, this also assumes that investments are easily scalable and can be sliced into small parts. Some investments do not have this property. Thus financing the cooperative needs complementary instruments especially if large up-front investments are necessary. Typical financing of young and quickly growing companies by external equity investors are not available for cooperatives. Therefore, their growth will be slower but also more sustainable than the growth of other companies, because it depends on the number of members, i.e. customer demand.

Cooperatives as an Organizational Solution for Platforms in the Sharing Economy

In the section "Defining and Characterizing the Sharing Economy" we explained that platforms are essential for the sharing economy and these platforms exhibit a tendency towards monopolization. It has also been shown that these monopolies cannot be contested and the pricing behaviour will not be disciplined by potential competition. Creating countervailing market power by aggregating the demand (or supply) of the platform users is also hard to implement, since another trait of the sharing economy is the atomistic structure of their users, who bring small units of demand and supply to these platform markets. Moreover the application of regulation against the abuse of market power is a lengthy process and hard to implement. It is doubtful whether these actions could be successful and unclear how these actions could look like. Splitting up a platform in order to increase competition will reduce the positive indirect network externalities and will shrink the benefits that the users can receive from the platform. A price control as another regulatory instrument would also be hard to implement. Thus, the problem remains that on the one hand people wish to have these platforms for exchanging goods or information, which will increase their welfare, and on the other hand the platforms will automatically monopolize, which will be detrimental for the users of the platform.

In the section "Basic Economic Characteristics of Cooperatives" we have shown under which circumstances cooperatives are a suitable solution to increase the individuals' welfare. Cooperatives are able to mitigate the problems stemming from the monopolies by combining consumers (or suppliers) and the monopoly in one company. Thus, we suggest that platforms could take the form of a cooperative that is owned by its users. In contrast to an administrative answer by applying competition law the organizational solution of forming a cooperative could maintain the positive effects of the platform (positive indirect network externalities) and at the same time could control the vertical dependencies on the monopolistic platform. Three different types of cooperatives are feasible solutions for platforms of the sharing economy.[19]

Type Ia: Suppliers (or Consumers) Jointly Own the Platform

In this first model one side of the market owns the platform, for instance the suppliers of goods found a cooperative, which operates the platform. In a (fictitious) example we could assume the Uber drivers own the Uber platform. Even if the platform gains market power, the exploitation of the suppliers is limited by the fact that the platform is owned by suppliers. So at most they would exploit themselves. Thus, the negative effects of the platform's market power would be eliminated. The missing disciplining competition effect on the platform would be substituted by the vote channel within

---

[19]Type I and type II cooperatives resemble the peer-to-peer sharing and the asset-hubs by Demary (2015) or Rauch and Schneider (2015), p. 11.

the cooperative. Even if the management of the cooperative would try to increase prices at the expense of the suppliers, the members could intervene by voting against the management in their function as owners of the platform to improve their relationship to the platform in their function as customers. Changes of the platforms offerings are not enforced by market pressure (e.g. offers by other platforms, which could not exist due to the characteristics of the production technology of platforms), but directly through interventions by the members, who can influence the scope and the quality of the platform's service. Appropriately implemented, a cooperative will have a superior relation to its customers (here: the suppliers), because they own the platform cooperative. Necessary information flows between the customers and the platform are facilitated, since the customers' reticence to reveal the information is reduced due to their ownership relation. They are benefitting themselves by revealing the information and consequently are improving the functioning of the platform. This information flow could only be hampered by free-rider behaviour of some members. Since all members benefit from the information flows even if they do not contribute to the information flow, their incentives to actively provide the information decrease. Therefore, additional transparency between the members, rules and communication are necessary to stabilize the information channel, which improves platform's performance.

The type Ia cooperative only solves the market power problem for one side of the market. For the other side if the market (here: the consumers) the market power problem remains. The relevance of this problem depends on the structure of the two-sided market. As mentioned in the section "The Economic Characteristics of Platforms" the platform operator has to balance the two sides of the market in order to create a virtuous circle by applying fees to the two sides. In many platforms just one side of the market has to pay the fees, while the other side may use the platform for free. In the case of such a platform that offers its service for one side of the market without charging the customers the market power problem is not existent for the customers on this side of the market. Therefore, a type Ia cooperative would be an appropriate solution for the sharing economy platform and mitigates the problems that are associated with the operation of such a platform.

The structure of the members will also influence the success and the functioning of the platform. As mentioned in the explanation of cooperatives more homogeneous member structures will facilitate the functioning of the platform, since it results in more similar member needs and wishes. These similar needs will facilitate the decision making of the members to operate the platform. In order to create value for both sides to the two-sided market which is operated by the platform a large number of members is necessary. However, many participants in the platform increase the probability of more heterogeneous members and thus will complicate the operation of the platform. This effect can be mitigated, if the platform offers simple interlinking services with only limited additional services. The more complex the operations of the platform become and the more services the platform offers, the more relevant heterogeneous members will be for the decision making costs. Take the example of Uber. A simple service that Uber offers is the connection of people who need a ride and the car owners who will offer the ride by the Uber-developed app. But Uber could extend its offerings. They could add insurance services for the car owners on their platform or could try to improve the social security service for the drivers. While most drivers will easily agree on the connecting app, there will be divergent opinions on the insurance issues, because some drivers enjoy social security protection because they are offering rides as a hobby, while others offer their service in a more taxi-driver-like fashion and would need these additional services, which leads to conflicts in determining the platforms activities.

Type Ib: Suppliers and Consumers Jointly Own the Platform

In a type Ib cooperative not only one side of the market owns the cooperative, but the participants on both sides of the market become owners of the platform. This type is an atypical cooperative. In the past cooperatives formed among the individuals of one side of the market. Including both sides of the market is a new approach. There are only a few examples of such cooperatives available.[20] As mentioned before the market power problem can arise for both sides of the markets and is relevant if the platform charges prices for both sides of the market. Then both sides of the market would be subject to the exploitation by a monopoly platform and both sides would be interested in restraining the platform's pricing power. Thus, a membership available to both sides of the market would be the immediate consequence.

By integrating the members of both sides of the market in the cooperative the heterogeneity automatically increases. Demand side and supply side will have similar interests in having a platform for using or suppling goods, but as consumers and suppliers they will have opposing preferences with respect to numerous parameters. Most obvious are their opposing interests concerning the price of the platform service. While being guided by the pricing guideline for two-sided markets to internalize the positive indirect network externalities, both sides of the markets will be tempted to reduce their burden at the expense of the other side, which will hamper the frictionless working of the platform because it disturbs the internalization mechanism. Moreover, providing information to the platform in order to improve the platform services could imply the provision of this information to the other side of the market, which could use it to the disadvantage of the information providers. These opposing interests are significant challenges for type Ib cooperatives and the platform success will crucially depend on managing this conflict of interests.

---

[20]One example is OSADL eG. OSADL is a cooperative that produces open source software solutions for companies of the machinery industry. Members of the cooperative are companies from the machinery industry (demand side) and IT companies programming the software (supply side).

Type II: Suppliers or Consumers Own the Platform and Jointly Own the Goods

The type II cooperative refers to a different understanding of ownership. While for type I cooperatives we assume that the goods, which will be shared, are owned by the individuals, in a type II cooperative the goods will be property of the cooperative and the members of the cooperative will share the ownership of the goods by becoming a member of the cooperative. The joint ownership of type II substitutes for the individual ownership of type I cooperatives. Because of this movement from individual to collective ownership the type II cooperatives lack the typical peer-to-peer characteristic of other sharing platforms. Yet, it is still part of the sharing economy because the individuals share the use of the goods, but add the sharing of ownership of the goods to their sharing activities. This kind of "double sharing" will be applied if the acquisition and ownership of the goods is very expensive and individual ownership is not affordable. The joint ownership also implies that the platform does not show the usual indirect network externalities, because the supply is provided by the cooperative itself (i.e. jointly by the users). Instead we observe direct network externalities. On the one hand additional members may increase the cooperative's pool of goods, on the other hand the additional member are new competitors for the limited number goods in the cooperative. So in the case of shared ownership the platform has a different nature and different economic characteristics. Nevertheless the dependency issues remain. Since the consumers are not able to own the goods individually, they depend on the supply by third parties, which again could have monopoly or oligopoly characteristics. Therefore, a cooperative will protect against exploitation as long as disciplining market mechanisms are not available. Other renting solutions are conceivable but could create new dependencies for the users.

Because the cooperative owns the (mostly expensive) goods the type II cooperative of sharing is usually confined to local areas but could grow into larger regions or countrywide over time. Therefore, due to this anchoring of the platform in the real economy it does not exhibit the characteristic quick platform expansion. Nevertheless, the type II cooperatives look back to a long tradition. In the agricultural sector joint ownership and joint use of machines has been common for centuries. Another example is Mobility, a Swiss car renting cooperative, which owns a large pool of cars and rents out these cars to their members.

Although the cooperative model is very convincing in containing the effects of the platform's market power especially for the type I cooperatives, there are some significant disadvantages of this model in implementing it for platforms in the sharing economy. Due to the indirect network externalities and the implied economies of scale, it is necessary that the platform grows quickly in order to generate these network externalities that benefit the platform users. This is in contrast to the ownership function of cooperative members, where customers have to become owners and contribute capital to the platform. Especially those users having free access to the platform will not be willing to listen to lengthy explanations about platform ownerships, rights and duties and they will be even less inclined to contribute capital.

Because the cooperative model requires more explanation and a monetary contribution, it hampers the quick growth of the platform, which is detrimental in a market, where speed is one of the success factors.

Moreover, some of the platform models of the sharing economy need some upfront investments, e.g. to buy infrastructure or to advertise the platform in order to become a winner in the platform competition. Again such investments are harder to finance for a cooperative that covers its financing needs by the equity provided by the members. The cooperative—like any other company—can of course use debt for financing but also the debt financing depends on the amount of equity that is provided by the members.

It will crucially depend on the individuals' preferences whether these impediments will restrict the use of cooperatives as a governance scheme for platforms. Up to now the convenience of easy access to platforms and the overwhelming opportunities they offer seemingly outweigh the benefits of further control over the monopolist. Nevertheless, recent scandals like the data abuse at Facebook may be a starting point to rethink these preferences, which would open the way for more complex governance structures.

Conclusion and Practical Implications

The sharing economy is an interesting new way to allocate existing goods among people. It is not creating new markets but the platforms of the sharing economy are able to bring new suppliers and consumers to the markets and give them beneficial access to these markets. Nevertheless, these platforms exhibit production characteristics that tend to monopolize market structures. In order to overcome the problems of monopolies without losing the advantages of platforms we analysed the applicability of cooperatives as an organization of the platforms. Organizing platforms as cooperatives eliminates the negative monopoly effects of the platforms, while the positive platform effects are preserved. Thus, the cooperative is—theoretically—the superior type of organization for platforms of the sharing economy. However, different markets of the sharing economy may require different cooperative structures which are subject to some disadvantages of the cooperative like heterogeneity of the members or a detrimentally slow speed of growth. Thus, further introspection into different types of markets and innovative financing mechanisms of platform cooperatives is still needed.

Although the idea of having a cooperative ownership is—up to now—purely theoretical, it should encourage a broader discussion of the platforms' governance structures. Due to the immanent competition restricting characteristics of platforms the currently existing platforms are not able to fully exploit the opportunities of the new technologies that are used in these platforms and they are dangerously redistributing rents from the individuals to the monopolistic platforms. The growing relevance of peer-to-peer activities will also require a rethinking of the economics how individuals form there buy-or-rent decisions.

References

Armstrong, M. (2006). Competition in two-sided markets. *RAND Journal of Economics, 37*(3), 668–691.

Anderson, Ch. (2006). *The Long Tail, New York*.

Clemons, E. K., Reddi, S., & Row, M. C. (1993). The impact of information technology on the organization of economic activity: The "Move to the Middle" hypothesis. *Journal of Management Information Systems, 10*(2), 9–35.

Coase, R. (1937). The nature of the firm. *Economica, 4*(16), 386–405.

Demary, V. (2015). Competition in the sharing economy. Institut der deutschen Wirtschaft, IW Policy Paper No. 19, Cologne.

Dittmann, H./ Kuchinke, B. (2015): Ordnungsökonomische Aspekte der Sharing Economy. In *ORDO – Jahrbuch für die Ordnung von Wirtschaft und Gesellschaft* (Vol. 66, pp. 243–262).

Fraiberger, S., & Sundararajan, A. (2015). Peer-to-peer rental markets in the sharing economy. NET-Institute Working Paper No. 15-19.

Hart, O. (1995): Firms, Constracts, and Financial Structure, Oxford.

Horton, J. J., & Zeckhauser, R. J. (2016). Owning, using and renting: Some simple economics of the "Sharing Economy". NBER Working Paper No. 22029.

Katz, V. (2015). Regulating the sharing economy. *Berkeley Technology Law Journal, 30*(4), 1067–1126.

Malone, Th. W. (2004). *The Future of Work, Boston*.

Malone, Th W, Yates, J., & Benjamin, R. I. (1987). Electronic markets and electronic hierarchies. *Communications of the ACM, 30*(6), 484–497.

Monopolkommission. (2016). Wettbewerb 2016. Einundzwanzigstes Hauptgutachten, Baden-Baden.

Peitz, M. (2006). Marktplätze und indirekte Netzwerkeffekte. *Perspektiven der Wirtschaftspolitik, 7*(3), 317–333.

Peitz, M., & Schwalbe, U. (2016). Kollaboratives Wirtschaften oder Turbokapitalismus. *Perspektiven der Wirtschaftspolitik, 17*(3), 232–252.

Picot, A., Dietl, H., Franck, E., Fiedler, M., & Royer, S. (2015). *Organisation – Theorie und Praxis aus ökonomischer Sicht*, 7th ec. Stuttgart.

PwC. (2016). Assessing the size and presence of the collaborative economy in Europe. http://ec.eu ropa.eu/DocsRoom/documents/16952/attachments/1/translations/en/renditions/native.

Rauch, D. E., & Schleicher, D. (2015). Like Uber, but for local governmental policy: The future of local regulation on the "Sharing Economy". George Mason University Law and Economic Research Paper Series, Research Paper No. 15-01.

Rochet, J-Ch., & Tirole, J. (2006). Two-sided markets: A progress report. *RAND Journal of Economics, 37*(3), 645–667.

Sundararajan, A. (2014). Peer-to-peer businesses and the sharing (collaborative) economy: Overview, economic effects and regulatory issues. https://smallbusiness.house.gov/uploadedfi les/1-15-2014_revised_sundararajan_testimony.pdf.

Williamson, O. (1985). *The economic institutions of capitalism, New York et al*.

Chapter 10
How Collaboration and Digitization Transform Large Project Business

Klaus Backhaus and Ulf König

Introduction

Collaboration and digitization are two trending buzzwords which companies both put their hopes in and struggle to handle at the same time. There are statements that the digitization process will destroy complete business models, including even those of current market leaders (Loebbecke & Picot, 2015). While the effect of collaboration and digitization is well covered in scientific B2C literature and both industry experts as well as consultancies offer seemingly endless amounts of practical advice, little is known with regard to the B2B sector (Miller, 2012). Adding to the matter's complexity, the B2B sector is rather heterogeneous consisting of four fundamentally different business models (Backhaus & Voeth, 2014). Out of these four, the so-called large project business (LPB) has enjoyed the least coverage in existing literature and also shares the fewest communalities with the B2C sector, therefore making a particularly insightful object of investigation.

Based on these considerations, our paper poses the following research question: How do increasing levels of collaboration and digitization transform the principles of LPB? To answer this question, section "Fundamentals of Large Project Business (LPB)" delineates the concept of LPB and describe its modus operandi as compared to other B2B business models. Section "Collaboration as a Key Characteristic of LPB" gives special focus to the role of collaboration, which has already been crucial in the past and which gains even more importance in today's globalized world. Section "Enlargement of Collaboration Partners in Times of Digitization" narrows down the effects of collaboration and digitization to three concrete examples: contract

K. Backhaus (✉) · U. König
WWU - University of Muenster, Münster, Germany
e-mail: backhaus@wiwi.uni-muenster.de

U. König
e-mail: ulf.koenig@uni-muenster.de

© Springer International Publishing AG, part of Springer Nature 2019
K. Riemer et al. (eds.), *Collaboration in the Digital Age*, Progress in IS,
https://doi.org/10.1007/978-3-319-94487-6_10

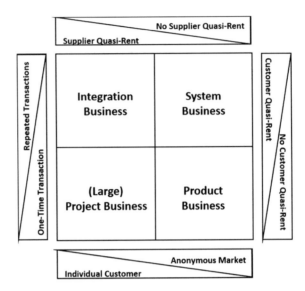

Fig. 10.1 Typology of B2B Business Models (Backhaus & Voeth, 2014)

negotiation, organizational charts, and advanced tools. Finally, section "Conclusion" closes with a short conclusion. Our contribution is to provide one of the first analyses of the impact of collaboration, digitization, and their interplay from a B2B and especially LPB perspective based on three clear-cut examples, which we deem highly illustrative of the forces at work. In contrast to the widespread belief that digitization impacts B2C businesses earlier and more strongly than their B2B counterparts (Backhaus & Voeth, 2014), we show that there is plenty of evidence against this cliché.

Fundamentals of Large Project Business (LPB)

In light of the broad range of B2B products, companies, and industries observed in practice, several authors such as Kleinaltenkamp (2001), Plinke (1997), and Richter (2001) have proposed typologies to structure the field. One of the most widely accepted typologies comes from Backhaus and Voeth (2014) and distinguishes between four different B2B business models along the following dimensions: (Fig. 10.1)

(1) Individual customer versus anonymous market: B2B customers can be either very few and therefore well identifiable or many and therefore more anonymous. The latter resembles B2C market structures as B2C consumers are almost always too many to e.g., develop intense seller-buyer relationships, truly customize products, and target them with personalized marketing messages.

(2) One-time transaction versus repeated transactions: B2B customers may either buy only once or repeatedly.

(3) Supplier quasi-rent versus no supplier quasi-rent: Suppliers may have or have not quasi-rents. The quasi-rent describes the supplier's investment specificity and therefore the switching costs, which can increase productivity while also restricting asset application possibilities. In particular, quasi-rents are defined as "[…] the excess of value over its salvage value, i.e., its value in its next best use to another renter" (Klein, Crawford, & Alchian, 1978).

(4) Customer quasi-rent versus no customer quasi-rent: analogous to (3).

The resulting four business models can be described as follows:

(1) The product business is characterized by an anonymous target market, one-time transactions, and the absence of both supplier as well as customer rents. In essence, this boils down to selling commodities. Typical examples are screws or computer hard drives. This business model shares the most similarities with classical B2C business models.

(2) The system business is characterized by an anonymous market, repeated transactions, no supplier quasi-rent but the presence of customer quasi-rents. Typical examples include office furniture and SAP software as products are complementary to each other and form a modular system. Once one has decided to make the initial purchase, there is a lock-in effect due to switching costs with regard to follow-up purchases.

(3) The integration business is characterized by few, identifiable customers, repeated transactions, and the presence of both supplier and customer quasi-rents. A typical example is an automotive supplier building a production line for a given OEM. Both the supplier as well as the OEM are highly dependent on the other party as reflected by the presence of mutual quasi-rents.

(4) Lastly, LPB as the subject of this paper is characterized by few, identifiable customers, one-time transactions, and the presence (absence) of supplier (customer) quasi-rents. Typical examples include rolling mills, power plants, and offshore wind parks, which are all technically complex systems of high monetary value (Backhaus & Voeth, 2014). Products are custom-made for each customer resulting in non-reciprocal quasi-rents on the supplier's side. To compete against the relatively small number of worldscale competitors in LPB, a company needs different technical and commercial competencies that vary from customer to customer.

Since LPB has rarely been addressed in existing literature so far and since it shares the least similarities with classical B2C business models, it represents a suitable object of analysis for this paper.

Collaboration as a Key Characteristic of LPB

Central Impact Factors

Managing LPB regularly means to bring together process and product know-how from different technical areas (like mechanics, mechatronics and electrical works) and companies on a project-specific basis. Moreover, the customer requires an individual solution that works reliably and meets the defined targets (e.g., "allowed downtimes" or "minimal output"; Backhaus & Voeth, 2014; Günter, 2013). Although project-specific competence mergers were historically the main reason for the broad and intensive collaboration in LPB, a large set of other reasons to collaborate has emerged in the meantime. Figure 10.2 contains a list of those reasons which Backhaus and Gnam (1999) consider as central impact factors in this context.

This non-exhaustive list of reasons to call LPB a collaborative business explains/accounts for the growing sizes of supplier coalitions (Backhaus & Gnam, 1999). In particular, the highlighted criteria #1, #3, #5 and #8 mainly determine size and structure of the alliances (see the following sections for an explanation why these criteria have led to coalitions with more and smaller members).

If one takes out these four dominant criteria, five criteria remain. These five criteria as a cluster are named "miscellaneous" not because they are less important, but their importance varies from situation to situation (Backhaus & Gnam, 1999). If patents are relevant, they are a strong argument in that situation. In other settings, patents

No.	Label	Short Description
1	Pooling of Know-how	Single supplier does not have enough Know-how to manage the project alone
2	Risk sharing	If the total project risk is too high to be handled by one supplier
3	Financial structuring	LPs regularly need an efficient financing structure that only can be realized, if one can get credit insurance in foreign countries which is linked to deliveries from that country these makes is necessary to join the coalition
4	Wanted by customer	The customer asks the supplier to include a special supplier into in the coalition
5	Local manufacturing	Legal prescription to produce parts of the order in customer country
6	Patents	Enlargement of partners because a technology is needed that is owned by a special supplier
7	Capacity enlargement	LP is too big for one supplier
8	"Cheapening"	Looking for partners who can "cheapen" the project-costs
9	Competitor reduction	By collaborating between competitors the number of competitors can be reduced
10	...	

Fig. 10.2 Reasons for collaboration in LPBs (Backhaus & Gnam, 1999)

may not be a driver at all. See Fig. 10.2 for a detailed description what the potential drivers are and how they contribute to the effect of growing collaboration units.

LPB and the Four Dominant Criteria

Criteria #1 (Pooling of Know-how) and #3 (Financial Structuring) are considered to be dominant because they are relevant with almost every order. As we have already pointed out, know-how pooling is the basic criterion that historically led to the effect of collaboration within LPB (Backhaus & Voeth, 2014; Backaus & Gnam, 1999). Furthermore, almost every LP has to be order financed which is why suppliers have to find credit agencies (e.g., private banks or other special institutions that are prepared to finance industrial projects like the IBRD, International Bank for Reconstruction and Development, shortly called World Bank).

To finance a project in dimensions of a billion dollars or even more, these institutions ask for international credit insurance (Backhaus, Brüne, & Wiegand, 2013). In all exporting countries, government supported public credit insurances have been installed providing exporters with the demanded credit risk coverages. These serve as a prerequisite for getting credits.

As all credit agencies—the German credit insurance company is called Euler-Hermes—have only limited budgets for individual countries, suppliers are often forced to get insurance and financial support from those countries that still have disposable budgets (Häberle, 2002). The supplier has to put together piece by piece like a puzzle in order to construct a complete financing and insurance package (financial engineering; Backhaus & Voeth, 2014). However, driven by political considerations, national insurers often ask supplier coalitions for national manufacturing in order to stimulate their local economies. This requires suppliers to make the local player a member of the supply consortium (Häberle, 2002), thereby enlarging the coalition (criterion #5).

Another supply-sided problem is the "Cheapening Criterion" (criterion #8). The rationale behind this criterion is as follows: to offer a competitive price, it may be a solution to find partners from countries with lower price levels. As a consequence of both the criteria "local manufacturing" and "cheapening", the project manager sometimes has to integrate partners from 20 countries or more in order to obtain the required financial package, which in turn makes collaboration ever more complex (Siepert, 1987).

Enlargement of Collaboration Partners in Times of Digitization

As we have shown, the number of coalition partners in LPB has always been larger than in other types of projects. In times of globalization and quickly developing economies in emerging countries, this number tends to grow even bigger. As a second megatrend, digitization has proved to be an omnipresent force with enormous potential of disruption. These two developments have some severe consequences for the mechanics of LPB. With large projects that have a two-digit number of consortial partners, managing the supplier alliance in times of digitization is a challenge. It gets even more complicated when—as often observed in practice—partners are not only more numerous, but come from different countries. The following sections will analyze in detail three illustrative effects of increased levels of collaboration and digitization on LPB, respectively: contract negotiation, organizational charts, and advanced tools.

Negotiating the Contract: Key to Legal Aspects

As customers and collaborating partners are located all around the world, the consortium is embedded into diverging legal frames (Backhaus & Gnam, 1999). In theory, the supplier should therefore have legal knowledge with respect to the specialties of almost every country in the world. As this is impossible to realize, players in LPB have developed contractual designs that enable the partners to build their own statute regulations and thus do not have to recur on the general rules of national legislation. It is this contract, which shall give the answer on any question that may arise. Exceptions become relevant only in those cases where national regulation is mandatory (e.g., in case of exclusion of liability or gross negligence) or if a claim comes up which is not accounted for in the contract. In these cases, the legal answer will be given by the respective national law. As it can be seen, a good contract is of mayor importance in LPB. But what makes a contract a good one? This is a question of perspective: we distinguish between a customer contract (CC) and a supplier contract (SC). The CC addresses the outer relationship between the customer and the seller as a whole, while the SC is mainly directed towards the inner relationship between coalition partners. The CC (also called "vertical contract") defines rights and obligations that may become relevant between supplier and customer, usually following a four-chapter-structure that can be taken as a check list during customer-supplier negotiations (for more details see Backhaus & Uekermann, 1990):

(1) Technical solution
(2) Commercial conditions
(3) Contract execution
(4) Breach of contract

The SC relates to two groups of rules, namely those

(1)   which deal with regulating how to internally handle claims stemming from the CC (example: who is responsible for a delayed delivery and how to handle the claim?),
(2)   regulating intra-coalition claims and obligations without a customer claim being involved (example: employee of supplier A damages the equipment of supplier B. If there will be no general delay from that event, A and B still have to be clear about their legal rights and obligations.).

Importantly, the SC as the inner relationship cannot contain paragraphs that do not match the conditions of the CC as the outer relationship (e.g., the CC promises a penalty in case of delay, but the SC frees all partners from paying). Thus, the SC is valid only if it matches the conditions of the CC, which raises the need for homologation of both contracts.

The Effect of Larger Coalitions—New Liability Concepts

As outlined before, today's supplier coalitions tend to grow big, which moves the SC into the center of attention. As the number of consortium partners increases, the order volume per partner naturally has to shrink. This makes it necessary to develop new liability concepts on the supplier side since traditional liability rules based on the no-fault-principle do not work anymore (Backhaus & Molter, 1984): Imagine a consortium with 10 partners handling a penalized EUR 100m project. The partners have agreed on the following contract clause addressing the consequences of a delay in delivery time: "The supply consortium will deliver hard- and software specified in Appendix A of this contract until March 15, 2020. In case of delay the suppliers will pay a penalty of 1% of the order volume per delayed week up to the maximum of 10% of the order volume if the delay lasts 10 weeks or longer". What does this mean for the penalty to pay in case of being 10 weeks late (worst case)? Assumed the 10 partners all have the same portion of the EUR 100m order volume (EUR 10m) and one partner is responsible for the delay, he has to pay the entire penalty which also amounts to EUR 10m—eating up his entire order volume.

As this is unreasonable, we need another concept for growing alliances. Such a concept could be the pre-liability concept (PLC): the basic idea is to split all liabilities in pre- and post-liabilities (see Fig. 10.3; Backhaus & Molter, 1984). The consortium member, who has caused the delay, is liable for an a priori determined part of the damage value—regularly the liability percentage defined in the customer contract, not on the entire order volume but rather on his own order volume. The rest will be paid according to the respective order shares of the coalition members. This concept socializes parts of payments for damages among the partners. Empirical analyses of new risk distributions have shown that besides the traditional liability concept based on the no-fault-principle, three alternatives can be observed in practice (see Fig. 10.3).

Liability Rule	Effective Burden of Contractual Penalty Referring to the Share of Order	Non-Responsible Consortial Member	Responsible Consortial Member	Key	
1.	**No Fault:** The responsible consortial member is solely liable	—	$p_i = p_g * \dfrac{100}{q_i}$	b	Penalty distributed as the remainder among all partners
2.	**Payment-Related:** The responsible consortial member is pre-liable for .... percent of the amount to be paid to the customer Remainder according to the shares of order	$r_j = \dfrac{b * p_g}{100}$	$p_i = p_g \left[\dfrac{b}{100} + \dfrac{e}{q_i} \right]$	e	Penalty to be paid by responsible partner beforehand
3.	**Penalty-Related:** The responsible consortial member is pre-liable for up to an amount of .... percent of the amount of his/her share of order – Remainder according to the shares of order	$r_j = p_g - \dfrac{t * q_i}{100}$ $p_g \geq \dfrac{t * q_i}{100}$	$p_i = p_g + t \left[1 - \dfrac{q_i}{100} \right]$ $p_g \geq \dfrac{t * q_i}{100}$	p_g	Maximum penalty as percentage of total order value
4.	**Multiplier:** Pre-liability by a consortial quota-based multiplier	$r_j = \dfrac{100\, p_g}{100 + q\,(v-1)}$	$p_i = v * \dfrac{100\, p_g}{100 + q\,(v-1)}$	p_i	Penalty of responsible partner i in percent of his/her order value
				q_i	Share of the responsible partner i of the total order value in percent
				r_j	Penalty of the non-responsible partner j as percent of his/her order
				s_j	Share of non-responsible partner j of the total order value in percent
				t	Percent of the value of share of order to be paid by the responsible partner as pre-liability
				u	Percent of the value of share of order to be paid by the non-responsible partner
				v	Multiplier of the percentage of the consortium-based share

Fig. 10.3 Different liability rules (Backhaus & Molter, 1984)

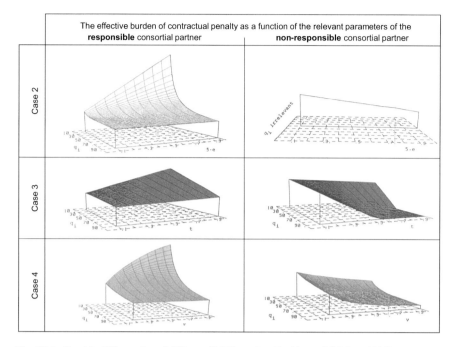

Fig. 10.4 Graphical illustration of different liability rules (Backhaus & Molter, 1984)

Column 2 specifies the liability effects depending on the SC. Column 3 (4) describes the liability effects of the different cases on the non-responsible (responsible) consortial members. Regarding the regulations of the pre-liability, they seem to be quite similar. However, looking at Fig. 10.4 as the graphical representation of the formulae in Fig. 10.3, it becomes clear that the effects of cases 2–4 on the penalty to be paid vary to a high extent. Simulating the effect of variations in the two parameters q_i (order share of the responsible consortial member) and the liability rule shows that their influence is in fact non-linear, except for case 3. Why is that? Case 3 is the only variant where the non-responsible partner can avoid any payment at all. Case 4 in comparison with case 2 shows that growing pre-liability rates in combination with shrinking consortial shares may lead to considerable higher payments.

The Effect of Digitization—Software-Aided Contract Negotiation

With an ever-bigger number of consortial partners, increased importance of the SC, and sophisticated liability rules, negotiation of such contracts has become a highly complex endeavor. While negotiation research has been the exclusive domain of game-theorists, economists, psychologists, and management/marketing scholars for decades, computer science and artificial intelligence (AI) have entered the arena with the advent of digitization. Historically, the application of AI in the context of negotiation is rooted in computers' ability to win complex games such as chess (Hsu, 2002) or poker (Spice & Allen, 2017) against human opponents. For any such game, it can be assumed that there is a winning strategy—the Nash Equilibrium, as game theory calls it (Nash, 1950). In order to identify this winning strategy, computers can teach themselves which actions to take (and which not) by means of reinforcement learning and Bayesian belief update processes, i.e. practicing trillions of games against a clone of itself (Gershgorn, 2017; Zeng & Sycara, 1998). Especially playing poker resembles a LPB-like negotiation as both situations are characterized by high levels of uncertainty with regard to variables such as the counterparty's cards or negotiation goals—something called "imperfect knowledge" in game theory.

Inspired by such developments in the field of gaming, a broad body of literature on autonomous software agents in negotiations has emerged. The investigated issues range from the effect of different algorithms on negotiation outcomes and welfare to the role of different bidding strategies (e.g., Faratina, Sierra, & Jennings, 2002; Ros & Sierra, 2006). Since the aim of our article is to illustrate the impact of collaboration and digitization in LPB on a macro level, a detailed review of the various kinds of algorithmic implementation would exceed our scope. It must be noted, however, that machine-machine negotiations, as investigated in the majority of these publications, represent a rather unlikely scenario both today and in the near future (Yang, Falcao, Delicado, & Ortony, 2014). In contrast, machine-human negotiations become more likely as technology advances. In such an environment, having the computer negotiate with business partners, sub-contractors, and customers may imply both benefits as well as threats: on the one hand, a well-trained software agent may close better deals than even the most experienced senior executive, e.g. because—unlike humans—AI is not prone to psychological biases such as loss aversion (here and in the following, Lin & Kraus 2010). In case of a lack of experienced negotiators, AI may still compensate for weakly trained negotiation skills and poorly qualified employees. Before actual negotiations, AI could also serve for training purposes in order to obtain the required skills. On the other hand, the process of negotiation oftentimes is a deeply human one and especially in the case of business partners and sub-contractors, it may represent the beginning of a long-lasting relationship. This may get overshadowed by perceptions of anonymity and mistrust as a result of having the computer negotiate. However, AI can adopt various strategies such as tactically disclosing negotiation goals to appear more human-like (Yang et al. 2014) as well as making multiple simultaneous-equivalent offers or delay acceptance in order to better understand the counterparty's preferences and achieve a win-win situation (Yang, Singhal, and Xu 2014). Using these and similar strategies has shown to both improve the negotiation outcome (e.g., in terms of individual utility, joint utility, or distance to Pareto-efficient solution) and the human's attitude towards the software agent, thus opening the door for a fruitful collaboration in the future.

Fig. 10.5 Alternative legal forms of supplier coalitions (Backhaus & Voeth, 2014)

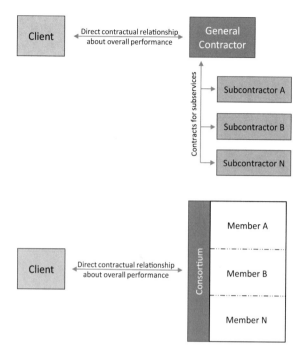

Changing the Organizational Chart

A basic decision in any alliance has to be made on the legal handling of different forms of cooperation. Basically we differentiate between two legal forms:

(1) General contractor model
(2) Project-specific consortium

For the differences between general contracting and a consortium see Fig. 10.5.

The general contractor is characterized by being the only representative of the supplier coalition to sign the customer contract (Backhaus & Voeth, 2014; Günter, 2013). Therefore, the general contractor is also the only one who has a direct contractual relationship with the customer. For the fulfilment of the contract, the general contractor places orders with sub-contractors. However, these sub-contractors are not liable for the delivery of the complete system, but only the general contractor.

In turn, a consortium can be understood as an unregistered company characterized by "joint and several liability". This means that each partner of the consortium is fully liable for any damage that the consortium as a whole or any of the involved partners may have caused (Backhaus & Voeth, 2014).

		General contracting	Consortia
Benefits	for clients	- only one negotiating partner - overall risk under one roof	- performance shares can be negotiated directly - liability basis increases
	for suppliers	- personal contribution is free determinable with a general contractor - free choice of subcontractors - reference advantage	- risk share decreases for all suppliers - direct client contact not just for the general contractor but for all members of a consortium (reference) - financing aids may be used, if as a requirement all direct client contacts are given
Disadvantages	for clients	- maybe lower liability basis at the supplier - if own know-how is great, in some circumstances it might be mandatory to give up performances which could be self performed	- more negotiating partners - must be able to judge the interface problems
	for suppliers	- if delivery conditions can not be passed on - bigger risk for the general contractor	- higher costs through coordination requirements - direct liability access to all members of a consortium

Fig. 10.6 Advantages and disadvantages of legal forms (Backhaus & Voeth, 2014)

The Effect of Larger Coalitions—Tendency Towards Consortia

Both legal forms have advantages and disadvantages. These are demonstrated in Fig. 10.6. While coalitions with smaller numbers of coalition partners may favor the consortium type of organization, growing numbers of consortial partners may make this type unattractive for various reasons (here and in the following Backhaus & Voeth, 2014):

(1) The supplier network becomes less transparent and the individual partner has less control. Therefore, many partners refrain from being made responsible for possible failures, which they had no power to prevent from happening. This development reinforces the need for new liability agreements.

(2) Coordination effort increases exponentially the more partners participate in a consortium leading to high friction loss and major inefficiencies. This is already a problem in the inner relationship between suppliers and can reach dramatic dimensions with regard to the outer relationship between customer and supplier.

(3) As a sub-domain of (2), negotiation effort increases with more partners joining an alliance.

The Effect of Digitization—Platform-Driven Partner Identification

Due to the trend of ever-larger alliances, which in turn make consortial forms of organization less attractive, the general contractor model gains increasing popularity. However, finding suitable sub-contractors in the traditional, offline way can represent a major challenge for many general contractors due to two primary reasons: first, as noted before, such networks may reach difficult-to-manage dimensions due to often-times very specialized customer requirements, which implies that a high number of sub-contractors has to be identified. Second, since each project is unique, one can rely only partly (if at all) on existing networks and former relationships. Here is where digitization comes in: apart from providing cheap, quick, and easy-to-use research possibilities such as Google's search application, which is increasingly used by B2B purchasers to gain information about business partners (Backhaus, Bröker, Brüne, & Gausling, 2013; Backhaus, Brüne, & Wiegand, 2013), digitization has paved the way for what is known as online reverse auctions (ORAs)—online platforms where sub-contractors bid for contracts (Sashi & O'Leary, 2002). Finding business partners via ORAs has shown to save time, effort, and ultimately costs because better candidates are identified at lower prices (Emiliani, 2000). However, attributing these achievements to digitization would be a premature oversimplification considering that traditional offline tenders have a similar effect. The digitization-induced advancement may rather be found in the surrounding service landscape, which not only helps to find suitable sub-contractors but guides collaboration at virtually every stage of the project in a way that would not be possible for offline tenders. For instance, the Oracle-owned platform GradeBeam offers contractors a matching algorithm, which refines the distribution of bid invitations to sub-contractors and thus helps reaching the most relevant ones (here and in the following, Oracle, 2016). Further down the process, GradeBeam provides pre-qualification services for shortlisted candidates, thereby reducing the risk of making a false choice due to lack of experience and/or heavy information asymmetries. Even later in the process, once the sub-contractor has been found, GradeBeam offers performance tracking and success evaluation far beyond the phase of tender preparation all the way through until the project's end. Finally, all data associated with this collaboration process and its different stages is collected, analyzed, and visualized in a central database at the general contractor's disposal. Looking at potential drawbacks of using such ORA platforms, it has to be noted that some contractors might have security and privacy concerns. Especially in the context of sensitive infrastructure or defense projects, business partners will be less willing to share information of the described extent with platform owners.

The above example shows not only how digitization radically alters the way sub-contractors can be found today—it also documents the manifold benefits and a potential downside for general contractors. However, ORA platforms function as two-sided markets, which are characterized by two distinct customer groups, to which the platform sells two different products (Rysman, 2009). While general contractors represent the first customer group, one also has to take into consideration the sub-contractors' interests as addressed in the following: on the positive side, suppliers also benefit from a highly convenient and time-efficient way to learn about new business opportunities, tools for smoother communication, and ultimately reduced cost of sales (Smeltzer & Carr, 2002). In addition, the above mentioned matching algorithms could provide proactive recommendations on which projects to bid. This would not only maximize success probability but also allow especially small sub-contractors to focus their limited resources only on projects, which match their specific competencies. On the negative side, this kind of new transparency is not available to the focal sub-contractor exclusively and therefore most likely increases competition (Smeltzer & Carr, 2002). Higher competition may in turn lead to lower prices and smaller profits for suppliers. Further, there is a certain risk to put effort into an ORA when in fact general contractors are not interested in a real offer but only seek to understand the market dynamics in order to increase negotiation power for a deal with a different supplier. In conclusion, the benefit-risk tradeoff appears less favorable for sub-contractors than for general contractors as there are fewer adjacent services and increased competition.

Advanced Tools

Another consequence of a growing number of coalition members is the need of owning adequate management tools and an appropriate culture in many—especially—supplier coalitions. While there seems to be a complete lack of literature on the impact of company culture in the context of LPB, a hardly overseeable offer of tools for project management is available. Googling for the term "project management tool" ends up with more than 14 million hits with software solutions in the lead. The tools encompass time- and cost-optimizing concepts as well as tracking systems or interface systems that concentrate on integrating the project management tools into other systems like ERP or PPS.

The Effect of Larger Coalitions—Software Standardization

The main priority of any LPB project manager is to ensure smooth coordination between the different business partners participating in the project. Problems of communication, supply chain alignment etc. have the potential to cause severe project delays, which would be penalized as outlined previously. To avoid this, a whole array of tools is at his or her disposal and although most of them are to some extent software-based as explained above, specific forms of organizations including responsibility distribution or feedback culture should also be mentioned in this context.

   To come up with a coordinated system, interfaces between these various software solutions need to be aligned. The probability that different software packages are used and consequently that their interfaces are not (fully) compatible rises with a larger number of consortial members. This phenomenon is not limited to LPB and in fact, most people may have experienced incompatibility issues in their personal life—however, in practice, the cost of this problem is often underestimated and literature is silent about its severeness. To solve this issue, there exist three main approaches:

(1) The first solution is to keep the number of different systems as low as possible in order to avoid compatibility problems. This requires neither changes nor effort from the software developers' side, but LPB companies need to find a (possibly difficult-to-reach) consensus regarding which tools to apply.

(2) The second solution is to aim for interface standardization such that the software packages themselves can be kept, but the intersections become fully compatible to each other. This approach requires significant investments on the software developers' side while users can stick with their familiar routines.

(3) The third solution is to develop new tools that are fully compatible by nature, such as browser-based software. New tools would require considerable effort from both developers as well as users. Since these services have emerged along with the progress of digitization and heavily rely on technologies such as cloud computing etc., they will be discussed in more detail in the next chapter.

The Effect of Digitization—Virtual Organizations

A virtual organization can be considered as an alternative to conventional forms of corporate organization involving physically detached and disseminated entities connected through digital technologies (Gupta, 1997). Originally, the concept was used to describe service-like organizational constellations where value creation is more dependent on immaterial skills and knowledge rather than physical machinery (The Economist, 2009). However, in times of ever-larger consortia spread across the globe, virtual organizations have also turned into the backbone of collaboration between LPB partners. This development was enabled through the emergence of various new technologies aiming at the reduction of collaboration barriers: for instance, cloud computing has paved the way for ubiquitous, simultaneous, and instantaneous access to shared resources through storing documents, applications, and services on centralized webservers (Hassan, 2011). Relying on this technology, applications like Google Docs allow multiple authors to edit a document simultaneously and let the authors observe the others' changes in real time (Google, 2017). So-called wikis are another tool which is based on a cloud-like idea that has gained widespread popularity: Wikis are websites whose content is contributed by a potentially unlimited number of authors, who are not defined in advance and who typically do not have a leader (Encyclopedia Britannica, 2007). Authors do not need any website programming skills as the infrastructure is provided in form of a browser-based text editor without further add-ons (Leuf & Cunningham, 2001). In addition, wiki entries are connected to each other via hyperlinks, which promotes meaningful topic association. Invented by computer programmers Bo Leuf and Ward Cunningham in 2001, the Hawaiian word "wiki" means "quick" (Leuf & Cunningham, 2001). The most famous wiki is probably wikipedia.org ranking among the top ten most visited websites globally since 2007 (Alexa, 2017). In the case of LPB, companies operate private wikis as knowledge management resources, notetaking tools, community websites, or intranets.

Both these examples, Google Docs and wikis, show how LPB consortia can organize themselves virtually by means of digital tools. What are the effects of such developments? On the one hand, there are effects rooted in the organizational change and on the other hand, there are effects stemming from the concrete application of the above mentioned tools. Regarding the former, virtual organizations clearly increase corporate flexibility, agility, and responsiveness as business partners do not have to resort to more bureaucratic forms of collaboration (Maccoby, 1991). What is more, virtual organizations as a whole as well as the separate members can better exploit their comparative advantages as they can focus on their core competencies and pool the remaining requirements (Igbaria & Tan, 1998). Isaca (2001) further found that virtual organizations are 30–50% more productive on average and significantly less prone to errors, which ultimately also leads to cost savings. These advantages stand in sharp contrast to the challenges that come along with virtual organizations. These mainly stem from the danger to neglect human nature in an increasingly anonymous process of collaboration: first, virtual interaction implies reduced face-to-face contact and therefore more room for misunderstandings. Lee (2014) observes lower levels of communication intensity in virtual organizations compared to physical ones, which is generally viewed as detrimental with regard to the project's success. In addition, Lee (2014) shows that participating partners are oftentimes confronted with a latent clash of organizational cultures, which does not get addressed as diligently as in other forms of cooperation such as post-merger integration in M&A. Lastly, Lee (2014) points out that virtual collaboration tends to hinder the cultivation of interpersonal relationships and trust among business partners.

On a lower level, the usage of digital collaboration tools such as cloud-based and cloud-like technology (wikis) also triggers various effects which go beyond the general ones presented above. On the one hand, collaboration has become more democratic and hierarchies have flattened since contributions to wikis etc. can be made on the spot without being filtered before. In fact, Leuf and Cunningham (2001) emphasize that wiki authorship must not be limited to experts in the traditional sense as content should be written by users for users. As a second consequence, reading what others have contributed in real time may result in higher levels of inspiration and creativity for the author's own contribution as it resembles idea generation approaches such as the 635-method (Rohrbach, 1969). This may ultimately lead to higher output quality at increased speed. On the other hand, having various authors edit and manipulate content and data simultaneously oftentimes results in redundancies and poor structure. In the worst possible case, the absence of revision and control can even lead to erroneous content being disseminated. This is why version control systems (VCSs) as another popular tool were called into existence: VCSs originally come from the field of software engineering, where a programming code is created in teams and needs to be reviewed by the other team members before implementation. The application tracks the changes to any given document and signs them with a timestamp, such that erroneous parts can be removed by retrieving a previous version. At the simplest level, this involves only saving a new copy of the document whenever a change has been made. At the more sophisticated level, a project can be partitioned into trunks and branches that can be approved, discarded, merged, or separated further while also recording meta data such as authorship, comments, tags etc. In conclusion, since the threats of using cloud-based and cloud-like collaborative infrastructure can be mitigated by deploying version control, the advantages will most likely dominate.

Conclusion

Collaboration and digitization are omnipresent buzzwords in today's business world. While numerous publications, consultancies, curricula etc. address the undisputable effect of these two phenomena on B2C industries, the B2B sector and especially LPB tend to fall off the radar. LPB has always been characterized by the demand for close collaboration and while some of the resulting consequences were happily embraced in practice, others were largely neglected. However, the situation has changed with the rise of digitization and there are interaction effects between both phenomena that cannot be ignored any longer. Yet, we did not come across any publication dedicated to the effect of digitization and its interplay with collaboration in a B2B or LPB setting. This paper represents a first step towards filling this gap by contrasting how LPB used to operate (and to a large extent still continues to do so today) and how collaboration and digitization revolutionize this industry. Three examples are analyzed in particular: First, contracts now feature new forms of liability agreements and are negotiated by automated software agents. Second, there is a trend away from consortia in favor of general contractor models, which is supported by ORA platforms easing the search for and management of sub-contractors by providing a rich variety of surrounding services. Third, virtual organizations and digital collaboration tools alter the way how business partners collaborate on a day-to-day basis rendering physical contact (almost) needless. While these three examples may not be the only changes brought by digitization into LPB, they nicely illustrate the disruptive potential coming along with these forces. As our work is purely conceptual, we hope to stimulate further studies into this direction that may also provide empirical proof and quantification of the outlined effects.

References

Alexa. (2017). The top 500 sites on the web. Retrieved November 7, 2017, from https://www.alex a.com/topsites.

Backhaus, K., Bröker, O., Brüne, P., & Gausling, P. (2013). Digitale Medien in B2B-Beschaffungsprozessen - eine explorative Untersuchung. Working Paper No. 52, Institut für Anlagen und Systemtechnologien, Westfälische Wilhelms-Universität Münster.

Backhaus, K., Brüne, P. A., & Wiegand, N. (2013). Auftragsfinanzierung und Financial Engineering. In M. Kleinaltenkamp, W. Plinke, & I. Geiger (Eds.), *Auftrags- und Projektmanagement* (pp. 137–173). Wiesbaden: Springer Gabler.

Backhaus, K., & Gnam, P. (1999). *Vertragsmanagement im internationalen Anlagengeschäft*. Berlin: unpublished manuscript.

Backhaus, K., & Molter, W. (1984). Auswirkungen verwirkter Pönale - Finanzielle Konsequenzen alternativer interner Haftungsregelungen bei konsortial errichteten Industrieanlagen. *ZfbF, 36*(3), 183–199.

Backhaus, K., & Uekermann, H. (1990). Projektfinanzierung: eine Methode zur Finanzierung von Großprojekten. *Wirtschaftswissenschaftliches Studium, 19*(3), 106–112.

Backhaus, K., & Voeth, M. (2014). *Industriegütermarketing*. München: Verlag Franz Vahlen GmbH.

Emiliani, M. L. (2000). Business-to-business online auctions: Key issues for purchasing process improvement. *Supply Chain Management: An International Journal, 5*(4), 176–186.

Encyclopedia Britannica. (2007). Wiki. Retrieved November 7, 2017, from https://www.britannica.com/topic/wiki.

Faratina, P., Sierra, C., & Jennings, N. R. (2002). Using similarity criteria to make issue trade-offs in automated negotiations. *Artificial Intelligence, 142*(2), 205–237.

Gershgorn, D. (2017). How a poker-playing AI is learning to negotiate better than any human. Retrieved November 07, 2017, from https://qz.com/907896/how-poker-playing-ai-libratus-is-learning-to-negotiate-better-than-any-human/.

Google. (2017). Google Docs—Create and edit documents online, for free. Retrieved November 7, 2017, from https://www.google.com/docs/about/.

Günter, B. (2013). Projektkooperationen. In M. Kleinaltenkamp, W. Plinke, & I. Geiger (Eds.), *Auftrags- und Projektmanagement* (pp. 383–422). Wiesbaden: Springer Gabler.

Gupta, J. N. D. (1997). *Association for Information Systems Proceedings of the Americas Conference on Information Systems*, 15–17 August 1997. Indianapolis (pp. 417–419).

Häberle, S. (2002). *Handbuch der Außenhandelsfinanzierung*. München, Wien: Oldenbourg.

Hassan, Q. F. (2011). Demystifying cloud computing. *The Journal of Defense Software Engineering*, 16–21.

Hsu, F.-h. (2002). *Behind deep blue. Building the computer that defeated the world chess champion*. Princeton: Princeton University Press.

Igbaria, M., & Tan, M. (1998). *The virtual workplace*. London: Idea group Publishing.

Isaca. (2001). Understanding virtual organizations. Retrieved October 10, 2014, from https://www.google.com/url?sa=t&rct=j&q=&esrc=s&source=web&cd=1&ved=0ahUKEwjIksfM8__bAhVIOhQKHSDfAR8QFgg0MAA&url=http%3A%2F%2Fwww.vodppl.upm.edu.my%2Fuploads%2Fdocs%2FUnderstanding%2520Virtual%2520Organizations.docx&usg=AOvVaw3_-GWUkHkymm1CS2rOYUm-.

Klein, B., Crawford, R. G., & Alchian, A. A. (1978). Vertical integration, appropriable rents, and the competitive contracting process. *The Journal of Law & Economics, 21*(2), 297–326.

Kleinaltenkamp, M. (2001). *Business-to-business-marketing*. Wiesbaden: Gabler.

Lee, M. R. (2014). *Leading virtual project teams: Adapting leadership theories and communications techniques to 21st century organizations*. Boca Raton: Auerbach Publications.

Leuf, B., & Cunningham, W. (2001). *The wiki way: Collaboration and sharing on the internet: Quick collaboration on the web*. London: Pearson Education.

Lin, R., & Kraus, S. (2010). Can automated agents proficiently negotiate with humans? *Communications of the ACM, 53*(1), 78–88.

Loebbecke, C., & Picot, A. (2015). Reflections on societal and business model transformation arising from digitization and big data analytics: A research agenda. *The Journal of Strategic Information Systems, 24*(3), 149–157.

Maccoby, M. (1991). Closing the motivation gap. *Research-Technology Management, 34*(1), 50–51.

Miller, M. (2012). *B2B digital marketing: Using the web to market directly to business*. Indianapolis: Que Publishing.

Nash, J. F. (1950). The bargaining problem. *Econometrica, 18*(2), 155–162.

Oracle. (2016). How do general contractors find their subcontractors and why should you care? Retrieved November 7, 2017, from http://www.texturacorp.com/bidmanagement-blog/how-do-g eneral-contractors-find-their-subcontractors-and-why-should-you-care/.

Plinke, W. (1997). Grundlagen des Geschäftsbeziehungsmanagements. In W. Plinke & M. Kleinal-tenkamp (Eds.), *Geschäftsbeziehungsmanagement im Technischen Vertrieb* (pp. 1–62). Berlin.

Richter, H. P. (2001). *Investitionsgütermarketing: Business-to-Business-Marketing von Indus-triegüterunternehmen.* München: Fachbuchverlag Leipzig.

Rohrbach, B. (1969). Kreativ nach Regeln – Methode 635, eine neue Technik zum Lösen von Problemen. *Absatzwirtschaft, 12*(19), 73–76.

Ros, R., & Sierra, C. (2006). A negotiation meta strategy combining trade-off and concession moves. *Autonomous agent and multiagent systems, 12*(2), 163–181.

Rysman, M. (2009). The economics of two-sided markets. *Journal of Economic Perspectives, 23*(3), 125–143.

Sashi, C. M., & O'Leary, B. (2002). The role of Internet auctions in the expansion of B2B markets. *Industrial Marketing Management, 31*(2), 103–110.

Siepert, H.-M. (1987). Multinationale Anbietergemeinschaften in der Exportfinanzierung. In K. Backhaus & H.-M. Siepert (Eds.), *Auftragsfinanzierung im internationalen Anlagengeschäft* (pp. 145–162). Stuttgart: Poeschel Verlag.

Smeltzer, L. R., & Carr, A. S. (2002). Reverse auctions in industrial marketing and buying. *Business Horizons, 45*(2), 47–52.

Spice, B., & Allen, G. (2017). Upping the ante: Top poker pros face off vs. artificial intelligence. Retrieved November 7, 2017, from https://www.cmu.edu/news/stories/archives/2017/january/po ker-pros-vs-AI.html.

The Economist. (2009). The virtual organization. Retrieved November 7, 2017, from http://www.e conomist.com/node/14301746.

Yang, Y., Falcao, H., Delicado, N., & Ortony, A. (2014). Reducing mistrust in agent-human nego-tiations. *IEEE Intelligent Systems, 29*(2), 36–43.

Yang, Y., Singhal, S., & Yunjie, X. (2014). Alternate strategies for a win-win seeking agent in agent-human negotiations. *Journal of Management Information Systems, 29*(3), 223–256.

Zeng, D., & Sycara, K. (1998). Bayesian learning in negotiation. *International Journal of Human-Computer Studies, 48*(1), 125–141.

Chapter 11
The First (Beer) Living Lab: Learning to Sustain Network Collaboration for Digital Innovation

Frank Frößler, Boriana Rukanova, Stefan Klein, Allen Higgins, Yao-Hua Tan and Séamas Kelly

Introduction

There is a gap in our understanding of the social structures and collaboration processes that sustain Living Labs, even as they gain attention as real-life experimentation settings for developing and testing innovative technology. This study offers an in-depth analysis of the first living lab of the ITAIDE research and development programme (Tan, Bjørn-Andersen, Klein, & Rukanova, 2011).[1]

The Beer Living Lab was designed as a platform for customs innovation.[2] The problem addressed is the paradox of facilitating trade while maintaining control. Governmental, legal and regulatory environments all have a role in safeguarding the public good by controlling supply chains while at the same time facilitating economic activity. The on-going challenge for both business and government is how to innovate

---

[1] ITAIDE: Information Technology for Adoption and Intelligent Design for E-Government.

[2] Earlier versions of this article were presented at the 20th Bled eMergence conference (Froessler, Rukanova, Klein, Tan, & Higgins, 2007) and portions published (Rukanova et al., 2011; Klein, Higgins, & Rukanova, 2011).

F. Frößler · A. Higgins (✉) · S. Kelly
University College Dublin, Dublin, Ireland
e-mail: allen.higgins@ucd.ie

F. Frößler
e-mail: ffroessler@gmx.de

B. Rukanova · Y.-H. Tan
Delft University of Technology, Delft, The Netherlands
e-mail: B.D.rukanova@tudelft.nl

Y.-H. Tan
e-mail: y.tan@tudelft.nl

S. Klein
WWU - University of Muenster, Münster, Germany

© Springer International Publishing AG, part of Springer Nature 2019
K. Riemer et al. (eds.), *Collaboration in the Digital Age*, Progress in IS,
https://doi.org/10.1007/978-3-319-94487-6_11

in regulated environments. Control of security, tariffs, excise and taxation raises the risk of duplicating or contradicting administrative, informational and technical needs. The need to enable transactions and traffic without losing control must accommodate the complexity of multi-stakeholder environments straddling these public and private domains.

In the Beer Living Lab we found that the social, attitudinal, performative, linguistic processes were crucial to the initiation and management of a network of collaboration. Our analysis reveals the importance of negotiation, sense-making, and knowledge brokers. Living Labs demand subtle, complex social performances from their participants to produce the effect of an inter-organisational network. The case highlights the importance of the practice of knowledge brokers and the varying activities which must be performed at different stages of the life cycle. It also makes a conceptual contribution by elaborating the concept of network practices on a social level, emphasising the importance of responding to contingencies of network collaboration over time.

What Are Living Labs?

A living lab is "a test environment for cyclical development and evaluation of complex, innovative concepts and technology, as part of a real-world, operational system, in which multiple stakeholders with different background and interests work together towards a common goal, as part of medium to long-term study" (Lucassen, Klievink, & Tavasszy, 2014).

Living labs were pioneered by William Mitchell at MIT's Media Lab and School of Architecture and City Planning (Eriksson, Niitamo, Kulkki, & Hribernik, 2006) and have since been initiated in many different domains. A living lab is a "naturalistic environment instrumented with sensing and observational technologies and used for experimental evaluation" (Intille et al., 2006). In particular, the approach mandates interventions—building and experimenting with prototypes in live environments (Abowd et al., 2000).

The approach has been described as a "research methodology for sensing, prototyping, validating and refining complex solutions in multiple and evolving real-life contexts" (Pierson & Lievens, 2005). Positioned as real-life experimental settings for creating and evaluating new/changed technology, processes, and work practices; they suspend old rules to test new ones, to play with the possibilities of new social and organisational behaviours.

Living Lab Cases: Social, Spatial, Temporal Contexts

Imperfect links between academia, policy, industry and societal sectors are blamed for innovation blocks (Burbridge, 2017) for which Living labs are offered as a solution (Canzler, Engels, Rogge, Simon, & Wentland, 2017). Unblocking the mutual flow of

Table 11.1 General characteristics of Living Labs research designs

Dimension	Description
Focus on innovation	Acting to introduce novel social, organisational and technological objects
Broad setting	Comprise many people, organisations, locations, and extended duration
Multiple methods employed	Characterised as multidisciplinary research and development. Methods are disparate and ontologically distinct
Theoretical foundations varied	No one dominant theoretical foundation. Different domains may juxtapose but are not integrative. The contribution is to preserve theoretical complexity and distinctiveness of situations

Source Klein, Higgins, & Rukanova, (2011)

knowledge between university and business is the focus of urban living lab initiatives in Europe (Grotenhuis, 2017; Voytenko, McCormick, Evans, & Schliwa, 2016).

They have been used for whole-city trials of new technology applications; of electric vehicles in Mlaga (Carillo-Aparicio, Heredia-Larrubia, & Perez-Hidalgo, 2013), for social geo-spatial mapping in Mexico (Sandoval-Almazan & Valle-Cruz, 2017).

As systemic experiments in social innovation they have been used to conduct trials linking geographically and culturally distant sites between China and Finland (Tang, Wu, Karhu, Hämäläinen, & Ji, 2012). They have been used to experiment with new modes of access and engagement between rural SMEs and central government in France, Greece, Latvia and Spain (Luccini and Angehrn, 2010). Business and communities in Spain have been seeded with new technology incubators, to experiment with it in a purely exploratory fashion (Gascó, 2017).

These examples explored novel combinations of technological apparatus (digital ecosystem), with technology in use (so called experiential computing) in an experimental social/spatial/temporal context (Nyström, Leminen, Westerlund, & Kortelainen, 2014). There is agreement that Living Labs refer to real-life, naturalistic settings for testing or evaluating concepts and/or technologies. They enable learning using in-the-wild settings as a bridge between the laboratory and the lived world; an open, uncontrolled yet *focused* mode of public experimentation; (see Table 11.1).

The duration of Living Labs may also be open-ended and stakeholders (e.g. technology providers, business and public organisations, users, and researchers) involved the whole time (Niitamo, Kulkki, Eriksson, & Hribernik, 2006). Consequently, they activate an emergent attitude to design and innovation processes.

Open Innovation

Not all problems addressed by technology are purely technical in nature, yet the political mind often misreads the power of technology. Even so, it is liberating to indulge in blue sky or magical thinking in order to address difficult problems. Echoing the idea of democratised innovation, a Living Laboratory mixes up the conventions of R&D (von Hippel, 2005). Instead of pushing innovation, designs may be shaped by emerging demands (Pierson & Lievens, 2005). Prototypes are adapted as users employ them in unexpected ways. Users and stakeholders become the source of innovation (Eriksson, Niitamo, Kulkki, & Hribernik, 2006; Pierson & Lievens, 2005; Henriksen, Rukanova, & Tan, 2008).

Open innovation initiatives seek new ways of identifying value and value propositions around new arrangements of technology, product and service service (Äyväri & Jyrämä, 2017). A focus on value implies attending to new ways of working, new hybrids of product/service, new user behaviours and emerging needs (Björgvinsson, Ehn, & Hillgren, 2012). They demand an intense focus on user involvement, on the co-creation of a good through the application of prototype arrangements to explore feasibility.

Living labs may also have a dark side. There is a tension between economic innovation and social innovation (Vasin, Gamidullaeva, & Rostovskaya, 2017). So-called SmartCities initiatives (Schaffers et al., 2011) have been accused of unrestrained data gathering from citizens in Dutch cities (Naafs, 2018). Therefore, researchers need to ask; whose interests are served by these experiments in systemic innovation? The aspiration for living labs is for *all* stakeholders to be involved. The systemic characteristics of living labs should enable actors to develop or uncover beneficial social innovation. Social innovation in this sense occurs by *involving* the public in collaborations that address social needs.

Contributing to the Living Labs Literature

Much of the literature on Living Labs focuses on definition and justification, offering few insider accounts to aid and inform those involved in starting and running them (Budweg, Schaffers, Ruland, Kristensen, & Prinz, 2011). We seek to contribute to addressing this gap; to develop a better understanding of the practices, processes and social dynamics that support the initiation and subsequent management of Living Labs. As '*development to research*' initiatives we need better tools to understand how to successfully start them, how to galvanise actors, to achieve consensus, to enact and learn from collaborative innovation in the wild.

Theoretical Framework

What theories address an understanding of the origin of networks, of the situated, contingent local world in which people enact their organisations and networks, which they mesh together into bigger things? In a general sense, the term network is used to describe the structure of ties among actors in a social system (Nohria, 1992, p. 288). However, network studies tend to focus on the organisational or institutional level, offering little insight into how human actors initiate and enact to produce institutional and organisational structures. The following offers a practice theoretical view on the interplay between actors and institutional practices in order to better interpret the generative process of network collaboration.

A Practice Theoretical Perspective on Network Relationships

A growing body of research on network relations recognises the complementary character of rational actor relations and relational theories. However, such work mainly concentrates on the macro-, inter-firm level (Schultze & Orlikowski, 2004). The problem with macro analysis is that it neglects the practice of individual members of organisations engaging in and managing boundary spanning activities at the micro level. We adopt a structuration approach (Giddens, 1984) on the 'practice theoretical' dynamics at work in the formation, production and reproduction of network relations.

Structuration

Structuration argues that individuals enact social structure. The apparent force or structure of the social world comes about through recurring actions and interactions. Human actors employ their context, knowledge and assumptions to produce/reproduce social practices. The impression of social structure arises through repeated action; the performance of practices that enact ways of knowing the world. Organisations and power structures are constituted recursively through the expression of practices, for example: interactions, expectations of interdependency or reciprocity, norms of interpersonal relation, social protocols etc. They may extend to inter-organisational practices and in turn constitute wider social networks (considered to be network practices)—network structures performed by knowledgeable actors or agents (Sydow & Windeler, 1998). Thus, actor/agents such as managers do not rely solely on institutional power or the structural properties of networks but also draw upon the rules and resources of extra-organisational resources, civil structure, governmental and society. Simply by enacting institutionalised practices the members constitute/re-constitute professional, organisational and inter-firm networks (Schultze & Orlikowski, 2004).

A theoretical approach informed by structuration theory appreciates that it is individual members of organisations who enact boundary spanning practices and activity. The focus of research should shift therefore from abstract organisational entities to look more closely at the performance of individuals, their assumptions, norms, expectations, protocols and routines. Rather than limiting analysis to the inter-firm level, this approach attends to processual and contextual aspects encountered and performed by individuals along with their interpretive schemes, beliefs, norms, and power relationships. As our theoretical foundation it offers a principled means of explicating contradictions, conflicts and the dynamics of network organisation and collaboration. In the following, we shall extend the practice theoretical perspective by referring to the communities of practice literature. We elaborate on sense-making processes within communities and the role of human agents in facilitating knowledge exchange across different communities.

Communities and Networks of Practice

Modes of knowing within a community are also ways of acting (Wenger, 1999). Wenger uses the term negotiation to emphasise the productive process of meaning construction which is historical, dynamic, contextual and unique. Meaning is contin-uously negotiated over time as people experience the world and their engagement in it as meaningful. A community of practice engages constantly through the production and reproduction of shared meaning.

Members from diverse organisations who engage in the same practices may per-ceive themselves as a network of practice; a shared identity arising from common, overlapping or similar practices (Brown & Duguid, 2001). Although the connections within a network of practice are less intense than those within a community, they do share commonalities allowing knowledge to circulate. In such networks diverse knowledge and practices may challenge each community's beliefs. Organisations, consisting of multiple communities of practices, can use their myriad of beliefs as the impetus for creativity and innovation, by tapping into and utilising the diverse practices of its own communities (Brown & Duguid, 2000). New communities may derive from a network of practice if they succeed in creating new sources of coher-ence, joint enterprise, mutual engagement, and shared repertoires (Wenger, 1999).

The Knowledge Broker

Misunderstandings manifested during collaboration among different communities are balanced against actors' attempts to create coherence and bridge differences. Discontinuities, gaps or incoherence between different aspects of work may be evi-dent in the form of temporal, spatial or organisational breakdowns (Beth Watson-Manheim, Chudoba, & Crowston, 2002). By clarifying mutual expectations, they may overcome misunderstandings and mitigate issues introduced by discontinuities.

The pro-active engagement of human agents as knowledge brokers is positively related with attempts to bridge discontinuities between organisations and communities. Knowledge brokers help to generate shared tacit understanding among communities (Walsham, 2005) and increase awareness of other functional areas' working practices (Hayes, 2000). Brokers need sufficient knowledgeability of the practices, working cultures and discourses of each group if they are to phrase and reframe the interests of one community in a way which is meaningful to another (Brown & Duguid, 2000). Social legitimacy enables these agents to facilitate knowledge exchange and learning by way of linking and combining practices. Institutional practices such as boards, plenary sessions, formal meetings and the informal interactions that surround them are contexts for negotiating meaning among members from different communities. They offer the neutral ground in which participants produce mutual understanding and agreement (Wenger, 1999). If enacted frequently these engagements become institutionalised and give rise to new knowledge and practices specific to the delegation and its participants.

Based on this discussion a combined theoretical frame for analysing innovation in the BeerLL consists of the following. Structuration informs how action/interaction co-constitutes social structure. Practice theoretical perspectives offer ways of accounting for the performative dimensions of communities and networks. Communities of practice helps to understand the links between language and practice, the reifications of shared experiencing that occur all the time.

The Beer Living Lab

The following case provides a detailed inside account of the social dynamics of the Beer Living Lab. The analysis focuses on how its members generated shared understandings and galvanised action.

The Beer Living Lab was the first of a sequence of four living labs established under the ITAIDE research project which ran from 2005 to 2010 as part of the EU 6th Framework for research and development (Tan, Klein, Rukanova, Higgins, & Baida, 2006; Tan, Bjørn-Andersen, Klein, & Rukanova, 2011). These living labs created in-the-world environments for innovation experiments in areas impacted by government regulation and international standards.

The Beer Living Lab focused on export/import logistics of excise[3] goods. In the absence of tax harmonisation, the free movement of goods flowing through logistics networks and crossing borders within the EU creates difficulties for monitoring and controlling taxation. Yet detailed monitoring and controlling adds administrative burdens and costs to all involved.

---

[3]Excise duties are indirect taxes levied on licensed goods such as alcohol.

Research Site

Cross-border trade attracts the most demanding regulatory attention because of the value it produces and the risks it introduces (Henriksen Rukanova, & Tan, 2008). International trade must be monitored, reported and regulated or there is no control. Yet consequent layers of administrative burden inevitably add cost to trade and degrade supply chain efficiency. The Beer Living Lab asked how new technology might help to overcome contradictions between the desire for 'frictionless trade' against changing security and threat environments?

New technologies are seen to be key enablers. The Internet of Things (IoT), RFID, ubiquitous internet, GSM infrastructures, GPS telemetry, real-time monitoring; all offer the means to extend type and availability of trade information. These technologies promise the means to increase levels of supply chain control, efficiency and security. Administrative loads may be lessened by increased digital integration and information sharing between key actors in our trade supply chains, yet new forms of partnership or organisational relations may be needed in addition to new information technology (Rukanova et al., 2011).[4]

The Living Lab ran a series of live tests of whole systems for enhanced international trade. It brought together a makeshift partnership of actors in order to experiment with new tools and new ways of enacting legally regulated activities. The complexity of the Beer Living Lab's social network and relationships is implied in this snapshot at its launch (Fig. 11.1). This picture provides a tangible representation of the scale of living labs as multi-actor, multi-disciplinary, multi-sited collaboration and coordination initiatives. Identities of partners and institutional stakeholders are listed below with abbreviations used in the following case analysis:

Fig. 11.1 ITAIDE consortium members at the kick-off meeting held at the Free University Amsterdam. March 1–3, 2006. *Credit* Hans Modder and Allen Higgins

---

[4]The Tamper-Resistant Embedded Controller (TREC) smart seal for container security developed by IBM, and a SOA, enabled by the Electronic Product Code Information Service (EPCIS) open standard from the global standardisation organisation GS1.

1. BeerCo: Heineken N. V.
2. National Taxation and Customs Offices including:

   a. DTCA—the Dutch Tax and Customs office
   b. TCA2—HM Revenue and Customs
   c. TCA3—US Customs and Border Protection

3. Researchers from National Universities including:

   a. NU—Vrije University (Amsterdam)
   b. NU2—a joint team from University College Dublin and the University of Müenster.

4. Technology, integration, consultancy and standards setting organisations:

   a. TechProv—IBM
   b. TechProv2—comprised of GS1's EPCglobal, UN/CEFACT and the WCO.

5. Sea Carrier—Safmarine, a subsidiary of the Maersk container shippingline.
6. 3PL subcontractors, telecommunications systems, GPS infrastructure and other stakeholders with indirect relationships to the network.

Research Method

The case study follows the interpretive tradition (Walsham, 1995; Myers, 1997). We employed a process approach (Markus & Robey, 1988) which provides for a contextual analysis of the processes of change (Pettigrew, 1985). A narrative approach was used for the analysis and presentation of organisational processes (Pentland, 1999). Guided by the theoretical/conceptual lenses of narrative and critical discourse analysis (Boland & Tenkasi, 1995; Phillips & Oswick, 2012), we derived abstractions and generalisations, linking empirical details with abstract theoretical concepts. The analysis connected organisational structuring with collaboration and individual actions, negotiation and sense-making.

Data were gathered from different sources to build a comprehensive picture of the case including:

1. Participation in workshops
2. Brainstorming sessions
3. Individual interviews with project participants
4. Participant observation
5. Document analysis.

University researchers (from NU, NU2 etc.) attended all general meetings, and many of the interactive sessions involving the partners. General project meetings and formal interviews were recorded and minuted. Findings from analyses were later reported on and presented to participants for validation and as a means of gathering further feedback.

Table 11.2 Interviewee pseudonyms and roles

Pseudonyms	Interviewee roles
Ron	DTCA[a] process innovation group member and BeerLL coordinator
Joan	DTCA customs auditor
Steve	DTCA client coordinator for BeerCo
James	BeerCo[b] customs manager and company liaison with DTCA
Bob	BeerCo internal tax auditor
Jane	BeerCo logistics manager
Rolf	TechProv[c] technical coordinator for demonstrator development
Frank	TechProv customs subject matter expert
Chris	TechProv2[d] technical coordinator for interoperability and standards
Pat	NU[e] principal investigator and strategic project relationships
John	NU project manager (operational, administrative)
Bobby	UKTCA[f] customs officer and liaison with DTCA and BeerCo
Jack	Sea Carrier[g] executive manager for applications and services

[a]Dutch TCA—Tax and Customs Administrations of the Netherlands
[b]BeerCo—international brewing Co
[c]TechProv1—international computing services and hardware Co
[d]TechProv2—international computing services and hardware Co
[e]NU—national university
[f]UKTCA—HM Revenue and Customs
[g]Sea Carrier—an international shipping Co

Documentation analysed included EU and national policy documents, excise procedures, internal reports of TCA1, project reports etc. See Table 11.2 for a summary list of the main interviewees (pseudonyms) their organisations and roles. Participant interviews lasting between 1 and 3 h each were conducted throughout the project in order to continuously evaluate their perceptions and understandings.

The Beer Living Lab: Case Analysis

Pre-project Stage—Creating a Context

The idea for the living lab research programme was triggered when Pat, a university professor at NU in the Netherlands, attended a conference. Having previously prepared proposals but failing to obtain EU research funding, Pat had become acquainted with many officials in the various departments and agencies of the European Commission. It was pointed out to Pat that a recent call for EU-funded research had been announced in his area of expertise. However, he knew from past experience that breadth and depth of academic and industry expertise was a prerequisite for a credible proposal, so he identified a small group of academic partners with whom he had long-standing relationships and who had an interest in contributing to the research proposal.

They proposed adapting the Living Labs method in order to analyse complex cross-border trade and logistics challenges, and to respond by developing and studying the application of innovative information technology centred solutions. Stakeholders composed of businesses, governmental agencies, universities and technology providers would come together to create, trial and explore more or less radical interventions in areas that had been resistant to change and innovation.

Four Living Labs were envisioned: experiments in administrative control of tax and tax-exempt trade; secure real-time transnational multi-modal cold-chains; data sharing among ecosystems of SMEs centred on a large manufacturer; and a unified food data model for pan-European trade. Pat drove the first living lab, the BeerLL, in the Netherlands. First, he needed to involve a government agency, a company, and a technology provider. Throughout his career Pat had worked as a kind of knowledge networker. His personal interest in ideas around controlled borderless movements within the Customs Union attracted others in related organisations who believed in the potential for improvement, and his practice of making and maintaining professional connections embodied a nascent social network that was primed to crystallise around this project.

To gain interest from the government Pat got in touch with Ron whom he had known for more than 10 years. Ron had previously worked for the Customs department in Dutch TCA and had recently been given responsibilities for the "process improvement group" whose objective was to envision innovative IS solutions for the Dutch TCA.

Ron reacted enthusiastically to Pat's suggestion to join the project because the BeerLL seemed to fit well with his new responsibilities. They discussed the latest policies and initiatives impacting Customs and Taxation and started working on a problem definition for the research proposal.

Ron wanted the project to make an impact with a high volume of cross-border trade transactions. He had no direct customer contact, but he got in touch with a colleague (Steve), who was a client coordinator for a large beer producer (BeerCo) and was also responsible for leading an e-Business project within Dutch TCA. Steve became interested in contributing to Pat's research proposal as it was well aligned with his own e-business interests.

> We were enthusiastic [about getting involved]… on a higher level it looked like a new concept and we thought it is good also for the tax office to think about it. (Steve, Dutch TCA)

Steve contacted the Customs Manager at BeerCo (James), however, it took another year before BeerCo would commit itself to joining the project.

> BeerCo was not very enthusiastic at the beginning, they had to look at their costs, so they said, what's our benefit? So, we convinced them that benefit is a lot longer term. And they said, ok, we do it (Steve, Dutch TCA)

To enrol a technology provider, Pat drew upon the existing institutional link between NU and TechProv and established a relationship with a board member of TechProv.

At that time TechProv was conducting research and development into a new secure container seal technology with communication and sensor capabilities. TechProv was interested in setting up a pilot under realistic conditions and additionally saw an opportunity for strengthening the relationship with Dutch TCA and learn more about e-Customs.

Once Dutch TCA, BeerCo and TechProv became interested in the project, the universities began preliminary studies. The focused on revealing opportunities for improving cross-border trade. These interactions between NU, Dutch TCA, Tech-Prov, and BeerCo were crucial for establishing an initial understanding of the problem area.

> They (TechProv and Dutch TCA) were the real motivation. I only had to align the interests and to coordinate the whole thing but at any moment in time I did not have to push anything. Because it was so much aligned with the strategic objectives… And then the two managed to get BeerCo, not just involved, but to drive the process. (Pat, NU)

With financial backing from TechProv and BeerCo, and part funding from the European Commission, contracts for the project were signed. The funding signalled credibility and gradually other organisations became interested, believing that Pat would make a success of the project. Selecting the right partners proved to be crucial for the later success of the network. The network found its origin in Pat's existing relationships but expanded wider due to his constant 'networking', responding to serendipitous events, and producing action, all of which encouraged new players to become interested in the initiative.

Analysis and Redesign Stage

Analysis and redesign yielded a new choreography for collaboration. In the pre-project stage, rather than being held together by shared interests, the network was merely a collection of stakeholders attempting to pursue their own self-interests. During the analysis and redesign stage, three key processes became essential for engaging the wider network of actors in the project and making the network work. These processes took place during general meetings and group interactions. They included (1) establishing initial social capital and shared understanding; (2) collaborating with others on specific tasks; (3) sense-making discussions integrating new learning and knowledge among groups.

During general meetings, Pat and Ron acted as knowledge brokers in addition to their formal roles and were socially influential in the processes that took place. Pat's activities were focussed on mediation and translation between a network of actors, who had different interests and different understandings of the problem domain. While in the initiation stage only a limited number of people were involved in setting up the project, when the BeerLL formally started, the organisations sent whole delegations of representatives. Sense-making processes needed to start again, now involving a larger group of people. These early general meetings were crucial opportunities for creating shared understandings, a shared language and shared purpose. This also held true for the later stages when redesigns were negotiated and where Pat again took a very active role in the negotiation of revised solutions, making sure that the interests of all parties were considered.

The following episode illustrates Pat's sense-making interactions. At this point BeerCo was still sceptical about the proposal from Dutch TCA about the redesign. Pat listened, interpreted, translated, and rephrased suggestions and tried to find acceptable solutions.

> Pat: "So it would be a recommendation to EMCS[5] from our point of view that they are able to cope with an AIN message.[6] Basically, instead of imposing another message AIN is already in place and if the EMCS can be designed in such a way that it can take in an AIN message as input that will be a benefit for you?"
>
> James: "Yes, of course."
>
> Pat: "Your real advantage is that you don't have to build yet another system."
>
> James: "The real Single Window. That's really good."

The accumulation of hundreds of these small interactions involving Pat and continuously cultivated by him and others within the network ensured that the BeerLL remained aligned with the multiple strategic objectives of the organisations involved.

Ron too acted as a knowledge broker to stimulate innovation by gently questioning people's existing interpretations and re-framing the problem area.

> Ron is the key person when it comes to bringing innovation to the BeerLL... He was breaking taboos in the sense of questioning the traditional ways of working and assumptions underlying these ways of working (John, operational manager BeerLL, NU)

> Ron has a long-term view. He is able to distance himself from the specific pilot and provide a long-term perspective, which compelled BeerCo to go along (Rolf, BeerLL Pilot coordinator, TechProv)

With respect to the work groups that were formed, most of the time task allocation emerged naturally in the sense-making process in accordance with personal and institutional domain knowledge. While an overall resource plan for the project was sketched out, it was the responsibility of each organisation to make people and resources available on time for scheduled activities. This was not always an easy task as there were inherent differences in practices, such as perception of time and speed of work.

> For us this project was different than what we are used to. In this case [the BeerLL] sometimes we had to work fast to produce deliverables and sometimes we had to wait too long till the next phase. (Rolf, BeerLL Pilot coordinator, TechProv)

John in his role as operational project manager took a slightly more instructive approach to coordinating efforts and facilitating the mutual adjustment of partners' understandings.

---

[5]EMCS: Excise Movement and Control System. An EU customs system for monitoring the movement of excise goods.

[6]AIN message: AangifteInformatie; digital trade declaration information.

John (remarked in retrospective): "It worked well; when TechProv realised that it would work, but not the way they were used to."

The analysis and redesign stages were marked by a gradual growing sense of community among the participants. They began to feel that they 'were' of the BeerLL. They were developing their own jargon, terms and abbreviations borrowed from customs, logistics, manufacturing and technology. There was a growing sense that the project could make a difference, that the technology would influence the development of the next generation of systems.

The Pilot and Evaluation Stage

This period of the project might best be described as 'Living Labbing in the wild'. Shifting from the conceptual phase to the actual development of a pilot required further interaction and negotiation among the participants to decide on the scope of the pilot and the subset of information that was feasible to exchange in that setting.

> One of the main issues we encountered was to have BeerCo produce the correct files and help to interpret these files. This required close collaboration between TechProv and BeerCo (Rolf, BeerLL pilot coordinator, TechProv)

After agreement was reached, TechProv, Dutch TCA and BeerCo had to line-up resources. TechProv had to ensure that the back-end systems and smart-seals used to monitor the shipment were operational. BeerCo had to ship containers with excise goods to the US and UK. Dutch TCA had to train personnel to perform inspections according to the new procedures. Dutch TCA had involve US and UK customs so as to guarantee that the necessary checks of the cargo were carried out in line with the new procedures.

Everyone involved had to work closely together. Meetings were arranged to provide a holistic view and develop a shared understanding of the pilot. Sessions were arranged to develop the training and procedures for those who would be working with the new system in the field. This new operational phase opened up new realms of uncertainty and risk required the participating organisations to re-engage in sense-making activities.

Evaluation of the system started with another general technical meeting. The technical meeting was an opportunity to discuss issues that had occurred during the pilot, to identify areas for improvement, and even unexpected successes. This was followed by research interviews with the various stakeholders. The interviews gave people a chance to reflect on the process as well as make sense of the overall goals of the living lab.

> The process went very well. We were lucky to some extent; TechProv came at the right time with the innovative technology... for them the BeerLL was one of the first test sites of the

smart seal. Dutch TCA needed a test case for AEO[7] and SW[8] and they wanted to try out these concepts; we (the university) provided fertile ground (Pat, Strategic Manager BeerLL, NU)

When we started, my expectations were very low… During the project things became clearer and I became more positive… I think that the ideas and the BeerLL concept are very nice and I am enthusiastic about them. If it depends on me, this is the future. I cannot be more positive than that! (James, Customs manager BeerCo NL)

The change in mindset is the most valuable achievement from the BeerLL, the innovation lies in the major shift in thinking. (Joan, Customs auditor, Dutch TCA)

The eventual outcome of the Living Lab was not considered to be 'a finished product' or even the end result of a deliberately executed project plan. Instead a processual perspective helps us untangle how complex happenings and interactions produced relatively stable relationships in addition to a working system. These processes include; stabilising the network, initiating a cognitive shift towards a network strategy, and developing a supportive culture and practices.

The BeerLL began to be thought of as a platform for ongoing innovation among equal partners.

In a Living Lab you as government are not in a position to exercise power. You need other mechanisms to drive people. Companies will do something only if the return on investment is clear. (Ron, BeerLL coordinator for Dutch TCA)

Through their continuous engagement over time and against their historical and contextual backgrounds, the participants started to appreciate the fresh view the network offered. Understanding themselves as members of this network with its own unique identity brought about the sense of a joint enterprise with its own distinct understanding of the problem area. The process of generating common understanding was the precursor creating an innovative redesign scenario.

Living Labs really require a lot from everybody… if you have a relationship based on friendship, people will help each other; if they become very formal and calculate everything, then the whole thing will stop. In the BeerLL, all the partners made the extra mile to get the extra resources that were needed. (Pat, Strategic manager BeerLL)

The project eventually fulfilled the objectives of the pilot and evaluation as the EU funding wound up. But the BeerLL did not cease to exist rather, its members moved to respond to the opportunities that had been revealed.

The BeerLL provided a good starting point for discussions of how things could be done differently (Joan, Customs auditor, Dutch TCA)

Even after the formal project concluded the actors continued to engage in sensemaking processes, taking the lessons learned from the BeerLL to the next level, in pursuit of new goals. For Dutch TCA, the proof-of-concept from the BeerLL

---

[7]AEO: Authorised Economic Operator—a licensed business status for operating in the international supply chain.

[8]SW: Single Window for customs services.

provided instruments to engage in political process of institutional change. Although the BeerLL as a time-bound project was over, its impact persisted through follow-on initiatives.

Findings and Discussion

The BeerLL as a Network

The BeerLL falls under the broad definition of network as a "structure of ties among actors in a social system" (Nohria, 1992). However, it was distinct from an inter-firm network, such as strategic or R&D alliances, as it involved a heterogeneous set of actors from different domains, notably the private and the public sector, which did not share a common goal (as is the case in strategic alliances or value-added partnerships) nor did they form a formal partnership as such. Rather, the BeerLL was an instance of a much broader political agenda and innovation initiative involving many organisations and institutions.

It was difficult to draw clear boundaries around the BeerLL. For example, the Dutch TCA involved other national customs and tax administrations in the live tech-nology demonstrator. Consequently, more emphasis was needed in the early phases of setting-up the network in terms of developing a joint agenda (sense-making and negotiation) as well as designing the joint activities. Given the experimental nature of the joint activities, processes of reflexive monitoring needed to be established to facilitate learning leading to adjustments to the structure and goal of the joint activities.

While the BeerLL matched features of Living Labs more generally, it lacked the stability of a pre-existing social structure (e.g. an organisation, community, town, or city). Yet the openness of its scope was useful as it provided space for unexpected opportunities and areas for innovation. It offered a temporal conceptual space for a diverse collection of actors to attempt to reimagine their network of relations in response to digital innovation.

The BeerLL as Network Collaboration

As a network of collaboration involving of players with different goals within a broader problem field, the BeerLL actually benefitted from having goals that were not all clearly defined. Yet while ambiguity and openness gave flexibility, it also complicated gaining commitment from participants. Even the end result, the tech-nology proof-of-concept and live deployment, was only an intermediary product in pursuit of these further goals. As much as the outcomes remained quite open, it was difficult to steer the process and measure the outcomes. Thus, in the BeerLL we were confronted with moving targets concerning the clarity of goals, actors and results.

Key issues in the early stages were how to select partners and how to negotiate their involvement. Later, consensus forming among the participants was the challenge. The participants eventually agreed to more ambitious goals to run a whole-system proof-of-concept study under real world conditions. Yet the parties involved did not regard their relationship wholly as a 'partnership' as each pursued different goals, although all related to cross-border trade and logistics challenges.

Coalition Building as a Prerequisite for Collective Action

In a dynamic, open-ended environment, individual actors became active participants in enrolling new actors into the BeerLL. The initial legitimacy of the project was used to establish further, deeper involvement. They extended the technology capability with Geo-Fencing and real-time tracking and expanded the actor network by involving other TCAs and logistics suppliers. For these actors, social capital was critical to drive the negotiations and motivate a wide heterogeneous group of actors to provide resources and commitment to the joint activities. This reinforced our finding that key actors captured the interests of others through direct personal involvement and commitment. Individuals enact negotiation and sense-making, but they interpret it in terms of their institutional and organisational contexts.

Rather than developing collaborative relationships, the BeerLL aimed at exploring common ground for collective action under the conditions of mutual dependencies of stakeholders who operate in separate domains. These actors normally enact rather antagonistic relationships characterised by mutual suspicion rather than trust. Yet within the shared environment of the Living Lab they were empowered to explore new ways of achieving radically different ways of relating with each other. This had benefits for private and public-sector actors through new ways of mutual coordination; new action, activities and knowledge. The BeerLL was like a loose coalition, where the partners found a consensus (for the common good), even if it involved compromising some of their own interests.

A Lifecycle Perspective

Although the BeerLL was an experimental setting rather than a full-scale implementation, it was at the same time a real-world project in which real resources were spent to make it happen. We regard three aspects as crucial for the actual initiation of the BeerLL.

First, people and organisations enrolled in the network because they had formed an expectation that something would happen. This was based on Pat's networking, his boundary spanning and professional contacts. It was justified eventually by successfully gaining EU sponsorship for the research proposal. The consortium produced a perception of credibility and gave a signal that the initiative had high level institutional commitment.

Second, the funding that the EU provided turned out to be critical as it helped to initiate joint activities with others beyond the consortium. Modest financial supports allowed peripheral and central actors to meet and discuss how to engage in collective action. Support for travel and meetings enabled participants within all organisations a degree of budgetary independence from the constraints of their own organisations. Eventually, many invested additional resources to participate and learn from the living lab.

A third element which we found crucial for the initiation of the BeerLL was the behaviour of key people spontaneously acting as knowledge brokers. These knowledge brokers were also local initiators, the people who took the initiative, came-up with ideas and started the process of engaging with others, of linking organisations.

Network Activities and Practices

Initially the BeerLL was a fragile social/institutional network which could in principle have broken-down at any stage. We recognised how crucial the behaviour of knowledge brokering is to network collaboration. Pat and John kept the network together during the whole process through their involvement in overcoming discontinuities within the network (Beth Watson-Manheim et al., 2002). Importantly, knowledge broking is seen in dyadic, triadic and group collaboration performances. For example, Pat and Ron, acted as complementary knowledge brokers and carried out different activities throughout the whole process. In another example, John, the operational manager, Rolf in TechProv and Steve in DTCA came together as a kind of communications back-channel that helped to keep the network together. Pat, through his activities of initiation, mediation and translation, became instrumental in the negotiation and sense-making processes for everyone and this was crucial for keeping the fragile network together. Pat could assume and maintain this role as he had the status to do that (being a professor, as well the research project coordinator). He was politically sensitive and neutral, constantly searching for the common denominator. These characteristics enabled the others to accept him in his role as a knowledge broker. Ron too was active in sense-making and sharing knowledge among wider groups. In the early stages of the project he was fundamental in framing the initial problem of the BeerLL as he had deep knowledge of the domain. In the analysis and redesign phase, he focussed on innovation facilitation.

Tolerance Towards Ambiguity an Open-Ended Dynamic

In traditional networks, there is usually an expectation that the network will stabilise for a period and function steadily if maintained (Riemer & Klein, 2006). This was not the case in the BeerLL which was open-ended and dynamic. Nor was it the goal of the BeerLL to achieve a long-term stable state of operation for continuous activities. Its goal was short-term, to simply test proofs-of-concept. The prototypes needed only operate a short time. They changed, were tweaked and did not need to be sustained indefinitely. As each learning experience was discussed and made sense of, the network proceeded to undertake some new change. The social network embodied new learning leading to new goals e.g. recommending necessary changes to legislation or altering technology capability. The experimental character of the Living Lab was a strength because it allowed for trial and error. Failures became an inevitable part of the learning rather than something to be avoided.

Concluding Remarks

Previous research into Living Labs has concentrated on the objectives of these enterprises while neglecting to reveal the underlying social processes of their formation and management. Our research reveals Living Labs as social networks of collaboration and of practice. Participants must be therefore become sensitive to the interactive and social dynamics of the Living Lab setting.

By definition Living Labs lack well defined boundaries or predictive goals. They demand continuous sense-making and negotiation. They are fragile states of engagement and remain fragile throughout their life cycle. The success of a Living Lab is never secured, it is instead the result of continuous effort, of engaging in sense-making and knowledge broking activities. While a single case is insufficient for generalisation, this extensive study offers empirical evidence and contributes to a growing body of research shedding light on the social performances involved in and needed to sustain Living Labs and network collaborations more generally.

References

Abowd, G. D., Atkeson, C. G., Bobick, A. F., Essa, I. A., MacIntyre, B., Mynatt, E. D., & Starner, T. E. (2000). Living laboratories: The future computing environments group at the georgiainstitute of technology. In *CHI '00: CHI '00 extended abstracts on human factors in computing systems* (pp. 215–216). ACM.

Äyväri, A., & Jyrämä, A. (2017). Rethinking value proposition tools for living labs. *Journal of Service Theory and Practice, 27*(5), 1024–1039.

Beth Watson-Manheim, M., Chudoba, K. M., & Crowston, K. (2002). Discontinuities and continuities: A new way to understand virtual work. *Information Technology & People, 15*(3), 191–209.

Björgvinsson, E., Ehn, P., & Hillgren, P.-A. (2012). Agonistic participatory design: working with marginalised social movements. *CoDesign, 8*(2–3), 127–144.

Boland, R. J., Jr., & Tenkasi, R. V. (1995). Perspective making and perspective taking in communities of knowing. *Organization Science, 6*(4), 350–372.

Brown, J. S., & Duguid, P. (2000). *The Social Life of Information.* Harvard University Press.

Brown, J. S., & Duguid, P. (2001). Knowledge and organization: A social-practice perspective. *Organization Science, 12*(2), 198–213.

Budweg, S., Schaffers, H., Ruland, R., Kristensen, K., & Prinz, W. (2011). Enhancing collaboration in communities of professionals using a living lab approach. *Production Planning & Control, 22*(5–6), 594–609.

Burbridge, M. (2017). If living labs are the answer—What's the question? a review of the literature. *Procedia Engineering, 180,* 1725–1732.

Canzler, W., Engels, F., Rogge, J.-C., Simon, D., & Wentland, A. (2017). From "living lab" to strategic action field: Bringing together energy, mobility, and information technology in germany. *Energy Research & Social Science, 27,* 25–35.

Carillo-Aparicio, S., Heredia-Larrubia, J. R., & Perez-Hidalgo, F. (2013). SmartCityMálaga, a real-living lab and its adaptation to electric vehicles in cities. *Energy Policy, 62,* 774–779.

Eriksson, M., Niitamo, V.-P., Kulkki, S., & Hribernik, K. A. (2006). Living labs as a multi-contextual R&D methodology. In *Technology Management Conference (ICE), 2006 IEEE International* (pp. 1–8). IEEE.

Froessler, F., Rukanova, B., Klein, S., Tan, Y.-H., & Higgins, A. (2007). Inter-organisational network formation and sense-making: Initiation and management of public-private collaboration. In *20th Bled eMergence* (pp. 1–17).

Gascó, M. (2017). Living labs: Implementing open innovation in the public sector. *Government Information Quarterly, 34*(1), 90–98.

Giddens, A. (1984). The constitution of society. *Outline of the theory of structuration.* Cambridge: Polity Press.

Grotenhuis, F. D. (2017). Living labs as service providers: From proliferation to coordination. *Global Business and Organizational Excellence, 36*(4), 52–57.

Hayes, N. (2000). Work-arounds and boundary crossing in a high tech optronics company: The role of co-operative workflow technologies. *Computer Supported Cooperative Work (CSCW), 9*(3–4), 435–455.

Henriksen, H. Z., Rukanova, B., & Tan, Y.-H. (2008). Pactasuntservanda but where is the agreement? the complicated case of eCustoms. In *International Conference on Electronic Government* (pp. 13–24). Springer.

Intille, S. S., Larson, K., Tapia, E. M., Beaudin, J. S., Kaushik, P., Nawyn, J., & Rockinson, R. (2006). Using a live-in laboratory for ubiquitous computing research. In K. P. Fishkin, B. Schiele, P. Nixon, & A. Quigley (Eds.), *Proceedings of PERVASIVE 2006* (Vol. LNCS 3968, pp. 349–365). Springer.

Klein, S., Higgins, A., & Rukanova, B. (2011). *Network collaboration models* (Chap. 14, pp. 255–270). Springer, Berlin.

Lucassen, I., Klievink, B., & Tavasszy, L. (2014). *A living lab framework: Facilitating the adoption of innovations in international information infrastructures.* Paris: TRA.

Luccini, A. M., & Angehrn, A. A. (2010). egovtube: Web2. 0 collaboration to sustain innovation adoption in rural living labs. In *Technology Management Conference (ICE), 2010 IEEE International* (pp. 1–8). IEEE.

Markus, M. L., & Robey, D. (1988). Information technology and organizational-change—Causal-structure in theory and research. *Management Science, 34*(5), 583–598.

Myers, M. D. (1997). Qualitative research in information systems. *MIS Quarterly, 20*(2), 241–242.

Naafs, S. (2018). 'Living laboratories': The Dutch cities amassing data on oblivious residents. The Guardian.

Niitamo, V.-P., Kulkki, S., Eriksson, M., & Hribernik, K. A. (2006). State-of-the-art and good practice in the field of living labs. In *Technology Management Conference (ICE), 2006 IEEE International* (pp. 1–8). IEEE.

Nohria, N. (1992). Networks and organizations: Structure, form and action. Harvard Business School Press.

Nyström, A.-G., Leminen, S., Westerlund, M., & Kortelainen, M. (2014). Actor roles and role patterns influencing innovation in living labs. *Industrial Marketing Management, 43*(3), 483–495.

Pentland, B. T. (1999). Building process theory with narrative: From description to explanation. *Academy of Management Review, 24*(4), 711–724.

Pettigrew, A. (1985). *The awakening giant: Continuity and change in imperial chemical industries.* Basil Blackwell.

Phillips, N., & Oswick, C. (2012). Organizational discourse: Domains, debates, and directions. *Academy of Management Annals, 6*(1), 435–481.

Pierson, J., & Lievens, B. (2005). Configuring living labs for a 'thick' understanding of innovation. *Ethnographic Praxis in Industry Conference Proceedings, 2005*(1), 114–127.

Riemer, K., & Klein, S. (2006). *Network management framework* (pp. 17–66). Springer, Berlin, Heidelberg.

Rukanova, B., Baida, Z., Liu, J., Van Stijn, E., Tan, Y.-H., Hofman, W., Wigand, R. T., & van Ipenburg, F. (2011). Beer living lab–intelligent data sharing (pp. 37–54). Springer.

Sandoval-Almazan, R., & Valle-Cruz, D. (2017). Open innovation, living labs and public officials: The case of mapaton in Mexico. In *Proceedings of the 10th International Conference on Theory and Practice of Electronic Governance* (pp. 260–265). ACM.

Schaffers, H., Komninos, N., Pallot, M., Trousse, B., Nilsson, M., & Oliveira, A. (2011). Smart cities and the future internet: Towards cooperation frameworks for open innovation. In *The future internet assembly* (pp. 431–446). Springer.

Schultze, U., & Orlikowski, W. J. (2004). A practice perspective on technology-mediated network relations: The use of internet-based self-serve technologies. *Information Systems Research, 15*(1), 87–106.

Sydow, J., & Windeler, A. (1998). Organizing and evaluating interfirm networks: A structuationist perspective on network processes and effectiveness. *Organization Science, 9*(3), 265–284.

Tan, Y.-H., Klein, S., Rukanova, B., Higgins, A., & Baida, Z. (2006). ecustoms innovation and transformation: A research approach. In *19th Bled eConference, eValues* (pp. 1–14).

Tan, Y.-H., Bjørn-Andersen, N., Klein, S., & Rukanova, B. (Eds.). (2011). *Accelerating global supply chains with IT-innovation.* Berlin: Springer.

Tang, T., Wu, Z., Karhu, K., Hämäläinen, M., & Ji, Y. (2012). Internationally distributed living labs and digital ecosystems for fostering local innovations in everyday life. *Journal of Emerging Technologies in Web Intelligence, 4*(1), 106–115.

Vasin, S. M., Gamidullaeva, L. A., & Rostovskaya, T. K. (2017). The challenge of social innovation: Approaches and key mechanisms of development. *European Research Studies, 20*(2), 25.

von Hippel, E. (2005). *Democratizing innovation.* Cambridge, Mass: MIT Press.

Voytenko, Y., McCormick, K., Evans, J., & Schliwa, G. (2016). Urban living labs for sustainability and low carbon cities in Europe: Towards a research agenda. *Journal of Cleaner Production, 123,* 45–54.

Walsham, G. (1995). Interpretive case studies in is research: Nature and method. *European Journal of Information Systems, 4*(2), 74–81.

Walsham, G. (2005). Knowledge management systems: Representation and communication in context. *Systems, Signs & Actions, 1*(1), 6–18.

Wenger, E. (1999). Communities of practice: learning, meaning, and identity. Cambridge University Press.

Chapter 12
Living Infrastructure

Kai Reimers and Robert B. Johnston

Introduction

Infrastructure is widely regarded as a material system that coordinates the activities of diverse practices. On one view, the ideal for infrastructure is to mechanise sanctioned forms of interaction between practices pursuing different and often conflicting goals, such that the resulting whole forms a well-oiled machine operating under a negotiated highest common denominator (Edwards, 2010). On another view, infrastructure should become an un-noticed lowest common denominator, on the basis of which diverse practices draw meaning and support, but get out of each other's way and act as independently as possible (Hanseth & Lyytinen, 2010).

In this essay, we argue against the notion that infrastructure is a material enabler of *either* a tight *or* loose coupling of activities of diverse practices. Instead, we propose that when infrastructure provides a site for an 'opening' in which practices are held *at once* both near and apart—both already familiar and not yet familiar, both same and other, both resisting and accommodating—life under the influence of these practices is lived to the full. We call the resultant whole 'living infrastructure' to denote that it is both infrastructure *for* living and infrastructure *that* 'lives'.[1] We

---

[1] Hubert Dreyfus (2017) would say, in the same vein, that it 'shines'. See also Heidegger (1950/1971, p. 180).

K. Reimers (✉)
RWTH Aachen University, Aachen, Germany
e-mail: reimers@wi.rwth-aachen.de

R. B. Johnston
The University of Sydney, Camperdown, Australia
e-mail: robert.johnston@sydney.edu.au

R. B. Johnston
Monash University, Clayton, Australia

© Springer International Publishing AG, part of Springer Nature 2019
K. Riemer et al. (eds.), *Collaboration in the Digital Age*, Progress in IS,
https://doi.org/10.1007/978-3-319-94487-6_12

will argue that such infrastructure is an on-going achievement of becoming,[2] which requires nurturing to maintain its continued productivity, and vigilance against the three-fold threats of tokenization, colonization and mechanization: otherwise it will cease to 'live'.

First we present the Medieval European City Square as a motivating example of a living infrastructure. We will employ this exemplar to define the conceptual parts which together we take to constitute 'living infrastructure'. Next we introduce a contemporary empirical case from the German healthcare environment. This is the Federal Unified Medication Plan for medication therapy safety. We argue in detail that this is a nascent living infrastructure providing a site where a productive opening 'happens' between multiple practices involved in medication therapy safety. We analyse this 'happening' to further refine the notion of living infrastructure by establishing how this opening took hold, how it was kept open, and how it was kept productive. We conclude by briefly contrasting living infrastructure with the traditional view.

Conceptual Preliminaries

Our aim in this section is to provide an initial conceptual framework for discussing living infrastructure and the terminology we will employ in the remainder of the paper.

The Medieval City Square

The city square arose as an important part of the Medieval European city layout and provided an open area in which city inhabitants could conduct the various aspects of their daily public lives. Frequently, city squares arose around a public water-well that became their centre piece, and on their sides stood various institutional buildings—for instance a church, a market, the town hall, a school—that made available to the inhabitants important influences on the conduct of a rich city life—such as religion, commerce, government and culture/education.

The city square thus established the presence of different 'regions' of public city life to the inhabitants, but importantly, it also held regions with a natural antipathy (such and the spiritual and the corporal, or the personal and the social) apart. The geography of the square quite literally protects life in the square from domination by any one region of city life, by placing its institutional representatives on different bounding sides of the square.

We suggest that the medieval square provides a conceptual exemplar for living infrastructure—in this case infrastructure for public city life to be lived to the full.

---

[2]In other words, a process in the strong sense (Tsoukas and Chia, 2002; Langley et al, 2013).

The city square arises as an opening in the clutter of the city; it is maintained as an opening in city life because regions of that life are established as both present and distinct by its layout; and it is productive of a good life because it encourages a continual encounter and evaluation of the 'regions' of city life in the course of daily interaction, and thus a continual on-going evaluation of what a full city life *could be*. In the opening of the city square, the contrasting regions of life are established *as* regions, and a full city life lived in the presence of these regions is disclosed to those who dwell there.

The City Square as Living Infrastructure

In what follows we will draw on the city square exemplar to give an account of how infrastructure more generally can 'live' when it provides the site where such a productive opening can take hold. It 'lives' when such an opening 'happens', and this happening[3] is living life to the full. However, first we must take some care to point out in what respects the example instantiates 'a productive opening' as we see it, and what aspects of the example might lead the reader astray.

Firstly, it is not the square as a material entity creating an open physical space in the city, nor the geography of the square mediating the opposition of the institutional buildings, that we wish to identify with such an opening. That is, here we are not interested in the usual conception of infrastructure as a material structure that coordinates diverse activities. Secondly, we are not interested in the square as a politically negotiated creation of the institutions to demarcate their various territories in their subjects' lives. That is, we are not treating infrastructure as an outcome of social negotiation between 'stake holders' in city living.

Rather, we view the city square as making possible particular lived interactions of the city dwellers that *already* happen under the aegis of these institutions. Thus, the square as a built place is merely the 'site' where certain oppositions among the 'regions' of the overall concern of the square (that is, a full city life) already lived there, are made possible. By connecting and opposing the institutions that embody these regions of life in the built place, the opening that the square grounds establishes them *as* distinct regions of the life lived there. What is productive about the city square is not its spatial or institutional geography but the distinction-making function of its openness. It is the openness of the square—not the square as such—that we view as the 'opening'. The common concern enacted in the square, the regions of life founded by the square, the openness of the square, the square as the site of this opening, and the happening of this openness, are what together constitute living infrastructure (see Table 1).

Thus, facilitating a full city life is not simply a matter of building a square that coordinates or controls access to the separate, opposing institutions of life. Nor is it a

---

[3]We use 'happening' in line with Heidegger's notion of Ereignis (Polt, 2005)—a productive, dialectical, gathering event (in the extended sense of event).

Table 1 Conceptual parts that constitute living infrastructure

Concept	Definition	Example (City Square)
Concern	A concern defines that aspect of human existence with which the infrastructure deals	The concern is living life to the full in a city
Region	Regions are distinct aspects of the concern—they are distinct 'locations on a map' of the concern	The regions are the institutions of town life—religion, state, commerce, and education/culture
Opening	An opening is the establishment of productive distinctions between the regions of the concern	The establishment of distinctions between spiritual, corporal, individual and social aspects of a full city life
Site of an opening	Where a productive opening takes hold	The lived-in city square that provides the conditions of an opening between church, town hall, market and school to happen
The happening of an opening	How an opening takes hold, is kept open, and continues to be productive	For any particular city square this can only be uncovered by detailed historical scholarship

matter of regulating the real estate of the square to prevent institutional encroachment on the political balance of city life. Rather, it is a matter of creating the conditions under which a square as a region-defining opening can arise, be kept open, and can continue to be productive. Only then can the square become infrastructure that 'lives'. The nature of an opening that makes this happen is the issue that we take up in the remainder of the paper.

We have not created these ideas *ex nihilo*: our conception of the city square as a productive opening has been inspired by our reading of various works from the later philosophical period of Martin Heidegger, in particular the essays "Building, Dwelling, Thinking", "The Thing" and "The Origin of the Work of Art" (Heidegger, 1971).

Case Background

Thanks to advances in general living conditions as well as the medical sciences, people now live much longer but also tend to live with chronic and multiple diseases when they are old, a condition known as multi-morbidity. This condition, in turn, is associated with the continuous use of a cocktail of drugs, so-called poly-pharmacy. Healthcare systems in most developed countries, however, have been erected on the assumption that people fall ill only occasionally and then, for a limited time, use a drug targeted specifically at that illness. Healthcare systems are generally not equipped to cope with monitoring and continuously adapting medication regimes of multiple drugs taken over long periods. This often results in combinations of drugs which are ineffective, due to cancellation of their effects, or risky, if effects of drugs amplify one another in unanticipated ways.

In Germany, the term 'medication therapy safety' was coined for this issue as part of a national action plan published by the Ministry of Health in 2007. This 'National Action Plan for the Improvement of Medication Therapy Safety' has since been updated three more times with the current action plan covering the period 2016–2019. These plans are supported by a 'Coordination Group on Implementing and Updating the Action Plan for Improving Medication Therapy Safety', in the following just 'Coordination Group'. This group has met regularly about three times per year since the publication of the first action plan. The group comprises representatives of various national-level professional associations, the Ministry of Health, and patient groups. Initially, it was mostly physicians, as well as community and hospital pharmacists, who participated in the meetings as professional specialists. Later, members of a national nursing association, the national hospital association, and the federal association of panel doctors—concerned with administering the reimbursement of doctors—officially joined the group.

The structure of the various action plans has remained relatively stable over the years. Sections outline establishing awareness of the problem of medication therapy safety both among medical professionals and patients, creating a 'safety culture', and various more specific measures such as encouraging physicians to report side effects to a national registry, with each attracting funds from the Ministry of Health by competitive tendering. The implementation of some of these measures is the responsibility of the Coordination Group itself, including a project to design and distribute an information flyer for patients to increase awareness for the problem and to establish a safety culture. One idea was to include the template for a 'medication plan' in this flyer so that patients could create their own medication plans.

However, over time this idea took on larger proportions; the group began to discuss what is now called the 'Federal Unified Medication Plan' ('Medication Plan' in the following) as an information and communication tool for all those involved in the medication process. Eventually, the Medication Plan became part of a new law, the so-called e-health law, published in December 2015, obliging physicians from October 2016 to create and print out a medication plan for patients who regularly take three or more drugs. From April 2017, such medication plans must comply with a detailed specification of the Medication Plan. This includes a 2D barcode so that a patient's medication plan can be machine-read and updated. How this Medication Plan came to productively structure interactions among the practices of the Coordination Group is the focus of our case.

Case Materials

We draw on two kinds of empirical material. Our main source for reconstructing and interpreting the story of the Medication Plan is the published meeting minutes of the Coordination Group. Since the publication of the first action plan in 2007, the group has met 30 times. All 29 publically available meeting minutes were first read from last to first by one of the authors and then, in the reverse order, excerpted and summarized into four categories: (1) composition of the group; (2) discussions concerning the definition of medication therapy safety; (3) discussions concerning the medication plan; (4) other relevant aspects of the discussion.

The second empirical source is the experiences of one of the authors as a founder of the 'Aachen Learning Community on Innovative Use of IT in Drug Distribution' (Claßen et al., 2015), a group of healthcare practitioners that has met about twice per year since February 2012 and which mirrors the composition and concerns of the Coordination Group, albeit at the local level. Recently, this group has started a project to document and reflect on experiences of physicians, pharmacists, and patients with the Medication Plan through an ongoing series of reflective video conversations. Apart from using domain specific knowledge from one of the author's active participation in the discussions and activities of the Aachen Learning Community, we will also draw on findings from the first series of reflective video conversations.

Case Findings

In this section, we describe and interpret the story of the Medication Plan. The development of this case narrative has also contributed to developing the notion of living infrastructure as the happening of an opening and therefore serves to illuminate rather than just illustrate our basic concepts. The story of the Medication Plan thus serves a similar function to our city square example, namely, as an archetype of a general principle. While the city square metaphor was useful for deriving the basic concepts as defined in Table 1, the concrete contours of the happening of an opening could only be fleshed out through detailed historical analysis of a particular case. This led us to distinguish three issues that together reveal the happening of an opening:

1. How the opening took hold,
2. How the opening was kept open,
3. How the opening was kept productive.

While it would be tempting to associate these issues with distinct phases in a linear development process, we will argue later that they are better understood as constitutive parts of the happening of opening. Thus, in each sub-section below, we present an episode particularly appropriate to each issue and do not intend these to be read as chronological.

How the Opening Took Hold

In this section, we will document how the various practices making up the Coordination Group came to encounter each other in a way that opened up the possibility of talking about and probing into new ways, not entirely managed and controlled by physicians, for determining and adjusting the medication therapy of patients. Out of this re-orienting of the dialogue between practices arose the Medication Plan which, in turn, became a site for re-orienting the relationships between the practices, initially those of physicians and pharmacists, but later also of regulators and patients.

Traditionally, the relationship between physician and pharmacist is perceived to be asymmetrical, although that was not always the case (Schmitz, 1998). Accordingly, the pharmacist is supposed to merely follow the prescription written by the physician, dispensing the specific drug intended by the physician to the patient. Only in cases when a certain drug may threaten the life of a patient is the pharmacist expected and obliged to intervene in the physician's medication decision by refusing to dispense that drug. In addition, the pharmacist is supposed to look out for possible prescribing errors, for example where the names of two drugs are very similar. As these are exceptional situations, it is not customary for the pharmacist to seek to communicate with the prescribing physician and physicians tend to evade direct conversation with pharmacists about the medication of a particular patient.

This separation between the two practices is reflected in the institutional structure of the German healthcare system which has very few platforms where physicians and pharmacists are able to interact as professionals. To the extent that such institutionalized forums for the interaction exist, these are typically concerned with allocating resources and workloads but not with medication. The constitution of the Coordination Group was therefore an unlikely gathering because the participating practices, especially those of physicians and pharmacists, could come together under the aegis of a shared professional concern, namely medication therapy safety.

The idea of the Medication Plan evolved from an addendum to an information flyer for patients into an information and communication tool for all actors involved in medication. As such, the Medication Plan announces the possibility of more intense and frequent communication and cooperation between the various practices, in contrast to the then current one-directional information flow from physicians to patients, pharmacists, and nurses and relatives. However, the potential shift in how these various practices might be re-oriented through the Medication Plan was not explicitly discussed by the Coordination Group. Rather, discussions were about whether the information flyer should include a 'unified' medication plan as a template for patients or not. Physicians were initially opposed to that idea, arguing that *patients* should design a medication plan according to their needs.

The possibility that the medication plan might become a new information tool for *all those* involved in medication decisions marked a significant broadening of its purpose, here signified by our capitalization of the medication plan as 'Medication Plan'. Such a possibility was explicitly announced in the second ministerial action plan, published immediately after the group's eighth meeting. The second action plan also specified a measure to hold a workshop with software providers to 'implement' the Medication Plan in software systems for general physicians, community pharmacists, and hospitals. Thus, there was a clear intention to broaden the reach of the medication plan from an information tool for patients to these other practices, which would allow them to become involved in novel ways in medication processes. The action plan justified this new position by referring to the discussions in the Coordination Group; however, prior to the publication of the second action plan these discussions only referred to the medication plan as an addendum to the information flyer.

Even though there are no indications in the meeting minutes that the Coordination Group explicitly discussed using the Medication Plan for re-orienting the various practices, there must have been an openness for this possibility. Otherwise, the action plan could not have referred to these discussions to justify the idea that the medication plan was to become a new information tool for all practices involved in medication processes, since that implies a significant shift from current practice using the prescription as a one-directional information tool. It appears that another discussion, which occurred concurrently with the discussions of the Medication Plan, greatly contributed to creating this openness, namely, a discussion concerning the definition of key terms related to medication therapy safety. One important aspect of that discussion was a proposal to distinguish between 'undesired drug effects' and 'undesired drug events'. While undesired biochemical drug effects cannot be avoided, some undesired drug events can be avoided, for example, by changing the way or the time that a certain drug is taken. Making this distinction turned out to be important. For example, in one session the group had queried the federal association of physicians about whether the current education of physicians sufficiently addressed medication therapy safety. The association had replied in the affirmative, arguing that the topic of pharmacovigilance is firmly established in medical curricula. Pharmacovigilance, however, only addresses undesired drug *effects* but not undesired drug *events*, such as interactions between various drugs. The group therefore decided that there was a need to educate physicians about the difference between pharmacovigilance and medication therapy safety.

The distinction between undesired drug effects and events opened the possibility for a legitimate and substantial involvement of pharmacists in medication decisions. Pharmacists are recognized to be 'experts in drugs' and could therefore better fine-tune a certain drug regime to make sure that avoidable undesired drug *events* are indeed avoided: as long as only undesired drug *effects* (colloquially known as 'side effects') mattered, it was clear that only physicians should make medication decisions because only they could trade off side effects against intended effects.[4]

---

[4]It is interesting to note that the group maintained that distinction for a considerable time even after a European directive had re-defined undesired drug effects to include medication errors, a re-definition which effectively collapses the distinction between undesired drug effects and undesired drug events and which the group eventually incorporated into its glossary. However, even one year after the need for adapting to the European directive had been first discussed by the group, the group decided that a proposed project would only be funded if the distinction between undesired drug

We interpret these events as indicative of an opening taking hold. Initially, only a certain openness to an as-yet unspecified possibility of a new way of orienting the various practices is noticeable. This openness is manifest in both the readiness to see the Medication Plan as something more substantial than was initially envisaged, and in the making of the distinction between undesired drug events and effects. Both these manifestations announce the possibility of a more significant involvement of pharmacists and other practices in medication processes which, however, was not yet specified or even thematised. Yet, following the publication of the second action plan, the Medication Plan would become the main *site* for working out these new roles, which came to concern the relationship between patient and regulatory practices in addition to pharmacists and physicians. Thus, the 'taking hold' of the opening involved the *anticipation* of a possibility that had yet to be worked out and defined.

How the Opening Was Kept Open

In this section, we will describe (1) how, in the discussions within the Coordination Group, various efforts to 'appropriate' the Medication Plan by particular practices involved were fended off, and (2) how this keeping at bay contributed to working out the emerging re-orienting of these practices that the opening had already brought forth.

The composition of the Coordination Group had stabilized after the first few meetings to representatives of

- the Ministry of Health, which we here interpret as articulating the *regulatory* practices concerned with allocating costs and benefits within the healthcare system,
- the drug committee of the federal association of *physicians*,
- the federal associations of hospital and community *pharmacists*,
- an 'action platform for patient safety' which includes *patient* organizations but is dominated by healthcare professionals,
- and of federal *patient* and *nursing* organizations.

Thus, the group comprised five practices, namely those of regulators, physicians, pharmacists, patients, and nurses.

There were two kinds of moves to claim ownership of the Medication Plan which we characterize as attempts at 'appropriation' in the following, namely, (1) proposals to restrict its purpose, and (2) proposals to limit the leeway users have in filling in medication data.

The first type of appropriation gesture, proposals to restrict the purpose of the Medication Plan, aimed at positioning it primarily as a document for patients to help them comply with the instructions of physicians. Such proposals were successfully countered with the argument that the communication function of the Medication Plan

---

effects and medication errors is accepted and worked into the project proposal. Thus, the group maintained this distinction in the face of considerable external pressure to give it up.

is essential for improving medication therapy safety. The topic of these discussions was whether the Medication Plan should also include a 2D barcode. This barcode would facilitate communication between the various practices. For example, patients may also buy some Over-The-Counter (OTC) drugs when presenting a prescription to a pharmacist. The pharmacist could then read the 2D barcode into her system, add the OTC drugs to the Medication Plan, check for possible undesired drug events, and print out the updated and validated Medication Plan. On his next visit to the physician, the patient would present the updated Medication Plan again so that the data entered by the pharmacist are now available to the physician too. This might include information about why the patient has been dispensed the OTC drugs, thus facilitating a direct professional exchange between pharmacist and physician.

On two occasions, participants expressly opposed this inclusion of the barcode as part of the Medication Plan, arguing that the purpose of the Medication Plan was primarily to instruct patients. Opposition to the 2D barcode was articulated by the representative of the Ministry of Health, who argued that dropping the barcode would avoid the necessity of equipping physician practices with scanners. Also, the representative of the hospital association was against inclusion of the 2D barcode in the Medication Plan, arguing that pursuing purposes other than instructing patients about the right way to take drugs would increase the barriers to its adoption. These two arguments reflect concerns about the 'costs' of implementing the Medication Plan in physician practices and hospitals. However, restricting the purpose of the Medication Plan to ensuring compliance by patients would have also strengthened a traditional understanding of the role of physicians as having complete authority over the medication of a patient.

By fending off this closure gesture, the opening that had emerged in the initial meetings of the Coordination Group, as a potential re-orienting of the practices of pharmacist and physician, was kept open. This 'keeping open' did not just consist of rejecting a narrow understanding of the purpose of the Medication Plan, but also specified a way in which the professions involved in medication decisions might communicate with each other. This is significant since the traditional means of communication between physician and pharmacist, the prescription, does not allow for a 'talking back' of the pharmacist to the physician. Hence, fending off efforts to restrict the Medication Plan to a single purpose also helped to further clarify the relationship between physician and pharmacist and to elaborate the opening that had emerged as a potential re-orienting of these practice.

The second appropriating move concerned various proposals to use coding systems for automatically filling in medication data. Instead of entering plaintext into a particular field, users would have to enter a code into software that would retrieve and fill the field contents from an appropriate database. The range of possible entries into a data field would thus be significantly constrained as compared to a plaintext field. Specifically, pharmacists proposed to use codes for, among others, the fields 'active ingredient', 'suggestions for taking a particular drug' (e.g. 'before the meal'), and 'reason for taking a particular drug' (e.g. 'against high blood pressure'). The first field, 'active ingredient', concerns the relationship between pharmacist and physician, the second and third fields the relations between pharmacist, physician, and patient.

The proposal to use codes for the field 'active ingredient' was related to a prominent project located in East Germany. There, a different form of re-orientation between the professions of pharmacists and physicians was proposed and tried out. This project was initiated by the federal association of pharmacists, which is also an institutional member of the Coordination Group, and the federal association of panel physicians, which was often present as a guest in the Coordination Group meetings before becoming a regular member. The most important element of this project was an agreement that physicians only prescribe so-called active ingredients, the chemical substance that causes the intended as well as the unintended effects of a drug in the human body, and pharmacists then select the appropriate drug.[5] Within the East German project, a complex choreography of interactions between the physician and the pharmacist was designed that would produce a medication plan which reflected their joint decision making, which is then handed over to the patient. The two projects are thus similar but also distinct. The Medication Plan, as envisaged by the Coordination Group, is (also) a communication tool for pharmacist and physician; by contrast, the medication plan as envisioned in the East German project is seen as the *result* of such communication. Moreover, as part of that project the roles of physician and pharmacist are precisely defined and their communication is precisely choreographed. This vision would have transformed the Medication Plan into a mechanistic form of communication—a coordination mechanism. As such this vision would have threatened the Medication Plan as the site of an opening where new forms of orienting the practices involved could continually be discovered and tried out. While the Coordination Group did not thematise advantages and disadvantages of the East German model, it rejected the proposal to use a coding system for filling the data field 'active ingredient' on the grounds that no mature coding systems are available for that purpose, thus fending off the possible 'closure' that would have resulted from bringing the medication plan idea under the influence of the East German project.

Proposals, also by pharmacist members of the Coordination Group, to use codes for the fields 'suggestions for taking a particular drug' and 'reason for taking a particular drug' were also rejected because of concerns about possible misinterpretations of these codes, especially by patients. The requirement that the contents of the Medication Plan must be intelligible to patients was emphasized several times in the context of discussing the use of codes. The group decided to use plaintext for these two fields in order to prevent any kind of 'wrong interpretation' until sufficient feedback from real-life tests had evaluated whether codes are helpful for users. Through this rejection, the group thus made it clear that patients are to be involved as active users of the Medication Plan, without specifying what 'active use' really means. By

---

[5]Drugs whose patent protection has expired are normally offered by several manufacturers. These drugs, so-called generic drugs or just generics, differ in price but also in composition concerning additives and other substances, and probably in quality as well.

fending off the interests of professionals, pharmacists in this case, the group came to assign a positive role to patients as users of the Medication Plan.

We interpret these moves and counter-moves as an ongoing, dialectical working out of the opening. Efforts to appropriate the Medication Plan exclusively as an instructional device to ensure compliance by patients and as a tool to enforce a legalistic and technical version of medication management were fended off. These counter-moves, however, also produced a more nuanced picture of how the Medication Plan could function in a new form of interaction between the practices of physicians, pharmacists, and patients, while continuing to resist specifying how this interaction should or must look like on each occasion. Hence, the opening was kept open in these discussions and this also elaborated the re-orienting of the various practices involved.

How the Opening Was Kept Productive

In this section, we document how, as the Medication Plan was tested, distinctions characterizing the involved practices came to the fore that had been glossed over in prior discussions. Articulation of these distinctions led to a further elaboration of the re-orienting of practices involved in medication. Moreover, as the Medication Plan was thematised in practice, the concern out of which it emerged was also elaborated.

Projects to test the Medication Plan were announced along with the publication of the concept itself after the eighth meeting; however, the first test results were thematised only about five years later. As of October 2016, general practitioners are legally obliged to prepare and print a medication plan for patients who regularly take three or more prescription drugs, and as of April 2017 such medication plans have to be compliant with the specification of the Medication Plan published by the group, including the specifications for the 2D barcode.

A continuing theme throughout the discussions of the group relating to these tests and initial experiences with the Medication Plan concerned problems with the various coding systems for automatic data filling. While the group rejected proposals to use such coding systems for several fields, as described above, four fields can be filled automatically by drawing on a code system for drug names known as the 'PZN' which emerged in the 1970s and is maintained jointly by trade associations of pharmaceutical manufacturers, wholesalers, and community pharmacies (Wagner, 2005). The PZN code acts as a data key for retrieving further drug-related information from commercially operated databases, including the trade name of the drug as registered with the authorities, the name of the active ingredient, the pharmaceutical form (e.g. tablet or a liquid), and the quantity of the active ingredient in one unit. A further field concerns the medication schedule, when to take each unit of the medicine.

When creating a Medication Plan, a physician or a pharmacist could use their computer system to retrieve drug-related data from the databases of several data providers using the PZN as a key.[6] However, field tests consistently showed that there are differences between data providers in how such data are maintained, especially the 'active ingredient' and 'pharmaceutical form' but also the 'trade name' fields. As a result of these inconsistencies, the contents of the Medication Plan may change when it is scanned compared to when it is printed out again, even though the medication itself did not change.

While in their discussions of these problems the members of the Coordination Group were mostly concerned with the costs of making the various data sources consistent, the discovery of these inconsistencies was also productive. For example, the group decided to design their own classification system for pharmaceutical forms. This move was heavily criticized by the three main database providers who feared damage to their businesses. They meanwhile cooperated to make their own classification systems for the pharmaceutical form of drugs consistent. However, the Coordination Group decided that it would continue to maintain and make available its own classification system, arguing that contents used in the Medication Plan should be in the public domain. More importantly, the group also argued that all contents of the Medication Plan must be intelligible to patients, an argument that had been made in other contexts as well, as reported above. Thus, the discovery of these data inconsistencies also contributed to a further elaboration of the re-orienting of the practices involved in medication processes by reasserting the active role of patients in its use.

While most tests of the Medication Plan involving patients concerned questions of usability and legibility, a project of the Aachen Learning Community, in which one of the authors is actively involved, studied how the Medication Plan changes the relations of the various practices by conducting reflective video conversations with patients, pharmacists, and physicians. One finding from these conversations is noteworthy. It became clear that the Medication Plan can become an occasion to bring into view the medication of a patient *as a whole*. This was most clearly articulated by a diabetes patient, but also by the physician member of the Learning Community. The patient reported how the Medication Plan had enabled thematising her medication holistically in both her interactions with her physicians and her pharmacist. The most striking instance of this concerned her interaction with a neurologist. He had refused to create a Medication Plan for her on the grounds that he was not her family doctor. However, talking about the Medication Plan led him to review her medication, subsequently finding a medication error. Thus, the talk about the Medication Plan seems to have changed the way that he views or comports to the medication, namely now in a more holistic manner. A Medication Plan was eventually created and printed by her endocrinologist. This also included the medication prescribed by the other physicians (about 6) she regularly sees as well as OTC drugs. Her pharmacist then spent about half an hour going through the Medication Plan again. Both, her family

---

[6]While the 'e-health law' later specified that only physicians are obliged to create and print out a Medication Plan, earlier discussions in the group show that the group also envisaged that pharmacists can create and print a Medication Plan for patients. Presently, the role of pharmacists in creating and updating the Medication Plan has not yet become clear.

doctor and her pharmacist had initially responded rather negatively to her request to prepare and check her medication plan but then became rather enthusiastic about this. Overall, she feels that her medication has acquired a new quality—that of being reviewed and approved holistically—even in cases where the medication was not changed. Moreover, her family doctor began to be concerned with the way she takes certain drugs and has asked her to visit more often to follow up on her medication-taking practice. The patient described this as 'reining in' her drug taking practice, something that was not entirely unwelcome to her.

The physician member of the Aachen Learning Community confirmed these observations that the Medication Plan provides an occasion to concern oneself more intensively and holistically with the medication of a patient. In particular, he noted (our translation):

> My experience is that the correct filling-in of the Medication Plan requires a lot of work, a lot of thinking through; it also occasionally forces the physician to check whether everything written down there [on the Medication Plan] is still up-to-date, is it still necessary? On the other hand, it is an instrument which calls for a lot of dynamic, because the Medication Plan is normally valid only for a few weeks or months and is then changed and modified again, and this, on each occasion, requires a new thinking through of the plan and the medication. Of course, not everything will be changed, but everything must be critically evaluated, and this is an important process.

He also believes that the Medication Plan is important for both physician and patient. In addition, he sees a need to comply with regulatory intentions.

We interpret these experiences as showing that the Medication Plan is 'generative' in the sense that, in practical use and testing, it continues to generate discussions and discoveries, resulting in further re-orienting of the practices involved in medication as the opening is further elaborated. This elaboration results from an ongoing practical interpretation of the Medication Plan such that, as its possible uses and purposes come to be better understood, each participant also comes to understand their own practice better and in a more nuanced way.

Discussion

In this section, we will interpret the happening of an opening, revealed by the Medication Plan case above, as a dialectic process of opposing proximity and distance between the practices as regions of a concern. This overarching dialectic of *nearness* and *farness* can be analysed into three constituent dialectics, namely, between the *already familiar* and the *not yet familiar*, between the *self* and the *other*, and between *resistance* and *accommodation*. Each dialectic powers an aspect of the overall happening of an opening and we will describe these sub-processes in the following sub-sections. To bring out how and why these dialectical processes can be productive, we will also describe how the delicate balance of nearness and farness in each is in constant danger of being closed down.

Recursive Processes in an Opening

The dialectic of the *already familiar* and the *not yet familiar* is the most fragile and hidden of the three dialectics. It involves a *recursive* process because it is powered by the anticipation of a possibility which has *not yet* become manifest, but which must still be assumed to be sufficiently solid to become the *basis* for concrete action and to manifest itself as something familiar. For example, for the Medication Plan to be able to become a site of an opening, the members of the Coordination Group had to allow a possible reality for the Medication Plan to structure their discussions and thus, in a sense, to create the foundations for its own coming into existence. Consequently, there was a high risk that such intuitive action would not live-up to the expectations of participants or that it was ill-founded. As well as being productive this process creates a particular vulnerability and fragility of the opening as well.

The danger which constantly threatens to break the productive tension inherent in this recursive process is not that people refuse to allow a possible reality into their discourse—this may be the case, but would simply signify a lack of imagination—but rather, that the possible reality that announces itself in such discourse is seen merely as a 'token' for some intentions that cannot or should not in fact be expected to become actual. In other words, a rift is created between present reality and a purely symbolic world that cannot be bridged. In our example, that danger could have manifested in a discourse about the Medication Plan characterized by an expectation that the Medication Plan will never acquire any real meaning, even if used in practice. This would amount to the discussion acquiring such a token character. This danger of *tokenization* was ever present, not only in the initial discussions, but also throughout the testing of the Medication Plan and in its everyday use. Conversely, the opening for which the Medication Plan has become a site continues to be productive only if, throughout its conception and everyday use, an as-yet unknown and unfamiliar reality is allowed to structure the conversations about the Medication Plan and inform ways of using it. Since this recursive process accounts for the 'taking hold' of an opening, it follows that the taking hold is not a singular event after which an opening 'exists', but part of the *ongoing* becoming of the opening, and that there is an ever-present danger that relations between practices may become unproductive and the opening disappears.

Assertive Processes in an Opening

An opening is also at risk from efforts to take over control of it—to appropriate it. For example, pharmacist members in the Coordination Group have repeatedly attempted to transform the character of the Medication Plan into a primarily pharmaceutical document through proposals to add various fields that are especially important from a pharmaceutical perspective. Likewise, members of the pharmacist and the regulatory practices have attempted to transform the Medication Plan into a coordination mechanism by proposing a detailed choreography of interactions between pharmacist and physician which would impose a narrow technical understanding of medication processes on physicians. Such efforts, however, were opposed by other members and eventually fended off.

The interplay between appropriation moves and assertive countermoves are the manifestation of another kind of process at work in the happening of an opening. Again there is a dialectic at work here because, while counter-actions mainly served to keep practices from dominating or 'colonizing' the Medication Plan as the site of the opening, they also contributed to the further working out of the relationships between the various practices. Such assertive processes are thus powered by a productive opposition between 'oneself' and 'the other'. They are productive to the extent that engagement with the other not only contributes to a better understanding of the other but also to a better understanding of one's own role and possibilities. The danger is that the opening becomes 'colonized' by one practice that imposes its way of understanding and acting on the other practices to such an extent that there is no openness to alternate perspectives.

Generative Processes in an Opening

There is a third process in the happening of an opening which is highly significant for its productivity. It is powered by a dialectical encounter between the materiality of the site of the opening and the human agency of the practitioners. For example, in field tests it was discovered that certain medication schedules could not be captured by the Medication Plan. Such discoveries, however, were not interpreted as uncovering deficiencies in the 'design' of the Medication Plan that should and could be eliminated by re-designing the Medication Plan as an artefact. Rather, they were taken as clues that further meaningful distinctions needed to be made and somehow addressed. Tellingly, the Coordination Group appreciated the existence of more complex medication regimes while also resisting calls for re-designing the Medication Plan to capture such medication regimes more mechanically. Other examples concern the practical interactions of physicians and pharmacists with the Medication Plan, which led them to change their comportment toward it and to understand the medication of their patients in a more holistic manner.

We interpret such discoveries as resulting from a *generative* dialectic of resistance and accommodation in interactions between human agency and a certain 'material agency' of the site of the opening, as described by Pickering's mangle of practice concept (1995). For instance, when interacting with the Medication Plan, one does not just encounter a certain material artefact, but all the other practices involved in medication processes. Such encounters with the resistance offered by the site of the opening may thus be experienced as a form of 'practice resistance' (Johnston, Reimers, & Klein, 2016) that calls into question or renders problematic certain aspects of one's own interpretations and understandings. Accommodating to such resistance is generative because, by adjusting one's understanding and way of acting, the relationships between the various practices are further refined and elaborated. The danger consists in reconciling such discrepancies in a mechanical manner, for example, by re-designing the Medication Plan to accommodate every variation that occurs in practice. Another form of 'mechanizing' the Medication Plan would be to prescribe ways of interacting through it so tightly that human agency is entirely deleted, as envisioned by the East German project. In both kinds of mechanization, a seemingly straightforward mechanical 'solution' to an existing 'problem' would be 'implemented': the result would be to close down an 'opportunity' to generate new meaningful distinctions that support more nuanced productive relations between the practices.

In sum, the nature of an opening consists in a certain way of re-orienting the various practices to one another which is productive. Three dialectics are at work in this re-orienting: a recursive dialectic that allows an opening to take hold, an assertive dialectic that keeps multiple perspectives in play, and a generative dialectic the keeps the opening productive. Each dialectic process is powered by a distinct opposition at work among practices, namely, between the already familiar and the not yet familiar, between self and other, and between resistance and accommodation. As such, they are each aspects of a more general dialectic of nearness and farness. Together these dialectics hold the practices apart as distinct and autonomous regions of a concern, and *at the same time*, provide a site where creative tensions and new meaningful distinctions are kept in play through close productive interaction.

Conclusion

We set out to elaborate the notion of 'living infrastructure'. We drew on the example of the Medieval European City Square to suggest what a living infrastructure might consist of, and what might justify the adjective 'living' to distinguish it from traditional conceptions of infrastructure. The key idea is the notion that a living infrastructure becomes the *site* where an *opening* between certain *regions* of life, which share some *concern*, *happens*. This happening of the opening is an on-going process of nurturing and safeguarding certain productive oppositions between the regions of living that are at once recursive, assertive and generative in the sense developed in the previous section.

We then presented an empirical case of the Federal Unified Medication Plan for medication therapy safety in the German healthcare environment. By a careful interpretation of the case materials we sharpened our conceptual tools and showed that this Medication Plan provides a site where a productive opening happens between multiple practices involved in medication processes in pursuit of a common concern for medication therapy safety. Thus, like the City Square, the Medication Plan exemplifies our notion of living infrastructure, as displayed in Table 2.

Finally, we should briefly return to our comments at the beginning of the paper about the traditional conception of infrastructure as a material coordination system and relate them to the notion of living infrastructure. We will simply note, as discussed

Table 2 Our conceptual framework, the City Square and the Medication Plan compared

Concept	Definition	Examples	
		The City Square	The Medication Plan
Concern	A concern defines that aspect of human existence with which the infrastructure deals	The concern is living life to the full in a city	The concern is medication therapy safety
Region	Regions are distinct aspects of the concern—they are distinct 'locations on a map' of the concern	The regions are the institutions of town life—religion, state, commerce, and education/culture	The practices involved with medication—medical, pharmaceutical, patienthood, regulatory
Opening	An opening is the establishment of productive distinctions between the regions of the concern	The establishment of distinctions between spiritual, corporal, individual and social aspects of a full city life	The establishment of productive relations between distinct practices involved in medication processes
Site of an opening	Where an instance of an opening takes hold	The lived-in city square that provides the conditions of an opening between church, town hall, market and school to happen	An actual in-use Medication Plan that sustains a productive opening between physician, pharmacist, patient, and regulator/insurer
The happening of an opening	How an opening arises, is kept open, and continues to be productive	The city square as an opening happens through various on-going dialectical processes, which could be documented for any particular city square	The Medication Plan as an opening happens by: taking hold through a dialectic of the already familiar and the not yet familiar; being held open through a dialectic of self and other; and remaining productive through a dialectic of resistance and accommodation

in the previous section, that when an infrastructure becomes tokenized, colonized or mechanized the productive tension between the regions of life lived there closes down. The infrastructure is no longer a site that holds open practices as distinctive and productive regions of life lived to the full: at most, only a mere material coordination mechanism for coordinating the transactional elements of existence remains.

References

Claßen, A., Eisert, A., Everding, W., Grebe, I., Härter, S., Hildmann, R., et al. (2015). *Arzneimitteltherapiesicherheit im Spannungsfeld von vollständiger Medikationsübersicht, mündigem Patienten und individualisierter Medikation.* Göttingen: Cuvillier Verlag.

Dreyfus, H. L. (2017). Heidegger's Ontology of Art. In M. A. Wrathall (Ed.), *Background practices: Essays on the understanding of being.* Oxford, UK: Oxford University Press.

Edwards, P. N. (2010). *A vast machine: Computer models, climate data, and the politics of global warming.* Cambridge, MA: MIT Press.

Hanseth, O., & Lyytinen, K. (2010). Design theory for dynamic complexity in information infrastructures: The case of building the internet. *Journal of Information Technology, 25*(1), 9–19.

Heidegger, M. (1950/1971). The Thing. In Poetry, Language, Thought, translated by A. Hofstadter, New York: Harper & Row.

Heidegger, M. (1971). *Poetry, language, thought* (trans: A. Hofstadter). New York: Harper & Row.

Johnston, R. B., Reimers, K., & Klein, S. (2016). Performing research validity: A "Mangle of Practice" approach. In L. Introna, D. Kavanagh, S. Kelly, W. Orlikowski, & S. Scott (Eds.), *Beyond interpretivism? New encounters with technology and organization* (pp. 201–214). Cham, Switzerland: Springer.

Langley, A., Smallman, C., Tsoukas, H., & Van de Ven, A. H. (2013). Process studies of change in organization and management: Unveiling temporality, activity, and flow. *Academy of Management Journal, 38*(1), 1–13.

Polt, R. (2005). Ereignis. In H. L. Dreyfus & M. A. Wrathall (Eds.), *A companion to Heidegger.* Malden, MA: Blackwell.

Schmitz, R. (1998). Geschichte der Pharmazie: Von den Anfängen bis zum Ausgang des Mittelalters, Bd. 1: Eschborn: Govi-Verlag.

Tsoukas, H., & Chia, R. (2002). On organizational becoming: Rethinking organizational change. *Organization Science, 13,* 567–582.

Wagner, T. (2005). Interorganisationale Informationssysteme in der Distribution pharmazeutischer Produkte in Deutschland. In K. Reimers, T. Wagner, & A. Zenke (Eds.), *Fallstudien interorganisationaler Informationssysteme – Ergebnisse aus vier Branchen und vier Ländern* (pp. 43–78). Göttingen: Cuvillier Verlag.

Part III
Digital Commerce and Consumer Experience

Chapter 13
Consumer Search Patterns: Empirical Evidence, Competing Theories and Managerial Implications

Christopher P. Holland

Introduction

Consumer search is of crucial important to the functioning of markets and therefore plays a pivotal role in marketing theory (Engel et al., 1995). In a multi-channel context where shoppers have a wide range of sources of information for search, around 80% of shoppers have used the Internet for search purposes, and in specific markets such as airlines, telecommunications and electrical goods, over half of all purchases, regardless of sales channel, originated on the Internet (Holland & Mandry, 2015).

The digital marketplace is characterized by software and tools to facilitate the online search process, in particular search engines, social media and specialized comparison tools, which influence the search process of consumers and are critical elements in a digital marketing strategy where companies naturally seek to manage the search process in order to promote their own products (Chaffey & Smith, 2017). Companies must decide not only what level of spending should be allocated to the digital channel, but also how it should be allocated across myriad digital channels, including search engine optimization, paid search, social media campaigns and email or database marketing (Internet Advertising Bureau, 2012).

The focus of this paper is to present an overview of competing theories that seek to explain or at least model the online search process for brand selection, in the light of recent empirical evidence regarding online consideration sets and the related use of search engines. An inductive approach is followed whereby a focused set of empirical data of the online search is presented, followed by a discussion

C. P. Holland (✉)
Loughborough University, Epinal Way, Loughborough, Leicestershire LE11 3TU, UK
e-mail: C.P.Holland@lboro.ac.uk

C. P. Holland
University of Münster, Münster, Germany

© Springer International Publishing AG, part of Springer Nature 2019
K. Riemer et al. (eds.), *Collaboration in the Digital Age*, Progress in IS,
https://doi.org/10.1007/978-3-319-94487-6_13

of competing theoretical frameworks. The purpose is to provoke new discussion around this topic and foster more pragmatic and realistic thinking in order to inform managerial practice, which appears to be following an independent trajectory to academic thinking and research. A new model is proposed that is based on a synthesis of empirical evidence, an inter-disciplinary theory base and ideas and concepts from the business press.

Empirical Evidence

The dominant concept for modelling consumer search is the consideration set, which is composed of a set of brands that the consumer finds interesting and evaluates to inform a buying decision (Stigler, 1961; Howard & Sheth, 1969; Court et al., 2009). The consideration concept set has been widely used in marketing since the 1960s, (Frank & Massy, 1963; Massy & Frank, 1964; Ehrenberg, 1965; Silk & Urban, 1978; Narayana & Markin, 1975). It is important because consideration sets explicitly define competing products through brand choice and therefore define a set of competitors. This valuable information informs product design, differentiation, advertising and market positioning. The definition of a consideration set is based on the marketing literature (Hauser & Wernerfelt, 1990; Howard & Sheth, 1969) and is given as:

> A consideration set is defined as the range of brands that a consumer actively considers when making a purchasing decision.

Emphasis is placed on the adjective 'active' to denote some form of positive search and evaluation behaviour. This distinguishes the consideration set from the awareness set, the group of brands that a consumer is aware of but does not necessarily actively consider.

Pre-internet Search

The assessor database is the largest review of actual consideration sets pre-Internet and measures the consideration set for a wide range of consumer goods including soap, beer, coffee, shampoo and yogurt. The range is from 2.6 to 6.9, with an average of 4.12. Other studies also show relatively narrow search patterns, e.g. beer (3.5), mouthwash (1.3), deodorant (1.6) and toothpaste (2.0) (Narayana & Markin, 1975), coffee (3.3), tea (2.6) and beer (3.0) (Massy & Frank, 1964), fast food (5.4), gasoline (3.0) and soft drinks (5.06) (Brown & Wildt, 1992). The point about these results is that consumers typically only chose from a handful of options. The awareness set is those brands that consumers are of from the universal set of all brands within a particular market.

Table 13.1 Average consideration sets from six market sectors in UK and US *Source* Holland and Mandry (2013)

	Average size of online consideration set	
	UK	US
Car insurance	2.77	2.41
Airlines	2.57	2.60
Mobile phones	2.56	2.42
Auto-motive	2.44	2.22
Banking	2.43	2.38
Grocery	2.40	2.13

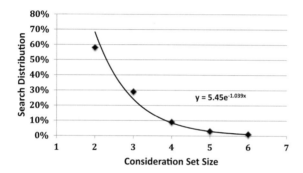

Fig. 13.1 The distribution of search consideration set for the US airline market

Online Consideration Sets

The Internet changes the search process by making potentially vast amounts of infor-mation, and therefore a wide range of options, available to the consumer. The use general purpose search engines and more specialized product search engines, termed digital comparison tools should also make the search process easier and faster by automating the collection and evaluation of a large set of brand data. However, those studies that have measured the online consideration set show clearly that not much has changed from the pre-Internet results shown above. If anything there has been a slight reduction in the consideration set, as measured using online panel data, e.g. see (Johnson et al., 2004; Zhang et al., 2006). The consideration sets for 6 market sectors from the US and UK is shown in Table 13.1, source (Holland & Mandry, 2013).

These consideration set sizes all fall within a narrow range between 2.13 and 2.77. Note that these results are averages, which masks the distribution of searchers. Taking the US airline market to illustrate the appearance of the distribution of searchers, see Fig. 13.1.

It can be seen that 90% of searchers only look at 2 or 3 websites, and that 10% conduct what could be termed an extensive search process, where 4 or more airline websites are viewed. The definition of an extensive search process may appear to be a little arbitrary, but it makes sense because in many consumer markets, there may only be around 5 or 6 brands with significant market share. The curved line is an exponential best fit. This is a good approximation though it is acknowledged that other skewed distributions such as power and geometric curves could also be applied.

All of the online results described above were based on an analysis of online panel data, which also showed another interesting outcome, that the searchers who looked at two or more websites accounted for approximately a quarter of all the users who visited any one of the websites within a competitive set. That is, three quarters of users visited one website, or one brand/competitor only. This could have been a very limited search activity, or more likely, to carry out some form of service such as e-banking, repeat grocery buying, topping up a prepay mobile phone or checking into an airline flight.

Search Engine Behaviour

By going back a stage in the search process to the use of search engines, a similarly narrow search pattern can be observed regarding the share of clicks garnered by the top ranking search results (Pan, 2015). These show that the top 3 rankings account for 75% of all clicks and that the first page accounts for approximately 90% of all clicks, i.e. it is a skewed distribution and could be modeled as a power curve in which the top rankings account for a disproportionately large percentage of the attention shown by searchers, measured by Click Through Rates (CTRs). Similar evidence is given from the online hotel industry, where search rankings show that the first page of results account for approximately half of all clicks, and the top 3 results account for half of all clicks from results displayed on the first page of results (de los Santos & Koulayev, 2017). Eye-tracking experiments also demonstrate a highly focused attention on the top results in early search engine results (Hotchkiss & Alston, 2005).

Interestingly, the search emphasis on the top results to the detriment of paying attention to lower-ranked results becomes even more pronounced on mobile devices, expressed by shorter search terms (Church & Oliver, 2011) and by steeper Click Through Rates (CTRs). The most plausible explanation is the smaller screen size of mobile devices compared to desktop search.

Why Do Narrow Search Patterns Matter?

The data almost speaks for itself. Narrow search patterns are the defining character-istic of consumer brand search, which has implications for advertising, entry of new competitors into mature markets, the frequency and extent of brand-switching, the nature of market share changes and the associated growth and decline of individual companies. It is therefore important to try and explain the nature of this search process and perhaps reevaluate what is sometimes taken as accepted wisdom, namely that consumers will perform economically rational searches until the benefits of additional information cost more than the expected search cost (Stigler, 1961). In an era when search costs are notionally very low because of the ease of access to a diverse range of information on the Internet and associated ideas around perfect competition in electronic markets (Malone et al., 1989; Anonymous, 2000), it seems reasonable to expect broad search patterns as the norm, so it is worth asking the question and reviewing other possible explanations.

Competing Theories

This section is not meant or claimed to be an exhaustive or even traditional literature review. Instead, it identifies thematic streams of research in an attempt to paint a broad picture of competing theories that might help explain narrow search patterns. Each stream of research is illustrated by a discussion of prominent papers that explain the logic, rationale and value of the approach in explaining the empirical evidence.

The theories are placed into two groups: (1) *Consumer-focused models*, theories that are primarily concerned with how the individual decision-maker behaves when searching and buying a product; (2) *Product-Market Models*, theories that seek to explain consumer behaviour based on the market context defined by the product characteristics, competitive strategies and offers of individual companies and the related market structure. In some ways this division is artificial because consumer-based theories will naturally take into account the market context. However, for analytical purposes and focusing on the individual theories, the grouping has merit because it identifies the two rather broad approaches to the problem. It also reflects the fact that the consumer-focused models do not explicitly take into account different market contexts, and theories that focus at a market level tend not be concerned with individual behaviour, but rather the overall pattern of choices as influenced by say market structure.

Consumer-Focused Models

The customer-focused models all attempt to model and explain how individual consumers behave and in particular how they conduct their search and evaluation of information. The idea of information processing models has a long tradition in psychology and marketing (Chestnut & Jacoby, 1978), information economics (Stigler, 1961), decision-making theory (Simon, 1955) and more recently in the attention economy (Davenport & Beck, 2001). It may also explain why consumers do *nothing*, i.e. exhibit inertia, measured by little or no search and remaining with their existing supplier (Jacoby et al., 1974).

Customers as Information Processing Systems

These theories are normally considered to be quite separate but it can be argued that they are all fundamentally looking at the collection, collation, analysis and evaluation of information in order to make a buying decision. Whether this is done from an economic perspective in which utility and costs are the main variables, or whether the focus is on understanding the process of cognition, or style of decision-making is of secondary importance. The merits of each theoretical approach for explaining narrow search patterns are evaluated.

Information Economics

The natural starting point is the seminal work on information economics (Stigler, 1961). This economic model of information search is very simple and elegant: a consumer incurs search costs for each additional piece of information that is sought and that each new piece of information has value. In the specific case of exploring prices for a particular type of product, say a car, then before the Internet, the cost of the search would be a combination of travel and time costs to visit a range of geographically dispersed car showrooms. The value of the additional information would depend on the price dispersion. After two searches, the consumer would make a decision on whether the expected value of additional search is greater than the cost of acquiring the information. An implicit part of this model is that the principal search cost is the cost of *acquiring* the information, rather than the cost of analyzing and making sense of it. Prima facie, the Internet dramatically reduces search costs (Anonymous, 2000; Malone et al., 1989), therefore one would expect the number of searches to be increased with the advent of the Internet and associated search tools. In a brand selection process, it is natural to expect consumers to conduct extensive search patterns because this would give them excellent market information, e.g. price, quality and availability, at relatively little cost. However, this is not generally the case and the theory appears to run contrary to the available evidence.

Decision-Making Style

A different approach looks at the decision-making style of individuals and argues that they fall into two broad groups: satisficers and maximizers (Simon, 1955; Karimi et al., 2015). Rather than assume that individuals behave in a rational manner and follow a mathematical economic model, it accepts that people have different psychologies. If this model is applied to the distribution of consideration set size in Fig. 13.1, it can be seen that just 10% of consumers can be classified as 'maximizers' and 90% as 'satisficers'. Given the paucity of data on the distribution of decision-making style pre and post Internet, it is difficult to make an empirical observation on the *effects* of the Internet on either group. It does appear though that the Internet has *not* transformed all consumers into standardized searchers with extensive search

Table 13.2 The attention economy measured by total time and visitor frequency

Airline	Average time in 1 month (min)	Average minutes per visit	Visitor frequency
Southwest Airlines Co.	15.4	6.8	2.3
Delta Airlines	29.7	10.0	3.0
American Airlines	20.3	7.4	2.8
United Airlines	24.1	8.2	2.9
JetBlue Airways	16.9	7.3	2.3

Source comScore October 2016

patterns. There remains a high variation in search behaviour and other factors beyond economics and psychology need to be studied.

Attention Economy

A relatively recent approach that explicitly considers the Internet is the attention economy concept (Davenport & Beck, 2001). The essence of the argument is that in economics, the abundant availability of information does not help us understand its consumption and instead the focus should be on what is limited, which is the attention of individuals. The idea that there is a fixed level of attention is novel because it places a limit on the search process that is not really acknowledged in the earlier research into information economics (Stigler, 1961), search in electronic markets (Malone et al., 1989) and psychology of search (Simon, 1955).

The attention economy also recognizes explicitly that a specific search problem for a consumer exists together with other activities that also demand attention and that in fact time is the limiting factor in search behaviour and this is what should be measured to evaluate consumer search and to measure the effectiveness of advertising campaigns (Voorveld et al., 2013). The idea has face validity for explaining why consumers fail to conduct extensive search, because they have very limited attention. Developing the theme on time as the currency of search, some additional data is shown in Table 13.2 on the amount of attention spent on the US airline websites.

The total average time spent in 1 month per website is between 15 and 30 min, with time per visit between 7 and 10 min. This is a relatively small amount of attention, especially when one considers that approximately 90% of customers look at just 2 or 3 brands (see online consideration set results in Table 13.1). Attention economy theory is important because it explicitly recognizes that consumers have a fixed, and therefore limited, amount of attention to spend across competing activities. The data in Tables 13.1 and 13.2 start to calibrate the actual level of attention spent on a specific task, i.e. searching for an airline ticket, and show that the airlines have two important challenges: (1) to be included in the consideration set; (2) to convert the searcher into a buyer in a short space of time. The attention economy is a powerful concept but it does not explain the variance in the search behaviour, nor does it fully explain why consumers expend so little time on evaluating important purchases such as flights, where economic theory suggests that a more exhaustive search process would be the norm (Stigler, 1961).

Prior Knowledge

An obvious explanation for expending so little effort is that consumers already have detailed knowledge about a market and are therefore confident that they do not need to conduct extensive search, measured by either the number of brands considered, or the amount of time spent on suppliers' websites. Satisficers appear to make up around 90% of the overall population based on the data shown in Table 13.1 and the associated analysis in Fig. 13.1. The limited search process can therefore be explained by a *combination* of prior knowledge and decision-making style, where those consumers with a high level of prior knowledge and who are also satisficers are expected to conduct less search than someone with low knowledge of the market and/or maximizers (Karimi et al., 2015).

Customer Inertia

In addition to existing customer knowledge, customers rarely start a search and buying process from scratch, i.e. they already have established patterns, or norms, for their behaviour. An important aspect of established patterns of behaviour is that customers generally have search inertia, i.e. there is a natural tendency for them to continue doing what they are already doing, or do nothing, unless something changes. There are clearly reasons to stay with the existing supplier or product: satisfaction with the existing supplier, laziness, risk aversion of new products and suppliers, feeling of entrapment, high switching costs, loyalty towards existing supplier, tie-ins from contracts, loyalty programmes and good value perception of the current product.

The point here is that it would be naïve to expect the majority of consumer behaviour to be characterized by extensive search patterns and associated switching between competing suppliers because there are clearly switching costs, risks and search effort involved in evaluating the market and switching from one competitor to another. A desire to buy a new product or switch from an existing supplier is normally a pre-requisite for search and indeed the most common strategy for consumers is to remain with their existing supplier (Johnson et al., 2004; Holland and Mandry, 2013).

Product-Market Models

The product-market models are distinctive from the consumer models because they are concerned with the product-market context, i.e. the product attributes and market characteristics such as industry concentration and supplier strategies, and how these directly affect consumer behaviour by determining, for example, the product risk, price, switching costs and what is available to consumers in terms of choice and market segments. For example, if there is limited competition within a market, then this will naturally be reflected by a correspondingly small average consideration set.

Industry Concentration

Industry concentration has long been recognised as an important indicator of competitive intensity (Besanko et al., 2009). The logic is that higher levels of industry concentration can potentially lead to excessive levels of market power for a small number competitors, and this limits competition in terms of price, innovation and consumer choice (Holland and Jacobs, 2015; Urban et al., 1984), or more accurately the numbers-equivalent of competitors is proportional to the range of brands open to consumers and is therefore proportional to the consideration set.

Market competition and evolution, for example the growth of successful companies, the demise of failed competitors, mergers and acquisitions and regulatory constraints, results in markets where there are only 4–5 significant brands, i.e. a small number of competitors enjoy a high collective share of the market. In markets where geographic specificity plays an important role, e.g. the US grocery market, industry concentration needs to be measured at a more local level within a specific *geographic area*, rather than at a national level.

Even in information-intensive markets such as insurance, physical distribution may be an important channel, which makes the availability of products through advisors an important consideration in consumer choice. For example, see the German retail insurance market, where brokers still control a large portion of the overall market. In online markets where a winner takes all dynamic operates, then the choice may be limited further still, e.g. the online app market for taxi services, where new entrants have quickly gained traction over the traditional business models and gained very high market shares very quickly.

The general point is that high levels of industry concentration are common in developed markets, and in new technology markets where network effects play an important role, then the markets mature quicker than traditional markets, and often result in even higher levels of concentration. This means that when one measures the number of brands that a consumer actively considers, industry concentration will limit the choice, which means that there may only be a handful of brands that are worthwhile considering.

Market Segmentation

Differentiation and segmentation of markets are crucial aspects of marketing strategy and even with broad market segments, e.g. premium and discount brands, this reduces the actual choice of brands that are suitable for a particular individual's needs and requirements. For example, in the UK grocery market, although there are 8 major brands with market share greater than 5%, if a consumer is only interested in value brands, then their choice is limited to just 2 companies Aldi and Lidl. Similar observations can be made in other international consumer markets, including airlines, insurance, mobile phones and clothes.

In conclusion, the successful segmentation of a consumer market in which the products from competitors are differentiated from each other and targeted at specific market segments, coupled with marketing communication from competitors that is known and clearly understood by consumers, is a very plausible explanation for small consideration sets in both offline and online channels.

Multi-Channel Search

A limitation of measuring the size of the consideration set in just one channel, the Internet, is that it may under-report what consumers actively consider based on their actions and behaviours in other channels. Retailers have even coined acronyms to describe such behaviour: ROPO, for research online purchase offline, and 'showrooming', often used in a derogatory or critical manner to describe the behaviour of consumers that inspect goods in showrooms and then buy them online, often at a cheaper price. The point is that most consumers will use a variety of channels for their information, which include online websites, physical stores, social media, electronic and face-to-face word of mouth, magazines and radio.

Digital Comparison Tools

Prima facie, the strongest explanation for small online consideration sets is that consumers use digital comparison tools to help them filter the total market into a smaller selection of possible brands, which are then researched in detail. In the travel market, search intermediaries such as Kayak and Expedia will scan a vast range of options based on a set of search criteria, e.g. destination, date and travel times, which circumscribe the market to reduce it to what is hopefully a more manageable problem for the consumer.

In this context, the value of the concept of the online consideration set could be questioned because consumer search processes are much more complicated in a digital-assisted world (Jacobs et al., 2017). However, if the consideration set concept is defined in terms of consumers visiting a brand's website, then there is very limited research that has explicitly considered the influence of digital comparison tools on direct search, i.e. direct visits by the consumer to the websites of competing brands.

Research using online panel data concluded that (a) not all consumers use digital comparison tools, and (b) those that do use digital comparison tools go on to conduct *more* direct search with airline websites than those that only did direct search (Holland et al., 2016). If the stimulating effect of comparison tools on direct search with airlines is replicated in other markets, then digital comparison tools can at best only offer a partial explanation of small online consideration sets.

Discussion of Competing Theoretical Models

The theories are evaluated with respect to their ability to explain the empirical results on search behaviour, in particular the small online consideration sets and the relatively small amount of attention spent on search measured by search time per brand per month. That is, their utility in terms of explaining search behaviour in the specific context of a product-market is the focus of interest, and search behaviour *in general* is not relevant and therefore beyond the scope of this paper.

Evaluation of Theoretical Models

Customers as Information Processing Units

Looking at customers as information processing systems is a very powerful concept because in an online environment, the search problem can be defined precisely and comprehensively in terms of information. Information economic theory could be used to predict extensive search patterns based on the idea of maximization and the fact that the Internet dramatically reduces search costs. However this makes two important assumptions about the nature of search costs and also about the expected value of further search that may not be true.

Information Economic, Search Effort and Price Dispersion

In the early models of search the focus was often on price information and price dispersion in the market (Stigler, 1961). It is very easy to compare price information so the main cost was in the collection of price information. In modern consumer markets there is often a bewildering choice of products and configurations of individual products, which make even the comparison of 'simple' price information very difficult (Swann, 2001). Search effort therefore has several components: collection; collation; analysis; comparison; and sense making. These apply to a wide range of information attributes, e.g. quality, suitability and price information, which need to be applied to a range of brand options. In addition, decision-making style, prior knowledge and industry concentration, may limit the expected value of further search because the consumer is only pursuing a satisficing solution, the consumer already has strong preferences for particular brands based on their prior knowledge and experience, and high industry concentration can also limit the available set of realistic options. Viewing the search problem in this light, it is quite plausible that consumers need to limit their brand selection to just 2 or 3 options in order to make a sensible trade-off between search costs and expected value from further search. The general point being made here is that previous comments and evaluations of information economic theory have not related the theoretical model to enough empirical evidence in order to *calibrate* it. Most commentators have therefore tended to under-estimate the cost of search and over estimate the value of further search.

Attention Economy

The argument outlined above is strengthened further by combining it with ideas from the attention economy, which explicitly states that total attention is a fixed amount, though it does not attempt to define or estimate the 'total' amount of time that is available (Davenport & Beck, 2001). Nonetheless, by making the limit of attention clear, it again suggests that the calibration of consumer behaviour requires more research and that in fact the total attention available for individual decisions may be much smaller than was previously assumed or implied, vide Table 13.2.

Customer Inertia

Customer inertia encapsulates a raft of additional consumer factors that help explain the apparent reluctance of consumers to switch from existing suppliers. These factors could be incorporated into an information economics perspective because they reduce the value of expected benefits. A practical approach to this concept is rather than get lost in the detail of *why* consumers exhibit inertia, it is easier and more straightforward simply to measure the extent of the inertia. For example, in an online market, the proportion of searchers to e-service tells us the proportion of the market that is actively looking at two or more competitors within a given time period. This is therefore a very robust measure of the proportion of potential switchers within a given market and therefore a good market indicator of the level of competition (Holland and Mandry, 2013).

Industry Concentration

Industry concentration limits the number of brands in the universal set and therefore will influence the size of the average consideration set. Similarly market segmentation will focus the attention of the consumer onto a related set of brands that suit their own particular requirements. The consumer may be aware of other brands but will not actively consider them because they are in effect operating in a distinct market, where the different market segments are heterogeneous from each other. Examples can easily be seen throughout Europe and the US in markets such as grocery, telecommunications and automotive markets.

Channel Interactions

There is strong evidence of important interactions between channels. In the case of search behaviour, information channels also include information sources such as radio, magazines and outdoor advertising. Returning to the problem of understanding the empirical data on consideration sets and search engines, the use of multiple channels could potentially mean that consumers consider brands in other channels in isolation from online search. However, given that the online channel has the lowest cost of search, it seems unlikely that consumers are using more expensive channels in isolation from the Internet though this would require empirical research. To understand the effects of multi-channel search requires consumer-focused research methods that track their behaviour and search patterns in their entirety, i.e. not just in one channel. The alternative hypothesis is that consumers look at the same brands or at least similar brands across multiple channels. On balance, multi-channel search behaviour does not therefore fully explain small online consideration sets.

The Customer Journey Metaphor

The customer journey model in which consumers move along a linear path in which a large range of options are reduced, i.e. a sales funnel (Engel et al., 1995) is an intuitively and appealing option because it appears to capture the essence of search behaviour, and can be used to guide marketing strategy, particularly to devise effective advertising campaigns. However, the simplicity masks important complexity, for example recursive search patterns (Court et al., 2009; Bughin et al., 2011), and differences in consumer and market characteristics (Howard & Sheth, 1969). The polar opposite to a linear customer journey would be one where the decision-maker is modelled as being buffeted, seemingly in random directions, as they are exposed to new information, advertisements and other external influences, influenced also by internal cognitive processing and evaluation of search information, prior knowledge and market perceptions. The truth probably lies somewhere between a simple sequence of stages and chaotic Brownian search motion.

Search Bricolage to Create an Information Mosaic

Would a synthesis of previous models be fruitful? This approach has been tried in the past. For example, there have been strong efforts at building intricate and comprehensive models of buyer behaviour based on how consumers search and evaluate competing offers dating back to the 1960s (Howard & Sheth, 1969). Although this particular model is theoretically elegant, it is almost impossible to operationalize and therefore use in a practical context. This is because the model attempts to be comprehensive in terms of variables and also includes the mechanisms of how the variables relate to each other.

It is important to first recognize the inherent complexity of the general search process and describe it in a realistic manner. Consumers search across multiple channels in an iterative manner, influenced by the nature of the search problem or buying decision, their personal traits and market characteristics. The Internet is not an ordered market-place, instead there is a diverse range of information from competitors, price comparison engines, agents, online advisors and social media, and it takes time and effort to create a semblance of order to information that is often difficult to locate, assess, evaluate and compare in a meaningful manner. Consumers search until they either make a buying decision or simply end the search process and do nothing.

Proposed Bricolage Search Model

The information processing model of consumers is apt, but consumers are not cold, rational, logical entities that systematically process, store, retrieve and reach optimal decisions. A better description of the search process may be to term it search brico-lage (Shih, 1998). Consumers rummage and delve for information in an improvised manner that is often more haphazard than planned, until they create an information-mosaic that is understood by the consumer, and a decision can be made. An illustrative diagram of the proposed bricolage search process is shown in Fig. 13.2.

Discussion of Bricolage Search Model

Search bricolage is distinct from an ordered, analytical approach, which is implicit in economic models of search (Stigler, 1961) and also in the marketing funnel concept (Engel et al., 1995), which both attempt to impose order and structure on search activity, which is described as a linear process. The main features of search brico-lage are that it explicitly models the search behaviour as an iterative (Court et al., 2009) and sometimes chaotic process, in which consumers piece together a picture or mosaic of the search problem based on separate fragments of information. The information mosaic is assembled from a diverse range of sources and is influenced by the characteristics of the consumer and the product-market context. An important prediction of this model is that the pattern from an individual search process would be characterised by a complex sequence of iterative search paths that is unlikely to have a clear, consistent and coherent logic to explain it. This is because in addition to a search strategy defined by consumer intent, objectives and purpose, the search pro-cess is also influenced by a combination of opportunity, spontaneity, available time

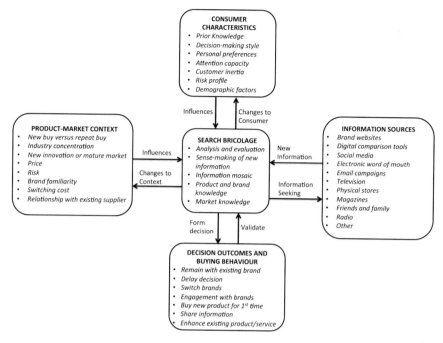

Fig. 13.2   Search bricolage: information sources, influences and outcomes

and random influences, rather like someone wandering through a range of market stalls or rummaging in a jumble sale.

The search process may result in changes to the product-market context as the consumer starts to understand their requirements and competing offers better. For example, after an initial review of the position, consumers may change the context because they decide to opt for a new technology innovation rather than a mature market, which could reset the search process. The act of searching also changes the consumer characteristics, for example by increasing the consumer's knowledge or modifying their preferences. The consumer continues to iteratively seek out new information, make sense of it, evolve the information mosaic in the context of the market and the consumer's own characteristics. Consumers make tentative decisions and then validate them to increase their confidence until a firm conclusion is reached and a decision outcome or buying action is made.

Conclusions

The pursuit of a general model of the search process is very ambitious and can be achieved at best in a broad-brush manner. This is because of the inherent complexity of the problem and the difficult of modelling and measuring the myriad of individual variables that affect the search process. The approach taken here is to propose a high-level model with search bricolage at its centre. The search context is defined by the product-market context and consumer characteristics. Search behaviour is modelled as a dynamic process in which consumers build up an information mosaic through search bricolage from multiple information sources. The search and evaluation of information could be highly structured but is likely to be rather haphazard in most cases. This results in tentative decisions that are iteratively validated, which eventually leads to a conclusion once the consumer is confident, or at least satisfied with their decision. Research into the detailed role and influence of individual factors such as risk, digital comparison tools, personal preferences etc. on the search process is important to develop a better theoretical understanding of how an individual factor(s) influences search, and this is the dominant research paradigm in management, where researchers from individual disciplines, in particular marketing, economics, information systems and psychology, attempt to understand and explain different aspects of the search process. However, it is also important to take a holistic perspective and at least attempt to conceptualise the problem in an integrative manner.

The main theoretical contribution of the proposed model is to argue that consumer search is not a scientific, rational method but is characterized by a bricolage process where consumers rummage for information in the jumble sale of information that is the Internet. Of course, there are large stalls in this market place, e.g. websites for the large brands, and there are agents to guide us around, i.e. search engines and digital comparison tools. But the point remains that the Internet is not an ordered place where information is neatly structured as per Yahoo!'s web directory concept launched in 1994 (Chekuri & Goldwasser, 1997), but rather an inter-connected jumble where the structure is determined by the content of individual web pages and hyper-text links between billions of separate documents and information sources. Consumers therefore employ a range of strategies in order to find relevant information without becoming overwhelmed by the volume and complexity of information, and the associated difficulties of sorting, organising and evaluating it. It is these broad search strategies, which are displayed as search patterns across large groups of consumers, rather than precise details of individual search behaviour, where most insights can be gained into the nature and extent of consumer search behaviour.

In terms of consumer traits, at an aggregate level and regardless of the product-market context, decision-making style (Simon, 1955) and attention economy theory (Davenport and Beck, 2001) hold most promise for describing and predicting consumer search behaviour. However, both theories suffer from a lack of detailed and accurate empirical information, and as a result of this lack of realistic data, there is very little *calibration* or testing of these models. The presentation of data in this chapter makes a small empirical contribution in this respect.

Managerial Implications

In a managerial context, the search process will be very specific and positioned within a particular market (e.g. telecommunications, airline, grocery), and most of the market context such as the maturity of the market, the value and risk of the purchase, will already be known and understood by managers. The focus of attention will therefore be on influencing the consumer search process through marketing communication. Looking at the online channel only, it is known from the empirical evidence presented in this paper and earlier research e.g. (Zhang et al., 2006; Johnson et al., 2004; Bellman et al., 1999; Holland & Mandry, 2013) that most consumers exhibit inertia in that they tend to stay with their existing supplier. Of those that search the market, the search process is narrow measured by the number of brands that are actively considered, and that consumers spend less attention than one might expect, in the case of the airline market this was less than 10 min per brand per visit within a one-month time period.

Market inertia favours high market share companies because market leaders have the most to lose by switchers. However, it is vital for all companies to at least maintain parity in advertising and awareness of their brands, to have a fighting chance of being included in the consideration set of searchers. Of course, this concept is not new and has been known for a long time in traditional advertising (Jones, 1990). What has changed though is the focus on understanding the nature of the information exchange between customers and competitors. To improve the allocation of online spending by companies requires a much better understanding of the search process and to have the skills and processes to take advantage of new data sources from web servers, online panels, search engine data, social media statistics and other newer forms of market intelligence that are based on online consumer behaviour.

The consumer search bricolage idea suggests that at a very detailed level, the search process may appear random. However, there will still be broad patterns, for example in segmentation of the market based on decision-making style and market trends such as the growth of discount or value brands. The complex nature of the search problem suggests that rather than adopt a specialist, single-discipline approach to investigate consumer behaviour, academic research *and* business research should follow a more inter-disciplinary approach and philosophy, which is in the spirit of research bricolage (Kincheloe, 2001). This requires collaboration across academic disciplines, and a recognition that a broad approach does not equate to a superficial analysis, but rather it seeks to be realistic and pragmatic in using concepts, tools and frameworks that are useful, regardless of their intellectual origins.

In an organisational context, managers should seek to avoid functional silos, for example between marketing and Information Technology or e-commerce functions, because the most valuable insights can be gained through collaboration between managers from different functional areas and the synthesis of types of data. This is especially true in a big data era where commercially valuable customer and market information is held in web server logs, online panel data and search histories, and can be combined with transactional data, market research data and managerial knowledge to create rich data sets and exciting opportunities to develop novel insights and strategies.

Acknowledgements I would like to thank my colleagues in decision-sciences, Information Systems, economics and marketing for their indirect contributions to this paper based on our extensive discussions about consumer search behaviour, in particular Dr. Nadia Papamichail, Dr. Sahar Karimi, Ms. Julia Jacobs and Prof. Gordon Mandry. Any errors or omissions are the sole responsibility of the author.

References

Anonymous. (2000). A thinkers' guide to internet economics. *The Economist, 355,* 64–66.

Bellman, S., Lohse, G. L., & Johnson, E. J. (1999). Predictors of online buying behavior. *Communications of the ACM, 42,* 32–38.

Besanko, D., Dranove, D., Shanley, M., & Schaefer, S. (2009). *Economics of strategy.* Wiley.

Brown, J. J., & Wildt, A. R. (1992). Consideration set measurement. *Journal of the Academy of Marketing Science, 20,* 235–243.

Bughin, J., Corb, L., Manyika, J., Nottebohm, O., Chui, M., de Muller Barba, T. B., & Said, R. (July 2011). *The impact of internet technologies: Search.* McKinsey&Company, High Tech Practice.

Chaffey, D., & Smith, P. (2017). *Digital marketing excellence: planning, optimizing and integrating online marketing.* Taylor & Francis.

Chekuri, C., & Goldwasser, M. H. (1997). Web search using automatic classification. In *Proceedings of the Sixth International Conference on the World Wide Web.*

Chestnut, R. W., & Jacoby, J. (1978). *Consumer information processing: Emerging theory and findings.* Graduate School of Business: Columbia University.

Church, K., & Oliver, N. (2011). Understanding mobile web and mobile search use in today's dynamic mobile landscape. In *Proceedings of the 13th International Conference on Human Computer Interaction with Mobile Devices and Services* (pp. 67–76). ACM.

Court, D., Elzinga, D., Mulder, S., & Vetvik, O. J. (2009). The consumer decision journey. *McKinsey Quarterly,* 11.

Davenport, T. H., & Beck, J. C. (2001). *The attention economy: Understanding the new currency of business.* Harvard Business Press.

De los Santos, B., & Koulayev, S. (2017). Optimizing click-through in online rankings with endogenous search refinement. *Marketing Science.*

Ehrenberg, A. S. (1965). An appraisal of Markov brand-switching models. *Journal of Marketing Research,* 347–362.

Engel, J. F., Blackwell, R. D., & Miniard, P. W. (1995). *Consumer behaviour* (8th ed.). Orlando, FL: The Dryden Press, Harcourt Brace College Publishers.

Frank, R. E. & Massy, W. F. (1963). Innovation and brand choice: The Folger's invasion. In *Proceedings of the American marketing association* (pp. 96–107).

Hauser, J. R., & Wernerfelt, B. (1990). An evaluation cost model of consideration sets. *Journal of Consumer Research, 16,* 393–408.

Holland, C., & Mandry, G. (2015). Online retailing. *The International Encyclopedia of Digital Communication and Society.*

Holland, C. P., & Jacobs, J. A. (2015). The Influence of the Herfindahl-Hirschman Index and Product Complexity on Search Behaviour: A Cross-sector Study of the US, Germany and UK.

Holland, C. P., Jacobs, J. A., & Klein, S. (2016). The role and impact of comparison websites on the consumer search process in the US and German airline markets. *Information Technology & Tourism, 16,* 127–148.

Holland, C. P., & Mandry, G. D. (2013). Online search and buying behaviour in consumer markets. In *46th Hawaii International Conference on System Sciences,* 10.

Hotchkiss, G., & Alston, S. (2005). *Eye tracking study: An in depth look at interactions with Google using eye tracking methodology.* Enquiro Search Solutions Incorporated.

Howard, J. A., & Sheth, J. N. (1969). *The theory of buyer behavior.* New York: Wiley.

Internet Advertising Bureau. (2012). IAB/ PwC UK Digital Adspend Study H1 2012. www.iabuk. net.

Jacobs, J. A., Klein, S., Holland, C. P., & Benning, M. Online search behavior in the air travel market: reconsidering the consideration set and customer journey concepts. In *Proceedings of the 50th Hawaii International Conference on System Sciences, 2017.*

Jacoby, J., Speller, D. E., & Kohn, C. A. (1974). Brand choice behavior as a function of information load. *Journal of Marketing Research,* 63–69.

Johnson, E. J., Moe, W. W., Fader, P. S., Bellman, S., & Lohse, G. L. (2004). On the depth and dynamics of online search behavior. *Management Science, 50,* 299–308.

Jones, J. P. (1990). Ad spending: Maintaining market share. *Harvard Business Review, 68,* 38–42.

Karimi, S., Papamichail, K. N., & Holland, C. P. (2015). The effect of prior knowledge and decision-making style on the online purchase decision-making process: A typology of consumer shopping behaviour. *Decision Support Systems, 77,* 137–147.

Kincheloe, J. L. (2001). Conceptualizing a new rigor in qualitative research. *Qualitative Inquiry, 7,* 679–692.

Malone, T. W., Yates, J., & Benjamin, R. I. (1989). The logic of electronic markets. *Harvard Business Review, 67,* 166–172.

Massy, W. F., & Frank, R. E. (1964). *Reprinted from the 1964 business and economic statistics section.*

Narayana, C. L., & Markin, R. J. (1975). Consumer behavior and product performance: An alternative conceptualization. *The Journal of Marketing,* 1–6.

Pan, B. (2015). The power of search engine ranking for tourist destinations. *Tourism Management, 47,* 79–87.

Shih, C.-F. E. (1998). Conceptualizing consumer experiences in cyberspace. *European Journal of Marketing, 32,* 655–663.

Silk, A. J., & Urban, G. L. (1978). Pre-test-market evaluation of new packaged goods: A model and measurement methodology. *Journal of Marketing Research,* 171–191.

Simon, H. A. (1955). A behavioral model of rational choice. *The Quarterly Journal of Economics, 69,* 99–118.

Stigler, G. J. (1961). The economics of information. *The Journal of Political Economy, 69,* 213–225.

Swann, G. M. P. (2001). Will the internet lead to perfect competition? *Business Economist, 32,* 6–15.

Urban, G. L., Johnson, P. L., & Hauser, J. R. (1984). Testing competitive market structures. *Marketing Science, 3,* 83–112.

Voorveld, H. A. M., Bronner, F. E., Neijens, P. C., & Smit, E. G. (2013). Developing an instrument to measure consumers' multimedia usage in the purchase process. *International Journal on Media Management, 15,* 43–65.

Zhang, J. J., Fang, X., & Liu Sheng, O. R. (2006). Online consumer search depth: Theories and new findings. *Journal of Management Information Systems, 23,* 71–95.

Chapter 14
A Tale of Two Cities: How High Streets Can Prevail in the Digital Age

Jörg Becker, Jan H. Betzing, Moritz von Hoffen and Marco Niemann

A Tale of Two Cities

> *"It was the best of times, it was the worst of times"*

Charles Dickens begins his 1859 novel "A Tale of Two Cities" by painting the contrasting scenes of Paris and London during the French Revolution. Fast forward about 250 years, research and practice have proclaimed the digital revolution and rung in the digital age (Brynjolffson & McAfee, 2014), but while the digital age might feel like the best of times for some city centers and their high streets, others feel left behind. We tell a tale set in the not so distant future of two cities and their high streets that could not be more different.

The Dark Side of e-Commerce

Its a cloudy February morning in Burnsley when Mr. Johnson prepares to have friends to his home to watch today's football derby. While having a coffee, he considers what has to be done and writes a to-do list. He checks how much beer and snacks are on

J. Becker · J. H. Betzing (✉) · M. von Hoffen · M. Niemann
European Research Center for Information Systems, Leonardo-Campus 3, 48149 Münster, Germany
e-mail: jan.betzing@ercis.uni-muenster.de

J. Becker
e-mail: joerg.becker@ercis.uni-muenster.de

M. von Hoffen
e-mail: moritz.von.hoffen@ercis.uni-muenster.de

M. Niemann
e-mail: marco.niemann@ercis.uni-muenster.de

© Springer International Publishing AG, part of Springer Nature 2019
K. Riemer et al. (eds.), *Collaboration in the Digital Age*, Progress in IS,
https://doi.org/10.1007/978-3-319-94487-6_14

291

hand and gets ready to go to the supermarket to stock up, but when he turns on the television in his living room, he notices that the TV is not responding to the remote control—and even the buttons on the television itself have no effect. After disconnecting and reconnecting the television, he is convinced that it is actually broken. He does not hesitate much before deciding to get a new one to save the evening. He talks himself into believing this was long due anyway and walks to the car.

He decides to pay a visit to the electronics store on Main Street, where he bought his television set some years ago. He pulls up nearby and searches the car's cup holder for some quarters to feed the parking meter. When he gets closer to the store, he notices that its neon sign and the store itself are dark. On the shop's door, he sees a notice that the store has been closed permanently. He peeks through the window and sees a torn banner that reads "We match any price!" He wonders where the shop owner, Mr. Wong Jr., might be working now. He had taken over the shop from his father only a couple of years before.

He turns away from the store and sees a well-known electronics retail store across the street and does not think twice before crossing the street and going in. Inside, a store associate greets him and asks if he needs help. Mr. Johnson states his urgent need for a new television. The associate raises his eyebrows as he apparently did not expect to be required. He reluctantly guides Mr. Johnson to the bank of televisions sets on display, and asks for his preferences and budget. When Mr. Johnson replies that he would like a television that is very bright and possibly anti-reflective because direct sunlight comes into his living room, the store associate hesitates before saying that he will have to check his computer for that. When he comes back a few minutes after, he shrugs and says that he could not find any information about anti-reflective televisions.

Meanwhile, Mr. Johnson has had a look around and has come to the conclusion that none of the televisions are right for him. He takes out his smartphone, browses to a popular e-commerce retailer, and looks at the best-selling televisions with the best average customer ratings. The top-selling product looks promising, as it has a matte display which he knows works well in direct sunlight. He shows the television to the store associate and asks whether they have it. The associate takes a note, goes to his computer again, and comes back a few minutes later with a printed offer. He hands the offer to Mr. Johnson, who gasps when he sees that the price is almost 200 GBP higher than advertised online and that it is not in stock but can be delivered in a week (or possibly longer). As Mr. Johnson does not want to cancel the derby party with his friends, he asks whether there is an option for same-day delivery at a higher price. The store associate smirks and shakes his head.

Mr. Johnson decides to try his luck elsewhere. On his way back to the car, he reads the shop signs along the street and notices that many of the shops he visited only a few years ago have vanished, their storefronts abandoned or replaced by faceless franchises, betting offices, and the like.

Back in his car, he uses his smartphone to search for electronics stores in Burnsley, but his search brings up only the store he has just left. He admits defeat and calls his friend to ask whether he would be willing to host the derby party at his place instead.

Back at home, he buys the television he wants online (at a 200 GBP savings) and renounces the high street.

In this future, traditional high street retail has lost. Pressed by e-commerce, local small businesses could do little more than engage in a price war. A downward spiral in prices resulted, and the effort was pointless because of the higher operating cost of brick-and-mortar stores compared to those of online players. Eventually, long-established retail businesses like Mr. Wong Jr.'s store closed down, and even the remaining chain stores struggle to meet customers' expectations.

The High Street Strikes Back

The sun rises above the hectic scramble of the Beckinsdale farmers' market on a Friday morning. Ms. Crawford finishes setting up her flower stand and awaits the first customers. She logs into Beckinsdale's city app—the Beckinsdale Companion—on her tablet, marks the stand's current location, and sets today's opening hours. She uses her tablet to take a picture of today's special offer, exotic pink lilies, and posts it to the local social network.

At the same time, Mr. Davis, a consultant from Beckinsdale's suburbs, plans his day. Since he has a new project coming up next week, he adds a new suit and a tie to his digital shopping list. He uses the Beckinsdale Companion to see if his favorite tailor is open today. While that shop is closed, he gets a recommendation for another boutique that carries the brand of suit he is looking for. He sees that his good friend, Ms. Paul, has marked the store as a favorite, so he sends her an instant message and asks about her experience with the boutique. Encouraged by Ms. Paul's positive response, he drives to the boutique with his toddler son in tow. As he reaches the city center, his phone directs Mr. Davis to a parking spot nearby. Because Mr. Davis registered his car with the Beckinsdale Companion, parking fees are automatically deducted from his account.

While Mr. Davis and his son are walking to the boutique, he receives an alert that the store has an unusually high number of customers right now, so his smartphone suggests making an appointment for a personal consultation in an hour, which Mr. Davis confirms. With free time to spend, Mr. Davis sits down with his son and opens the local social network to see what others in the area are doing. He browses through various posts, including Ms. Crawford's offer for lilies, and then sees that Ms. Paul has just checked into a coffee shop around the corner. He comments on her activity and decides to meet her. Because he knows his toddler gets bored in the coffee shop, he drops the boy at a high street childcare service the boy enjoys for a small fee. Remembering the lilies, he decides to bring Ms. Paul some flowers and locates Ms. Crawford's stand in the Companion. Guided by his phone, which interacts with Bluetooth beacons spread across the city, he navigates to the stand and buys the flowers. Then he drops in at the coffee shop and gives a pleasantly surprised Ms. Paul the lilies. As Mr. Davis pays for his coffee on his smartwatch, the barista offers him a complimentary cookie because this was his fifth visit to the coffee shop this month.

The hour having passed, an associate at the boutique greets Mr. Davis by name and directs him to a rack of suits. The associate needs Mr. Davis' exact measurements, but since the Beckinsdale Companion includes a data marketplace for retailers, he finds Mr. Davis' measurements, which another tailor took recently. Judging by Mr. Davis' shopping history, the associate gladly pays a small data-access fee, which will be paid to the tailor who provided the measurements. Mr. Davis authorizes the request for his suit measurements with a tap on his smartwatch.

After choosing his suit, Mr. Davis requests custom tailoring, so the associate asks whether he wants to wait for it in the store or use the local evening delivery service. Just then, Mr. Davis receives a push message from the child care center that his boy wants to be picked up, so Mr. Davis decides on the delivery option. Quickly, the associate suggests adding a matching shirt and tie from a partnering outfitter to the delivery. Unsure of the offer, Mr. Davis declines but asks the associate to send him the product details. The associate uses his tablet to finish the order, and Mr. Davis confirms the purchase with another tap on his smartwatch. He then heads to the childcare service and picks up his son. On their way back to the car, Mr. Davis receives an offer for free parking if he spends ten pounds or more at a nearby toy store. Pleased by this serendipity, he buys a small stuffed animal, and his parking fee is automatically reversed. At home, Mr. Davis opens the boutique associate's recommendations for the shirt and tie, and since they come with no additional shipping cost and free return, Mr. Davis places the order.

In the evening, Ms. Crawford closes her flower stand and checks to see how many people have seen her lily post and digitally engaged with her business. Shortly after, a courier delivers the consolidated business outfit to Mr. Davis home. Happy with the quality of the tailoring and the great recommendation for the shirt and tie, he posts a picture and a review of the boutique to the Beckinsdale Companion.

Although Mr. Davis' shopping trip is set in the future, the technologies that enabled him to streamline his day exist today. Our example shows how integrated services on the retailer and high street levels can facilitate hybrid digital and physical customer experiences. However, for the Beckinsdale scenario to become reality, high streets must first escape the inevitable downward spiral that we have described—perhaps exaggerated a bit—in the Burnsley case.

A Downwards Spiral in High Street Retail?

Ongoing digitization has had a significant impact on the traditional structures of high street retail as e-commerce and m-commerce's market share grows. While offline retail revenue grew slightly in Germany from EUR 427.6 billion in 2007 to EUR 486.5 billion in 2016 (HDE, 2017), e-commerce revenue increased almost five-fold, from EUR 10.9 billion in 2007 to 52.74 billion in 2016 (Furchheim et al., 2018). Although e-commerce accounted for only 13.2% of the business-to-consumer (B2C) retail market in 2017, the double-digit growth rates are projected to continue (Furchheim et al., 2018), challenging high street retail and especially small and medium-sized enterprise (SME) retail. As seen on Burnsley's high street, this trend manifests in abandoned commercial spaces that render the corresponding high street less attractive, leading to more businesses' failing. The market cannot compensate for such vacancies, and the high street gradually empties out (BBSR, 2017).

The retail market currently responds with omnichannel and "bricks-and-clicks" approaches (Brynjolfsson et al., 2013; Herhausen et al., 2015), where customers can switch seamlessly between channels and benefit from both the digital and the physical world. Nevertheless, most of such projects are executed by large retail chains that exclude the SME retailers that usually make up the majority of high street tenants. Large chain stores that branches at every other city center do not contribute to the attractiveness and individuality of a high street and may not be able to stop the high-street erosion process, even if they use omnichannel approaches. Instead, digitization must take place on the high street as a whole, where the high street's overall well-being influences its tenants and vice versa.

A suffering high street can be a critical issue for the whole city on multiple levels. The most obvious and direct consequences of a spiraling high street are economic, as fewer retail shops lead to dwindling sales, decreasing tax incomes, and lost jobs. An eroding high street also affects the social environment as the city becomes less attractive, which damages both the city's housing market and its tourism industry. To counter this development, the city must raise its high street's economic and physical attractiveness. Countermeasures include financial support for the retailers and construction projects to improve the city center's physical attractiveness. However, the extent to which an individual city's retailer suffers depends on factors like the city's population and its surrounding countryside (BBSR, 2017). While prime locations in attractive, large cities are expected to suffer minimally from the effects of the ongoing structural change in the retail industry, smaller cities—especially those that are near larger cities—are not expected to fare as well (BBSR, 2017).

In the past, SME retailers had limited competition and could use personalized services and individual assistance to justify a price premium. However, today spatial distance is bridged by e-commerce, and smart devices and ubiquitous Internet connectivity have made customers "informed, networked, empowered and active" (Prahalad and Ramaswamy, 2004, p. 5) with in-depth product information, price comparisons, and digital services literally at their fingertips. Without being constrained by opening hours or distance, customers can engage with online retailers 24/7 and receive personalized advice and recommendations from retailers, social shopping communities, and their own social groups. Thus, e-commerce and m-commerce have altered the long-lasting power relationships between customers and retailers (Hagberg et al., 2016) as customers increasingly engage in "research shopping" or "showrooming," visiting brick-and-mortar stores to look at products but buying online (Gensler et al., 2017). With ubiquitous access to shopping opportunities, the formerly sequential customer decision process is now a continuous, dynamic decision-making process, where customers continuously re-evaluate their decisions during and between every phase of the their journey (Faulds et al., 2018). Customers are empowered by using their mobile devices in stores to compare prices, research, and buy, freeing them from the retailer's influence (Parise et al., 2016). Most strikingly, a recent Forester survey revealed that only 29% of customers perceive store associates as knowledgeable (Murray, 2016), and a Motorola survey found that 61% of mobile shoppers believe their product knowledge exceeds that of store associates (Faulds et al., 2018).

Traditional high street retailers also suffer from spatial constraints in terms of both locality and shelf space, as their markets become increasingly diverse. In economic terms, this effect is typically discussed with reference to "the long tail" concept (Anderson, 2008), which describes the increasing availability of and demand for obscure or individualized products while each of the goods has only limited demand in a brick-and-mortar retailers' local market. To face the challenge, the retailer is required to stock a wide range of products for a limited local audience only, exposing it to high costs for stock keeping and low turnover. Therefore, online retailers that may cater to national or even global audiences have a strong competitive advantage, as their market for obscure or individualized products is much larger (Ahlers et al., 2018). Although it may seem pointless to consider the long tail with rarely sold products, for segments like books, rarely sold products are 30% of the market. Therefore, almost a third of brick-and-mortar retailers' potential profits are lost to the competition online.

Another threat for high-street retail that is lurking in the digital realm is customer analytics. Many local retailers determine their marketing and procurement options based on gut feeling and coarse insights into customer segments or marketing theory (Murray, 2016). Although large retail chains collect and analyze customer data, they are retailer-specific data silos that do not benefit the high street as a whole. The online competition understands the benefits of analyzing the data generated on their own platforms and from third parties and have almost perfected their analytics instruments to the point at which they can precisely recommend products and services to individual customers. Therefore, while a SME retailer typically relies only on intuition, experience, and interaction to assess a potential customer's needs, large e-commerce players draw from their huge accumulations of data to recommend products based on similar customers' purchases and preferences.

It is clear that e-commerce and increasing customer empowerment and expectations impact high streets and that the digital age will lead to further transformation of brick-and-mortar retail. High streets that understand these issues are seeking remedies to strengthen their position in the customers' buying processes. The next chapter outlines how digitization impacts and may be able to improve high streets' competitive position.

Digitization on the High Street

What can we learn from our two tales? What are the key elements for high streets to prevail in the digital age? Digitization refers to the "integration of digital tech-

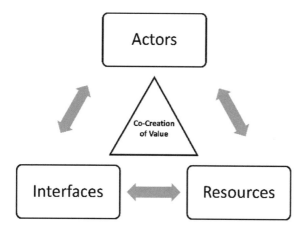

Fig. 14.1 Dimensions of digitization on the high street

nologies into everyday life" (Hagberg et al., 2016, p. 696), where analog activities are transformed digitally (e.g., a shift from parking meters to automatic billing of parking fees) and completely new activities emerge (e.g., mobile social networks). City centers and high streets are complex service ecosystems within which actors like customers, retailers, service providers, and local authorities interact and influence each other over time and space (Chandler & Lusch, 2015). Enabled and constrained by institutions and institutional arrangements, actors engage in the exchange of services in ever-changing constellations (Vargo & Lusch, 2016) to create "economic, financial, or social value or some combination of these" thereof (Chandler & Lusch, 2015, p. 6).

Digitization profoundly transforms the service setting, the channels, and the interfaces between actors, the roles and relationships between actors, the resources integrated into the service delivery process, and the creation of value (Hagberg et al., 2016; Vargo & Lusch, 2016). In the Beckinsdale example, the setting is not spatially bound to the actual high street but reaches into the personal spaces of the actors involved. Digital technology provides interfaces so actors can engage, free of temporal and spatial constraints. The Beckinsdale Companion and associated information systems, along with their interfaces, underlying processes, and governing mechanisms, are based on institutional arrangements between municipal entities, retailers, and service providers, so this digital platform facilitates the service ecosystem. We use the Beckinsdale example to discuss the transformative power of digitization for high streets using the lens of the Service-dominant logic (SDL) of marketing (Vargo & Lusch, 2016). Figure 14.1 depicts the dimensions we considered: service interfaces, resources used, actors and their roles and relationships, and the co-creation of value in service exchanges.

Interfaces

High street retailers traditionally deliver services in person-to-person interactions, but today they can also draw from a plethora of digital technologies to integrate the physical and digital worlds and provide new channels and forms of interaction (Willems et al., 2017). The ubiquitous mobile smart devices that are connected to the Internet have become central interfaces between actors (Bradlow et al., 2017; Faulds et al., 2018), and the notion of an actor also comprises technology itself (Hagberg et al., 2016). Glushko (2010) differentiates among seven contexts in which information-intensive service may occur, all of which can be found in the Beckinsdale example. High street retail is largely an information-intensive service, where "the information actions are responsible for the greatest proportion of value created by the service system" (Glushko, 2010, p. 21). For example, Ms. Crawford uses the Beckinsdale Companion in a self-service interaction to provide information on her flower stand, which then creates value for Mr. Davis, who uses the information in another self-service interaction to navigate to her stand. Transparent to the user, Mr. Davis' smartphone interacted with Bluetooth beacons in a back-end-intense machine-to-machine interaction. Although Glushko (2010) differentiates between location-based and context-aware service contexts, we maintain that most, if not all, digital services in the high street use actors' locations and other properties as context. In Beckinsdale, the main actors are constantly providing information to the underlying information system, either through proactive input, as Ms. Crawford did, or via sensor- and vision-based technologies.

Digitization in high street retail can, to some extent, be boiled down to the introduction of additional digital and physical touchpoints to the service system that allows actors to interact and co-create experiences (Brynjolfsson et al., 2013). With these touchpoints, retailers can influence and interact with their customers at every stage of the customers' journey. While Faulds et al. (2018) limited their unit of analysis to dyadic customer-retailer interactions, we widen the view to include third-party and municipal service providers. For example, the Beckinsdale Companion provides an interface between municipal parking services, retailers, and customers. Allowing customers to buy a toy in exchange for parking fees is one outcome of this additional touchpoint, which influenced Mr. Davis' customer journey and created value for everyone. The whole scenario depends on back-end analytical services, such as the service that allowed the toy store to send the promotion to Mr. Davis. In our example, there is also a local social network of high street actors that links customers with their reference groups and to other customers in their vicinity (Betzing et al., 2018).

Digital technologies also empower store associates in technology-enhanced person-to-person interactions (Glushko, 2010). The salesperson in the boutique was equipped with a tablet that provided information about the customer and created better value propositions by personalizing the service. Mr. Davis' use of his smartwatch to confirm the salesperson's requests also shows that these new channels and interfaces in the high street service system are bi-directional. These mobile touchpoints blur the boundaries between the public space and the customer's private space (Shankar et al., 2010), while multiple direct touchpoints to the retailer support its ability to satisfy the customer's information demands using the channel of his or her choice.

Resources

Traditional value creation in high street retail is based on selling products and services (Grönroos & Voima, 2013). The SDL shifts the focus from value-in-exchange to the co-creation of value in reciprocal interactions between actors (Vargo & Lusch, 2016). Vargo and Lusch (2008) defined service as "the application of specialized competences (operant resources–knowledge and skills), through deeds, processes, and performances for the benefit of another entity or the entity itself" (p. 26). This theoretical lens is reflected in many retailers' changing self-conceptions away from simply being sellers of goods to being problem-solvers and providers of experiences (Lemon & Verhoef, 2016). Consequently, operant resources become "the fundamental source of strategic benefit" (Vargo & Lusch, 2016, p. 8). On the digitized high street, data is the central operant resource.

In the Beckinsdale scenario, various actors make their data public, and the city itself pursues a "smart city" approach, where a municipal digital infrastructure gathers various information from the physical world. Increasing numbers of cities give open access to their cities' data, which can be used to provide smart digital services. In Beckinsdale, sensors and cameras measure the occupancy of parking spots and pedestrian flows on the high street, so these technologies can supersede traditional methods of customer behavior analytics, such as surveys and user shadowing in high streets. After Mr. Davis consented to having his data collected and shared, his smartphone tracks his movements in stores and around the high street to deliver location-based services. His information yields value on both the retailer and the high-street levels, as retailers can gain insights into their customer bases, personalize their services, and provide targeted advertisements. Think of the coffee shop that rewards Mr. Davis for re-visiting the store, and more advanced analytics even allowed the toy shop to infer Mr. Davis' needs from his trajectory, i.e., he parked with subject to public charges and later visited the child care services. On the high street level, pedestrian flows, hot and cold spots, and store migration can be analyzed to support marketing cooperatives and local authorities in their strategic and operational decision-making. Aggregated customer data even allows for (geo-)recommender systems that are similar to those customers already accustomed to in e-commerce. For example, based on his previous store visits, Mr. Davis got a recommendation for a boutique that he had not visited before.

High street retail can tap into many sources to digitize their offerings. Figure 14.2 shows the prevalent sources that retailers can already use, but high street retailers may see the technologies behind these data sources as difficult to integrate into their service systems and as suitable only for larger retailers. However, it is a misconception that the digitization of high street retail is fully dependent on investments in novel and potentially expensive technologies. In fact, retailers are often already

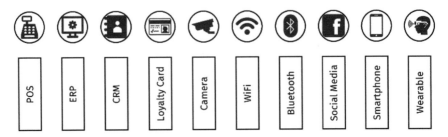

Fig. 14.2 Data (Re-)sources available for high street retail

in possession of the resources they need, such as point of sale (POS) terminals or enterprise resource planning (ERP) systems, which are valuable data providers (Li et al., 2012). Loyalty cards and customer relationship management (CRM) systems have been used for years to link customers to their transactions (Chen, 2014). In the Beckinsdale scenario, this information was made available to the boutique's salesperson, who was then able to recommend suits to Mr. Davis based on his shopping history.

Other operant resources can be found outside the high street and smart city settings. User-generated content from social media and rating and review sites are already publicly available in large quantities and—in the ideal case—provide honest and unbiased opinions (Kaplan & Haenlein, 2010). In the current setting, most content is user-generated and interactions between customers and other participants in the high street ecosystem. The local social network in the Beckinsdale example allows Mr. Davis to ask his reference group about the boutique, find a suitable gift, and learn about Ms. Paul's location. For retailers, user-generated content teaches them more about potential customers than is usually feasible during a regular customer interaction, as customers may not disclose the interests or upcoming plans to store associates but do so on their social media profiles (Stieglitz et al., 2014). Knowing their customers' personal preferences can be useful in creating better and more personalized recommendations and interactions. Thinking back to Mr. Davis and Ms. Paul, social media data could help Ms. Crawford to suggest Ms. Paul's favourite type of lilies to Mr. Davis.

Beyond the collection of data, most of the value of data marketplaces lies in its meaningful aggregation and integration. Given the vastness and diversity of data resources available, from highly structured data (ERP) to unstructured data (video, sensors), this task is complex, as information from various sources, some of which are not in the retailer's control, must be integrated to overcome retailer-specific data silos. Mr. Davis uses a digital shopping list and tracks his shopping history across stores, so the customer provides data to the retailer, which then can integrate and enrich it with the retailer's own data. Moreover, pioneer work has been conducted by heavily data-driven companies like Facebook and Google, which continuously develop more efficient systems to store, integrate and analyze collected data (e.g., Chen et al., 2016; Pedreira et al., 2016; Rendle et al., 2016).

The Beckinsdale scenario also shows that data is not only a resource that is shared and used freely, but under certain circumstances it is even a tradeable good. For Ms. Crawford it makes sense to publish her stand's details for free, since customers are not likely to be willing to pay for this data, and keeping it secret gives her no economic advantage. However, Mr. Davis' tailor has a financial interest in keeping his measurements secret (because of the investment made in obtaining the data), while the boutique owner has a financial interest in obtaining them (to avoid investing in taking the measurements himself). It should be clear, then, that both parties can maximize their utility by trading the data for money (Stahl, 2016). While selling what has been coined "information goods" would have been unthinkable only a few years ago—and may still be difficult for retailers who are involved primarily in selling tangible items—it has become an established and maturing reality (Schomm et al., 2013). Establishing data marketplaces and associated pricing mechanisms is not trivial (Stahl, 2016), but doing so can create additional revenue for retailers, regardless of their stores' operating hours. If data marketplaces are used as in the example, they can contribute to positive customer experiences across the high street.

Actors

The management and IS literature has studied information technology's potential to transform organizations for more than sixty years. Many theories, such as those related to organizational politics and culture, can be adopted to the high street ecosystem (e.g., Robey & Boudreau, 1999). We see political actors like single retailers and groups of retailers organized into marketing cooperatives that seek to exercise their power in shaping the high street to their benefit. Digitization on the high street level introduces new actors and changes the roles and power relationships of existing ones. New actors might provide services that contradict longstanding organizational culture and retail heuristics. For example, the boutique salesperson in Beckinsdale placed Mr. Davis' shopping experience and his needs over the short-term maximization of profits when he recommended a competitor's tie.

In Beckinsdale, a form of high street alliance changed the traditional mode of competition between retailers to one of cooperation, united by the common goal of a prospering high street (Gomes-Casseres, 1997). As known from online affiliate networks, the boutique might receive a provision for referring the customer. In a similar vein, the data marketplace allows retailers to exchange customer information. We maintain that platforms enable retailers to participate in digitization because of economies of scale and scope. Marketplaces and networks bring actors together and facilitate the exchange of services. Many digital encounters in the Beckinsdale example would be all but impossible for a single retailer who has limited financial resources and technical expertise. For example, why would a SME retailer publish a mobile app for his or her store? From a customer's standpoint, a central interface with which to receive information on retailers in the vicinity is more valuable than using a single retailer's app, about which a foreign visitor to the high street might not even be aware. The Beckinsdale Companion also strengthens the customer's role; we already saw how customer-facing digital technologies empower customers in their relationships with retailers. While generic third-party solutions for price comparison or product searches are out of single retailers' control, a central local platform like the Beckinsdale Companion can empower customers for the mutual benefit of the high street's stakeholders (Faulds et al., 2018).

The actors in Beckinsdale provide various types of services within the unified interface of the Companion. Customer-facing services are provided by the municipal authorities (e.g., parking), retailers (e.g., promotions), a local platform provider (e.g., beacon-based navigation, location-based recommendations), third-party service providers (e.g., local delivery), and other customers (e.g., the local social network). We also see that digital communication and coordination mechanisms support existing "offline" high street services, such as a child-care service. While a stable mode of cooperation between retailers, third-party service providers, and municipal bodies has been established in the Beckinsdale example, for other cities complex organizational questions arise: Who introduces a platform? What cost and revenue structures are available? What remunerations, sanctions, and governance structures exist? Who can provide a service to whom? How are collaboratively provided services delivered with regard to a steady level of service quality across providers? The Beckinsdale Companion provides a digital business directory that replaces the Yellow Pages that publishing companies traditionally provided, but will these companies run this digital counterpart, or are there new intermediaries? In Germany, we already see third parties who provide digital platforms and modules as white-label solutions that local operators can license. Moreover, the role of local marketing cooperatives might be affected as well. Rival cooperatives in some cities might result in both introducing digital services on high street level, but from the customer's standpoint, rival offerings that lack integration are inferior to a central, integrated service platform like the one in Beckinsdale. One might observe displacements and platform races that are similar to those that are occurring in mobile operating systems and programming languages.

(Co-)Creation of Value

Burnsley's retailers engaged in a price war and lost, while retailers in Beckinsdale understood that a price war is pointless and focused on other strategies instead (Brynjolfsson et al., 2013; Rao et al., 2000). Relevant kernel theories in marketing and customer behavior research include those related to customer satisfaction, service quality, customer relationship management, and customer engagement. Most prominently, research has suggested that retailers and other service providers focus on co-creating customer experiences to increase the customers' value perceptions (Betzing et al., 2018; McColl-Kennedy et al., 2015b).

Customer experience theory addresses customers' responses to retailers and other actors (McColl-Kennedy et al., 2015a). Based on a comprehensive literature review,

Lemon and Verhoef (2016) defined customer experience as the customer's "cognitive, emotional, behavioral, sensoric and social responses to a firm's offerings during the customer's entire purchase journey" (p. 74). Customers respond both consciously and unconsciously to encounters with retailers at multiple touchpoints and form their experiences dynamically over time.

With the introduction of new interfaces and service contexts (Glushko, 2010), we see digital customer experiences that are facilitated by interacting with technology (e.g., using a web-shop) and hybrid online-offline customer experiences, where analog and digital channels are mixed (McColl-Kennedy et al., 2015a). The SDL acknowledges that "value is always uniquely and phenomenologically determined by the beneficiary" (Vargo & Lusch, 2016, p. 8) so customers assess the co-created value by means of accrued interactions with the retailer and other actors (Tynan et al., 2014).

Value is dynamic in nature, as customers continuously re-evaluate their experiences along the customer journey with respect to the "purpose or objective that is directly served through product/service usage" (Lemke et al., 2011, p. 847). Consequently, high street actors cannot prepare canned experiences for customers to retrieve. To what extent service encounters serve the customer's experience is individual to the customer's perception and depends on external influences like the customer's personal cultural and social belief system (McColl-Kennedy et al., 2015b). For example, Mr. Davis consulted his friend Ms. Paul before visiting a store and might now associate the store with a positive social response even if he had never visited it. The creation of customer experience also depends on the customer's willingness to engage in co-creation, the other actor's responses, and the customer's perception of its value (McColl-Kennedy et al., 2015b), which can be further distinguished into "experiential/hedonic, symbolic/expressive and functional/utilitarian" (Tynan et al., 2014, p. 1062) types of customer value.

Mr. Davis' shopping trip is a high street experience comprised of intermingled experiences and customer journeys. Mr. Davis was willing to grant permission for a store to use his information, and he actively engaged in co-creation at multiple encounters. Based on his interactions with the local social network, Mr. Davis bought flowers and visited Ms. Paul, which addresses the social and emotional responses that lead to an hedonic experience (Tynan et al., 2014). Interactions with the boutique and its salesperson resulted in different types of customer value. Based on Mr. Davis shopping list, shopping history, and measurements, the salesperson responded efficiently to Mr. Davis needs, which resulted in a functional experience. Mr. Davis will use the suit and tie he bought as a form of outer-directed self-expression toward his new client, leading to a form of both expressive and social customer value.

In the end, not only have customer experiences been co-created, but the exchange of service have also yielded economic, financial, and social value for the high street actors (Chandler & Lusch, 2015). Central to the digital transformation in high street retail is the provision of seamless high street experiences, where all stakeholders collaborate to contribute to the experience (Faulds et al., 2018). Retailers are responsible for the co-creation of customer experience with their customers both within their store and on high street level with the help of digital technologies and interfaces.

How Will the Tale Continue?

We have seen that high street retail is in a transformation and that the digital age is both boon and bane for high streets. With omnichannel retail and hybrid digital high street services, the borders between digital and physical customer experiences are blurring, and manifold touchpoints and actors are competing at every point in the customer journey. In Burnsley, the high street retailers were not able to respond to the challenge of digitization, and their high street degraded.

Information systems research can make a positive contribution to addressing high streets' social, political, and economic problems. As seen in Beckinsdale, by transferring some of the benefits of e-commerce to the high street ecosystem and combining them with the integral benefits of physical brick-and-mortar retail, the local retailers can collectively make both digital and physical value propositions that go beyond e-commerce to foster lasting customer experiences. We envision that, on the way to becoming fully digital, high streets can evolve to using central digital platforms as an improvement over individual- and retailer-specific approaches. In this highly cooperative scenario, actors in the high street ecosystem have to join forces for the common good by converging data from retailers, customers, and municipal bodies on a central hub. Thus, value is created by a community of high street actors within a *digital platform ecosystem* (Tiwana, 2014).

Alliances and platform business models are in stark contrast to traditional high street retail business models, so they require that retailers undertake a mind shift. Much of the value created in the Beckinsdale example results less from selling goods and services than from high street actors' being intertwined in ever-changing constellations and united on a digital platform. Hence, traditional business models and strategies that are tailored to the creation of value only from the inside of an organization cease to be applicable.

Central digital platforms have an undeniable financial incentive: The investment required to create a fully digitized customer experience are daunting even for large Internet enterprises and chain retailers and are simply impossible for the average SME high street retailer. However, where individual budgets are insufficient, shared effort can go a long way. Since, digital retail online and on the high street is inherently data-driven, shared investment not only supports the transformation from traditional to digital but also widens the available data for local platforms. Strong digitized high streets might even draw online players back into the physical world. Bell et al. (2017) showed a trend in formerly pure online players' opening offline showrooms to increase demand and reach customers in person. Bringing high street retailers together on a single platform also vastly lowers the entry barriers for new or more risk-averse retailers by reducing the individual upfront financial investment and creating lagged benefits from instantaneous visibility. The inclusion of laggards in the platform ecosystem is beneficial for incumbent participants as well, as the additional retailers increase the high street's appeal by making the ecosystem more diverse and offering additional opportunities for value co-creation. At the same time, complexity for customers and retailers is reduced since all interactions are carried out via a single touchpoint, similar to a "one-stop shop," a central vision of e-government.

In the joint research project *smartmarket²*, a consortium of information systems, marketing, and service researchers from the universities of Duisburg-Essen, Paderborn, and Münster and industry partners, we are jointly designing and developing a central platform to accompany the physical high street ecosystem with digital services and to foster the co-creation of digital customer experiences. From a service marketing perspective, our future research will investigate how the co-creation of customer experiences influences customers in their decision processes, how different types of customers and segments react to digital interventions, and how customers evaluate these hybrid online-offline experiences.

Although digital customers expect personalized service from retailers, privacy concerns with regard to their location, shopping list, and purchase history remain. Future studies should investigate customers' privacy-related decision-making on collaborative platforms. Legal issues, such as those related to the EU General Data Protection Regulation (GDPR), and ethical considerations must also be taken into account. From an economic perspective, a digital platform requires a sound business model, multiperspective business processes, and a service provider that acts as an intermediary between high street stakeholders. In addition, the central platform influences power relationships on the high street, so future research should investigate how existing networks might evolve or disperse and how new alliances might form since, from a technological perspective, a central platform is a highly complex system that requires a sound architecture and interfaces to the various stakeholder systems.

Several challenges must be addressed before the digital high street is in a position to strike back, but cooperation and a central digital representation are paramount for the ability of high streets as a whole to prevail. In Beckinsdale, where rich information is available to all high street participants, the retail marketing heuristic "deliver the right message to the right person at the right time" is taken to a new level by means of hyper-relevant messages and value-added digital services across the high street. However, Bradlow et al. (2017) reminded us that "retailers will need to consider both the ethical and potential boomerang effects that many customers feel when products are hyper-localized" (p. 81). In the near future, we will see how innovative high streets set themselves apart from their less-innovative and purely "analog" counterparts. Information systems research cannot alleviate all problems high streets face, but they can help high streets meet the digital expectations of their connected and empowered customers—for the best of times!

Acknowledgements This essay was developed in the research project *smartmarket²*, which is funded by the German Federal Ministry of Education and Research (BMBF), promotion sign 02K15A074. The authors thank the Project Management Agency Karlsruhe (PTKA).

References

Ahlers, R., Bollweg, L., Lackes, R., Ruegenberg, A., Reza, A., & Siepermann, M., et al. (2018). Are local retailers conquering the long tail? A web usage and association rule mining approach on local shopping platforms. In *Proceedings of the Multikonferenz Wirtschaftsinformatik, MKWI '18*, Lüneburg, Germany.

Anderson, C. (2008). *The long tail: Why the future of business is selling less of more.* New York, NY, USA: Hyperion.

BBSR. (2017). Online-Handel – Mögliche räumliche Auswirkungen auf Innenstädte, Stadtteil- und Ortszentren. Tech. rep., Bundesinstitut für Bau- Stadt- und Raumforschung (BBSR) im Bundesamt für Bauwesen und Raumordnung (BBR), Bonn, Germany. http://www.bbsr.bund.de/BBSR/DE/Home/Topthemen/2017-online-handel.html.

Bell, D. R., Gallino, S., & Moreno, A. (2017). Offline showrooms in omnichannel retail: Demand and operational benefits. *Management Science* 1–23.

Betzing, J. H., Beverungen, D., & Becker, J. (2018). Design principles for co-creating digital customer experience in high street retail. In *Proceedings of the Multikonferenz Wirtschaftsinformatik, MKWI '18*, Lüneburg, Germany.

Bradlow, E. T., Gangwar, M., Kopalle, P., & Voleti, S. (2017). The role of big data and predictive analytics in retailing. *Journal of Retailing, 93*(1), 79–95.

Brynjolffson, E., & McAfee, A. (2014). *The second machine age: Work, progress, and prosperity in a time of brilliant technologies.* WW Norton & Company.

Brynjolfsson, E., Hu, Y. J., & Rahman, M. S. (2013). Competing in the age of omnichannel retailing. *MIT Sloan Management Review, 54*(4), 23–29.

Chandler, J. D., & Lusch, R. F. (2015). Service systems: A broadened framework and research agenda on value propositions, engagement, and service experience. *Journal of Service Research, 18*(1), 6–22.

Chen, C.-C. (2014). RFID-based intelligent shopping environment: A comprehensive evaluation framework with neural computing approach. *Neural Computing and Applications, 25*(7–8), 1685–1697.

Chen, G. J., Wiener, J. L., Iyer, S., Jaiswal, A., Lei, R., Simha, N., et al. (2016). Realtime data processing at Facebook. In *Proceedings of the 2016 International Conference on Management of Data, SIGMOD '16*, San Francisco, CA, USA.

Faulds, D. J., Mangold, W. G., Raju, P., & Valsalan, S. (2018). The mobile shopping revolution: Redefining the consumer decision process. *Business Horizons, 61*(2), 323–338.

Furchheim, G., Wenk-Fischer, C., & Manner-Romberg, H. (2018). E-Commerce â€" der neue Nahversorger? Tech. rep., Bundesverband E-Commerce und Versandhandel e.V., Berlin.

Gensler, S., Neslin, S. A., & Verhoef, P. C. (2017). The showrooming phenomenon: It's more than just about price. *Journal of Interactive Marketing, 38,* 29–43.

Glushko, R. J. (2010). Seven contexts for service system design. In P. P. Maglio, C. A. Kieliszewski, & J. C. Spohrer (Eds.), *Handbook of service science* (pp. 219–249). Springer.

Gomes-Casseres, B. (1997). Alliance strategies of small firms. *Small Business Economics, 9*(1), 33–44.

Grönroos, C., & Voima, P. (2013). Critical service logic: Making sense of value creation and co-creation. *Journal of the Academy of Marketing Science, 41*(2), 133–150.

Hagberg, J., Sundstrom, M., & Egels-Zanden, N. (2016). The digitalization of retailing: An exploratory framework. *International Journal of Retail & Distribution Management, 44*(6), 336–368.

HDE. (2017). Umsatz im Einzelhandel im engeren Sinne in Deutschland in den Jahren 2000 bis 2017 (in Milliarden Euro). Retrieved March 13, 2018, from https://de.statista.com/statistik/date n/studie/70190/umfrage/umsatz-im-deutschen-einzelhandel-zeitreihe/.

Herhausen, D., Binder, J., Schoegel, M., & Herrmann, A. (2015). Integrating bricks with clicks: Retailer-level and channel-level outcomes of online-offline channel integration. *Journal of Retailing, 91*(2), 309–325.

Kaplan, A. M., & Haenlein, M. (2010). Users of the world, unite! The challenges and opportunities of social media. *Business Horizons, 53*(1), 59–68.

Lemke, F., Clark, M., & Wilson, H. (2011). Customer experience quality: An exploration in business and consumer contexts using repertory grid technique. *Journal of the Academy of Marketing Science, 39*(6), 846–869.

Lemon, K. N., & Verhoef, P. C. (2016). Understanding customer experience and the customer journey. *Journal of Marketing, 80*(6), 69–96.

Li, H.-B., Wang, W., Ding, H.-W., & Dong, J. (2012). Mining paths and transactions data to improve allocating commodity shelves in supermarket. In *International Conference on Service Operations and Logistics, and Informatics, SOLI '12*, Suzhou, China.

McColl-Kennedy, J. R., Cheung, L., & Ferrier, E. (2015a). Co-creating service experience practices. *Journal of Service Management, 26*(2), 249–275.

McColl-Kennedy, J. R., Gustafsson, A., Jaakkola, E., Klaus, P., Radnor, Z. J., Perks, H., et al. (2015b). Fresh perspectives on customer experience. *Journal of Services Marketing, 29*(6/7), 430–435.

Murray, C. (2016). Real-time data drives the future of retail stores. Tech. rep., Forrester Research. Retrieved March 13, 2018, from https://retailnext.net/en/benchmark/real-time-data-drives-the-future-of-retail/.

Parise, S., Guinan, P. J., & Kafka, R. (2016). Solving the crisis of immediacy: How digital technology can transform the customer experience. *Business Horizons, 59*(4), 411–420.

Pedreira, P., Croswhite, C., & Bona, L. (2016). Cubrick: Indexing millions of records per second for interactive analytics. *Proceedings of the VLDB Endowment, 9*(13), 1305–1316.

Prahalad, C., & Ramaswamy, V. (2004). Co-creation experiences: The next practice in value creation. *Journal of Interactive Marketing, 18*(3), 5–14.

Rao, A. R., Bergen, M. E., & Davis, S. (2000). How to fight a price war. *Harvard Business Review, 78*(2), 107–116.

Rendle, S., Fetterly, D., Shekita, E. J., & Su, B.-y. (2016). Robust large-scale machine learning in the cloud. In *Proceedings of the 22nd ACM SIGKDD International Conference on Knowledge Discovery and Data Mining, KDD '16*, San Francisco, CA, USA.

Robey, D., & Boudreau, M.-C. (1999). Accounting for the contradictory organizational consequences of information technology: Theoretical directions and methodological implications. *Information Systems Research, 10*(2), 167–185.

Schomm, F., Stahl, F., & Vossen, G. (2013). Marketplaces for data: An initial survey. *ACM SIGMOD Record, 42*(1), 15–26.

Shankar, V., Venkatesh, A., Hofacker, C., & Naik, P. (2010). Mobile marketing in the retailing environment: Current insights and future research avenues. *Journal of Interactive Marketing, 24*(2), 111–120.

Stahl, F. (2016). High-quality web information provisioning and quality-based data pricing. Doctoral thesis, Westfälische Wilhelms-Universität Münster.

Stieglitz, S., Dang-Xuan, L., Bruns, A., & Neuberger, C. (2014). Social media analytics: An interdisciplinary approach and its implications for information systems. *Business & Information Systems Engineering, 6*(2), 89–96.

Tiwana, A. (2014). *Platform ecosystems: Aligning architecture, governance, and strategy*. Waltham, MA, USA: Morgan Kaufmann.

Tynan, C., McKechnie, S., & Hartley, S. (2014). Interpreting value in the customer service experience using customer-dominant logic. *Journal of Marketing Management, 30*(9–10), 1058–1081.

Vargo, S. L., & Lusch, R. F. (2008). Why 'service'? *Journal of the Academy of Marketing Science, 36*(1), 25–38.

Vargo, S. L., & Lusch, R. F. (2016). Institutions and axioms: An extension and update of service-dominant logic. *Journal of the Academy of Marketing Science, 44*(1), 5–23.

Willems, K., Smolders, A., Brengman, M., Luyten, K., & Schöning, J. (2017). The path-to-purchase is paved with digital opportunities: An inventory of shopper-oriented retail technologies. *Technological Forecasting and Social Change, 124*, 228–242.

Printed in the United States
By Bookmasters